STAR TREK™

THE ART OF JUAN ORTIZ

THE NEXT GENERATION

STAR TREK THE ART OF JUAN ORTIZ **THE NEXT GENERATION**
STD Ed. ISBN: 9781785653872
LTD Ed. ISBN: 9781785653971

Published by
Titan Books
A division of Titan Publishing Group Ltd.
144 Southwark St.
London
SE1 0UP

First edition: March 2017

10 9 8 7 6 5 4 3 2 1

Did you enjoy this book? We love to hear from our readers. Please e-mail us at: **readerfeedback@titanemail.com** or write to Reader Feedback at the above address.

To receive advance information, news, competitions, and exclusive offers online, please sign up for the Titan newsletter on our website: **www.titanbooks.com**

A CIP catalogue record for this title is available from the British Library.

Printed in China.

STAR TREK™

THE ART OF JUAN ORTIZ

THE NEXT GENERATION

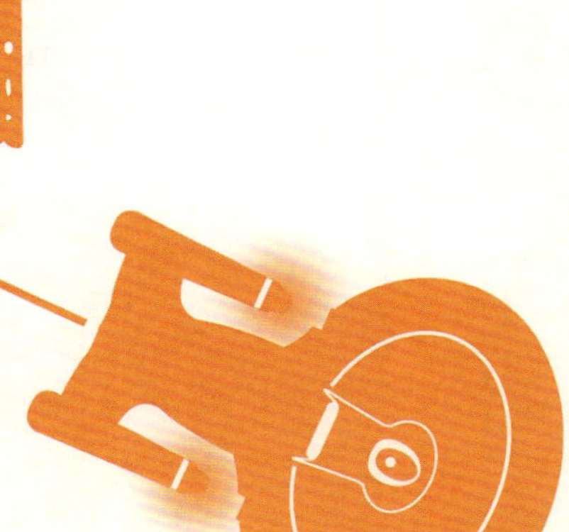

TITAN BOOKS

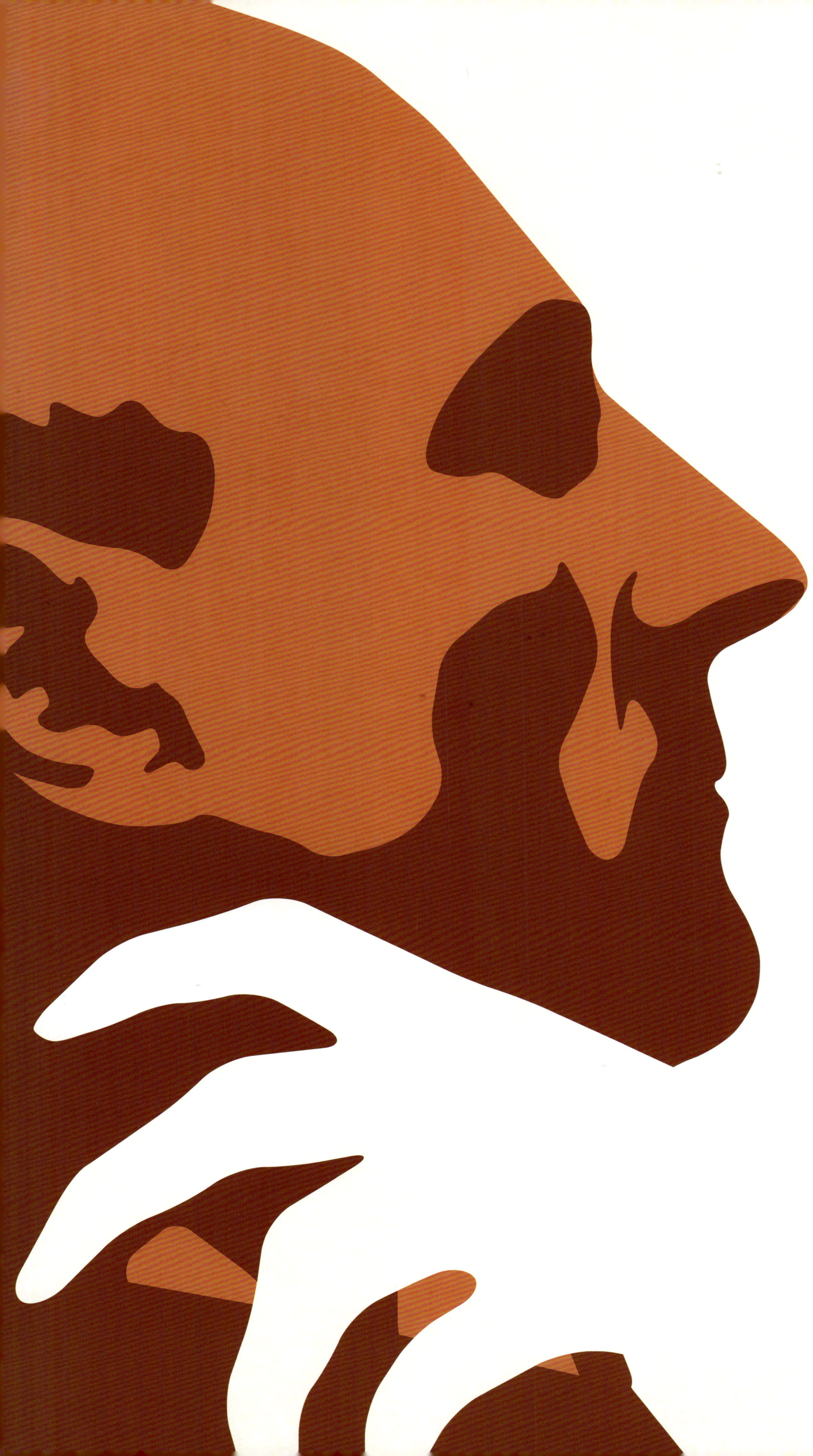

Contents

A Fresh Take for the Next Generation 6

Season One 14

Season Two 42

Season Three 66

Season Four 94

Season Five 122

Season Six 150

Season Seven 178

Episode Index 205

A Fresh Take For The Next Generation

An Interview with JUAN ORTIZ
by Nicola Edwards

> *"I just don't consider* The Next Generation *retro..."*

Your first book for Titan, *Star Trek: The Art of Juan Ortiz*, which came out in 2013, focused on the Original Series of the show. How different was the experience of creating that poster set from this one?

I grew up watching the Original Series from an early age, so most of the work was based on my memories. With *The Next Generation*, I had to re-watch many of the episodes. I also didn't reference much artwork from before 1970. I was mostly inspired by indie film posters, black-light posters, some rock/punk posters and a bit from comic books. For the most part, I tried to stay away from much of the retro look.

Interesting. Why did you want to avoid the retro look this time around? Did you feel like it was less appropriate for *The Next Generation* than for the Original Series and if so, why?

I just don't consider *The Next Generation* retro. Maybe because the last *Next Generation* film was only about fifteen years ago. And with the series having been in reruns for a few years now, I am being reintroduced to it on an almost daily basis.

What does the word retro mean to you?

Retro always meant mid-century to me. I guess you can consider the thirties through the seventies retro. It seems to be the time of the pop culture revolution. Comics, movies, cartoons, advertising, radio and TV shows. Much of what I

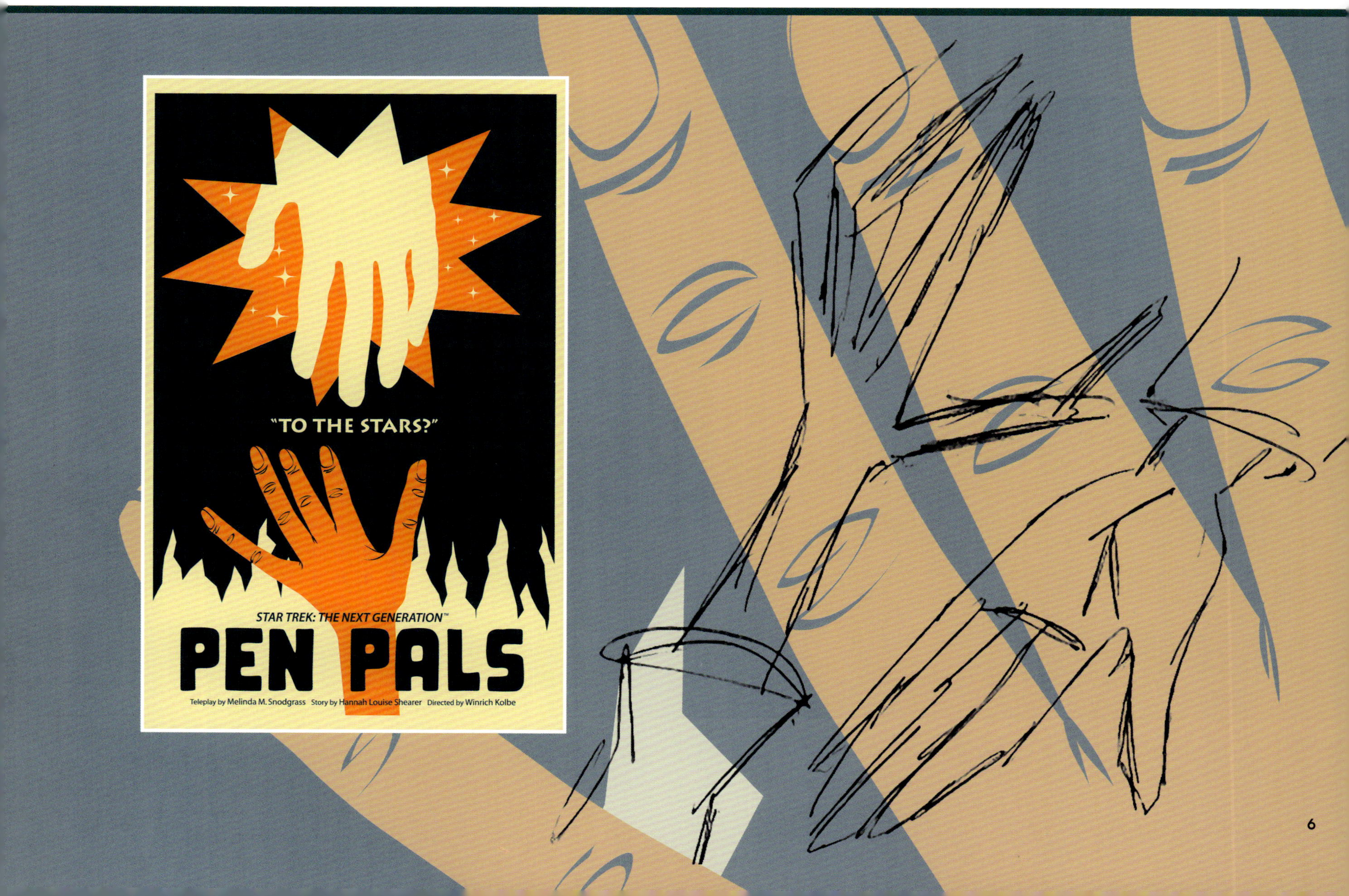

loved growing up. A lot of what was good decades ago is still good now. So why just leave it in the past? *The Next Generation* was all about that. Taking something old and polishing it off for a new generation.

Are there other *Star Trek* poster sets that you would like to create in future?

I created posters for the animated series about a year after the Original Series set. So far they've only been available as trading cards from Rittenhouse. There will also be a magnet set with my *Star Trek* film series, available sometime in 2016 at the *Star Trek* convention in New York. Those will be available from ReedPOP. And I am also currently creating a new round of posters based upon the new films. Those will be available for promotional purposes.

What's your favorite of all your movie posters and why?

I still like "A Private Little War" from the Original Series. I like how the negative space creates the central image. I didn't plan it that way but I like when the art takes me in a different direction than the one intended.

What is your favorite of your *Next Generation* posters and why?

"Peak Performance" is probably my favorite because I always wanted to incorporate a checkerboard into one of my designs, like some of my favorite sci-fi book covers. I also had fun creating the painterly background.

"...I like when the art takes me in a different direction than the one intended."

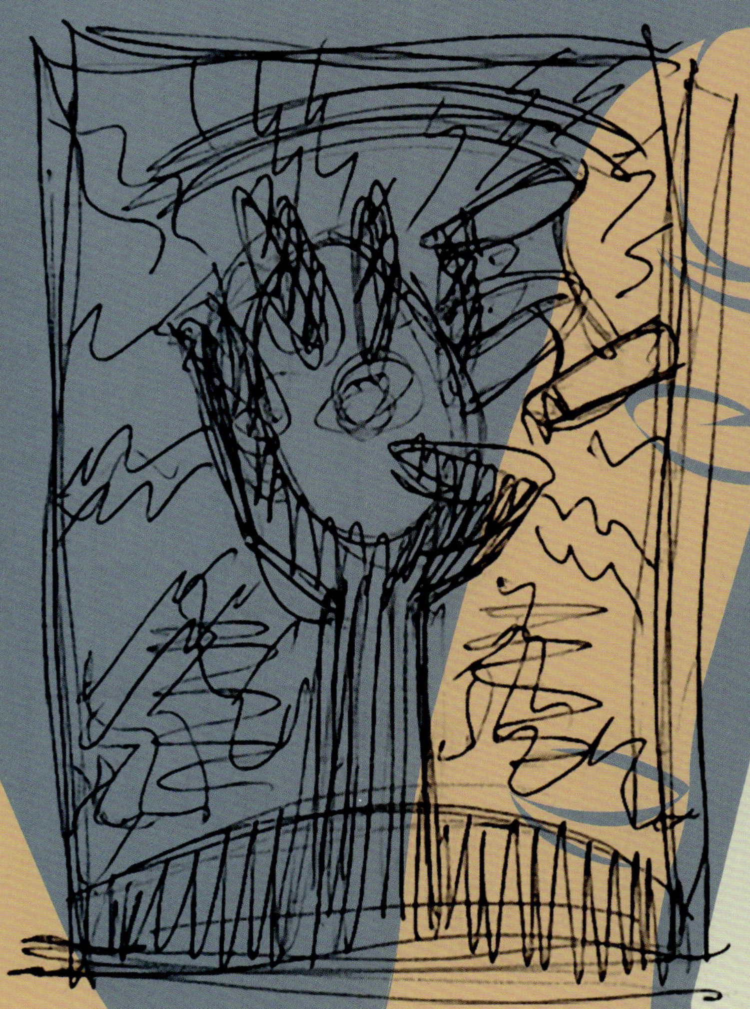

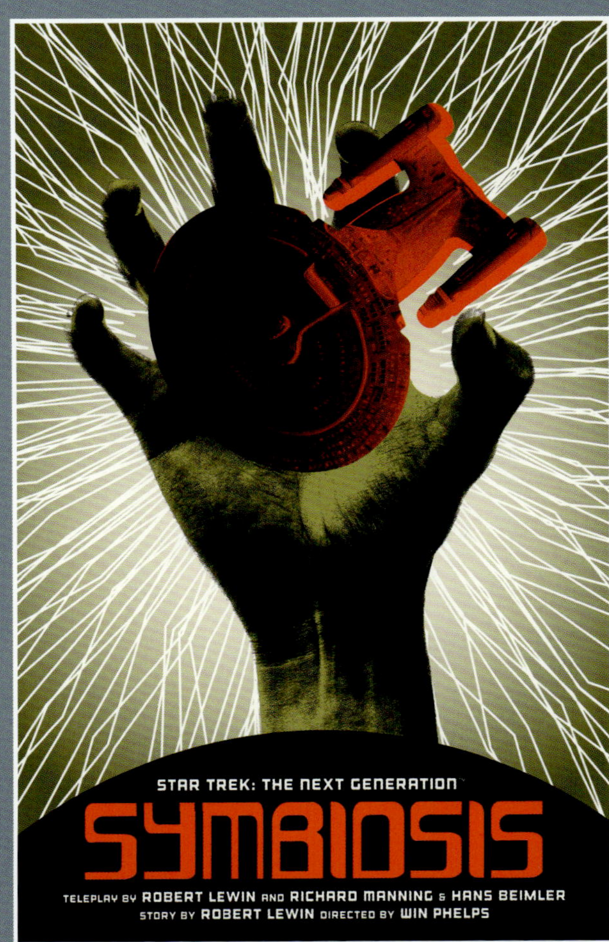

> *"...posters from my childhood are the ones that have made the biggest impact."*

Are there any posters by other artists that have inspired you or impacted on your work in a memorable way?

There are many posters and artists that have inspired me. The posters from my childhood are the ones that have made the biggest impact. Not all of them are film posters, either. I remember seeing black-light posters for the first time and having my mind blown. Now I own most of the Marvel Comics black-light posters by the Third Eye Company. The *Star Wars* poster by the Hildebrandt Brothers was another of my favorites. That one started me researching the old serial posters from the forties.

What's your favorite *Next Generation* episode and why?

It would probably be a draw between "The Inner Light" and "The Offspring." Both stories deal with science and technology, yet both are emotional because they are rooted in family.

Why did you not incorporate a flute into your "Inner Light" design?

That to me would have been the obvious choice. Which is why I didn't do it. Early in the episode, someone plants a tree. I knew instantly that the tree, along with Picard, would be my image.

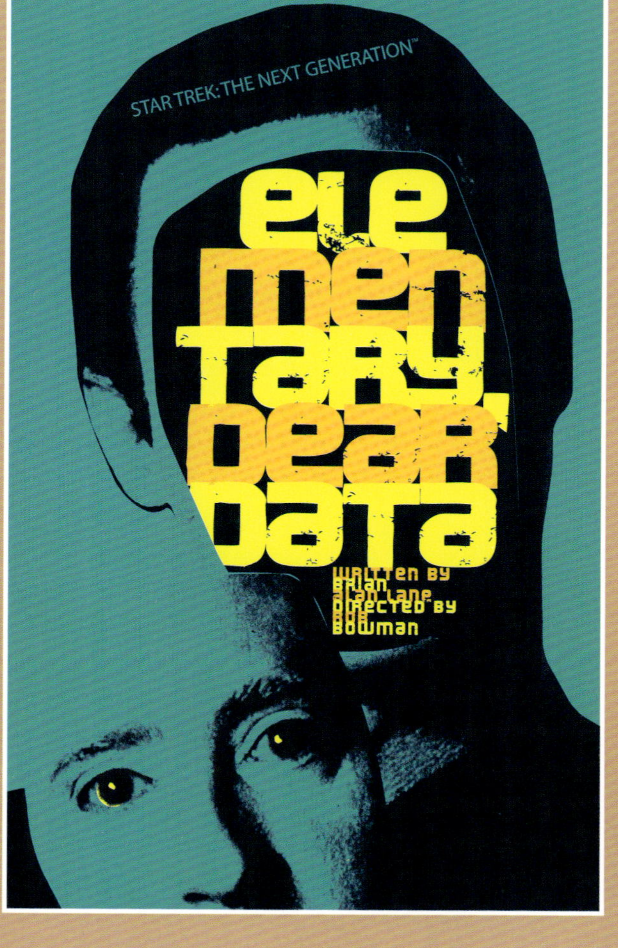

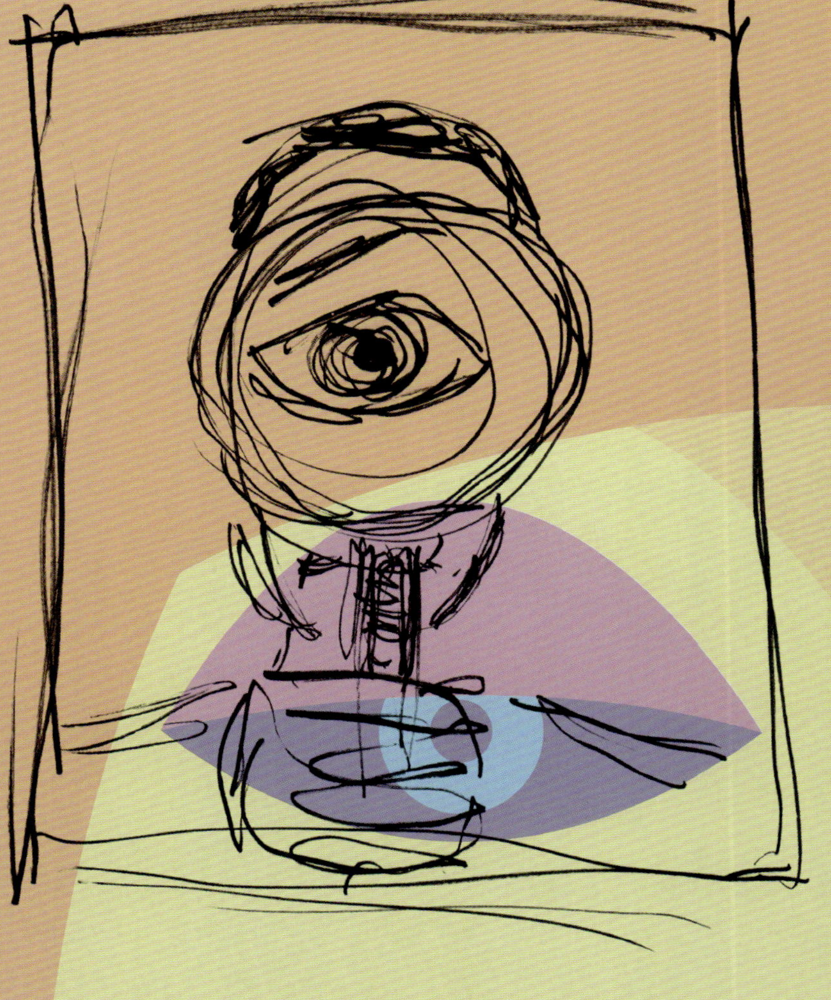

Were there any episodes you found particularly tricky to depict and, if so, why?

"The Outrageous Okona" was a difficult one. I wanted Data in some sort of stand-up situation but I also wanted to inject more of a *Star Trek* element. In the end, there proved to be too much happening. I'm not completely happy with the final results. Without a *Trek* element, this poster may as well be for *The Love Boat*.

Your work is very conceptual. Why do you think this is your preferred style and what do you think it says about you as an artist?

I just try to keep things interesting for myself. If I can create something that may have been a challenge for me, then I'm happy with it. I can understand movie studios creating posters based on what works for them, but I wanted mine to be different. And for that I needed to take chances. I think the conceptual aspect just grows out of the process of trying something different.

What does *The Next Generation* mean to you as a show? What did it mean when it was first on TV and has that changed now you're older?

I was already in my twenties when the series aired, but it was nice to see something new from the world of *Trek*, besides the movies. *The Next Generation* created many fans in the eighties and that number continues to expand. Looking back at when the show started reminds me of where I was and what I was doing back then. Which, for me, were not the best of times.

"...I just try and keep things interesting for myself."

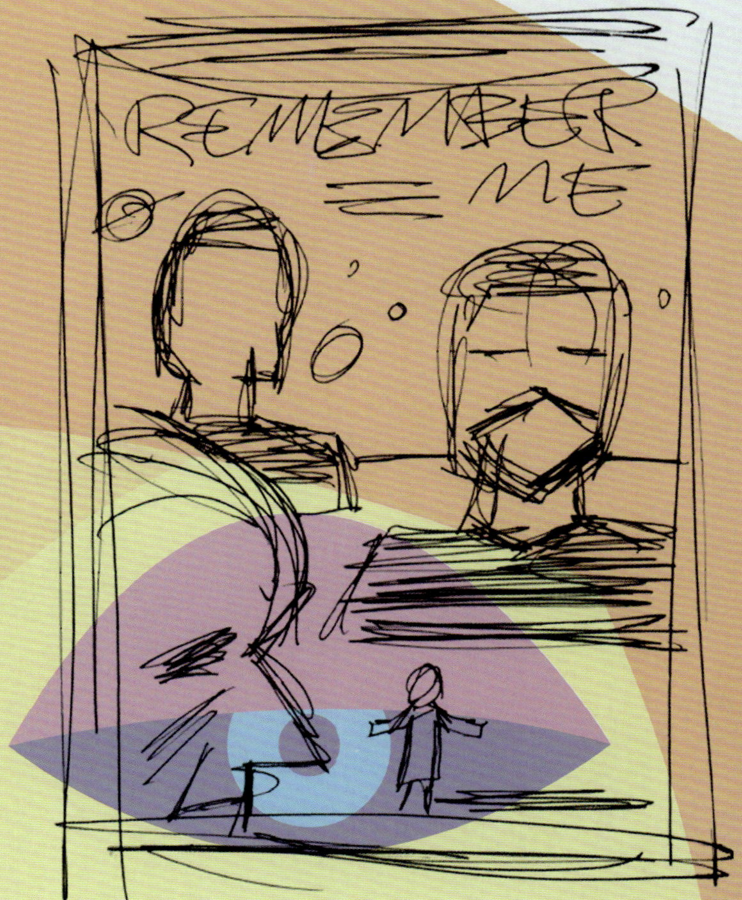

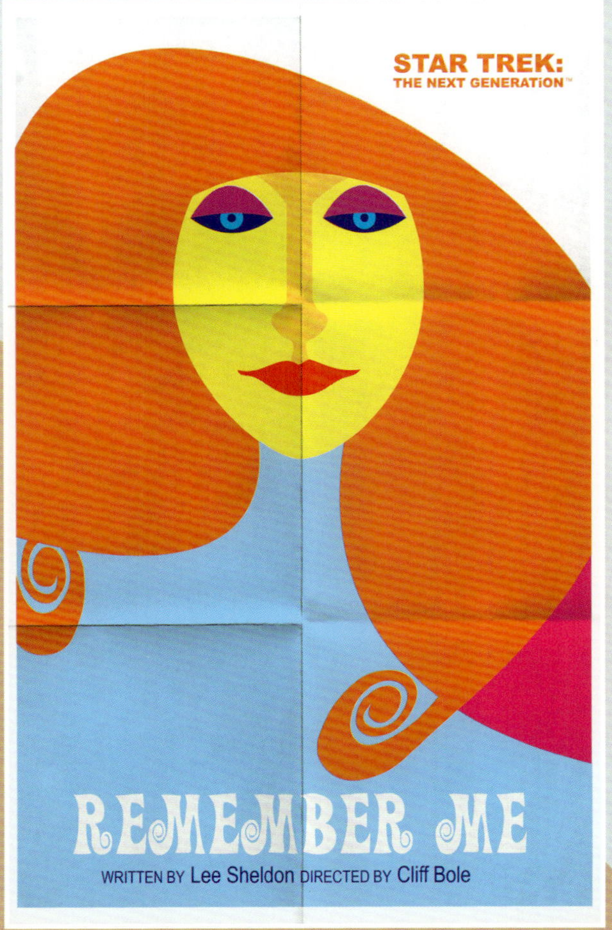

"When I create a piece of Star Trek *art, I'm reliving my past, a bit."*

A lot of people seem to feel like *Trek*, in its various incarnations, has accompanied them through both the good and bad periods of their life, partly by virtue of its longevity and partly because its themes are so human and universal. Is that true for you too?

When I think of a *Trek* series or film, it's almost impossible not to remember where I was or what I was doing back then. When I create a piece of *Star Trek* art, I'm reliving my past, a bit. The good with the bad. But life moves forward. *Star Trek* is about a better future. I went from being virtually unknown to having my work seen and admired in many countries. I may not have made a fortune but I am satisfied that, through my *Star Trek* work, I have enriched my life. That much I can take with me.

Is there anything about any of your posters that you think might be of interest to fans that isn't obvious when looking at them?

I remember reading about nanorobotics in an *OMNI Magazine* back in the seventies. So when it came time to design the "Evolution" poster, I thought back to that article and imagined what my cover for an *OMNI Magazine* issue would look like.

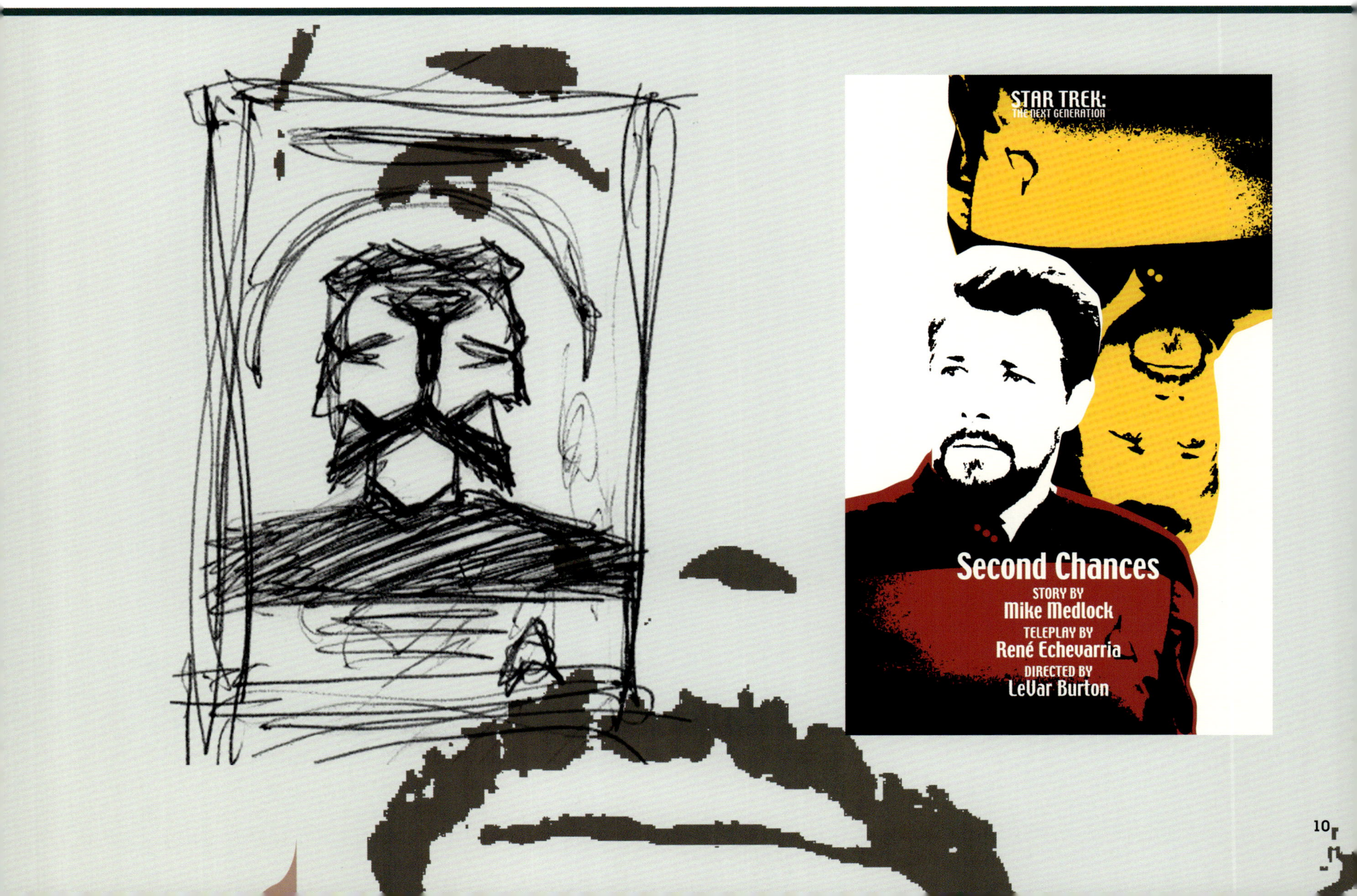

How does the colour treatment for your *Next Generation* posters compare to that for your Original Series posters and what is the thinking behind that?

I knew that I couldn't make *The Next Generation* look like my Original Series. I tried to keep the colors less faded or muted. But I also didn't want to go all eighties, either.

How important are lettering choices to your posters? What can you tell us about your decisions in this area?

The lettering is very important and in some cases the lettering is everything. With the Original Series, I didn't always use "retro" fonts. I used the fonts that were available to me. Whether they were considered retro or not, I sought not to limit myself. I approached the type with *The Next Generation* the same way.

How long does it typically take you to create a poster and does this vary much?

I like to work quickly. So once I have the idea, it may take about a day to execute. This will vary, depending on how familiar I am with the story or subject matter. With the Original Series, the ideas came quickly. So on some occasions, I was able to create three to five posters per day. There were days when I did the same with *The Next Generation* too, but that was mostly because of the approaching deadline.

"The lettering is very important and in some cases the lettering is everything."

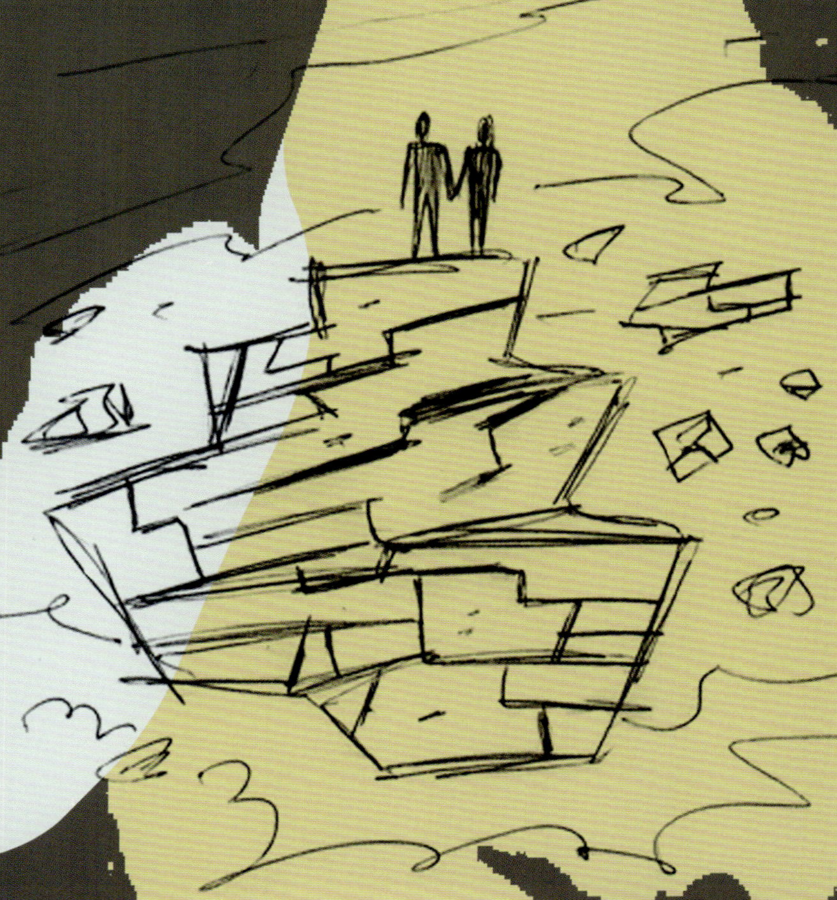

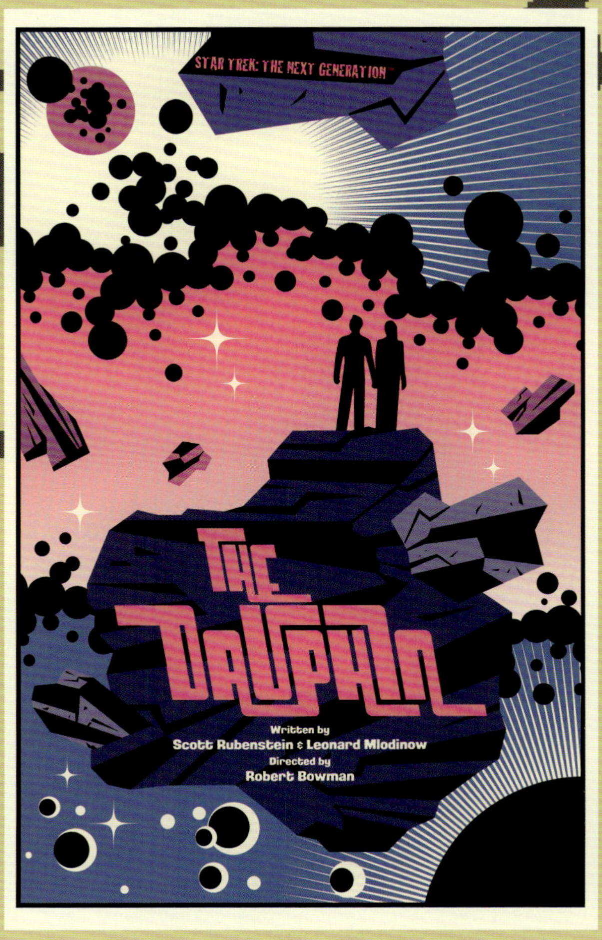

"...Trekkies have a special bond. Almost like a family."

What do you hope people get out of this collection?

I just want enough people to like them. They were originally created as a trading card set but I hope they translate well into the book format and eventually we may see a few actual posters. Although, I think the complete set may be a little too extensive for anyone's walls.

Who is your favorite *Next Generation* character and why?

I'm sure I'm like most people that will say Data. I just find the character interesting and he also illustrates how far science had evolved within *Trek*. I'm hoping the new series will stretch the science and technology even further.

Do you consider yourself a Trekkie and how do you feel about the Trekkie community in general? Do you think they are different from other fandoms and, if so, why?

I consider myself a sci-fi fan. Being a Trekkie is just one aspect of that. I don't know too many Trekkies, so I can't really speak from experience. I just feel that Trekkies have a special bond. Almost like a family. It's more of a belief and a way of life.

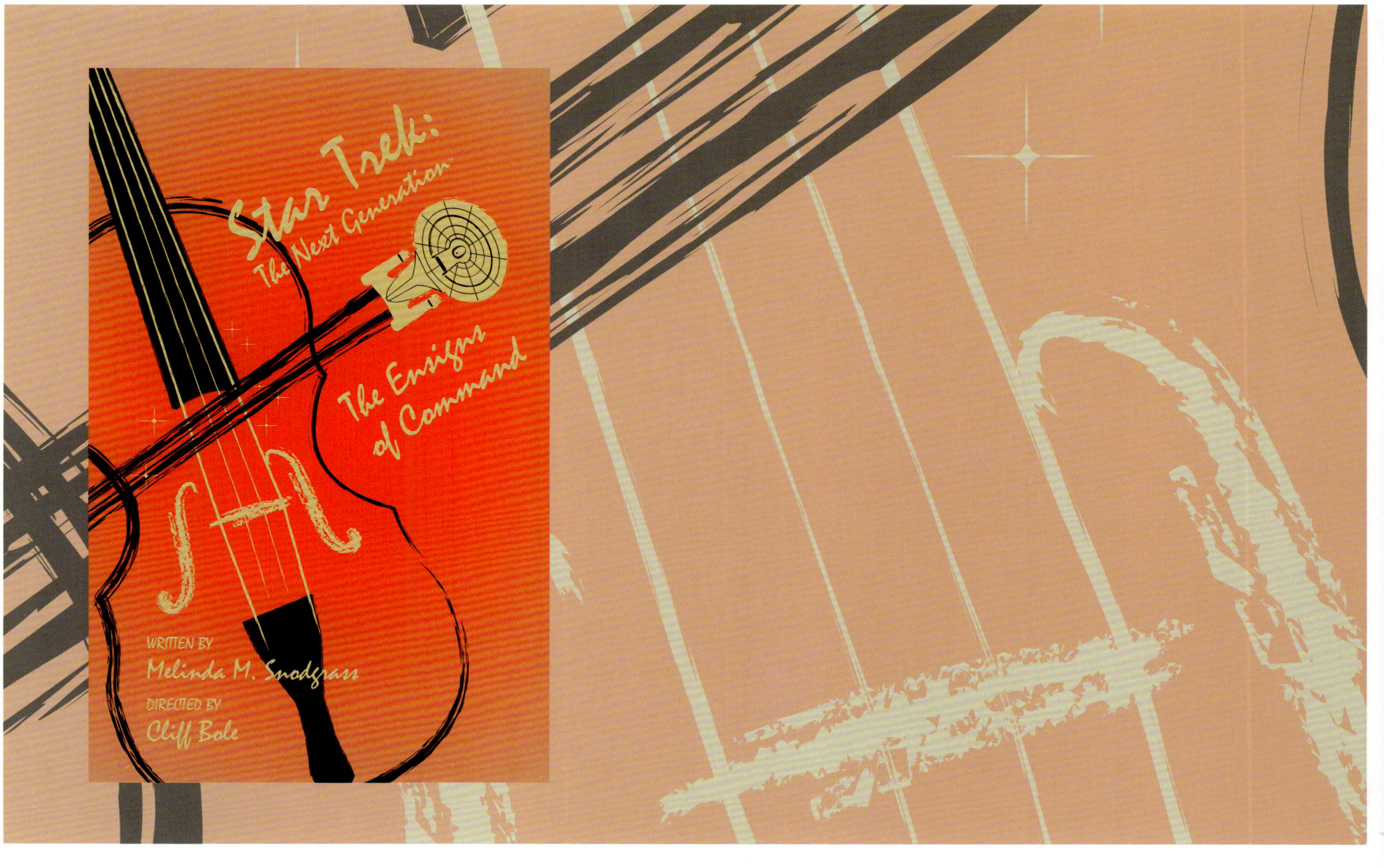

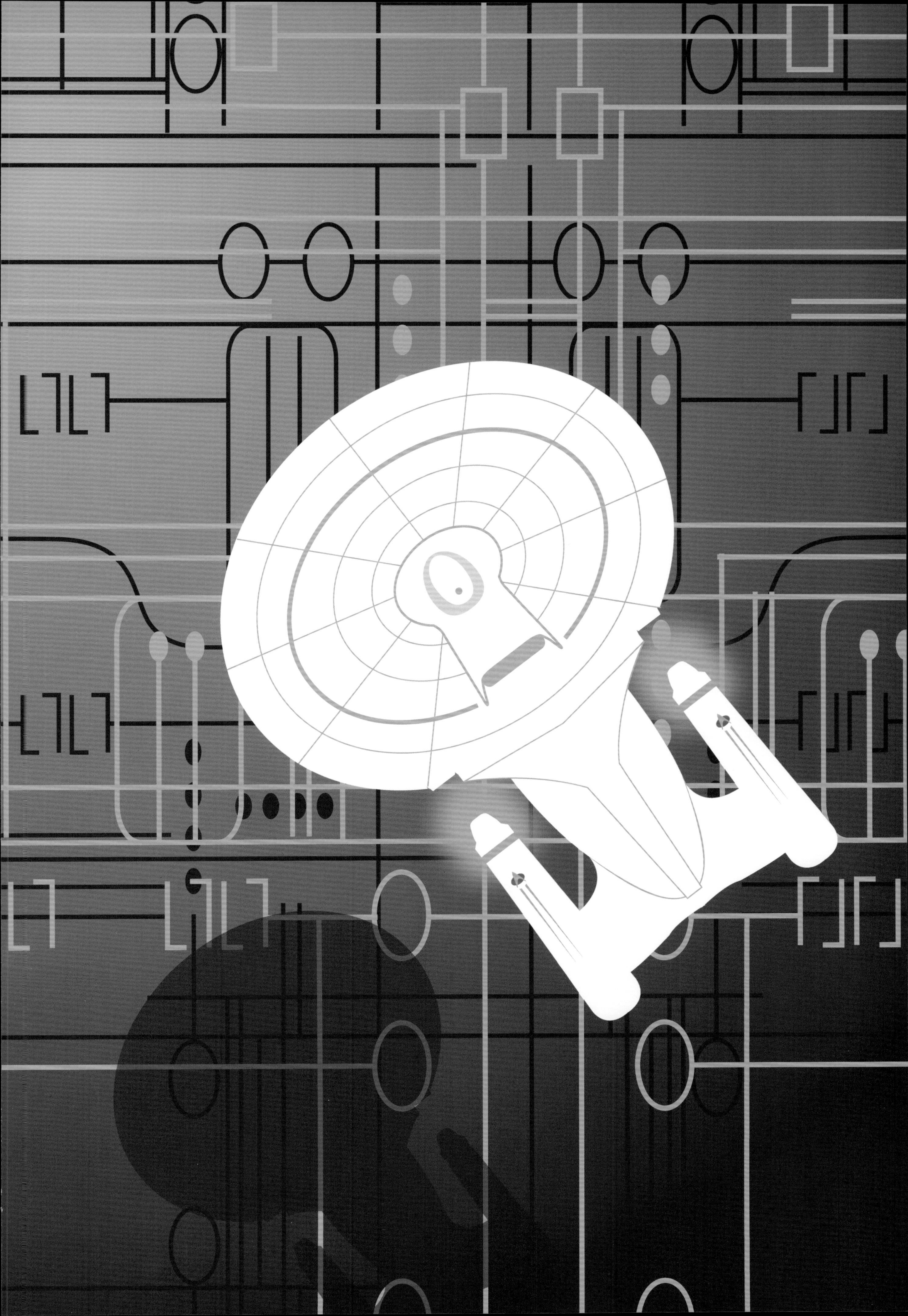

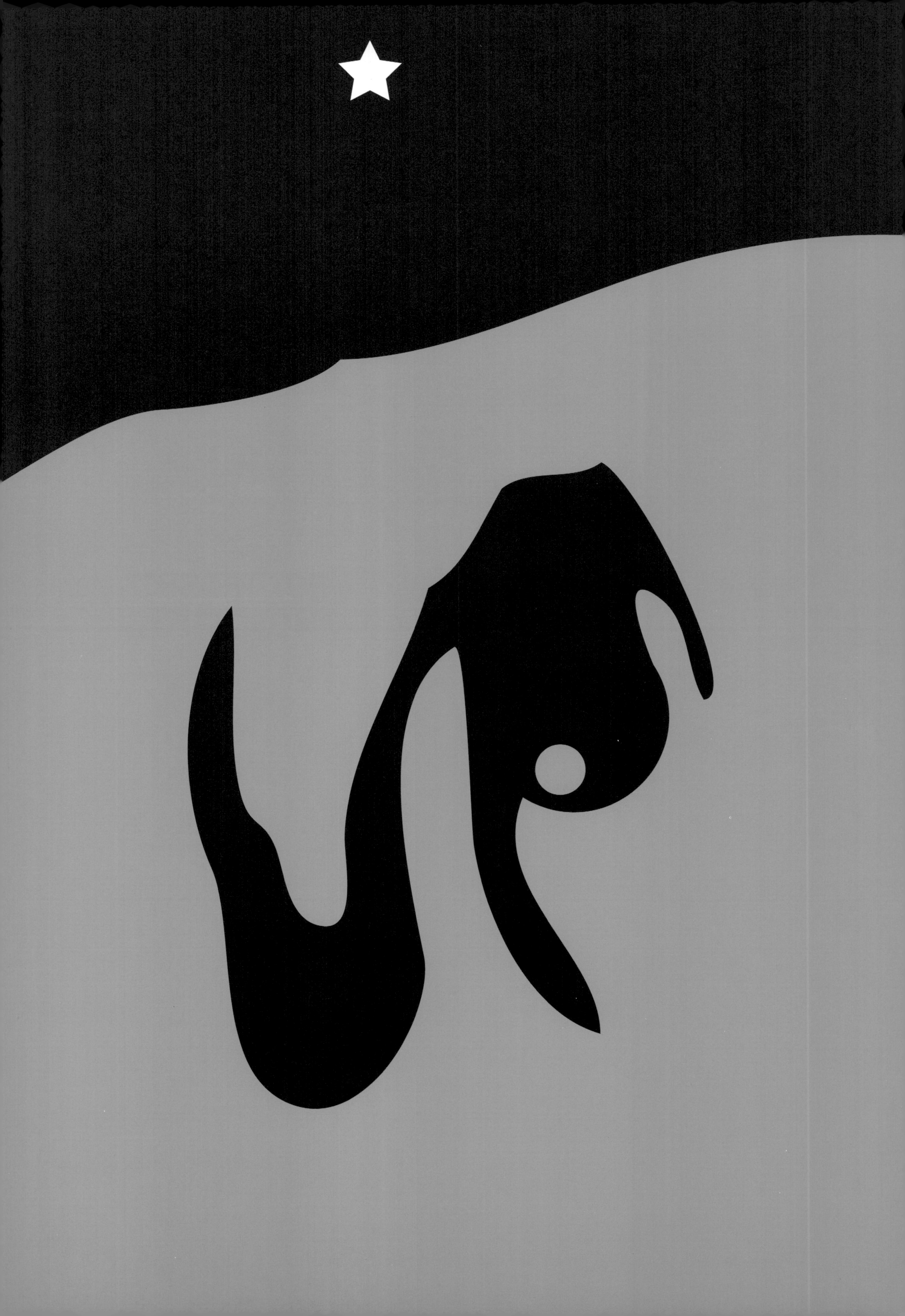

Season One

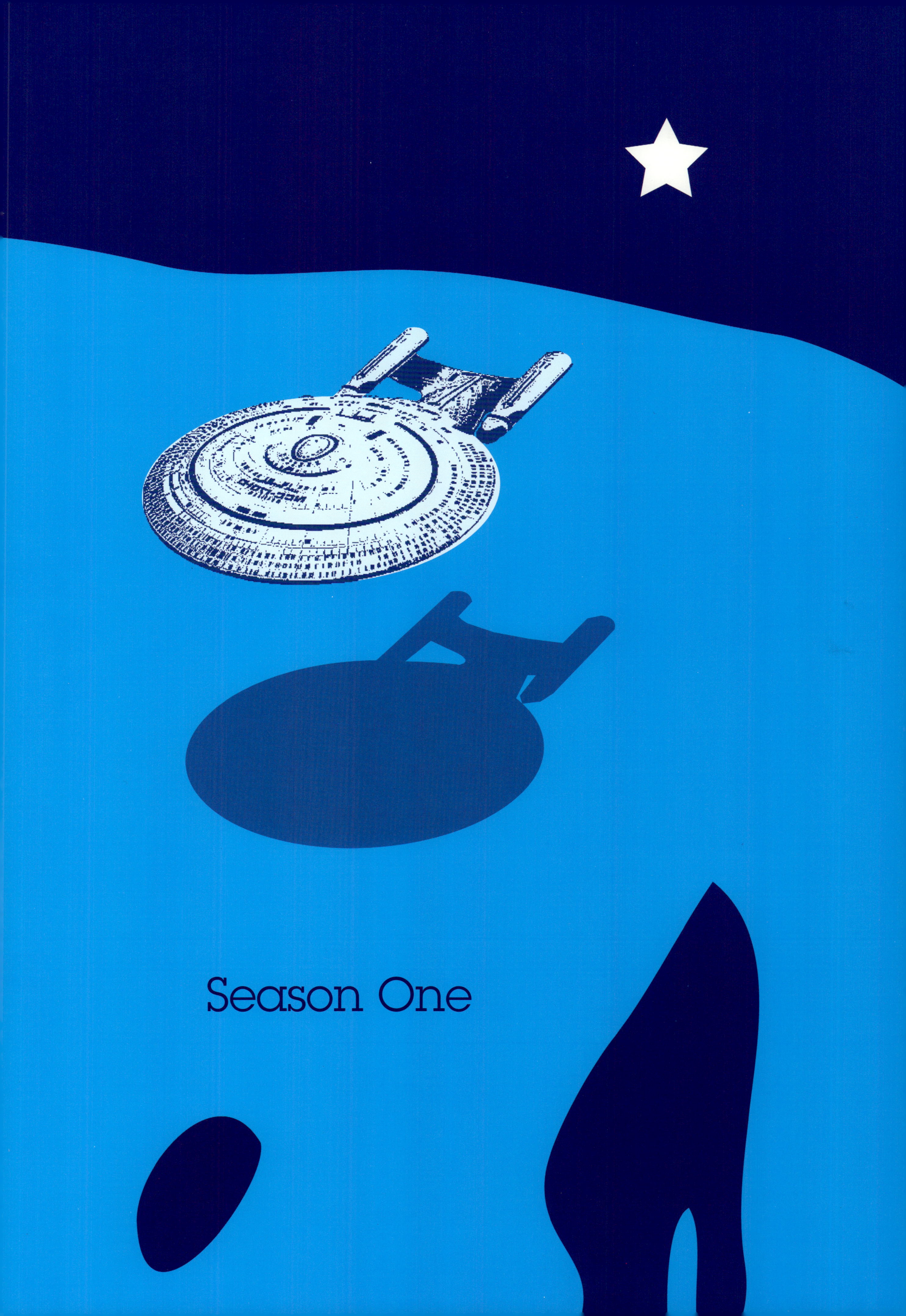

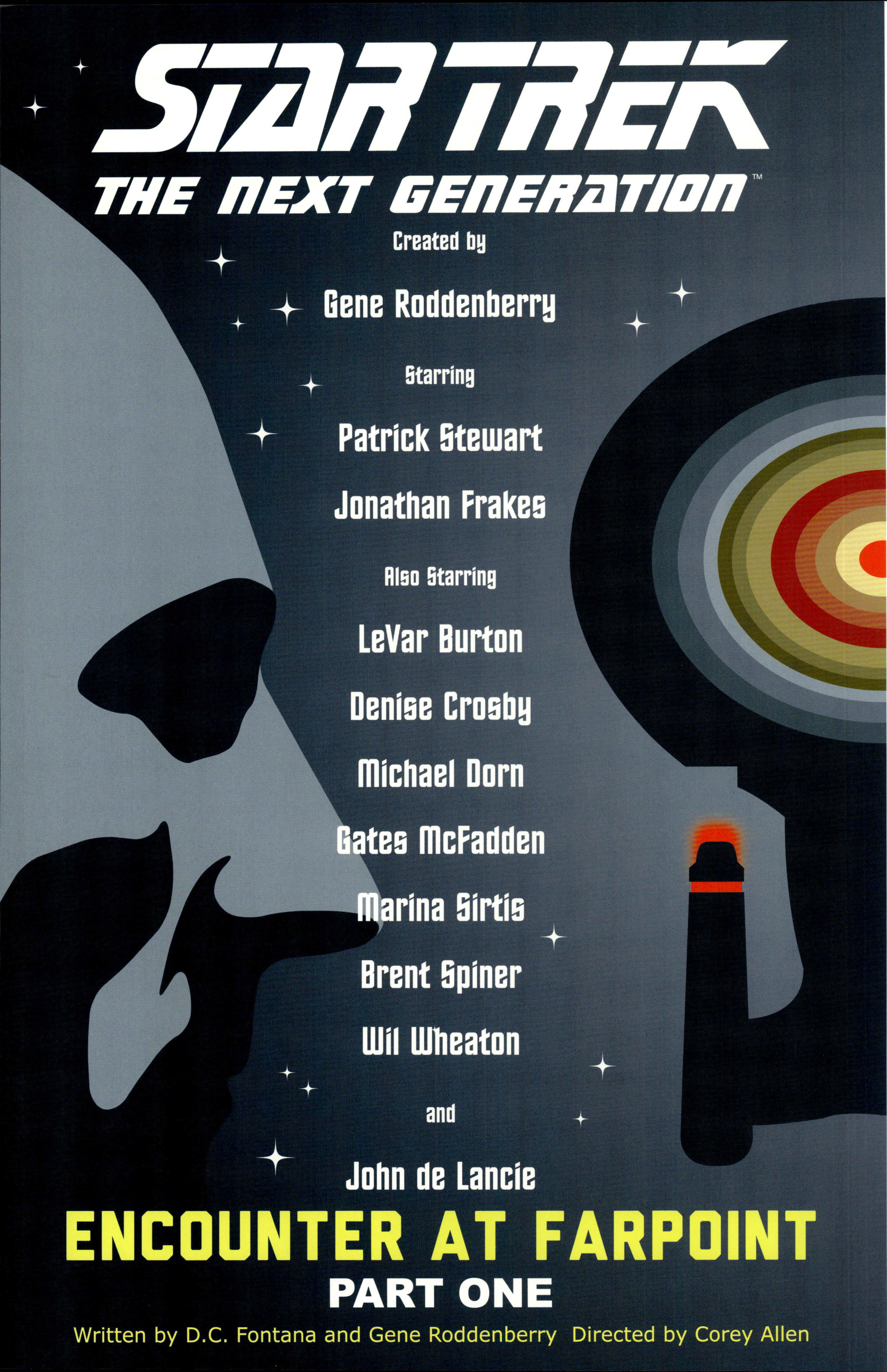
STAR TREK
THE NEXT GENERATION™
Created by
Gene Roddenberry
Starring
Patrick Stewart
Jonathan Frakes
Also Starring
LeVar Burton
Denise Crosby
Michael Dorn
Gates McFadden
Marina Sirtis
Brent Spiner
Wil Wheaton
and
John de Lancie
ENCOUNTER AT FARPOINT
PART ONE
Written by D.C. Fontana and Gene Roddenberry Directed by Corey Allen

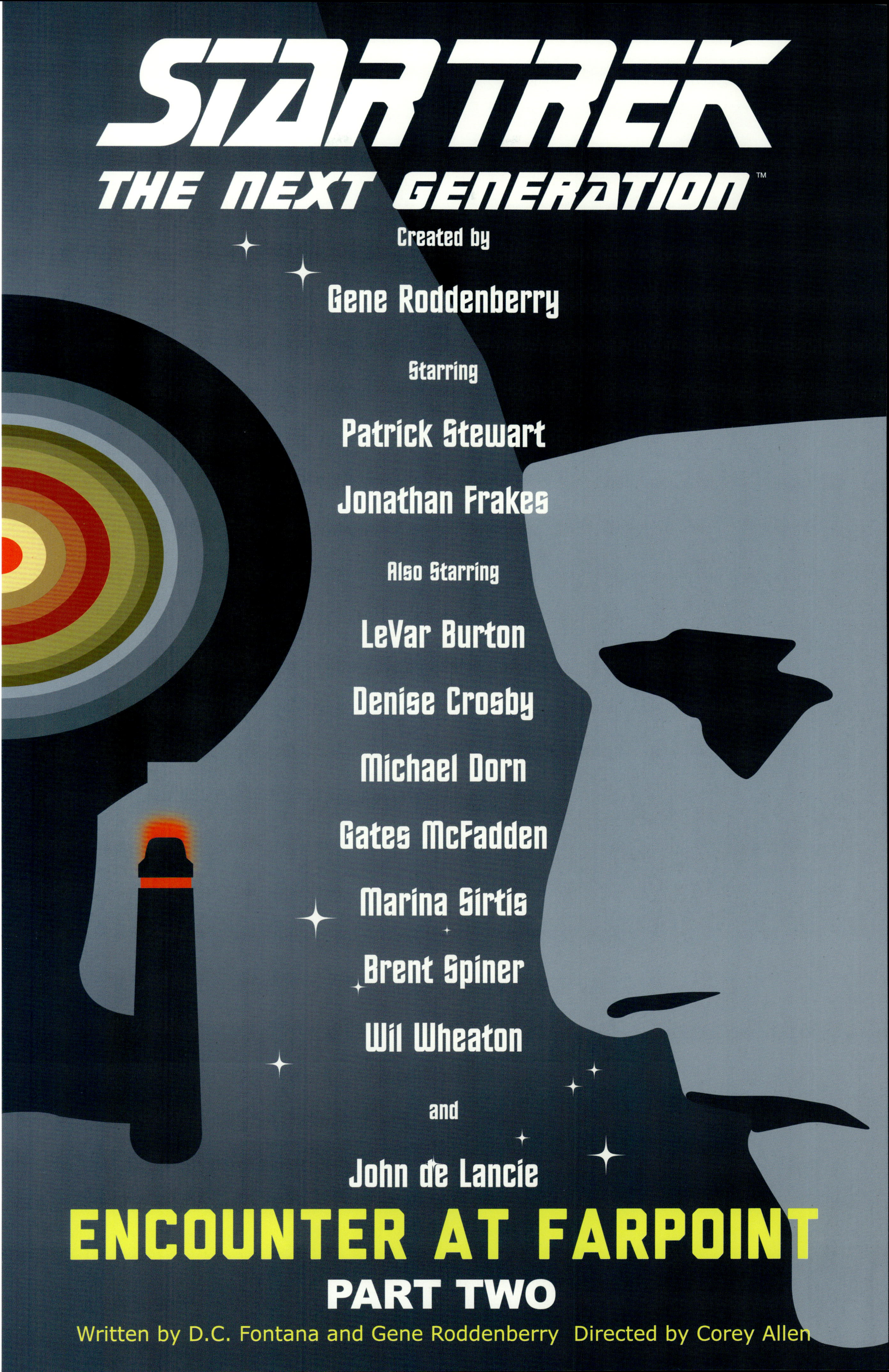
STAR TREK
THE NEXT GENERATION™
Created by
Gene Roddenberry
Starring
Patrick Stewart
Jonathan Frakes
Also Starring
LeVar Burton
Denise Crosby
Michael Dorn
Gates McFadden
Marina Sirtis
Brent Spiner
Wil Wheaton
and
John de Lancie
ENCOUNTER AT FARPOINT
PART TWO
Written by D.C. Fontana and Gene Roddenberry Directed by Corey Allen

STAR TREK:
THE NEXT GENERATION™
THE NAKED NOW

Teleplay By

J. Michael Bingham

Story By

John D.F. Black *and* **J. Michael Bingham**

Directed By

Paul Lynch

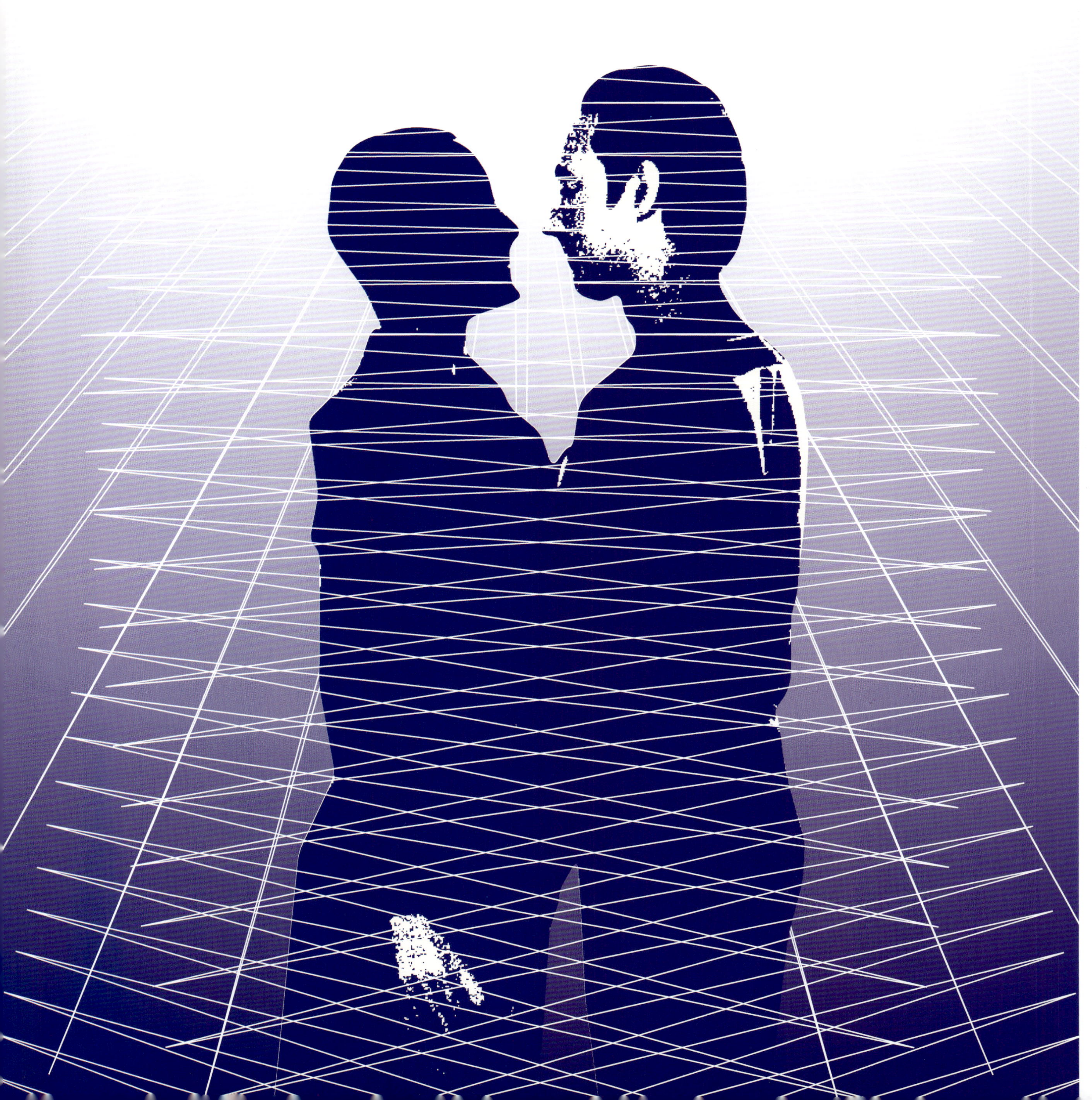

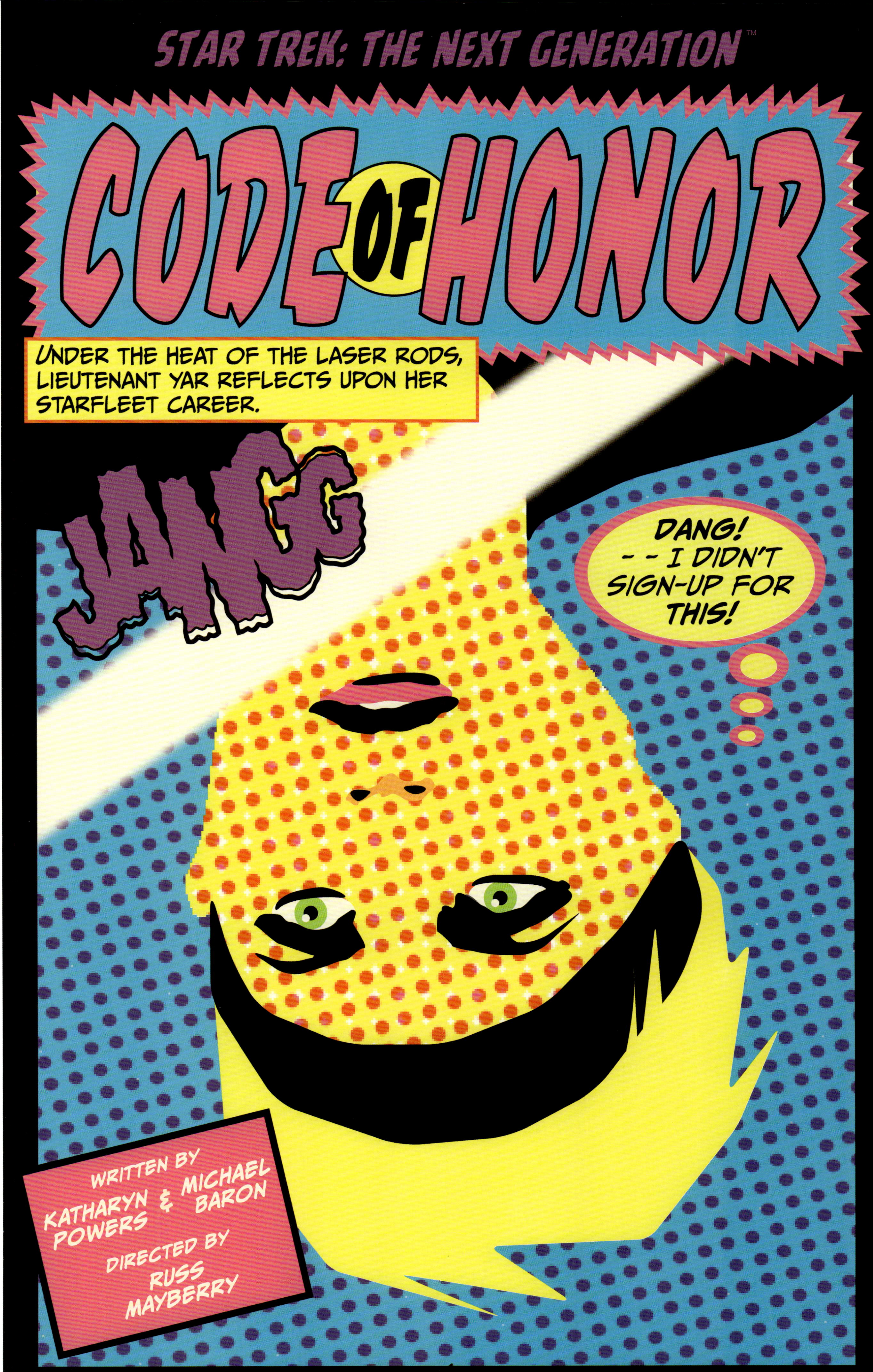
STAR TREK: THE NEXT GENERATION™
CODE OF HONOR
UNDER THE HEAT OF THE LASER RODS, LIEUTENANT YAR REFLECTS UPON HER STARFLEET CAREER.
JANG
DANG! - - I DIDN'T SIGN-UP FOR THIS!
WRITTEN BY KATHARYN POWERS & MICHAEL BARON
DIRECTED BY RUSS MAYBERRY

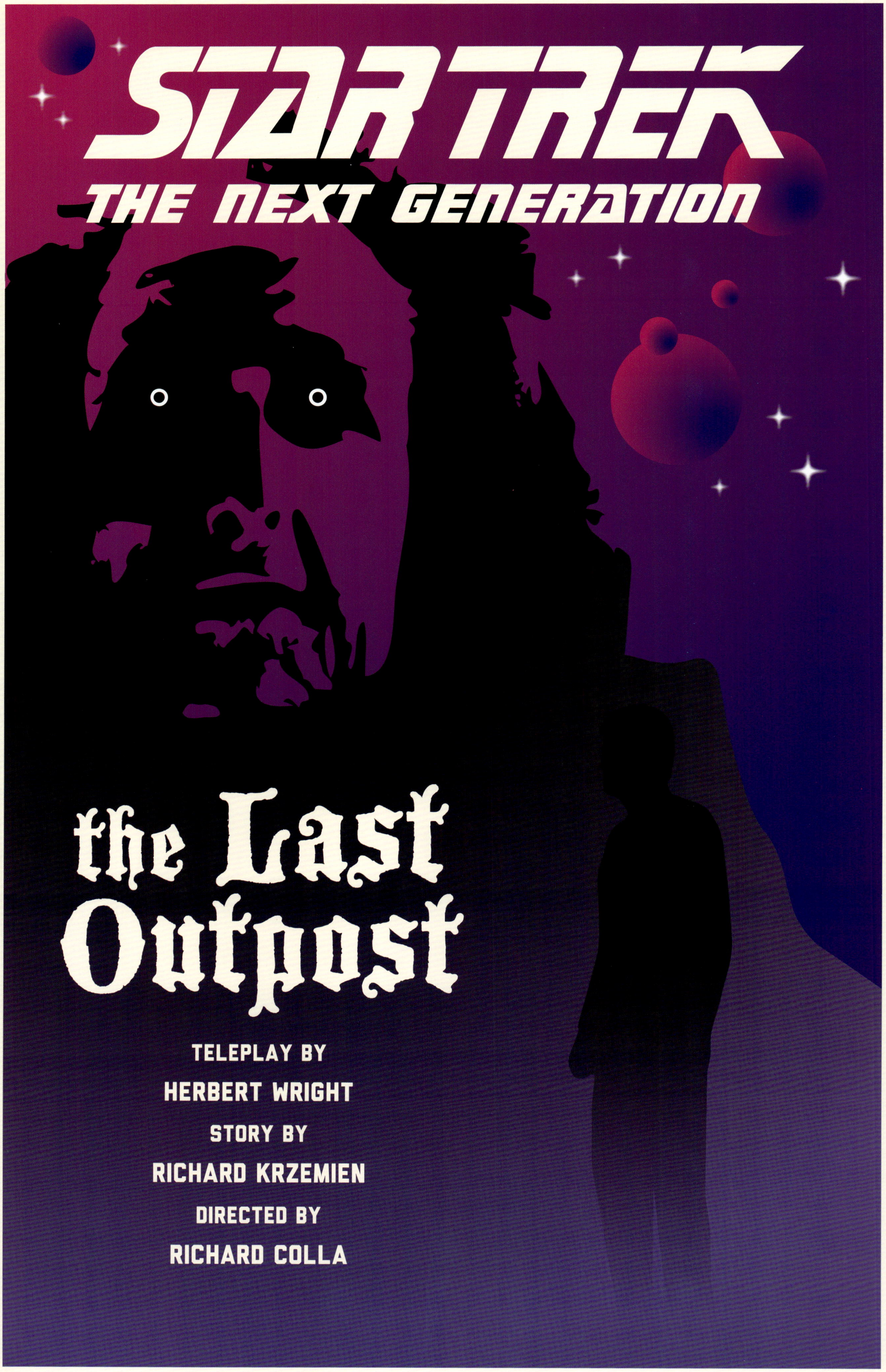
STAR TREK
THE NEXT GENERATION
the Last Outpost
TELEPLAY BY
HERBERT WRIGHT
STORY BY
RICHARD KRZEMIEN
DIRECTED BY
RICHARD COLLA

STAR TREK: THE NEXT GENERATION™

WHERE NO ONE HAS GONE BEFORE

Written by Diane Duane & Michael Reaves
Directed by Rob Bowman

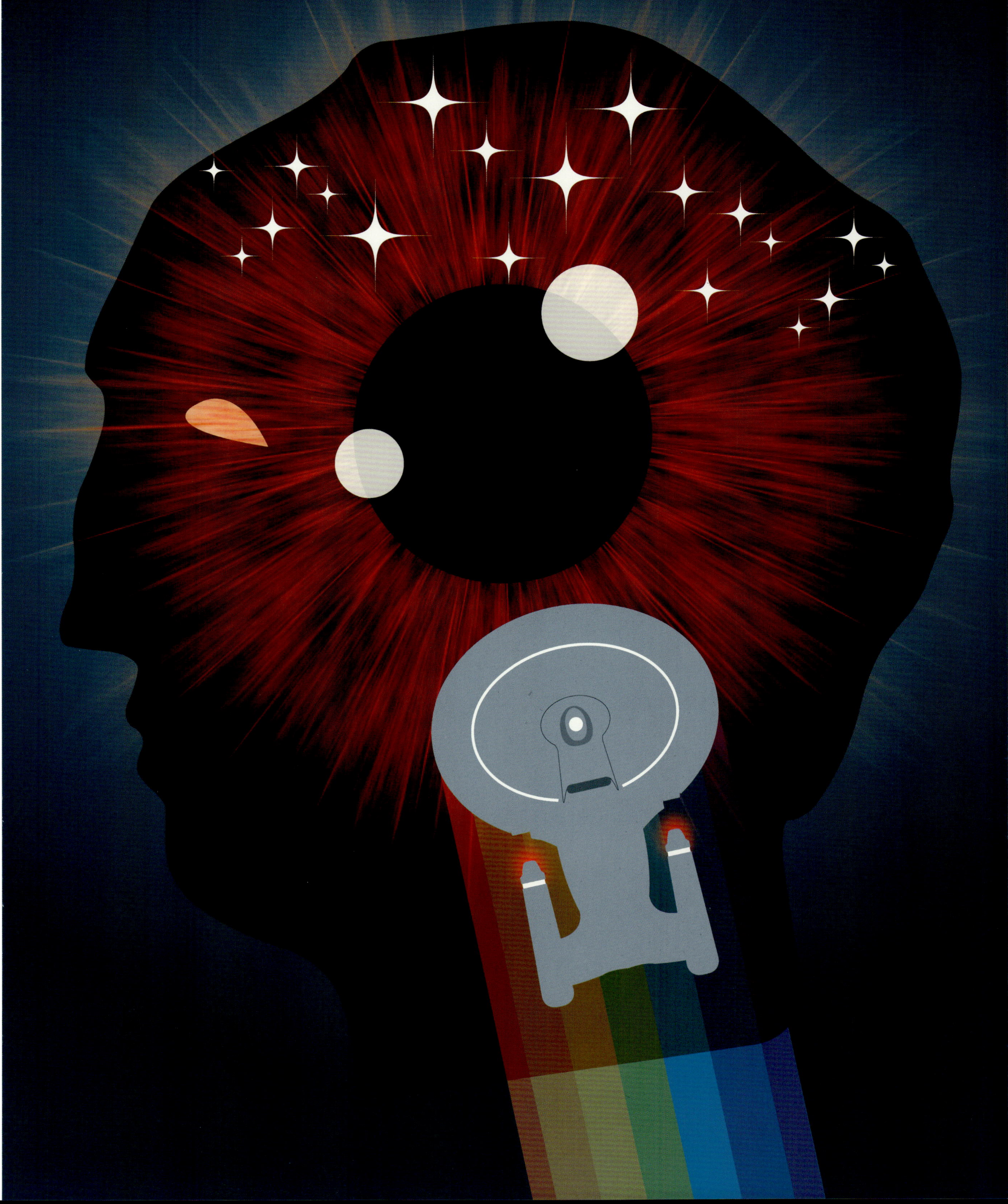

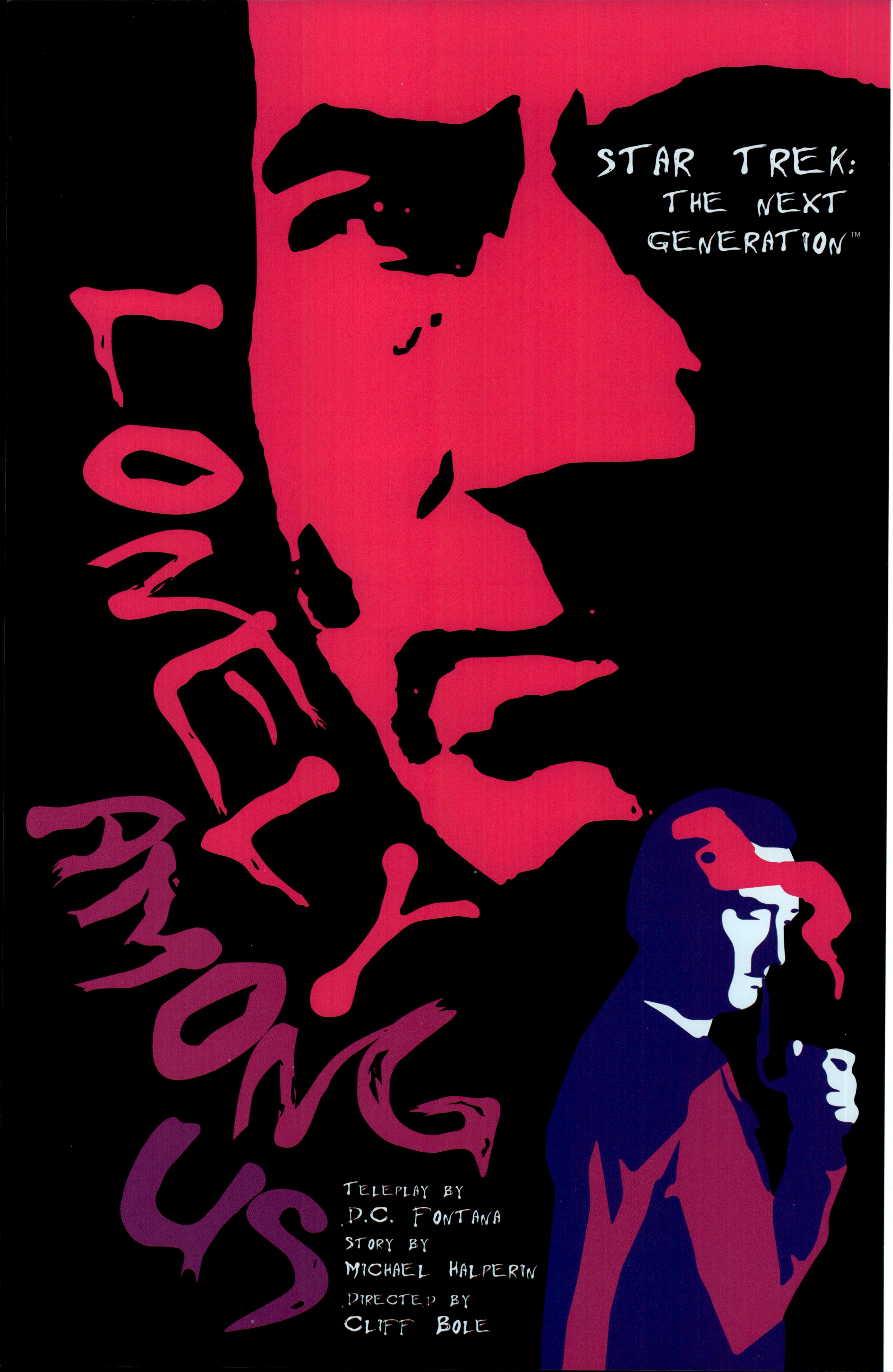
STAR TREK:
THE NEXT
GENERATION™
LONELY
AMONG
US
TELEPLAY BY
D.C. FONTANA
STORY BY
MICHAEL HALPERIN
DIRECTED BY
CLIFF BOLE

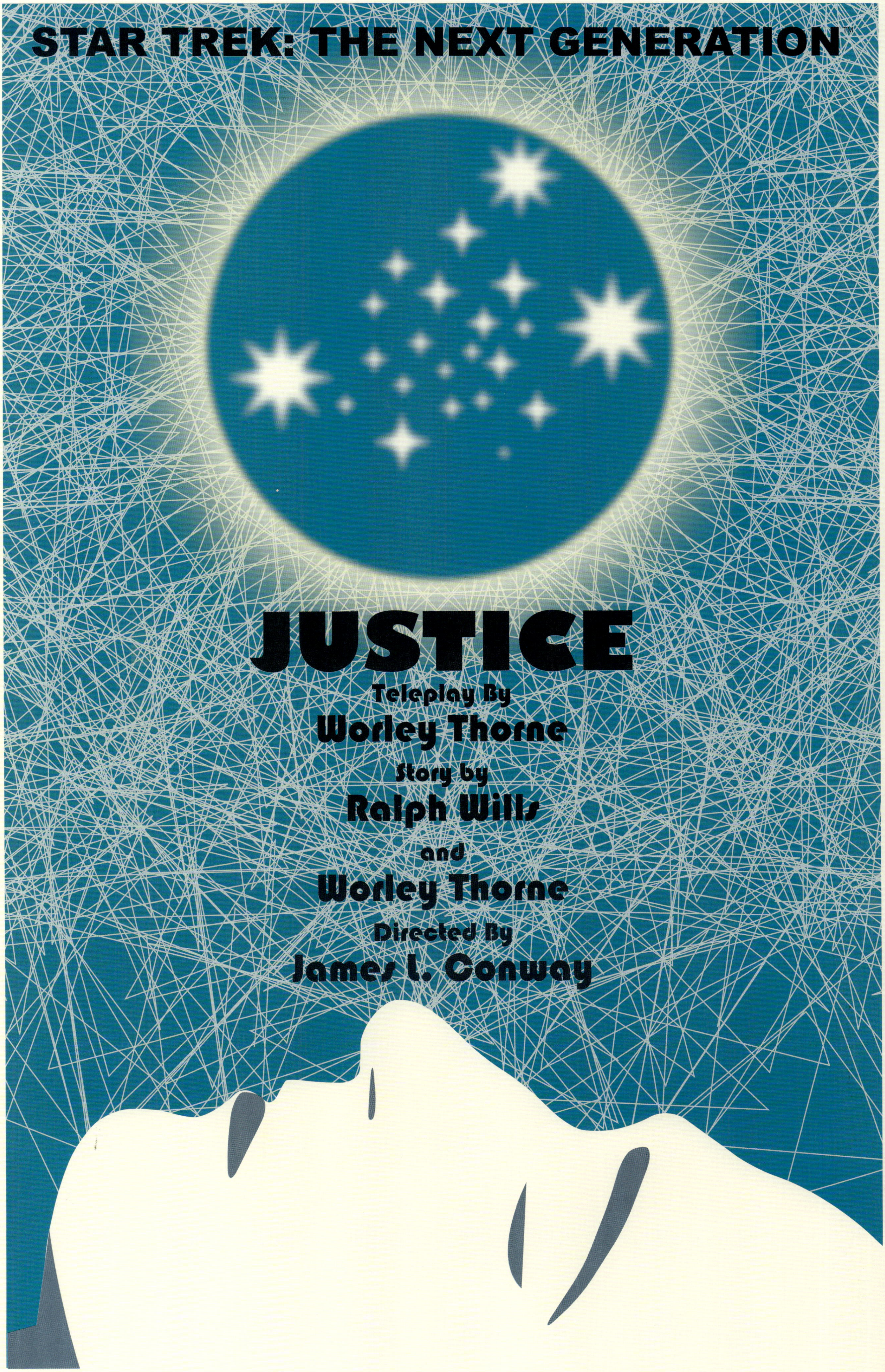
STAR TREK: THE NEXT GENERATION™
JUSTICE
Teleplay By
Worley Thorne
Story by
Ralph Wills
and
Worley Thorne
Directed By
James L. Conway

STAR TREK: THE NEXT GENERATION™

THE BATTLE

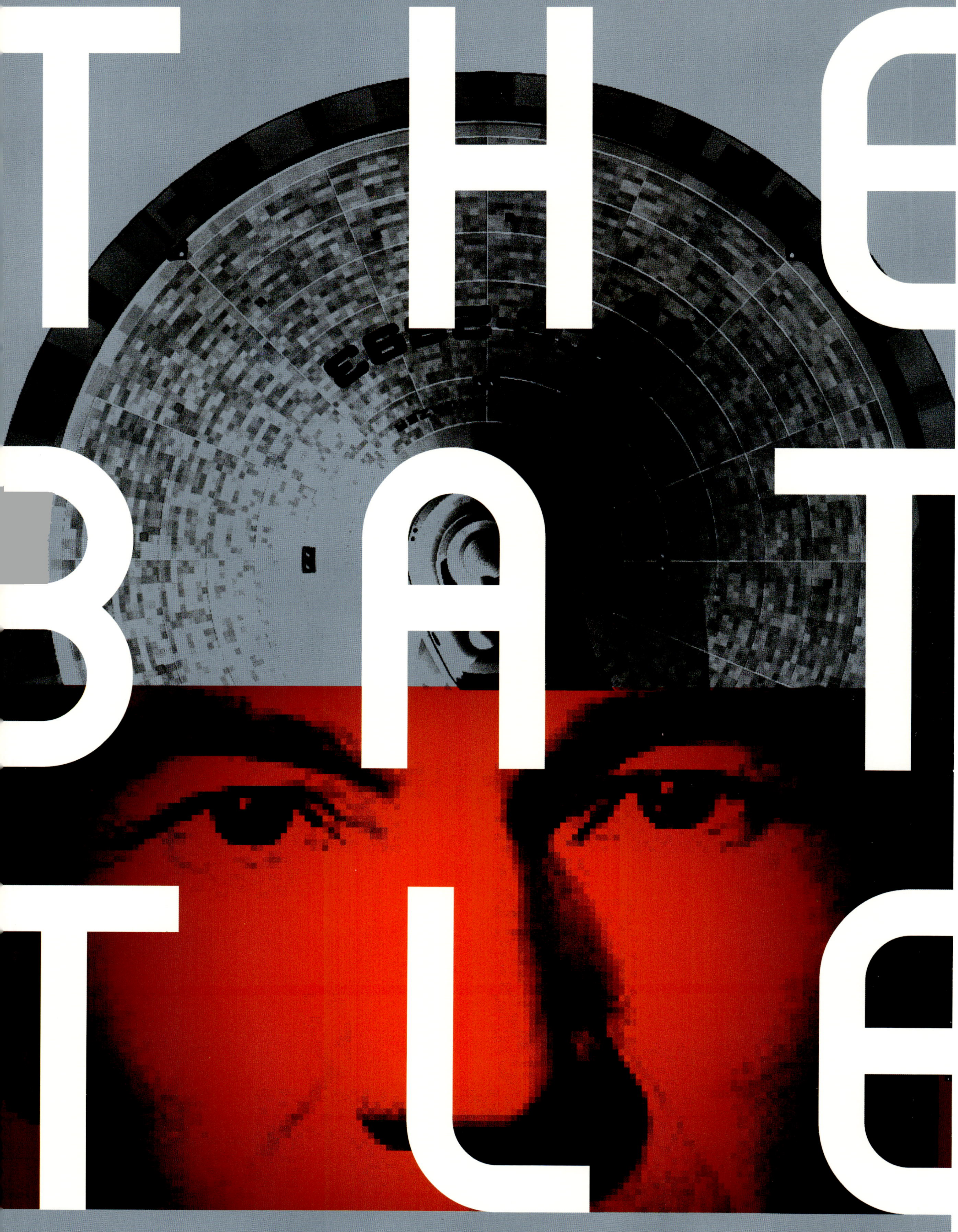

Teleplay by Herbert Wright

Story by Larry Forrester

Directed by Rob Bowman

Hide and

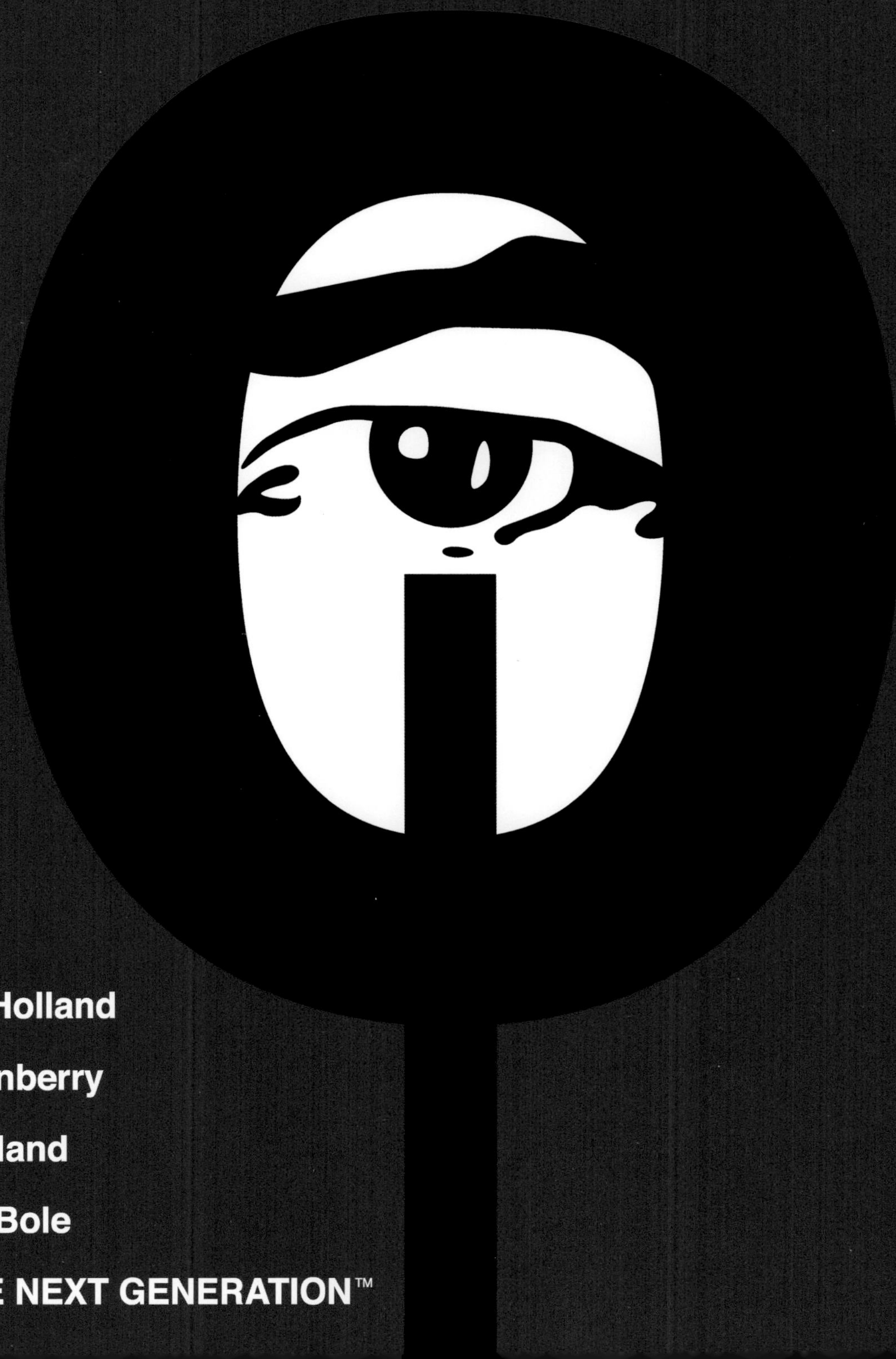

Teleplay by C.J. Holland

and Gene Roddenberry

Story by C.J. Holland

Directed by Cliff Bole

STAR TREK: THE NEXT GENERATION™

STAR TREK: THE NEXT GENERATION™

HAVEN

TELEPLAY BY

Tracy Tormé

STORY BY

Tracy Tormé and Lan O'Kun

DIRECTED BY

Richard Compton

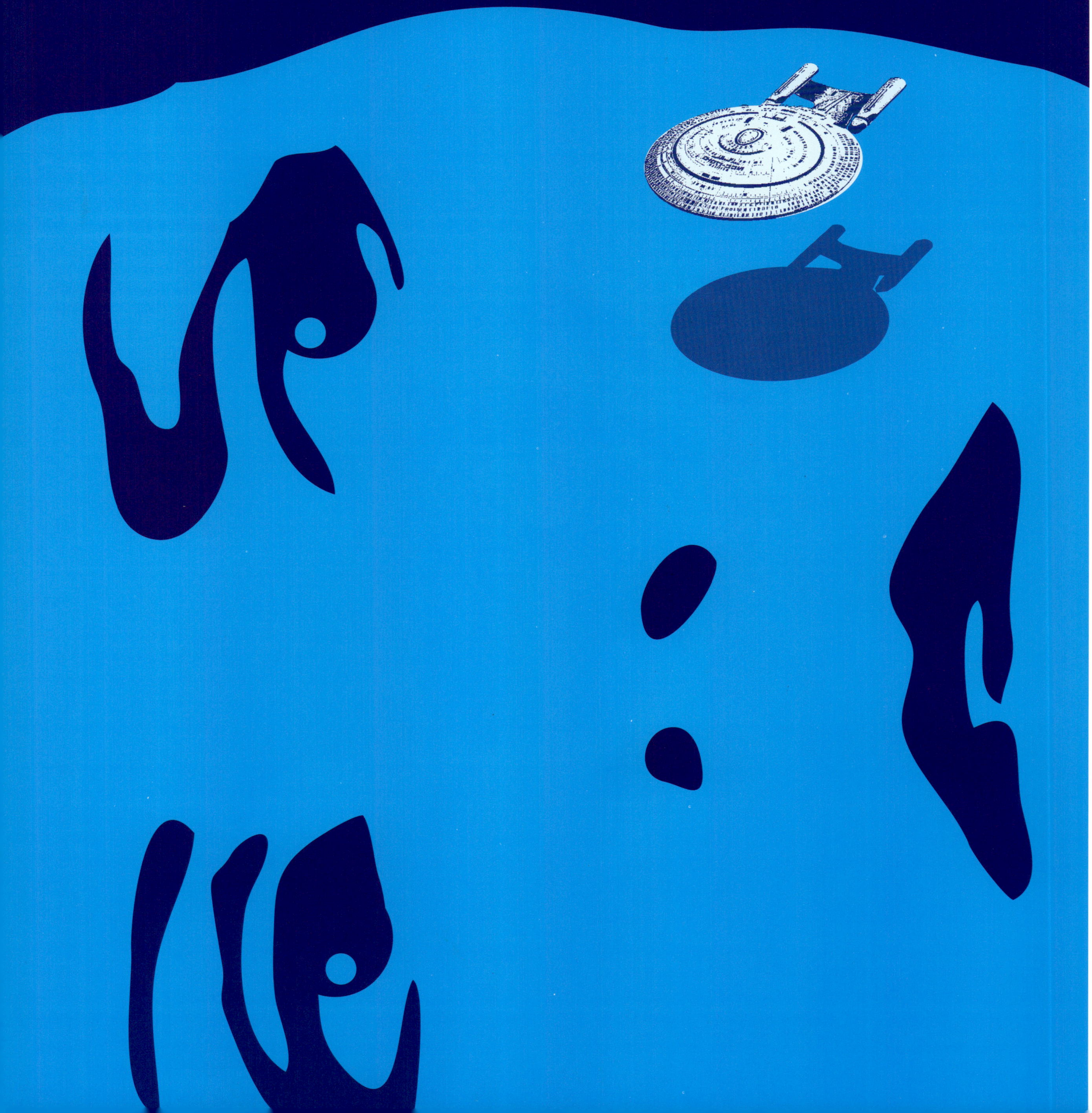

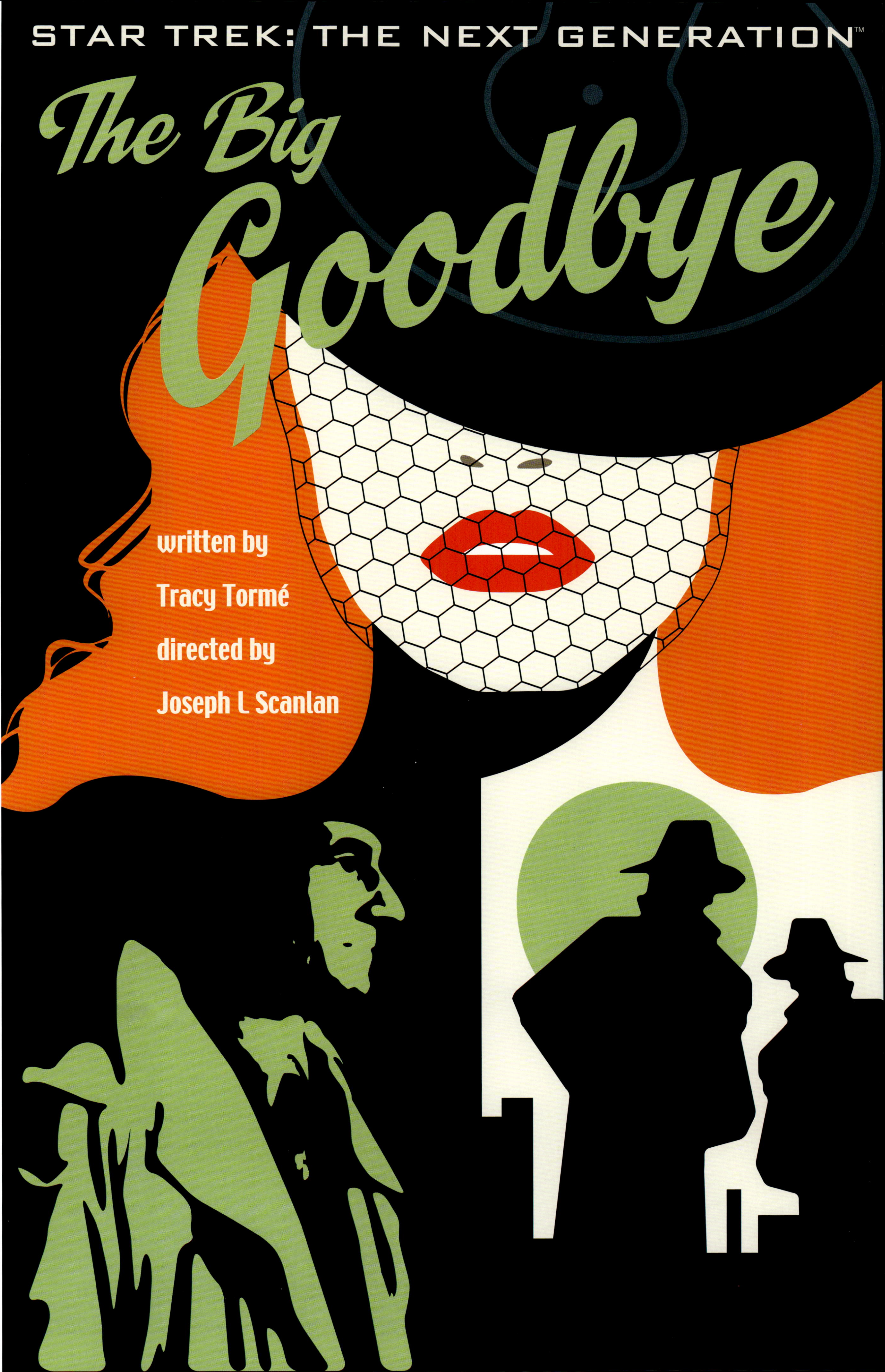
STAR TREK: THE NEXT GENERATION™
The Big Goodbye
written by
Tracy Tormé
directed by
Joseph L Scanlan

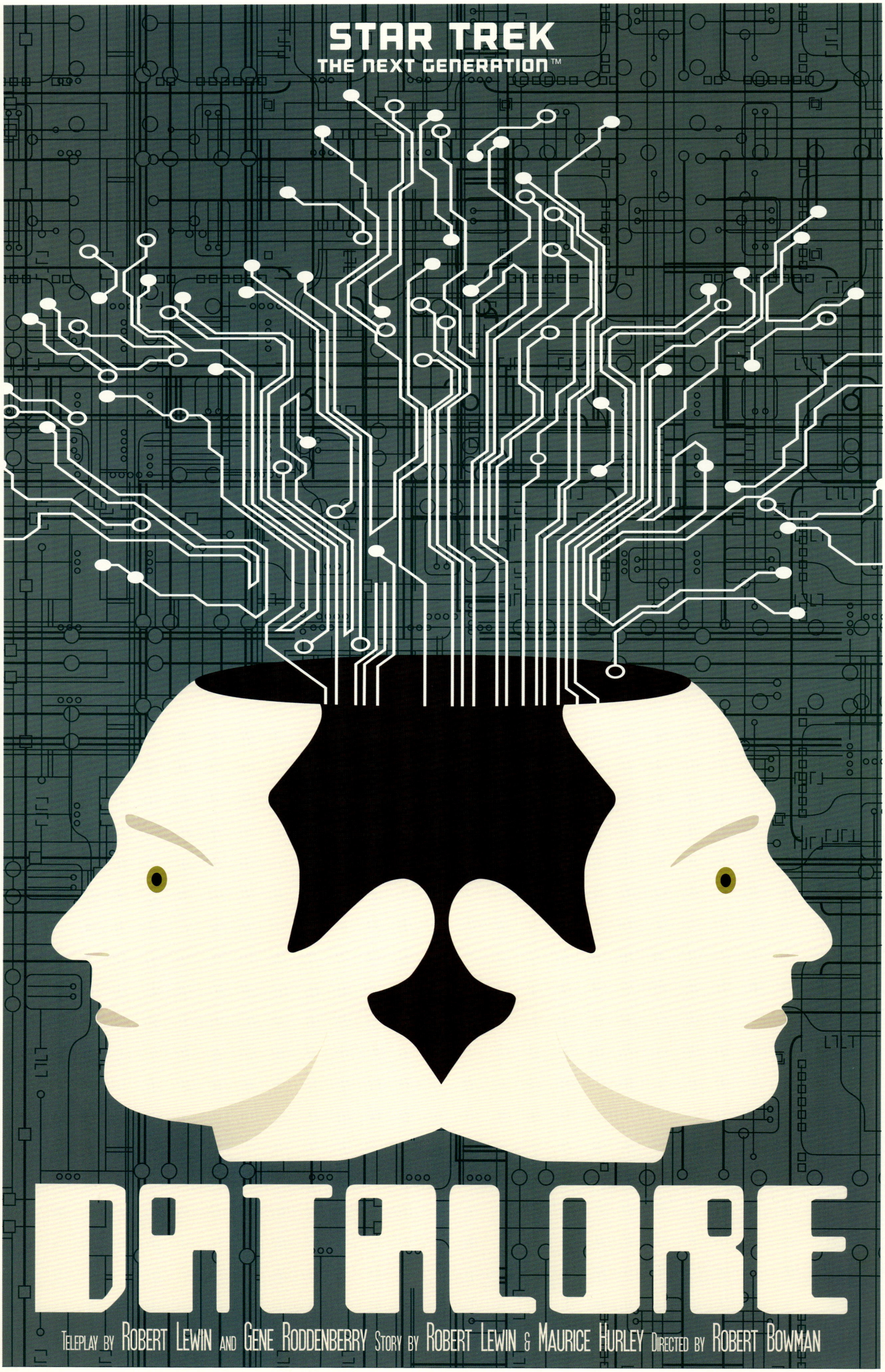
STAR TREK
THE NEXT GENERATION™
DATALORE
TELEPLAY BY ROBERT LEWIN AND GENE RODDENBERRY STORY BY ROBERT LEWIN & MAURICE HURLEY DIRECTED BY ROBERT BOWMAN

STAR TREK: THE NEXT GENERATION™

ANGEL ONE

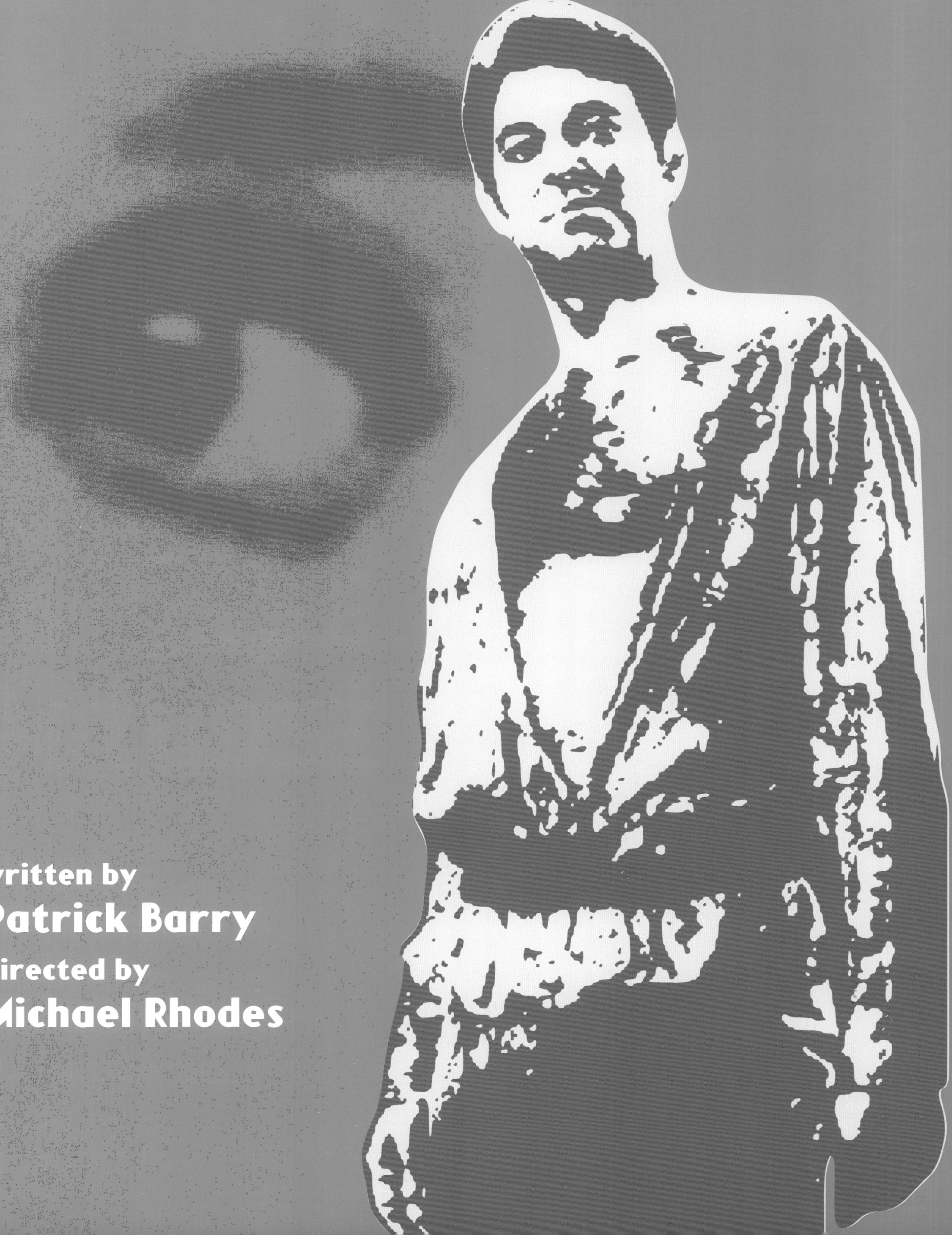

written by
Patrick Barry
directed by
Michael Rhodes

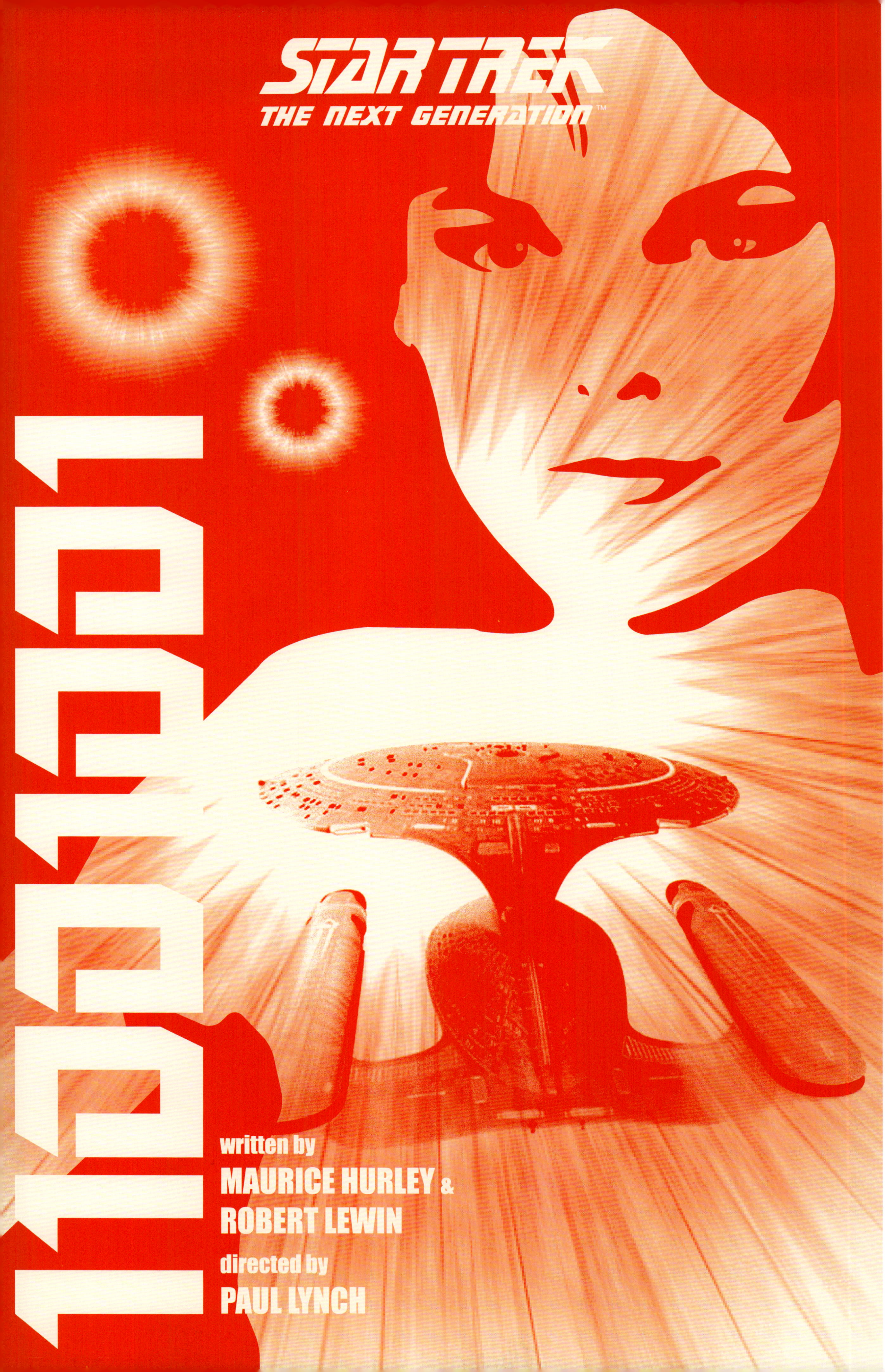
STAR TREK
THE NEXT GENERATION
11001001
written by
MAURICE HURLEY &
ROBERT LEWIN
directed by
PAUL LYNCH

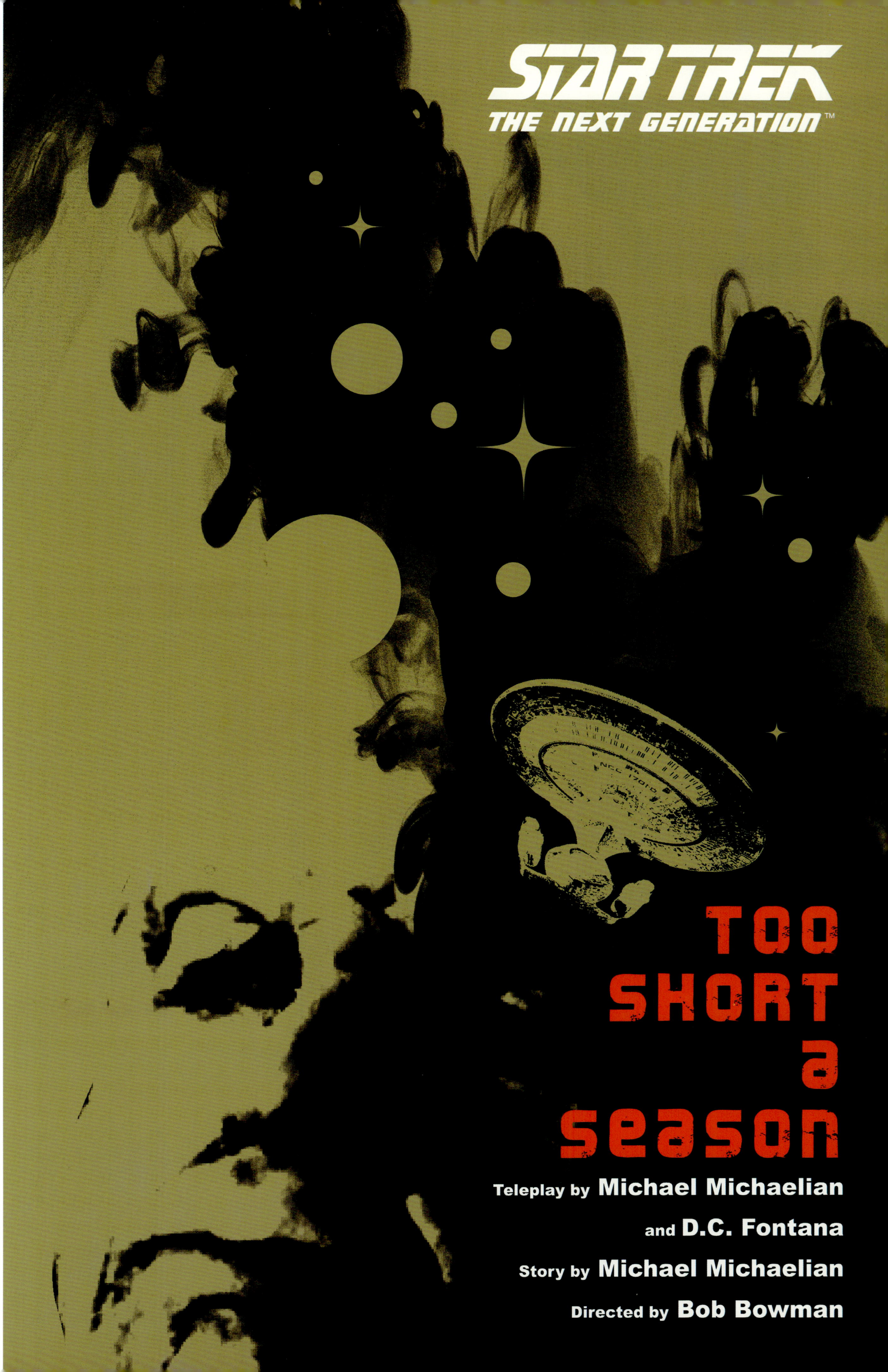
STAR TREK
THE NEXT GENERATION™
TOO SHORT a season
Teleplay by Michael Michaelian
and D.C. Fontana
Story by Michael Michaelian
Directed by Bob Bowman

STAR TREK
THE NEXT GENERATION™

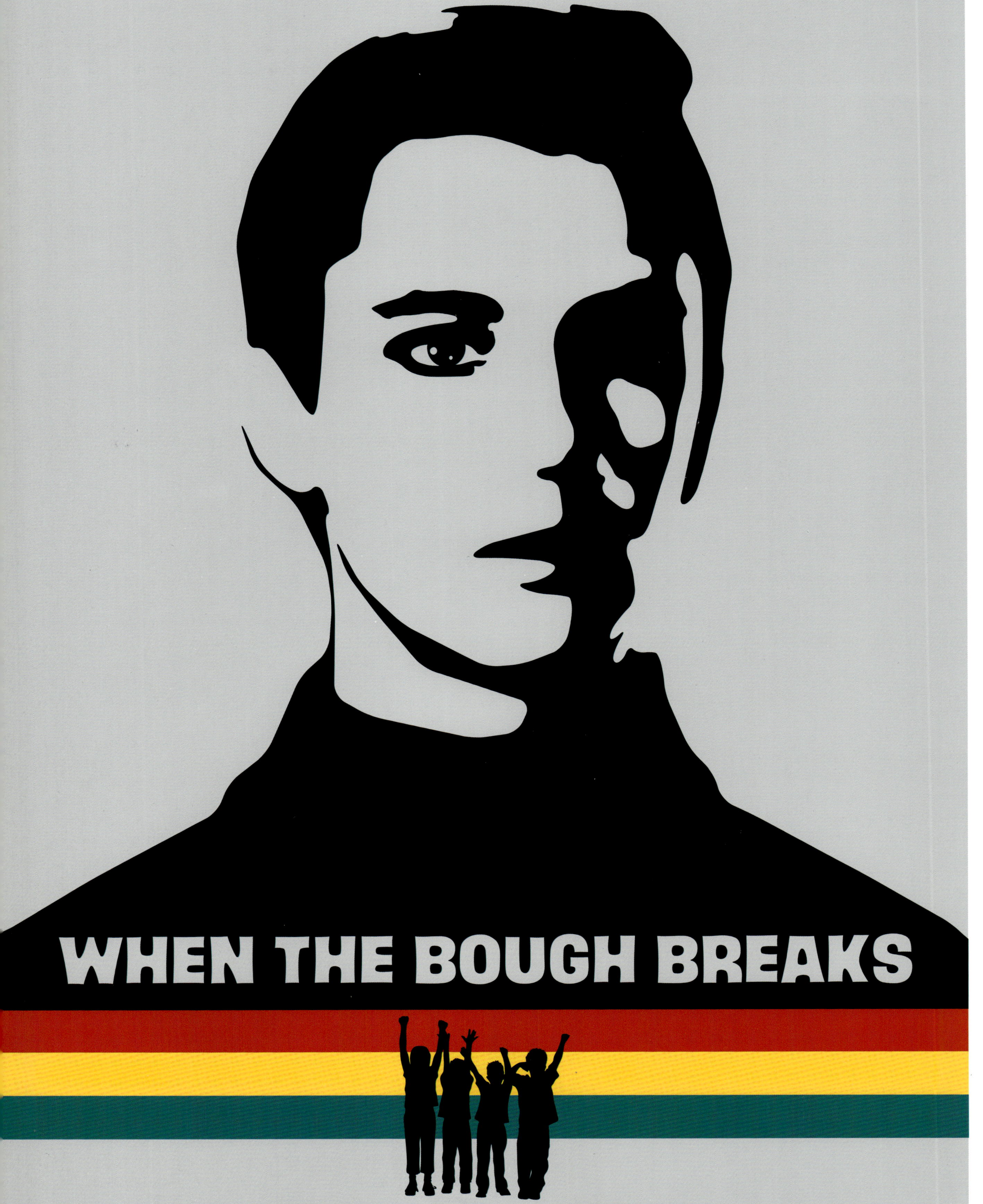

Written by Hannah Louise Shearer
Directed by Kim Manners

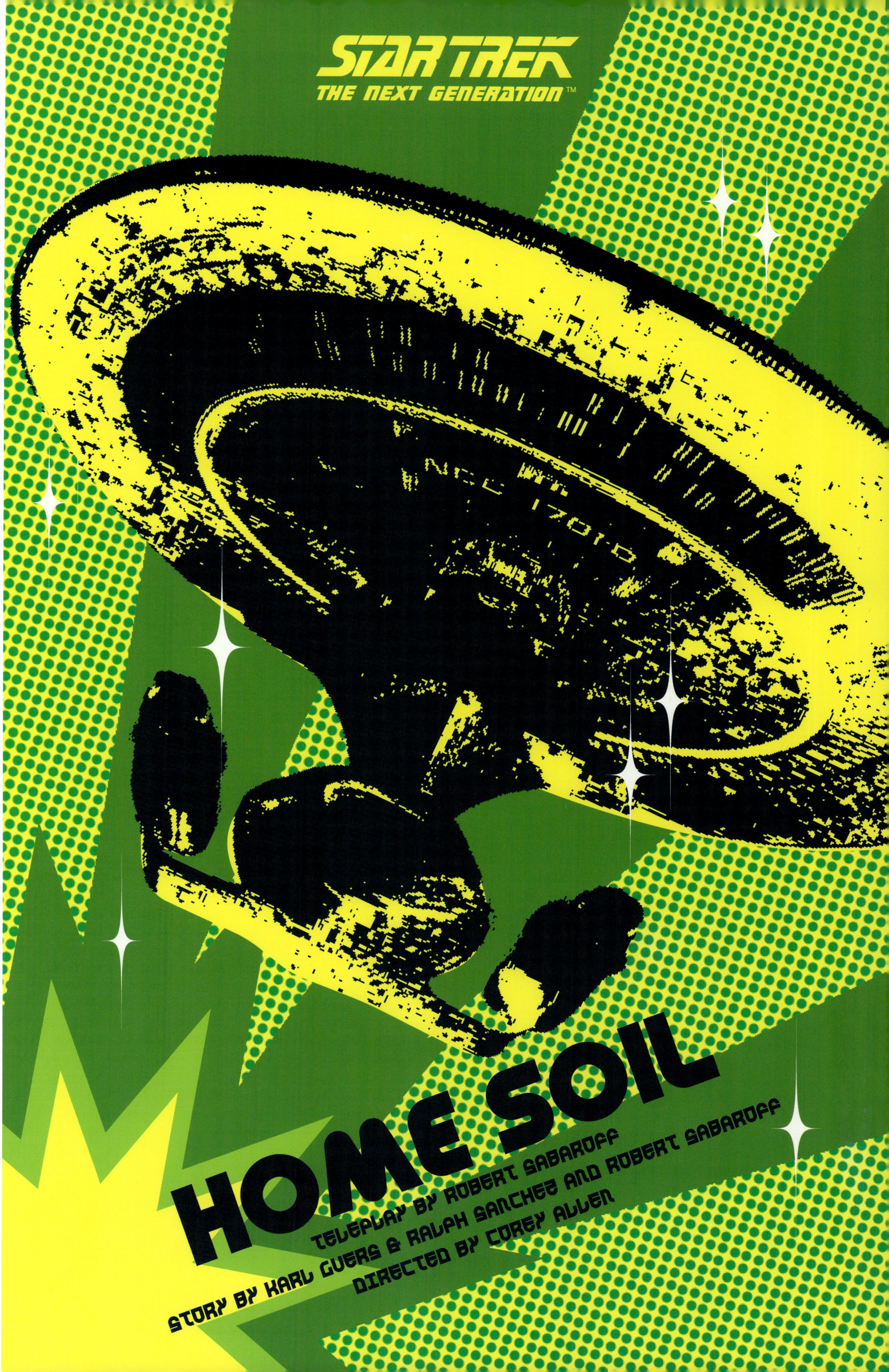
STAR TREK
THE NEXT GENERATION™
NCC-1701-D
HOME SOIL
TELEPLAY BY ROBERT SABAROFF
STORY BY KARL GUERS & RALPH SANCHEZ AND ROBERT SABAROFF
DIRECTED BY COREY ALLEN

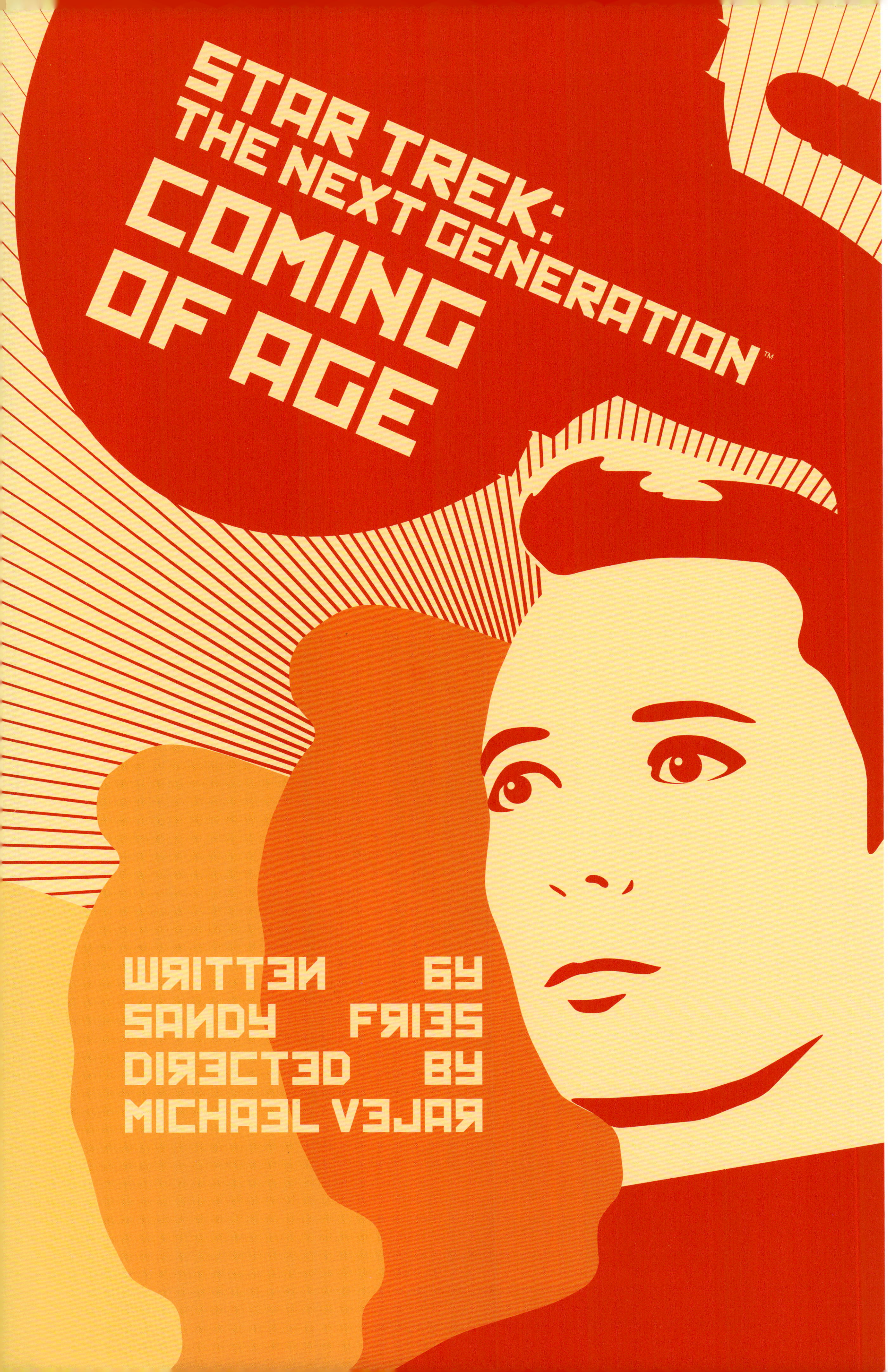
STAR TREK:
THE NEXT GENERATION™
COMING
OF AGE
WRITTEN BY
SANDY FRIES
DIRECTED BY
MICHAEL VEJAR

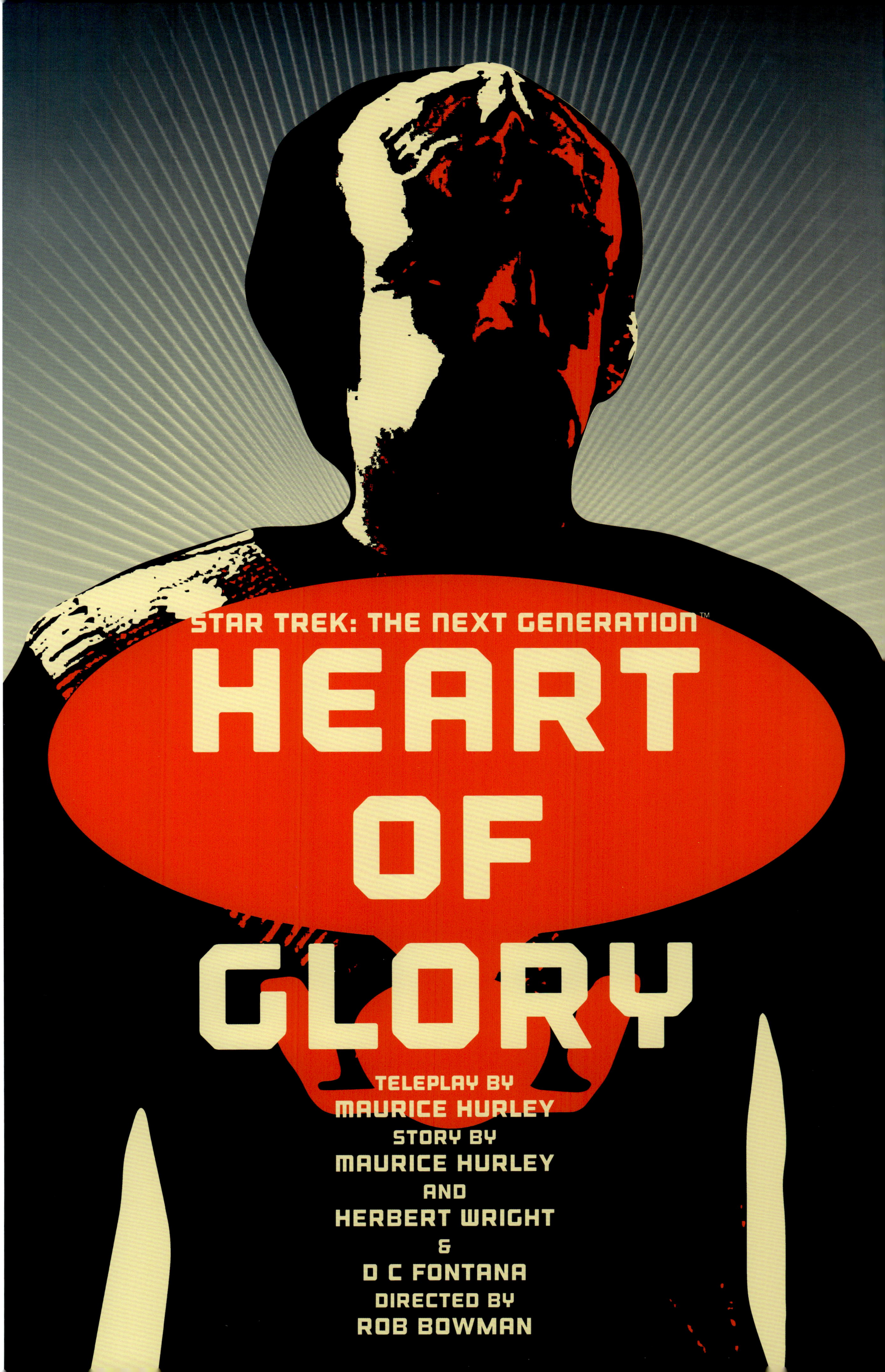
STAR TREK: THE NEXT GENERATION™
HEART
OF
GLORY
TELEPLAY BY
MAURICE HURLEY
STORY BY
MAURICE HURLEY
AND
HERBERT WRIGHT
&
D C FONTANA
DIRECTED BY
ROB BOWMAN

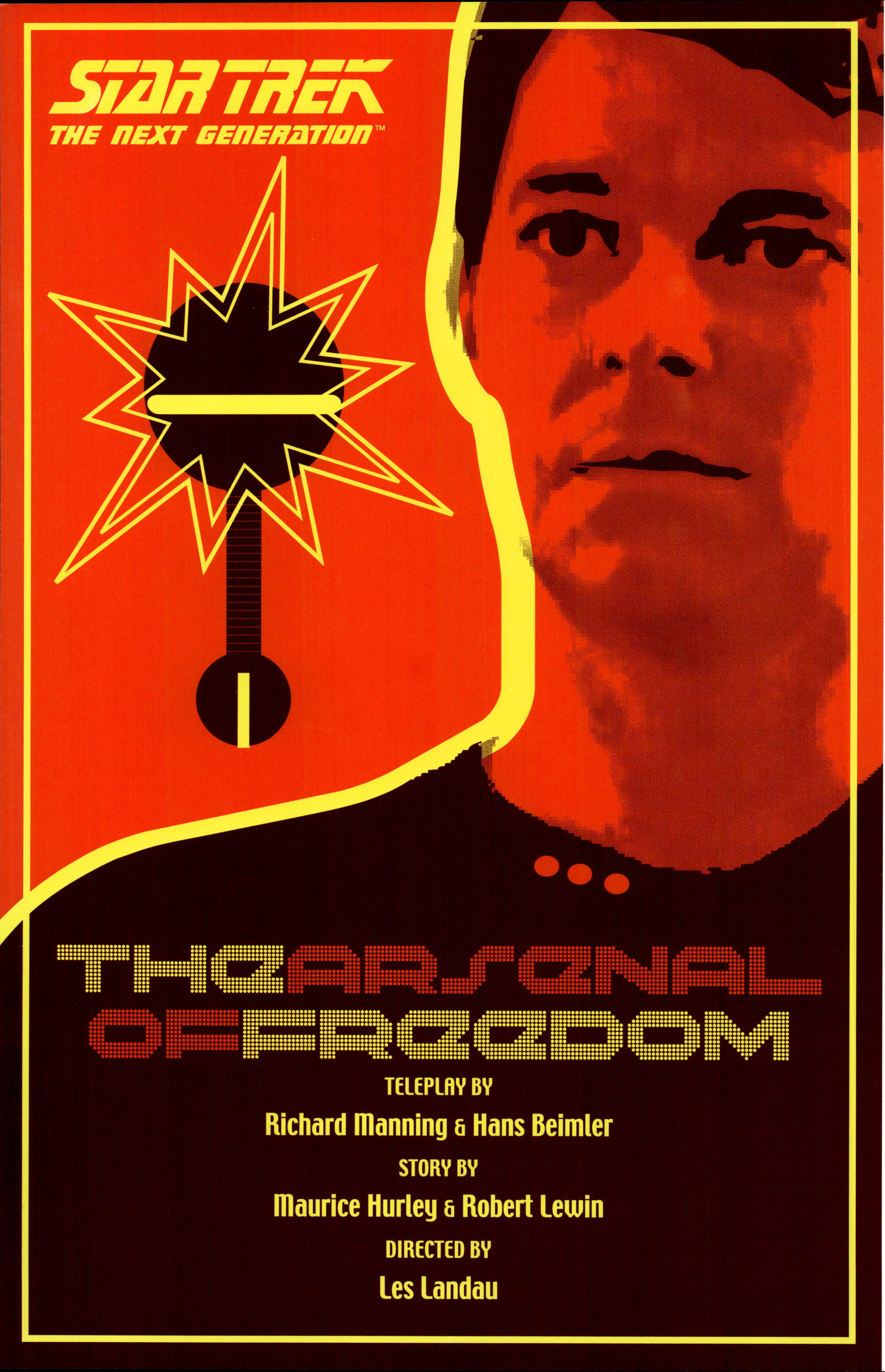
STAR TREK
THE NEXT GENERATION™
THE ARSENAL
OF FREEDOM
TELEPLAY BY
Richard Manning & Hans Beimler
STORY BY
Maurice Hurley & Robert Lewin
DIRECTED BY
Les Landau

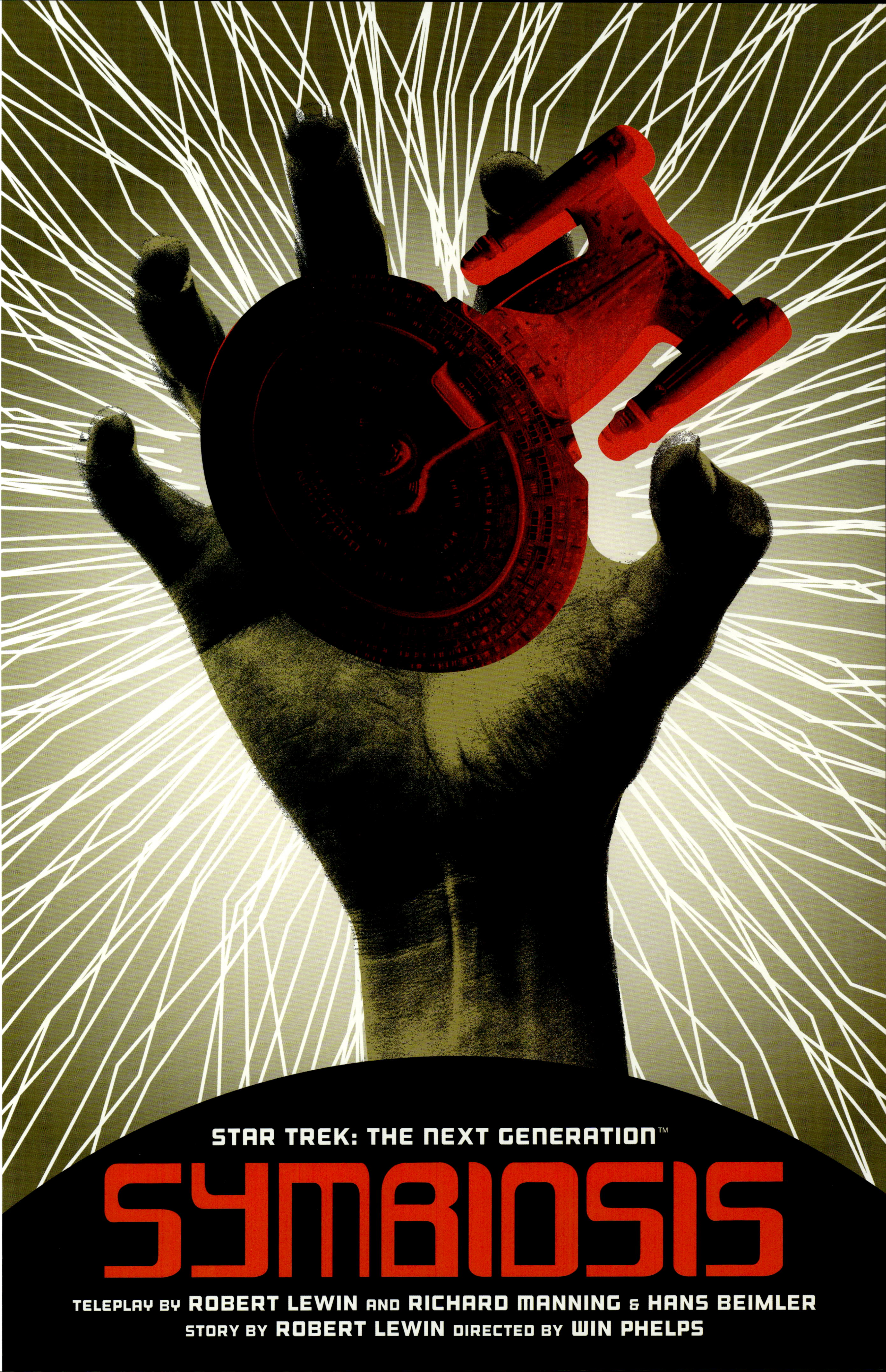
STAR TREK: THE NEXT GENERATION™
SYMBIOSIS
TELEPLAY BY ROBERT LEWIN AND RICHARD MANNING & HANS BEIMLER
STORY BY ROBERT LEWIN DIRECTED BY WIN PHELPS

STAR TREK
THE NEXT GENERATION™

SKIN OF EVIL

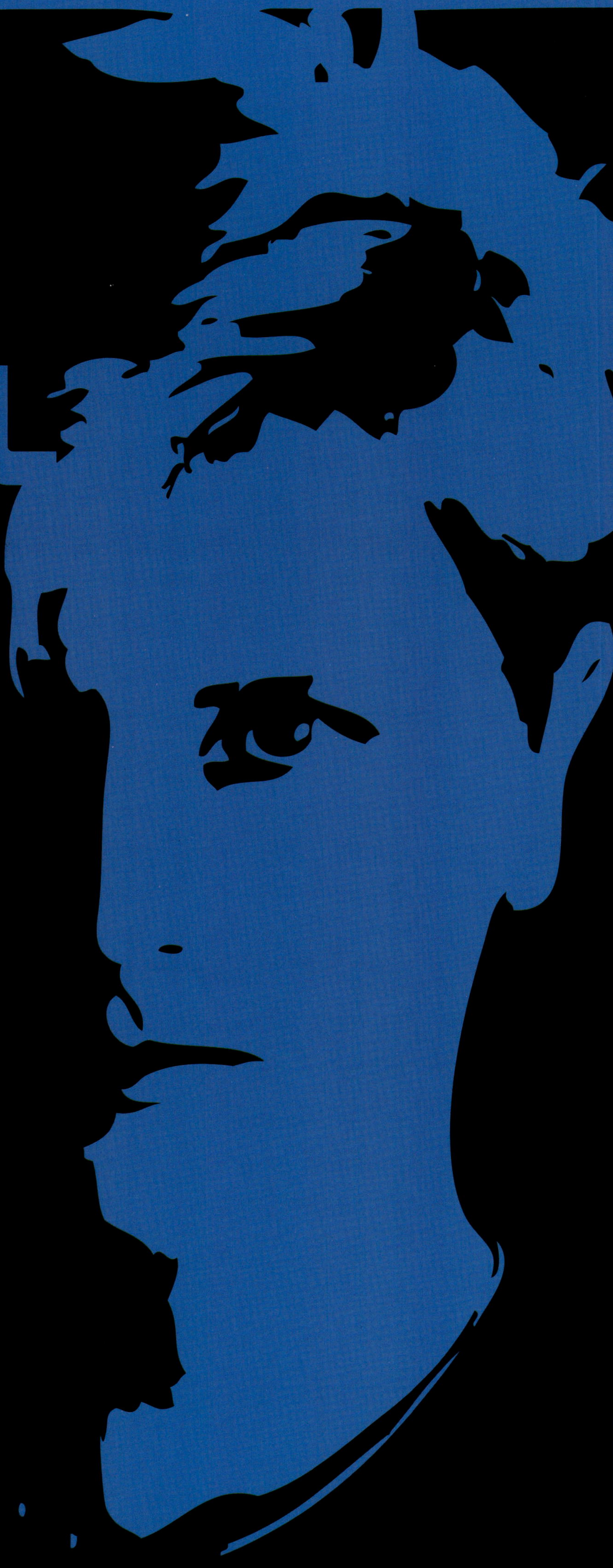

TELEPLAY BY

JOSEPH STEFANO

AND

HANNAH LOUISE SHEARER

STORY BY

JOSEPH STEFANO

DIRECTED BY

JOSEPH L. SCANLAN

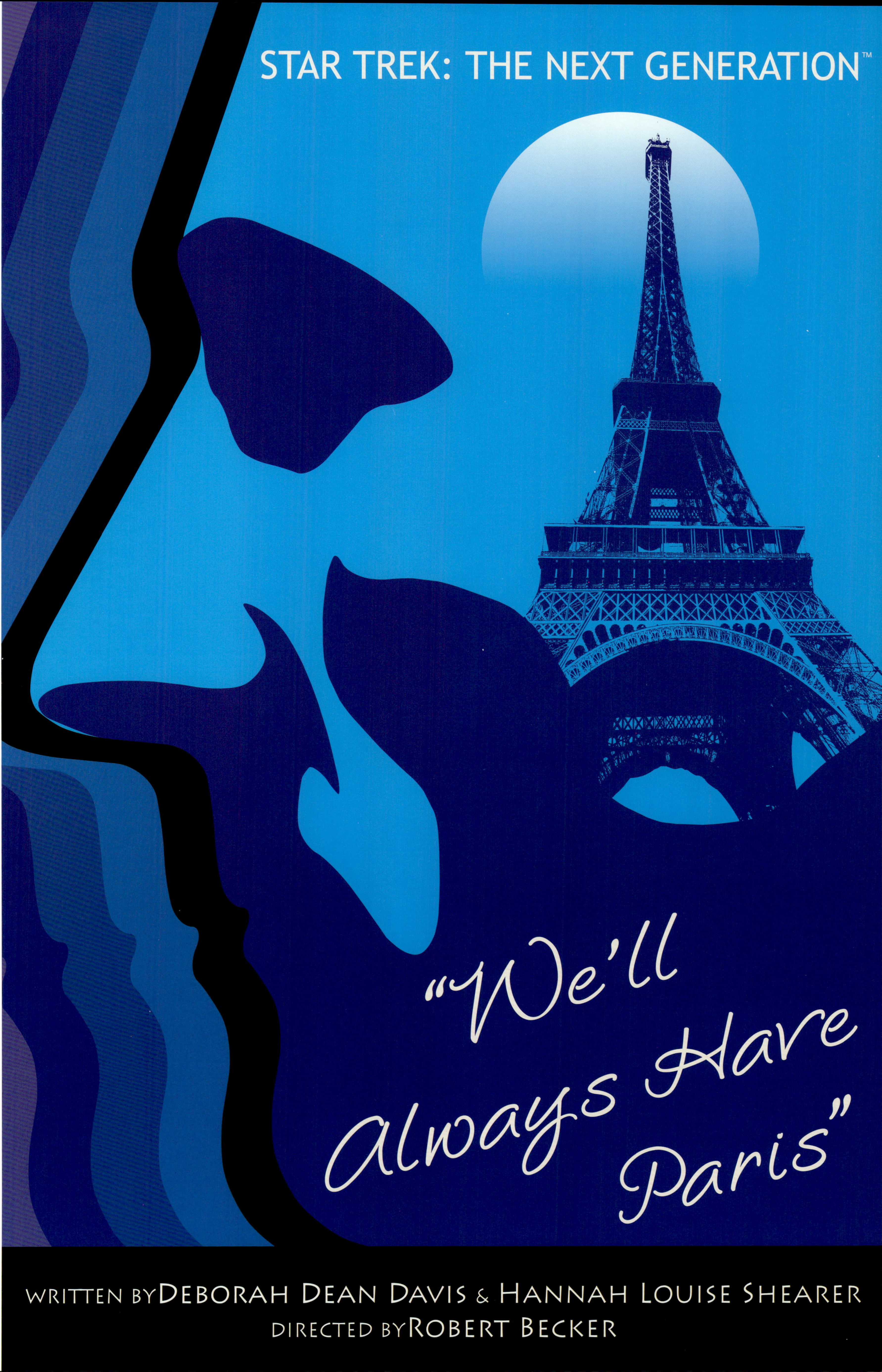
STAR TREK: THE NEXT GENERATION™
"We'll Always Have Paris"
WRITTEN BY DEBORAH DEAN DAVIS & HANNAH LOUISE SHEARER
DIRECTED BY ROBERT BECKER

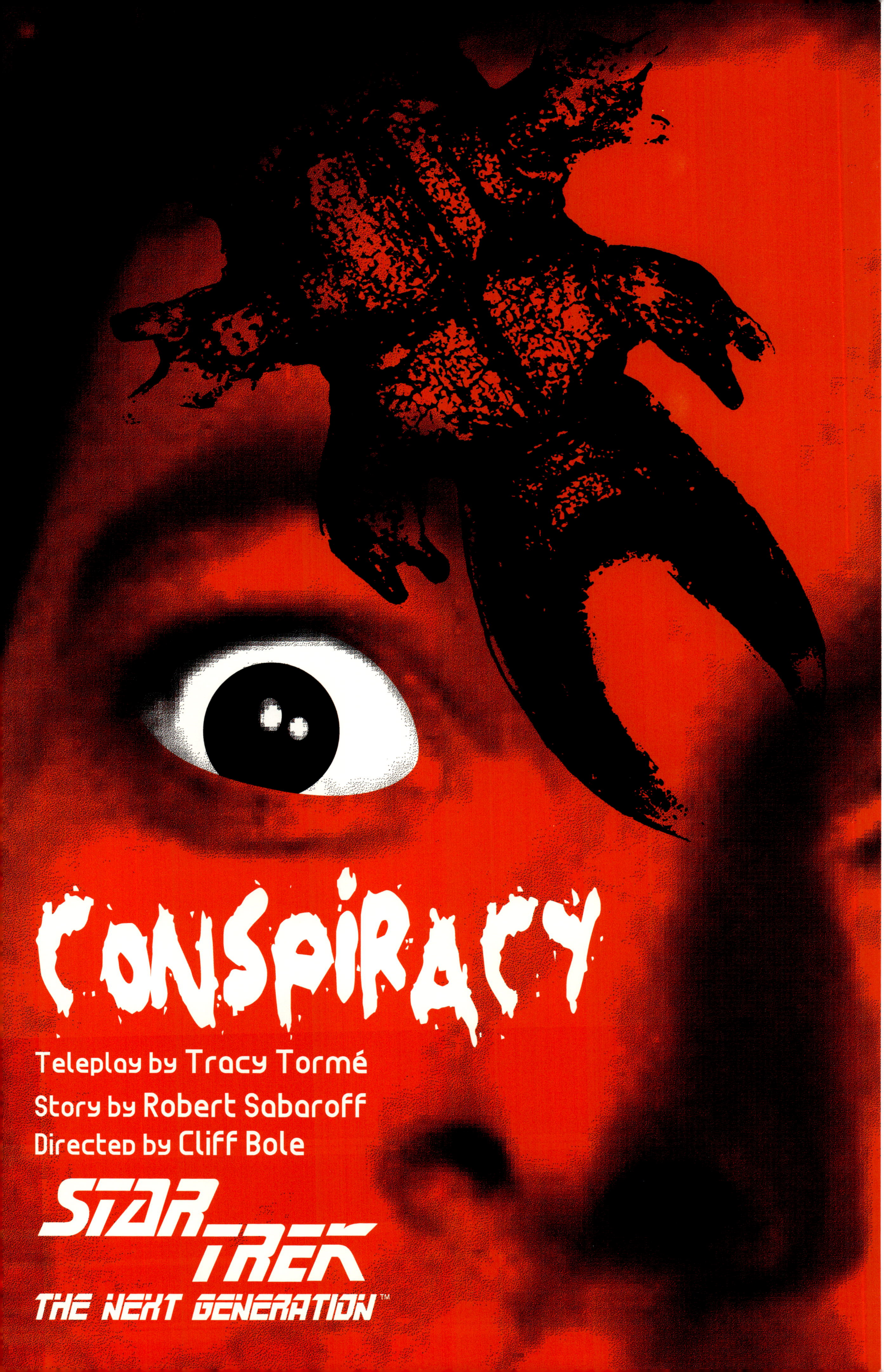

CONSPIRACY

Teleplay by Tracy Tormé

Story by Robert Sabaroff

Directed by Cliff Bole

STAR TREK
THE NEXT GENERATION™

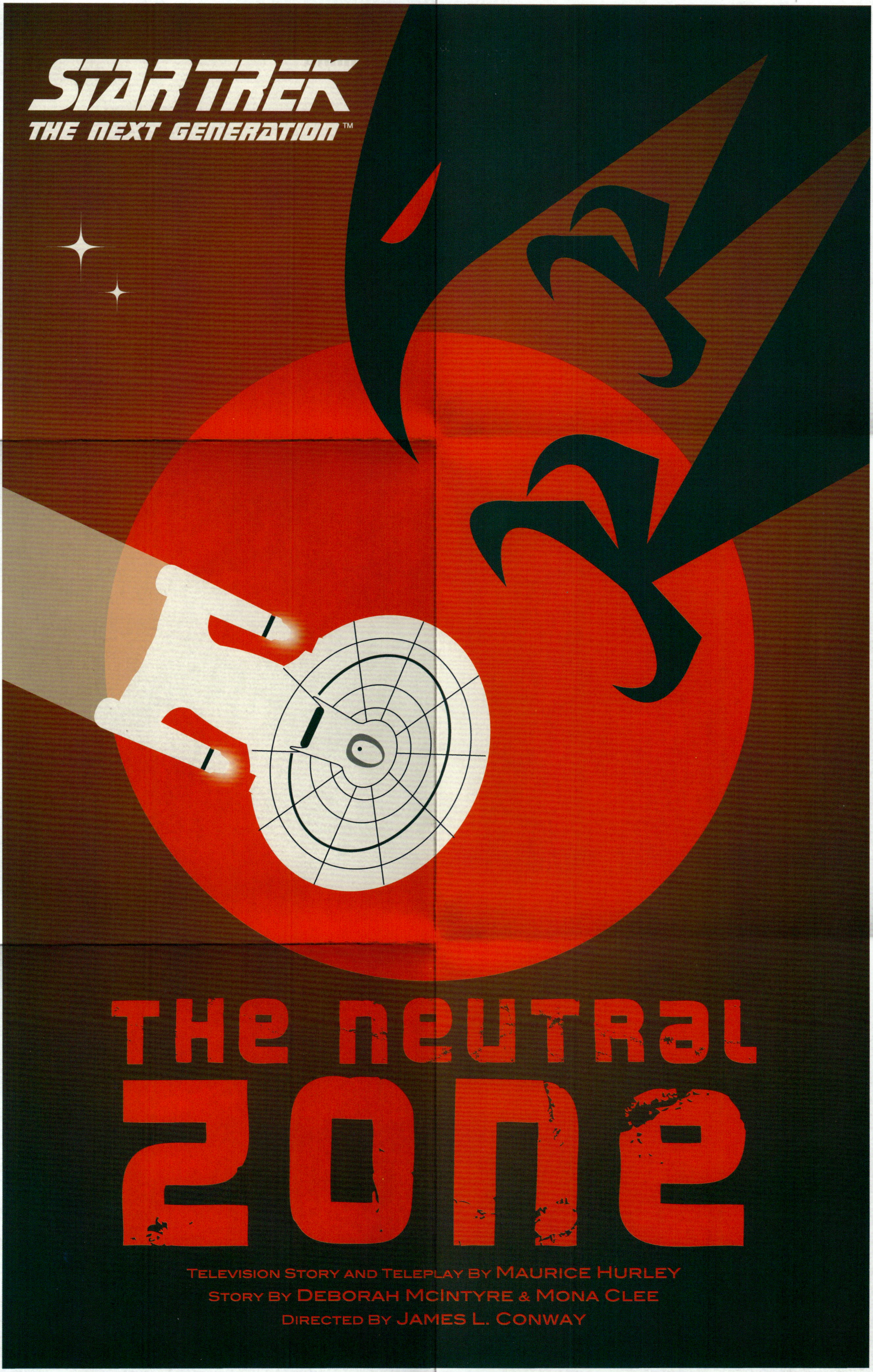
STAR TREK
THE NEXT GENERATION™
THE NEUTRAL ZONE
TELEVISION STORY AND TELEPLAY BY MAURICE HURLEY
STORY BY DEBORAH MCINTYRE & MONA CLEE
DIRECTED BY JAMES L. CONWAY

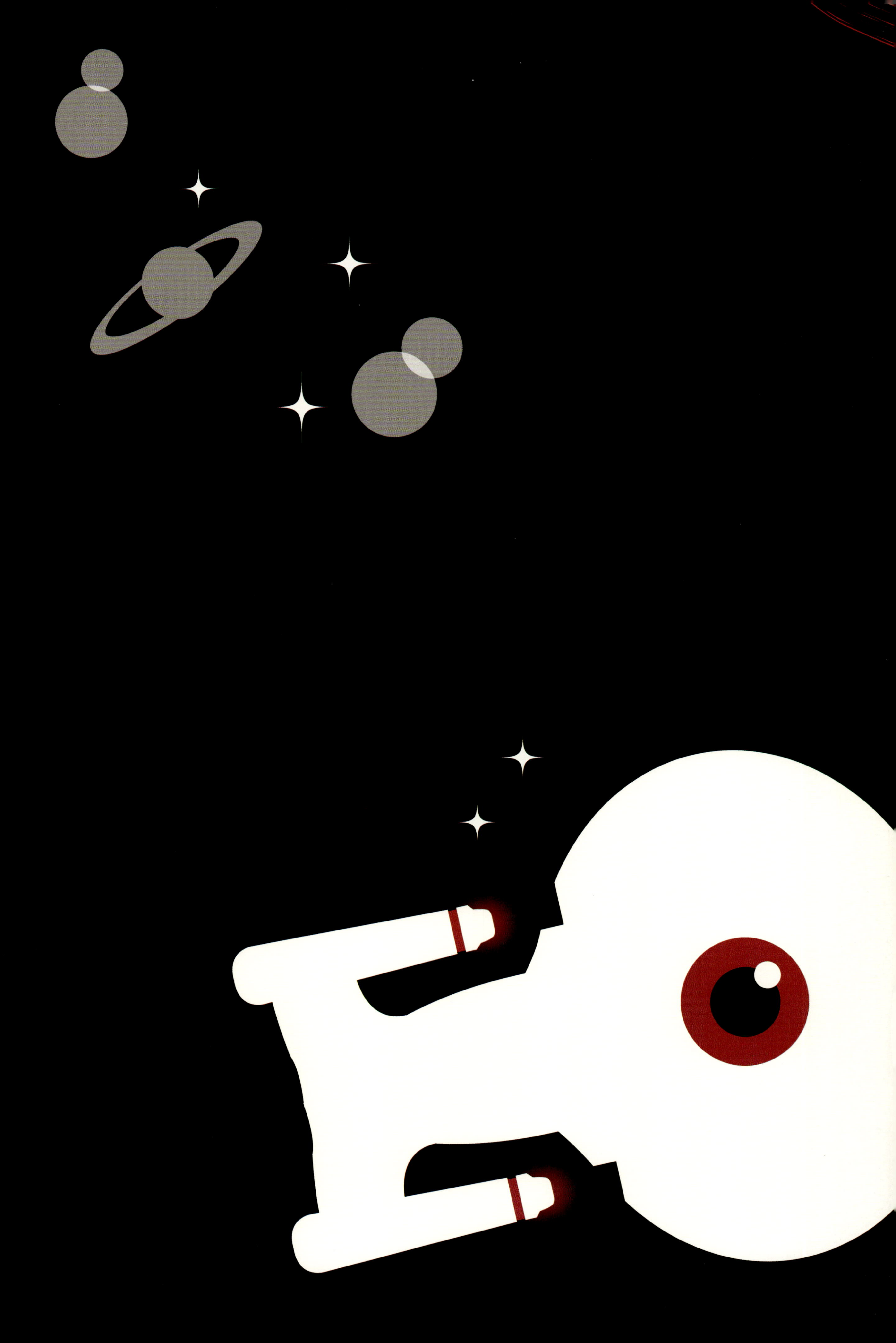

Season Two

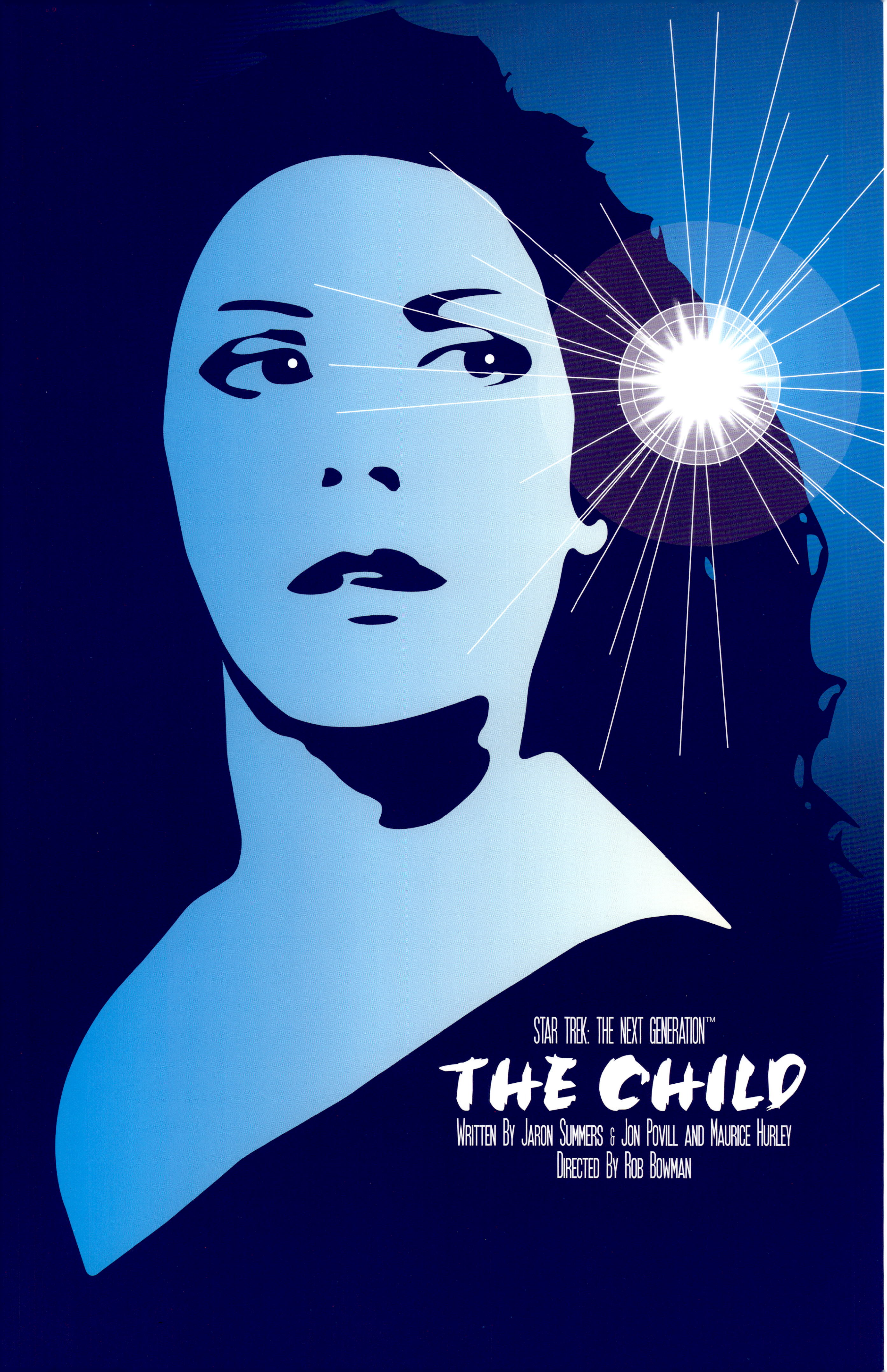
STAR TREK: THE NEXT GENERATION™
THE CHILD
WRITTEN BY JARON SUMMERS & JON POVILL AND MAURICE HURLEY
DIRECTED BY ROB BOWMAN

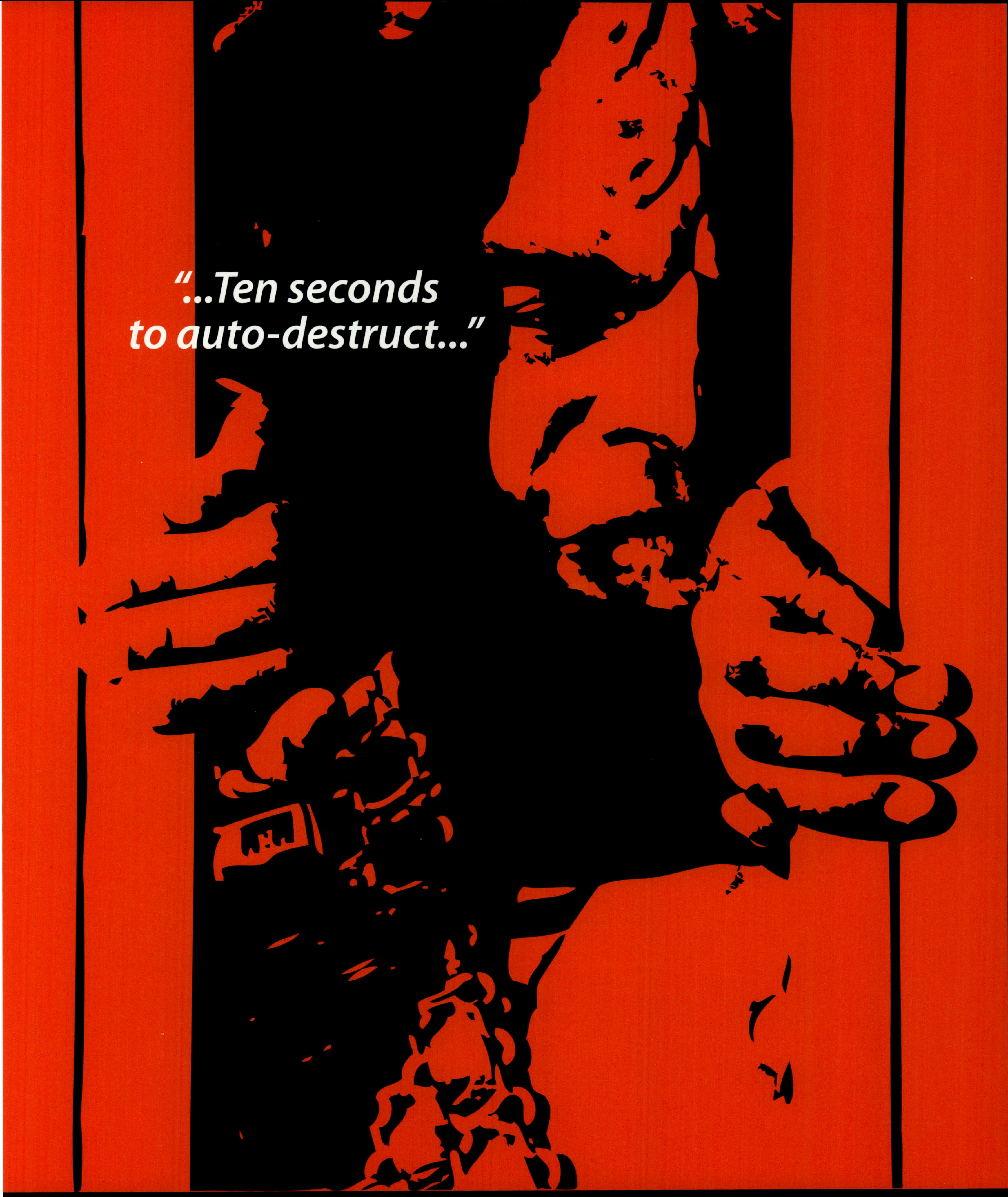

STAR TREK: THE NEXT GENERATION™

WHERE SILENCE HAS LEASE

Written By Jack B. Sowards   Directed By Winrich Kolbe

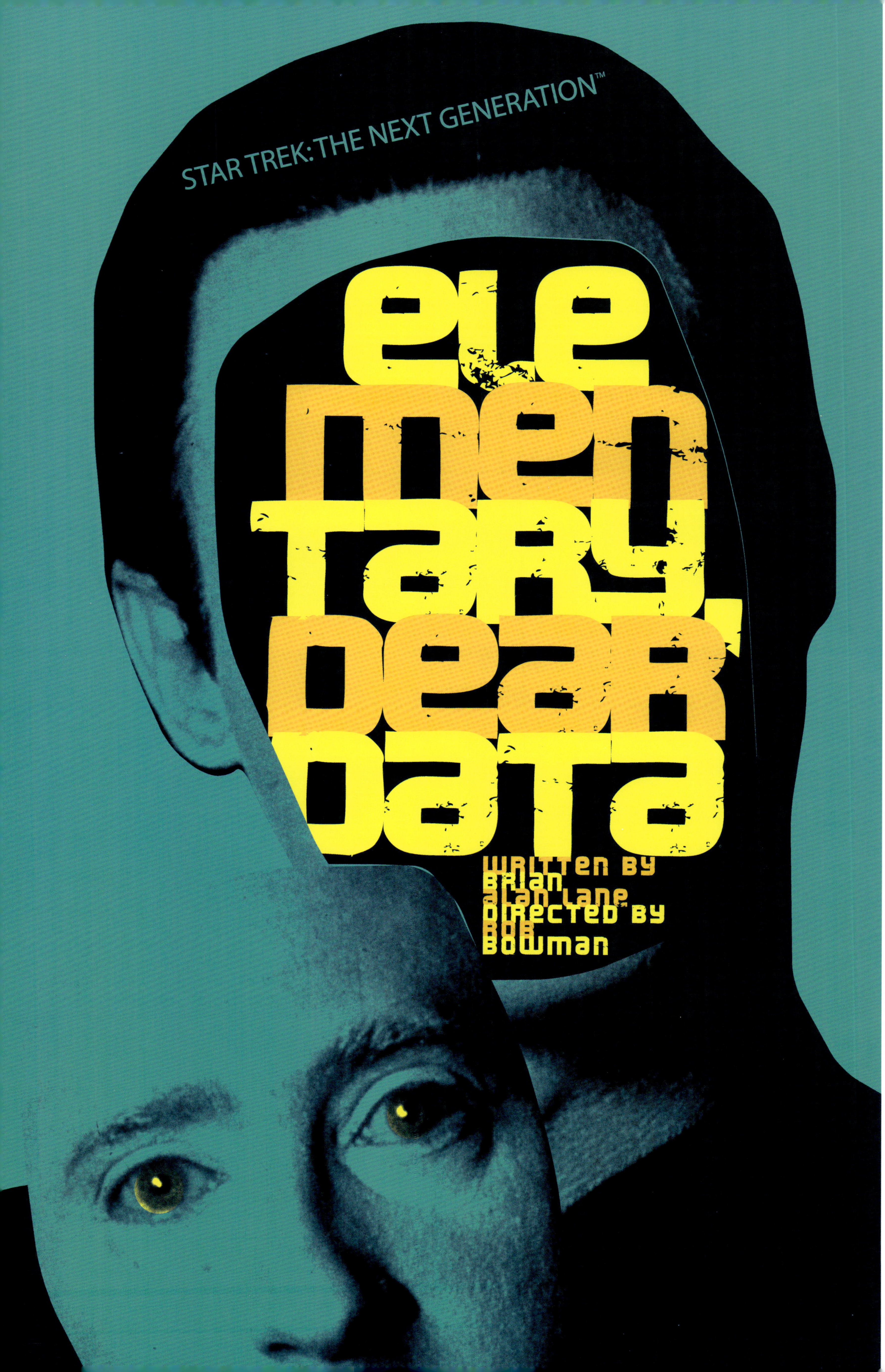
STAR TREK: THE NEXT GENERATION™
ele
men
tary,
dear
data
Written by
Brian
Alan Lane
Directed by
Rob
Bowman

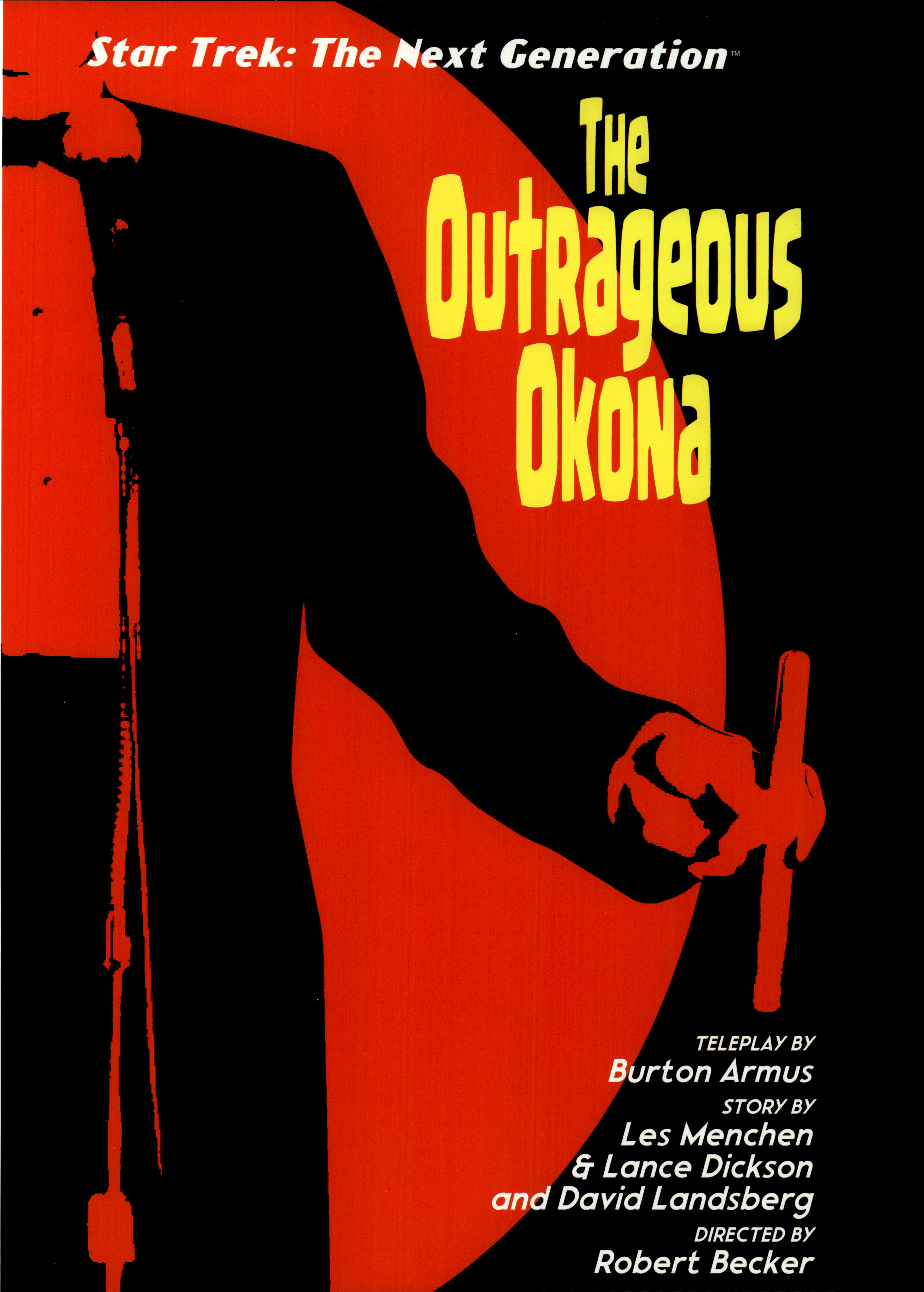

Star Trek: The Next Generation™

The Outrageous Okona

TELEPLAY BY
Burton Armus
STORY BY
Les Menchen
& Lance Dickson
and David Landsberg
DIRECTED BY
Robert Becker

STAR TREK: THE NEXT GENERATION™

LOUD AS A WHISPER

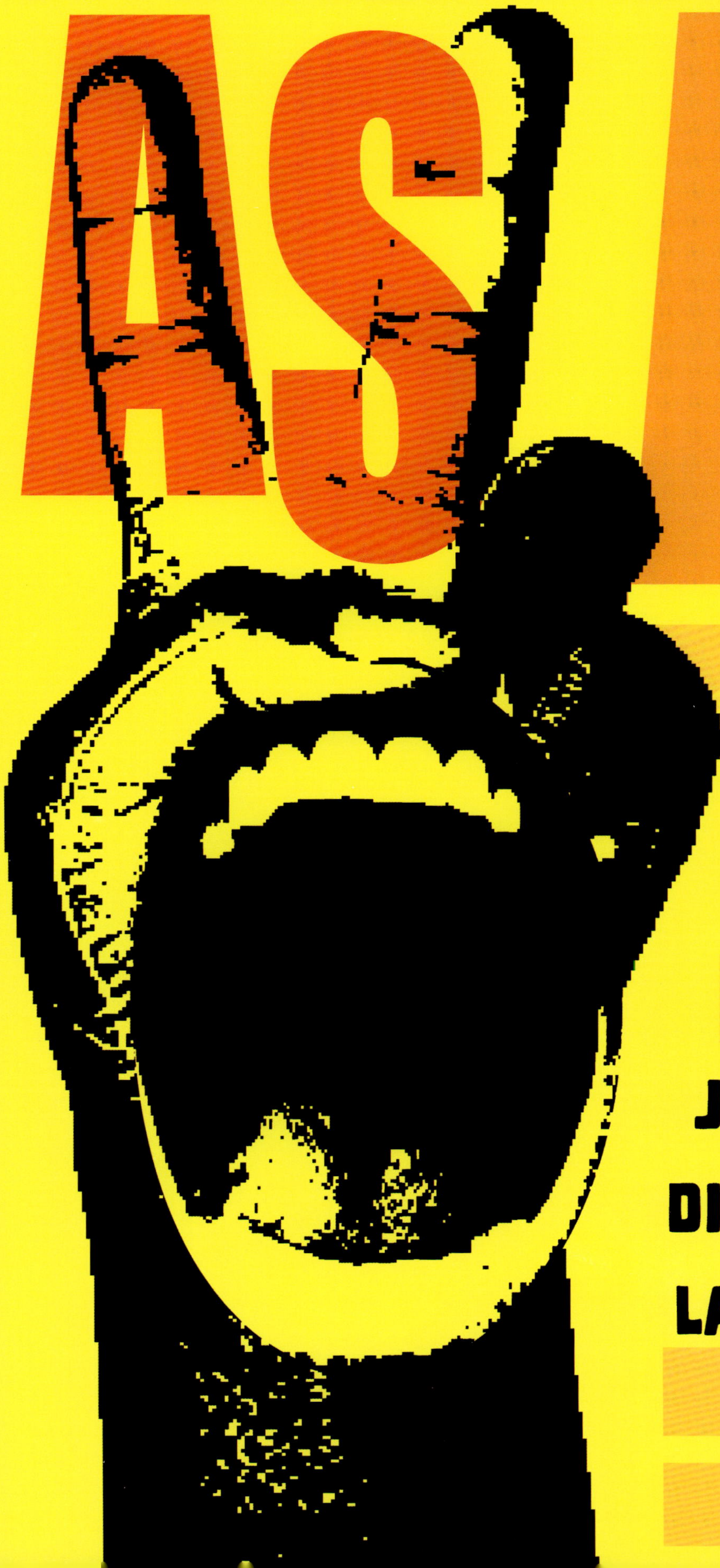

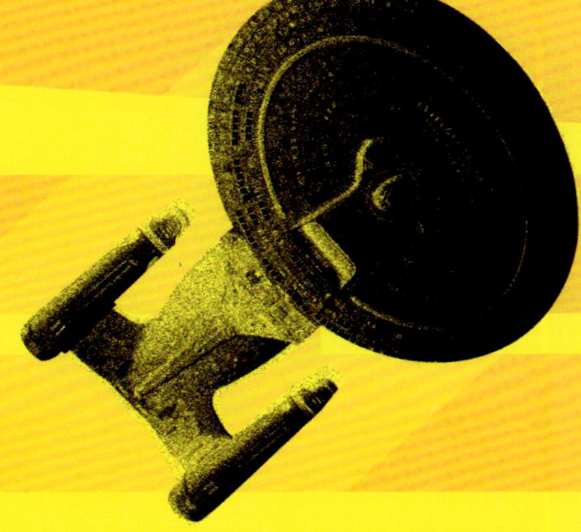

WRITTEN BY
JACQUELINE ZAMBRANO

DIRECTED BY
LARRY SHAW

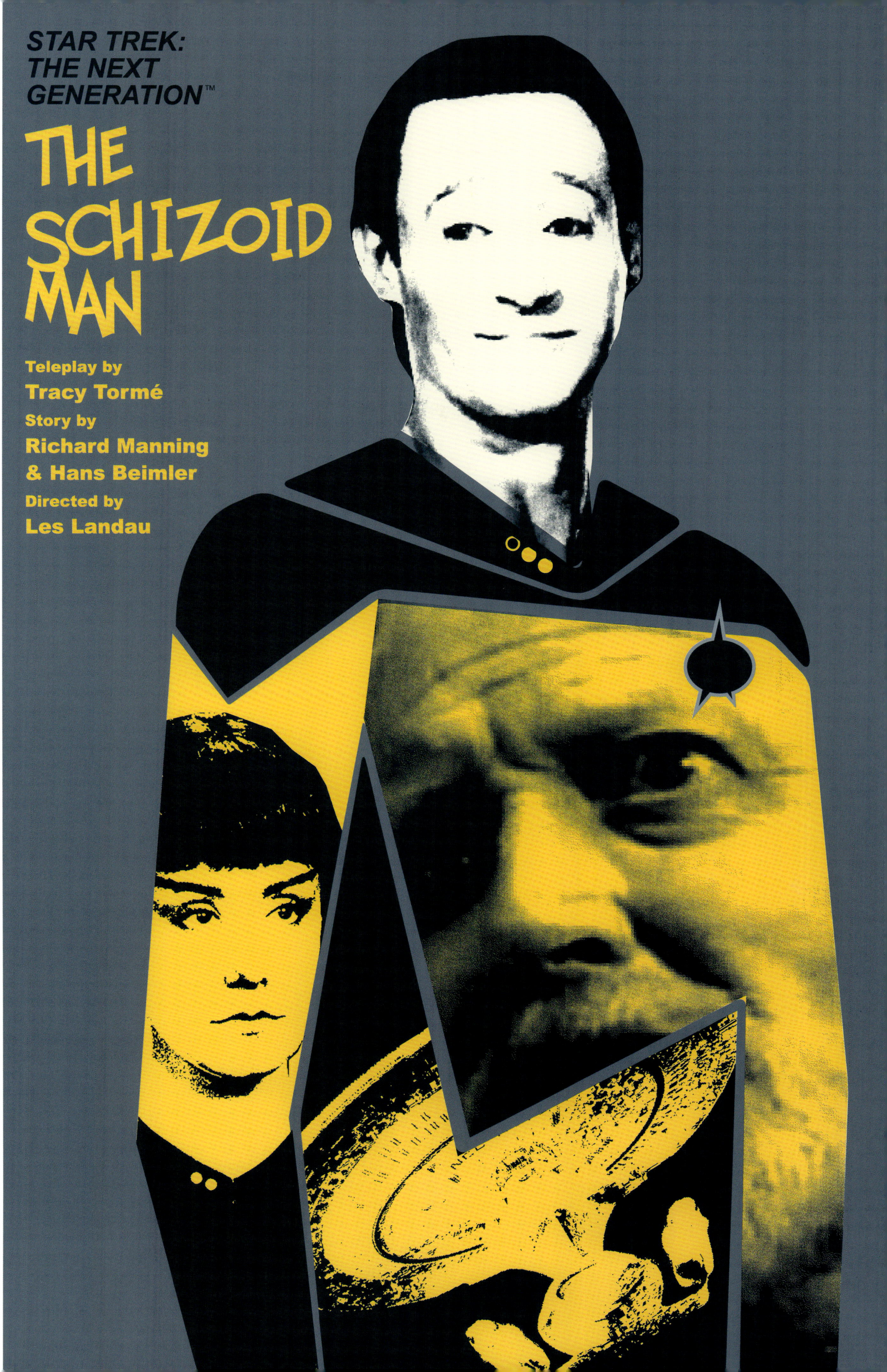
STAR TREK: THE NEXT GENERATION™
THE SCHIZOID MAN
Teleplay by
Tracy Tormé
Story by
Richard Manning
& Hans Beimler
Directed by
Les Landau

STAR TREK: THE NEXT GENERATION™

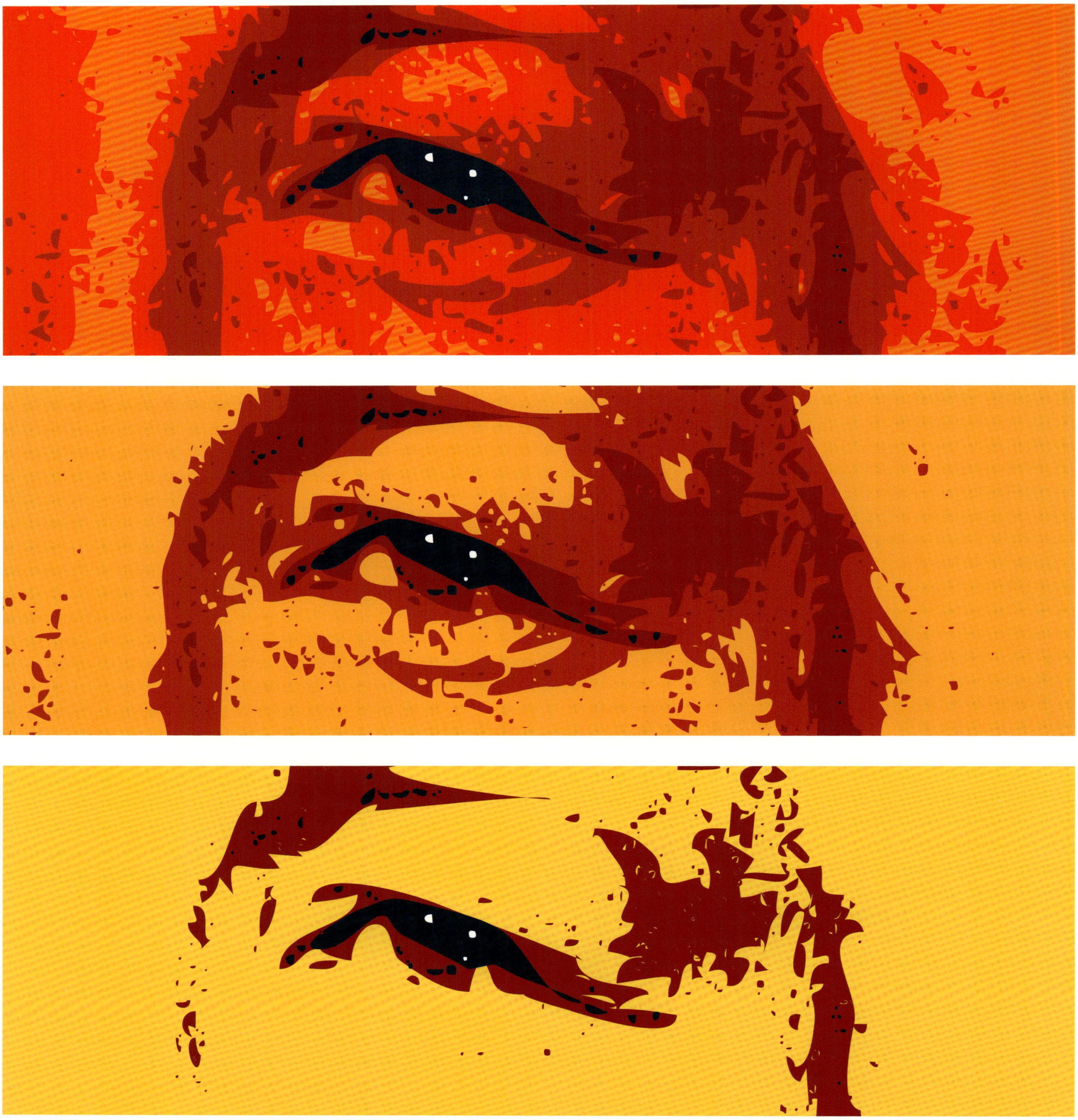

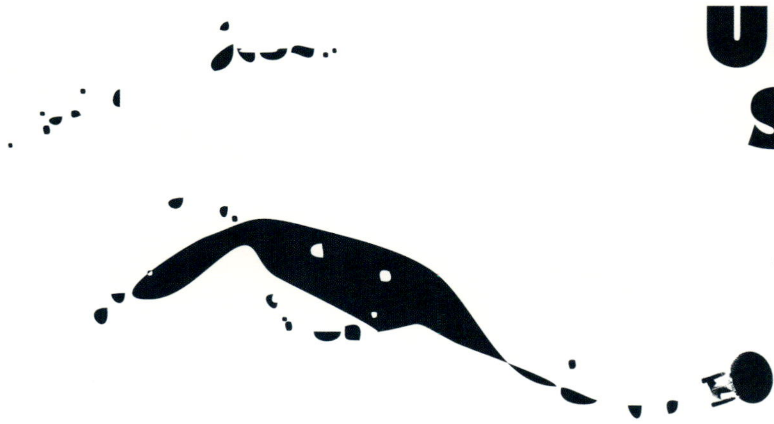

UNNATURAL SELECTION

Written by

John Mason & Mike Gray

Directed by

Paul Lynch

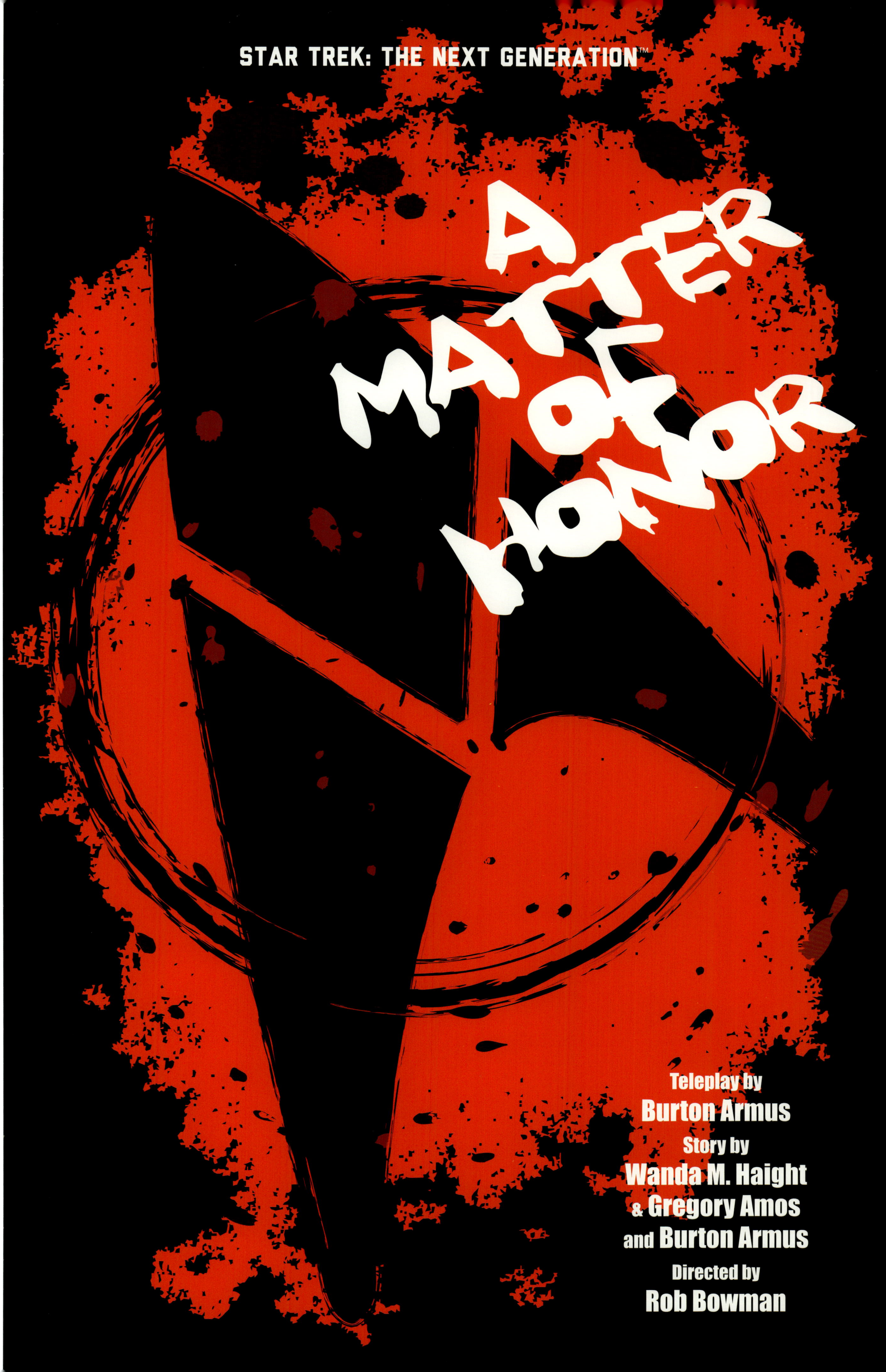
STAR TREK: THE NEXT GENERATION™
A MATTER OF HONOR
Teleplay by
Burton Armus
Story by
Wanda M. Haight
& Gregory Amos
and Burton Armus
Directed by
Rob Bowman

STAR TREK: THE NEXT GENERATION™

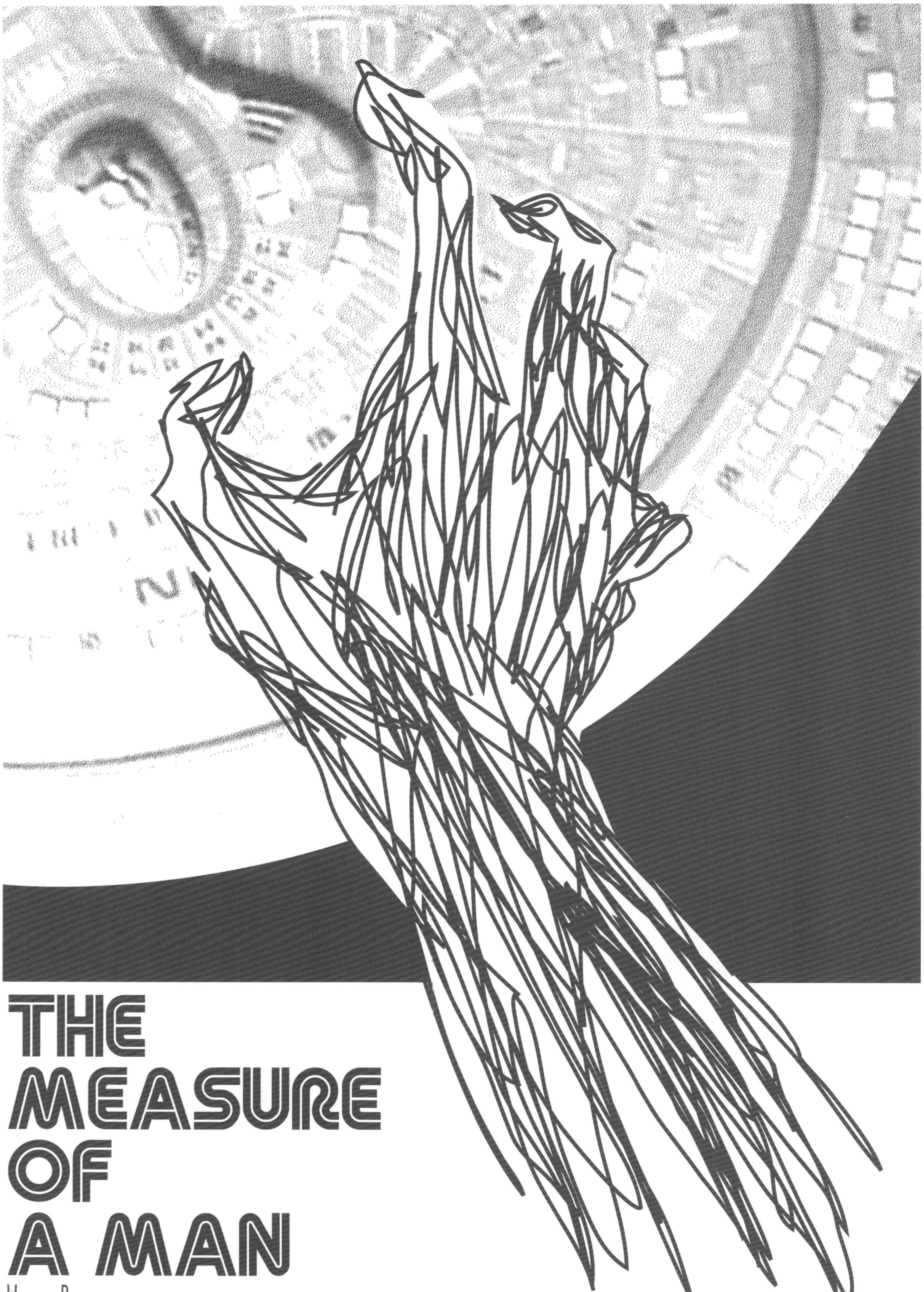

THE MEASURE OF A MAN

Written By

Melinda M. Snodgrass

Directed By

Robert Scheerer

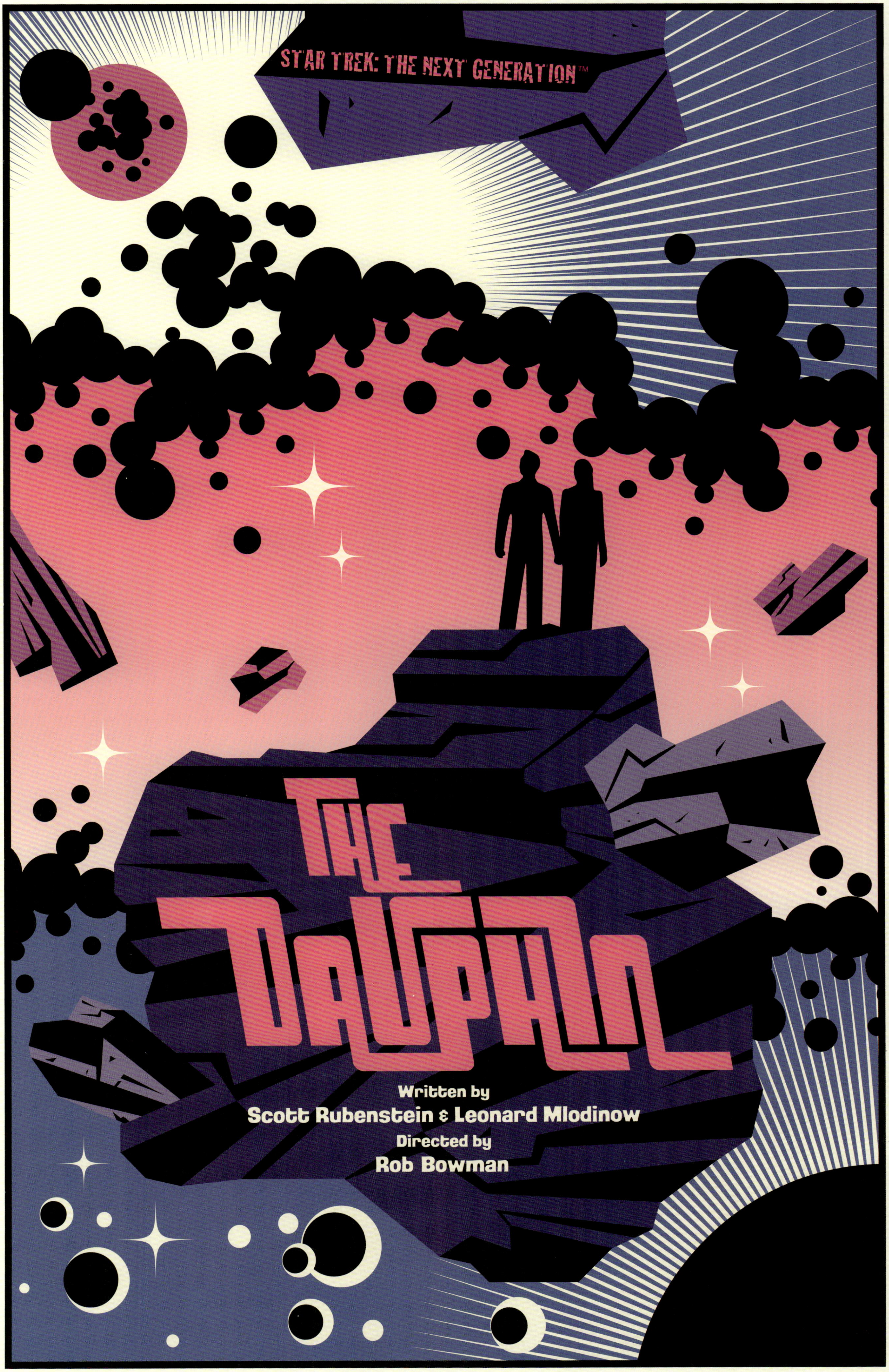
STAR TREK: THE NEXT GENERATION™
THE DAUPHIN
Written by
Scott Rubenstein & Leonard Mlodinow
Directed by
Rob Bowman

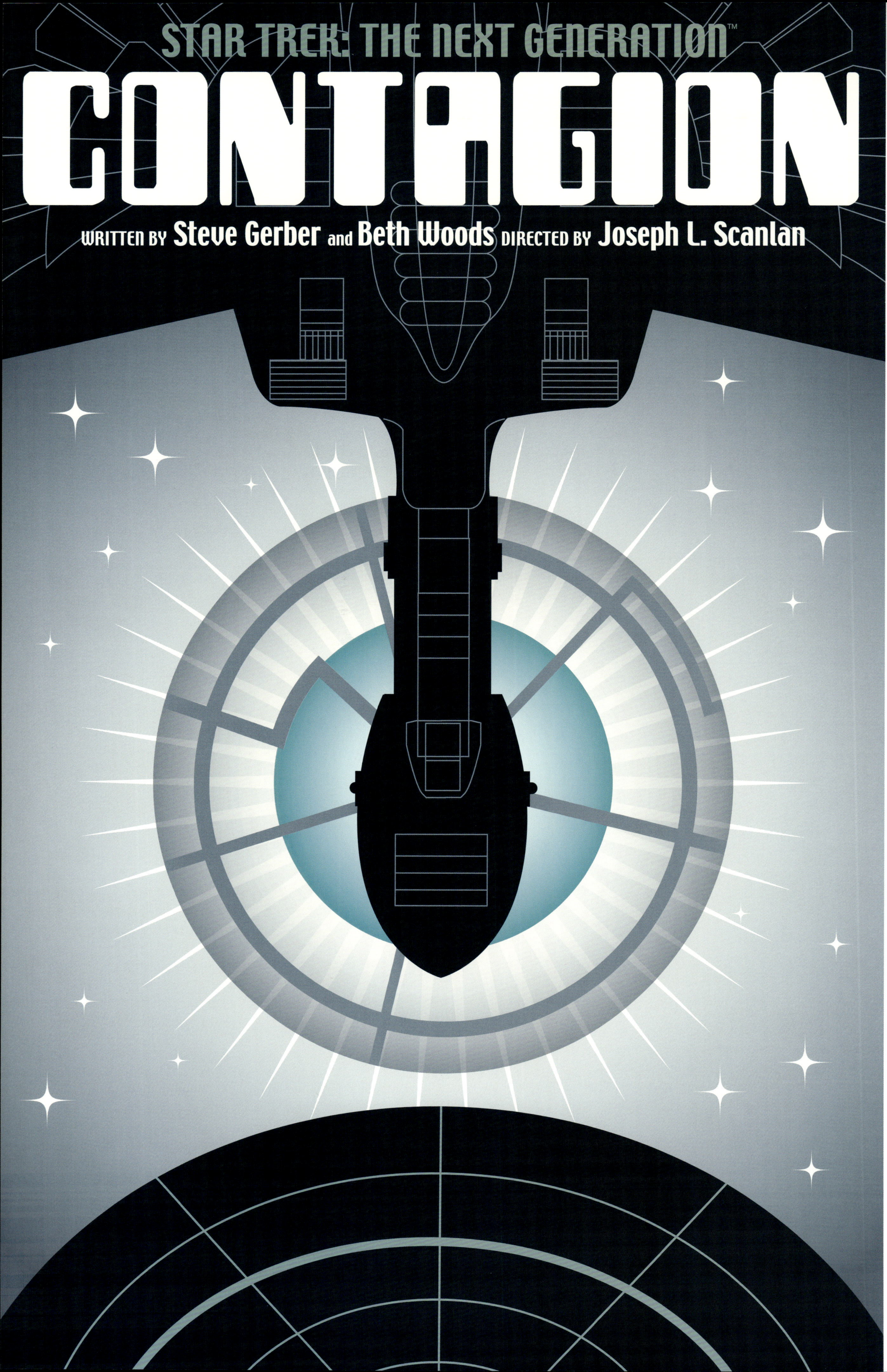
STAR TREK: THE NEXT GENERATION™
CONTAGION
WRITTEN BY Steve Gerber and Beth Woods DIRECTED BY Joseph L. Scanlan

STAR TREK
THE NEXT GENERATION™

The Royale

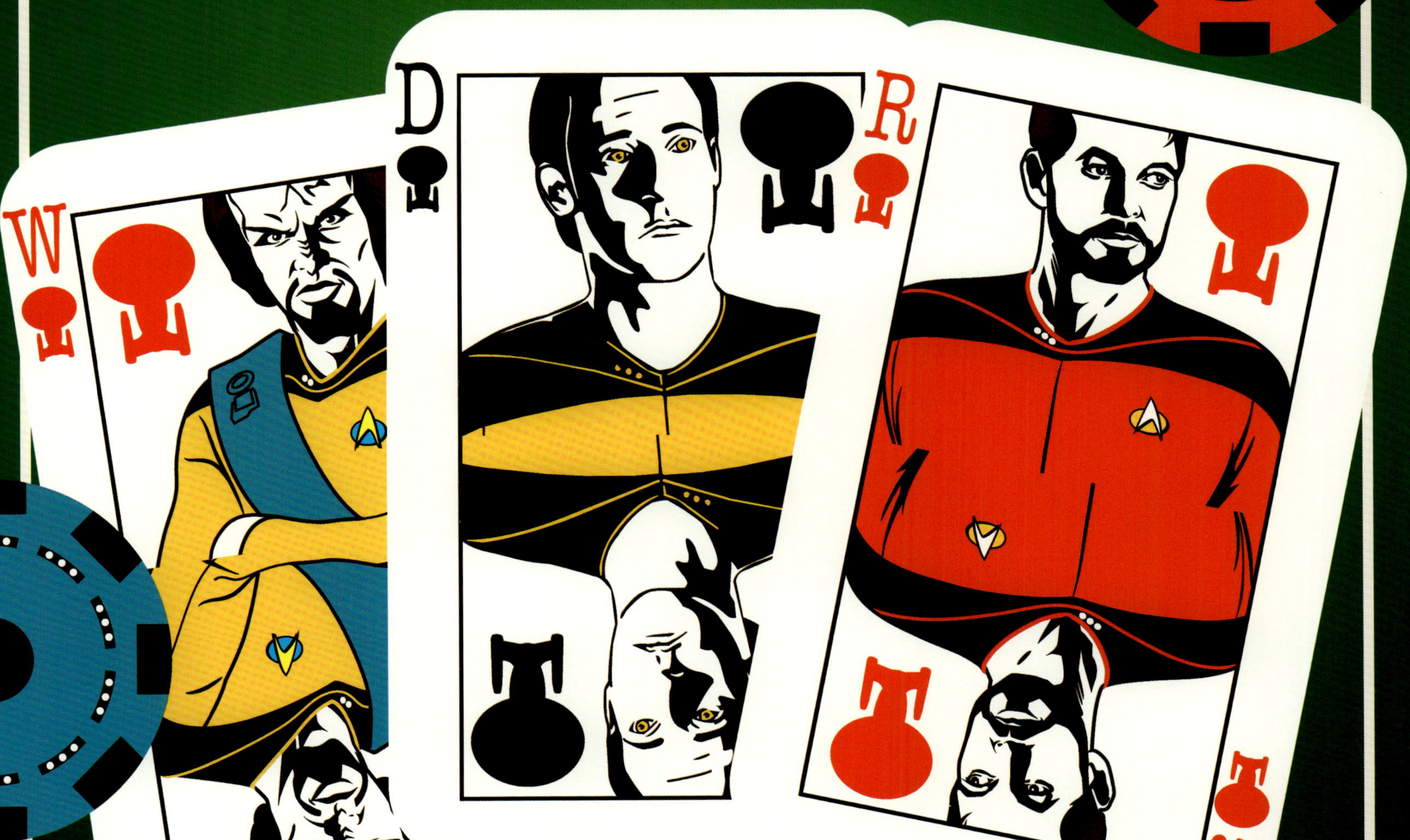

Written by Keith Mills

Directed by Cliff Bole

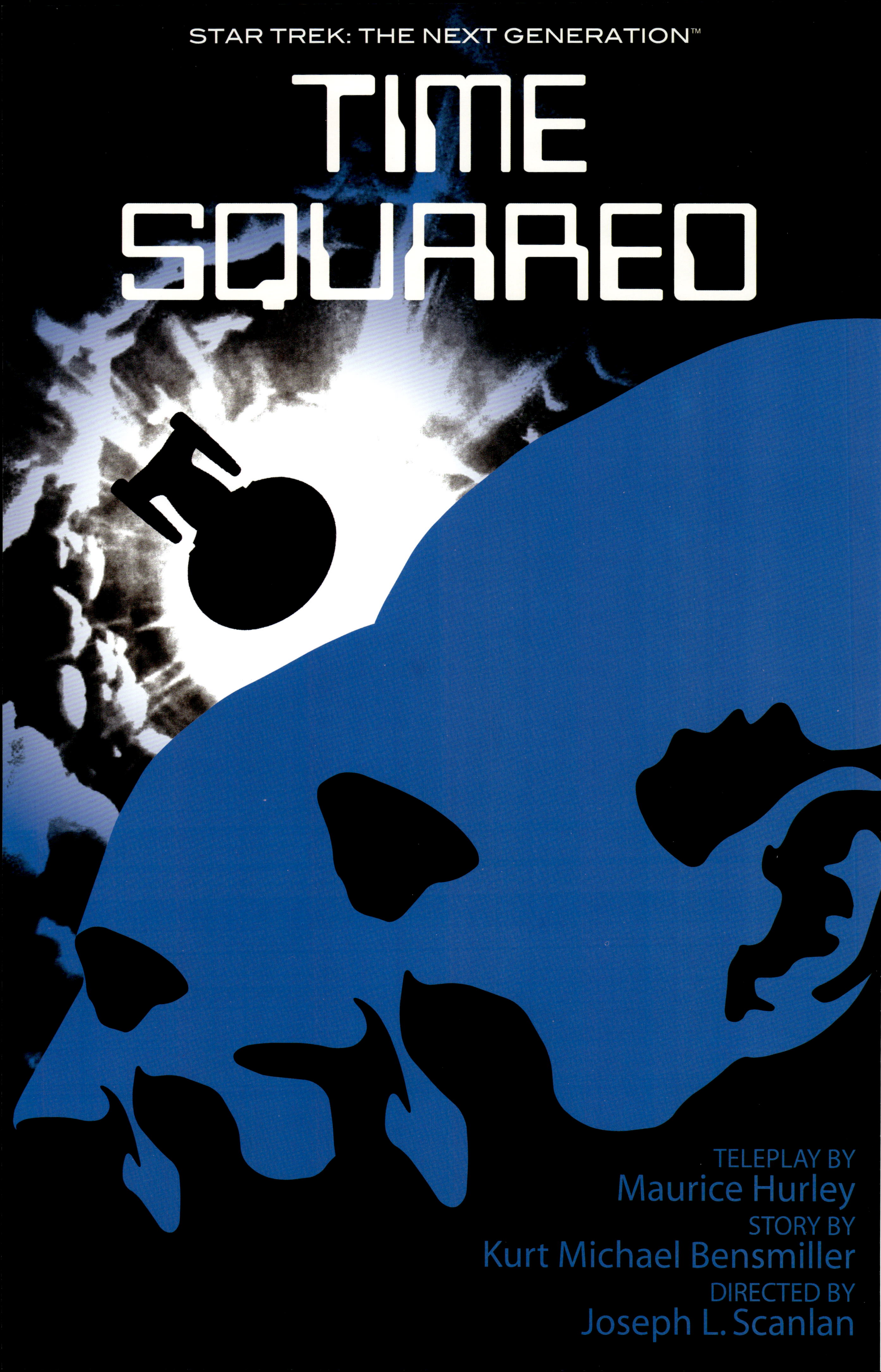
STAR TREK: THE NEXT GENERATION™
TIME SQUARED
TELEPLAY BY
Maurice Hurley
STORY BY
Kurt Michael Bensmiller
DIRECTED BY
Joseph L. Scanlan

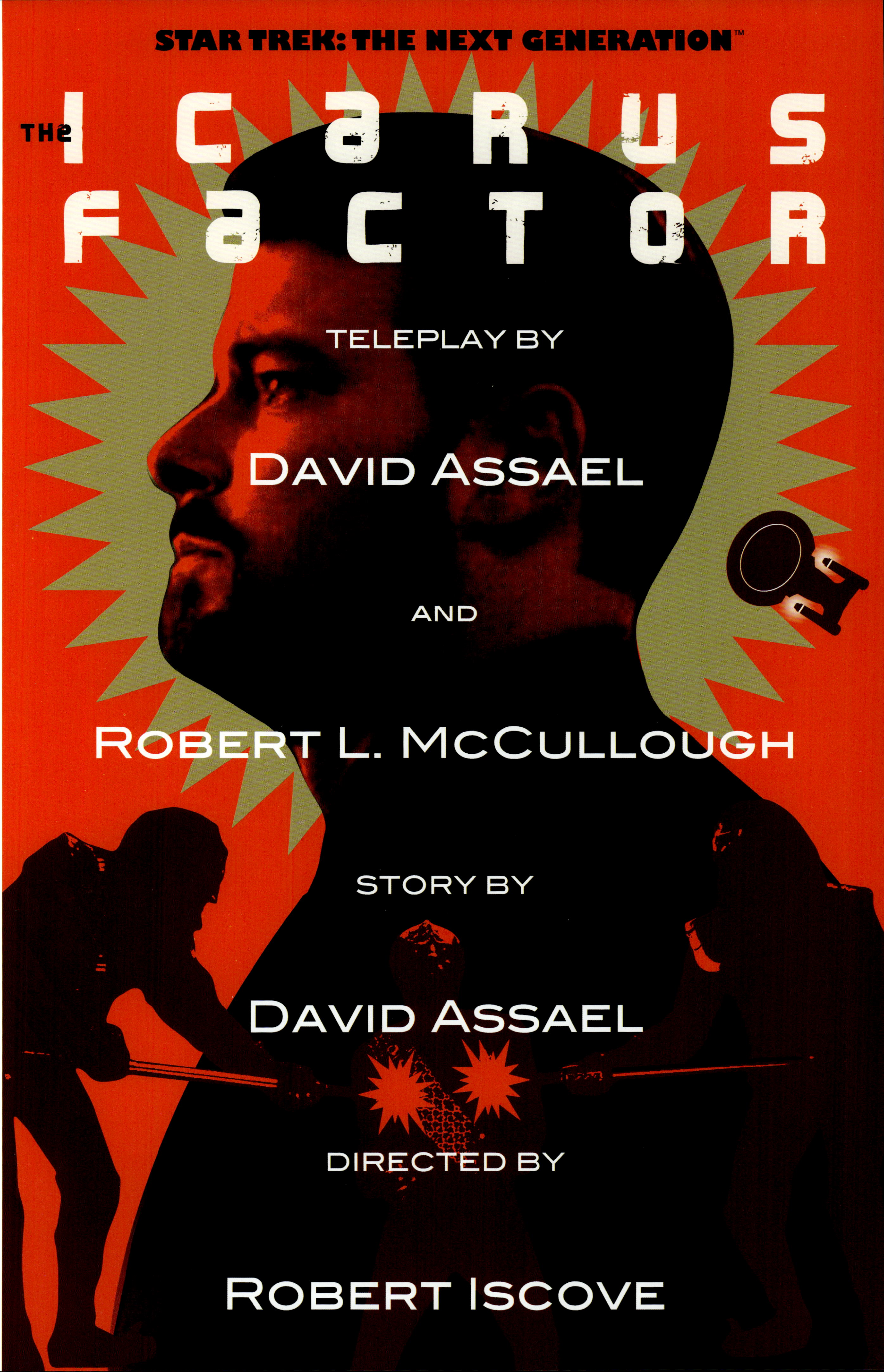
STAR TREK: THE NEXT GENERATION™
THE ICARUS FACTOR
TELEPLAY BY
DAVID ASSAEL
AND
ROBERT L. MCCULLOUGH
STORY BY
DAVID ASSAEL
DIRECTED BY
ROBERT ISCOVE

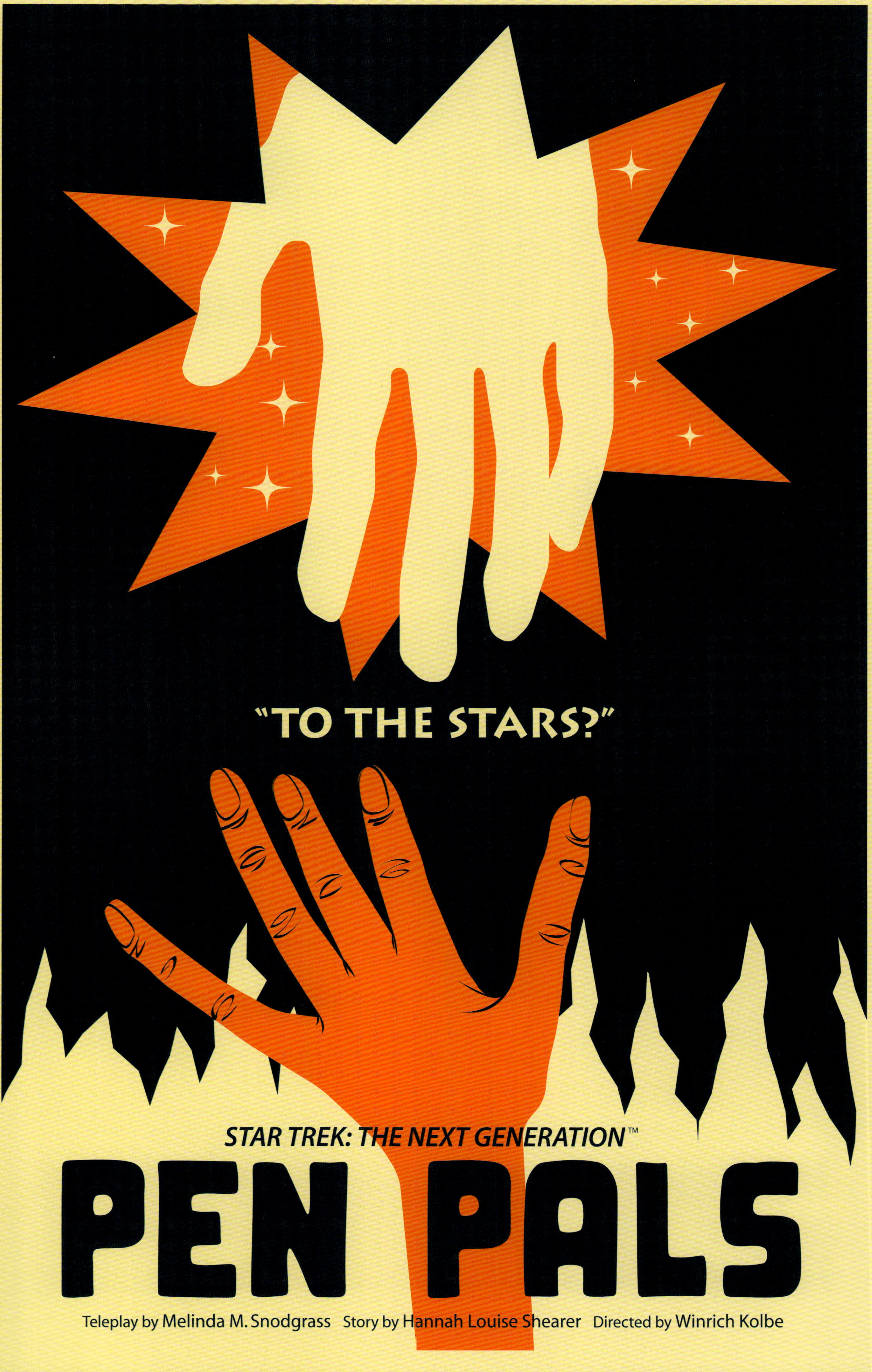

"TO THE STARS?"
STAR TREK: THE NEXT GENERATION™
PEN PALS
Teleplay by Melinda M. Snodgrass Story by Hannah Louise Shearer Directed by Winrich Kolbe

STAR TREK
THE NEXT GENERATION™

Q WHO

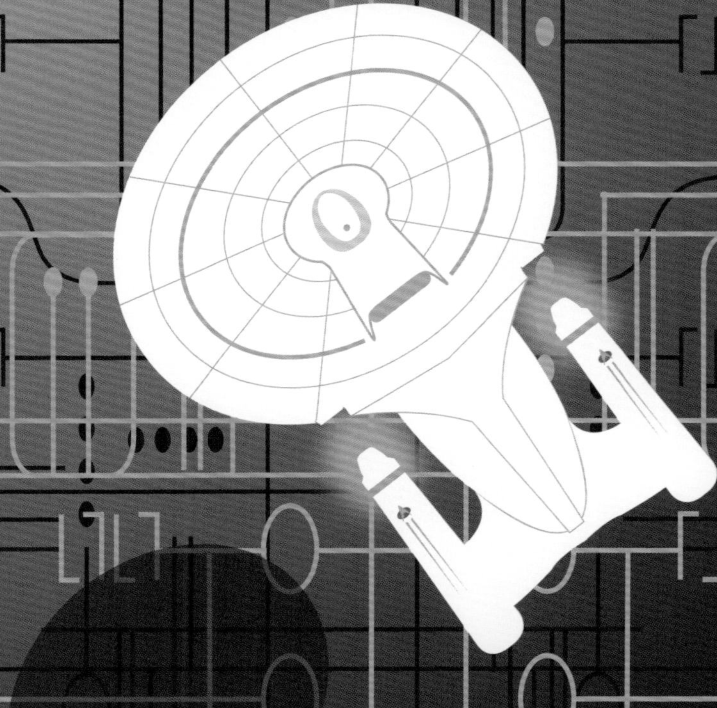

Written by
Maurice Hurley
Directed by
Rob Bowman

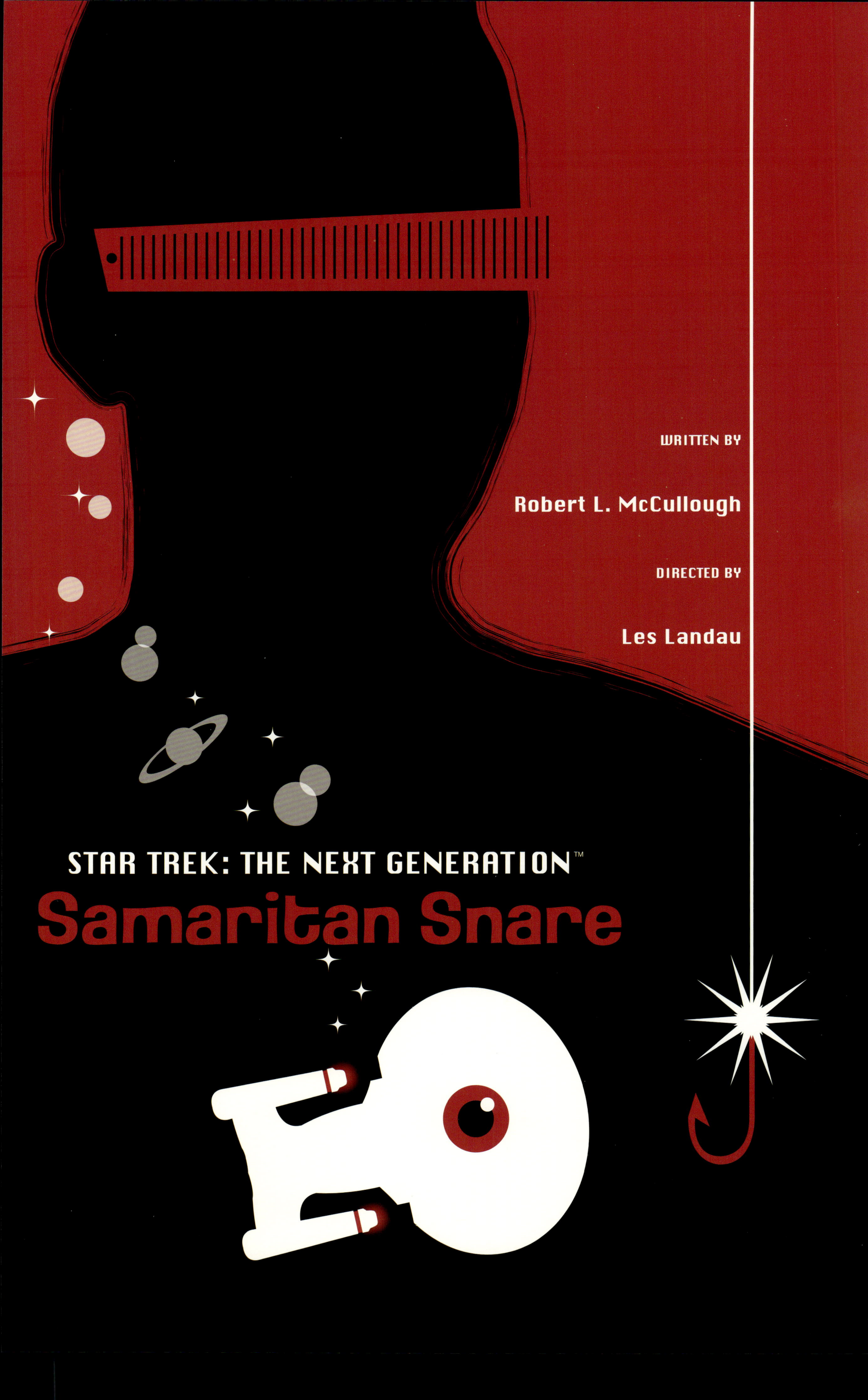
WRITTEN BY
Robert L. McCullough
DIRECTED BY
Les Landau
STAR TREK: THE NEXT GENERATION™
Samaritan Snare

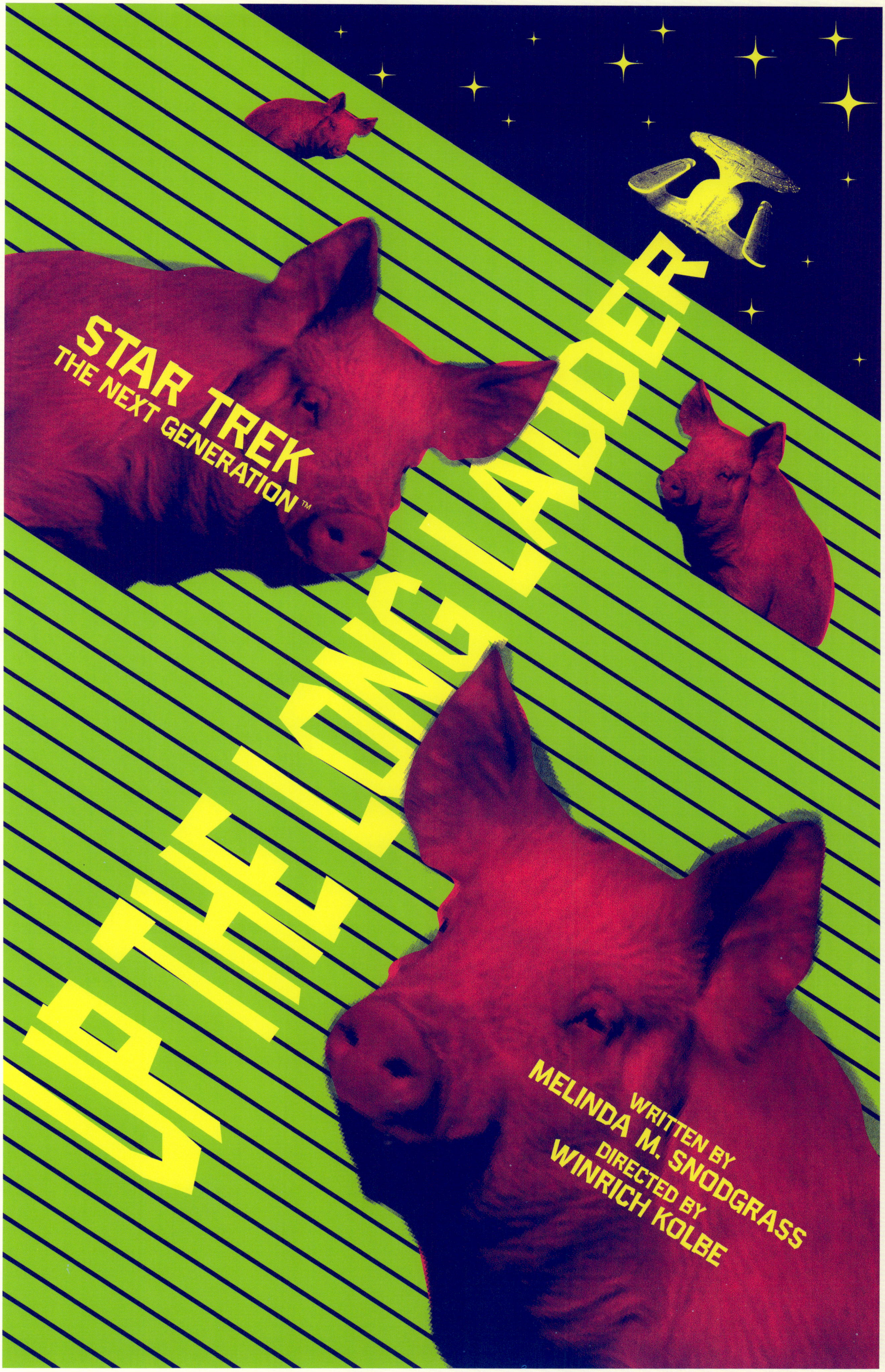
STAR TREK
THE NEXT GENERATION™
UP THE LONG LADDER
WRITTEN BY
MELINDA M. SNODGRASS
DIRECTED BY
WINRICH KOLBE

STAR TREK:
THE NEXT GENERATION™

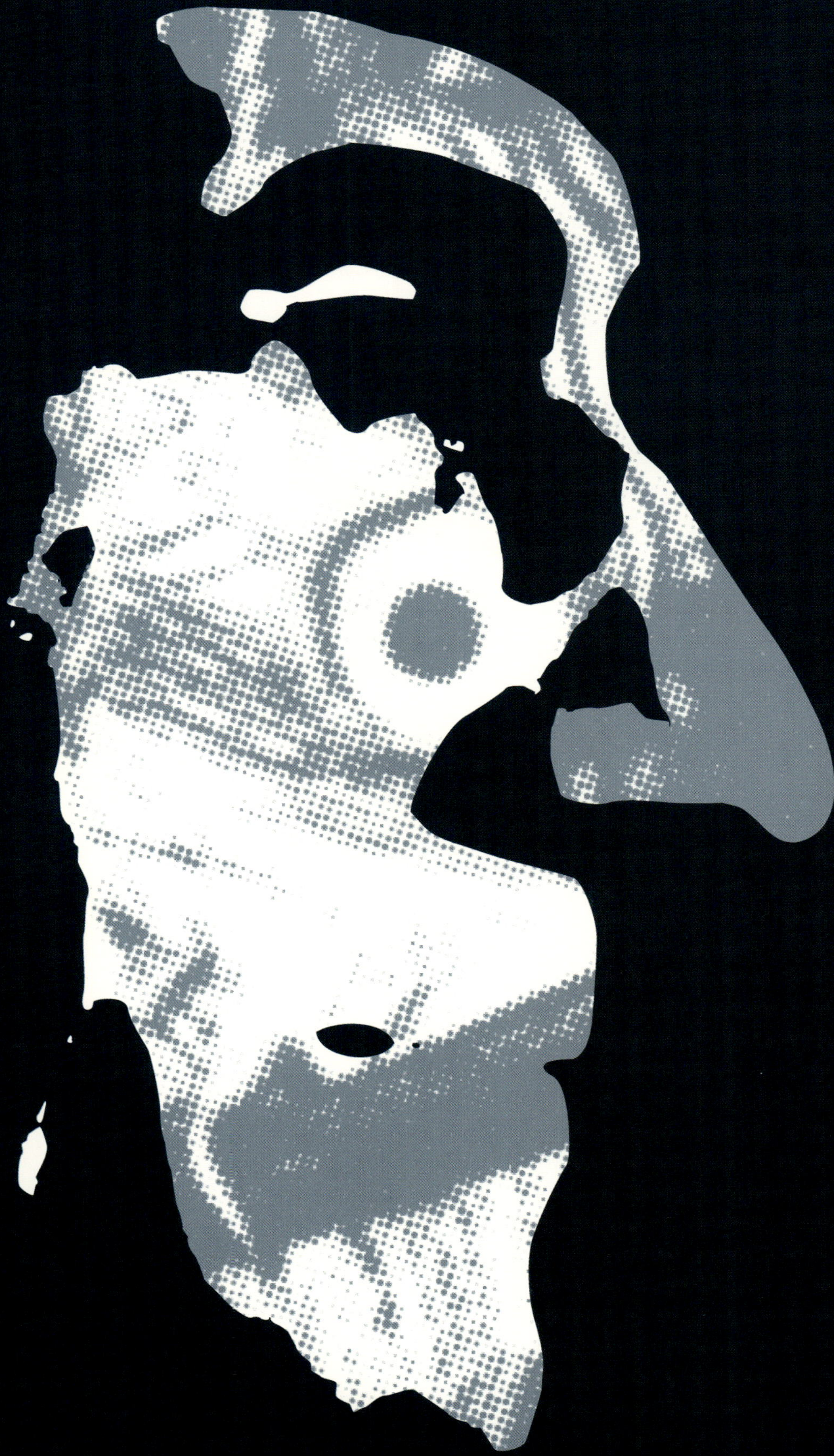

MANHUNT

WRITTEN BY
TRACY TORMÉ
DIRECTED BY
ROB BOWMAN

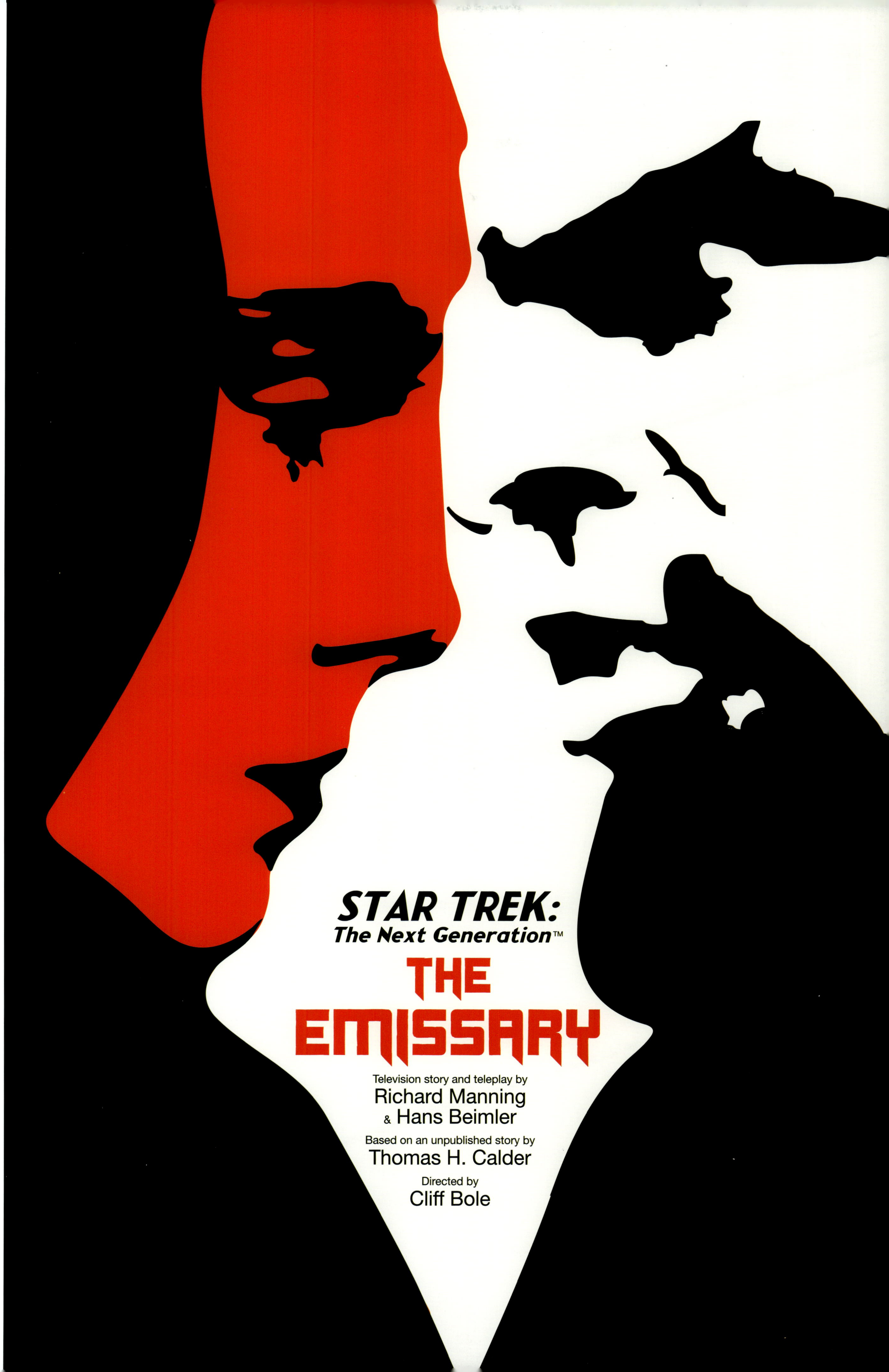
STAR TREK:
The Next Generation™
THE EMISSARY
Television story and teleplay by
Richard Manning
& Hans Beimler
Based on an unpublished story by
Thomas H. Calder
Directed by
Cliff Bole

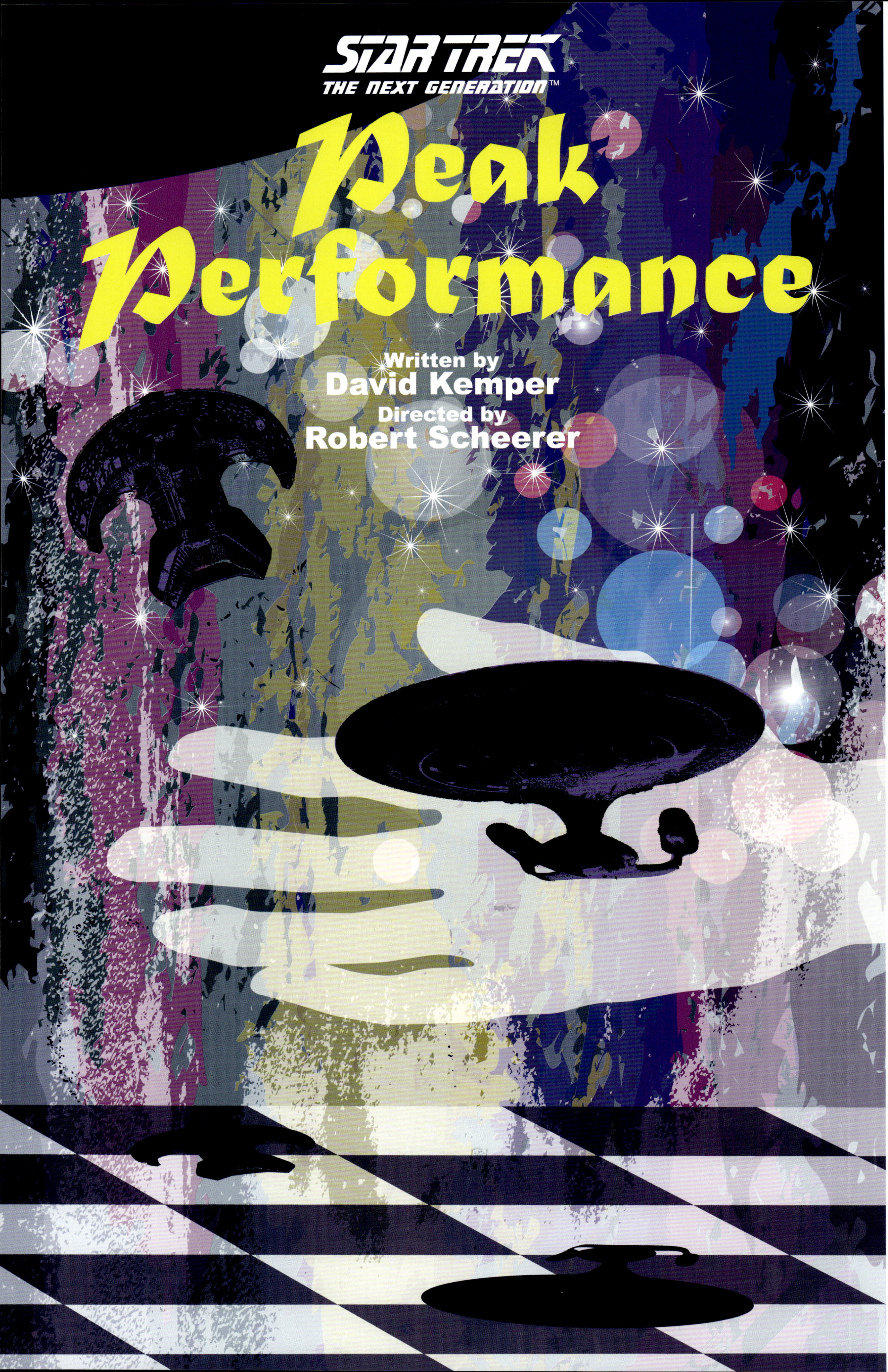
STAR TREK
THE NEXT GENERATION™
Peak Performance
Written by
David Kemper
Directed by
Robert Scheerer

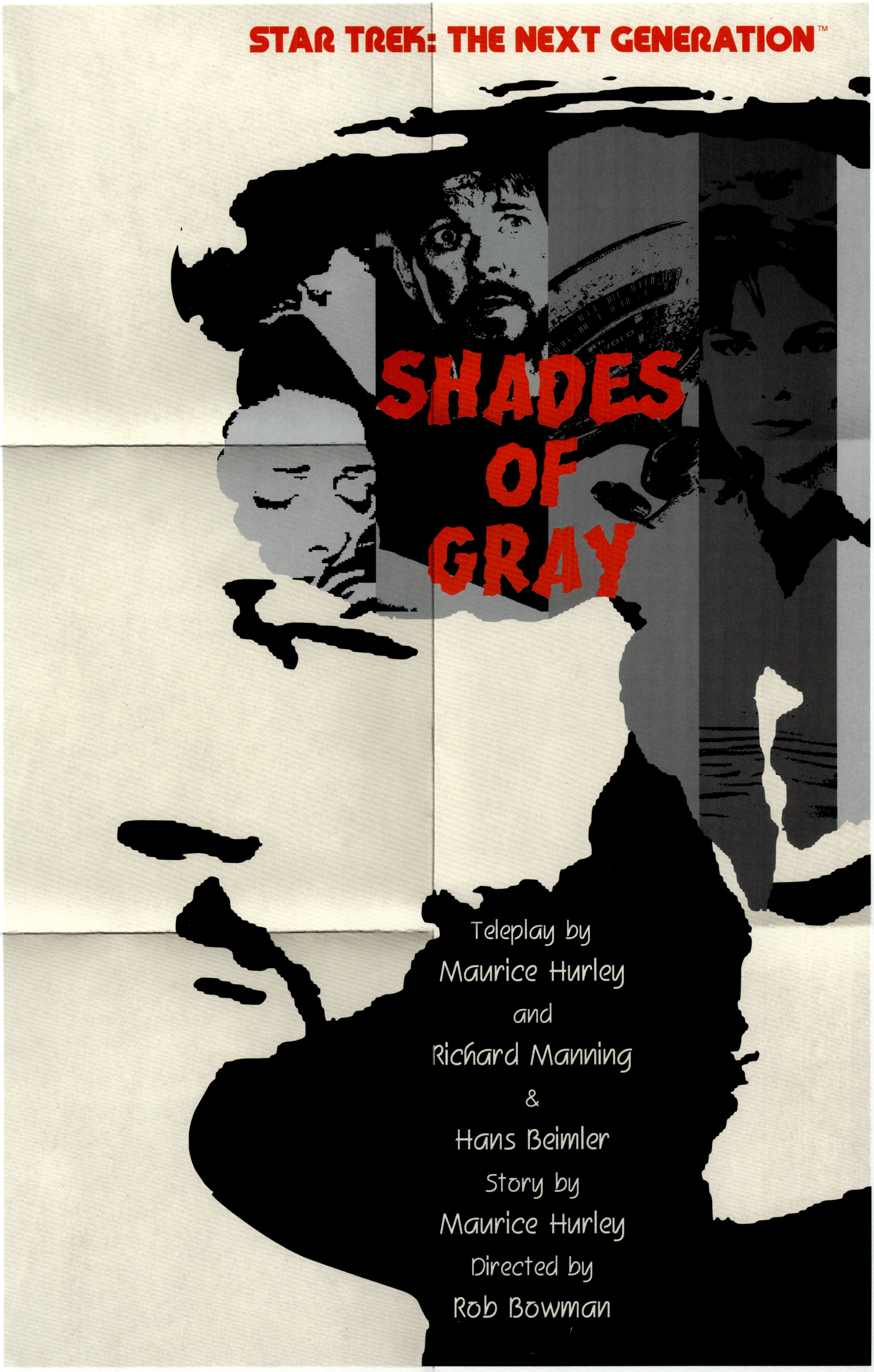
STAR TREK: THE NEXT GENERATION™
SHADES OF GRAY
Teleplay by
Maurice Hurley
and
Richard Manning
&
Hans Beimler
Story by
Maurice Hurley
Directed by
Rob Bowman

Season Three

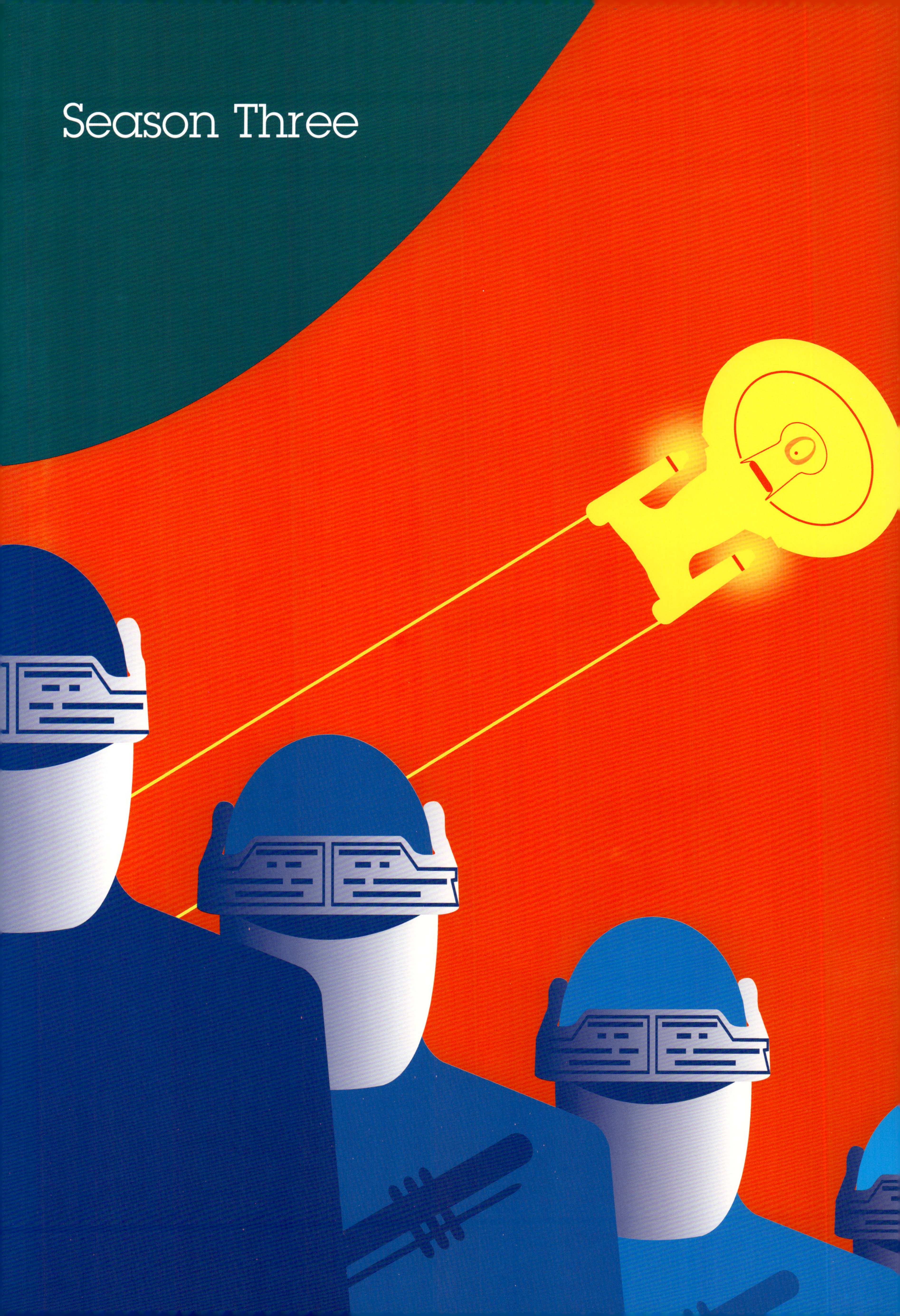

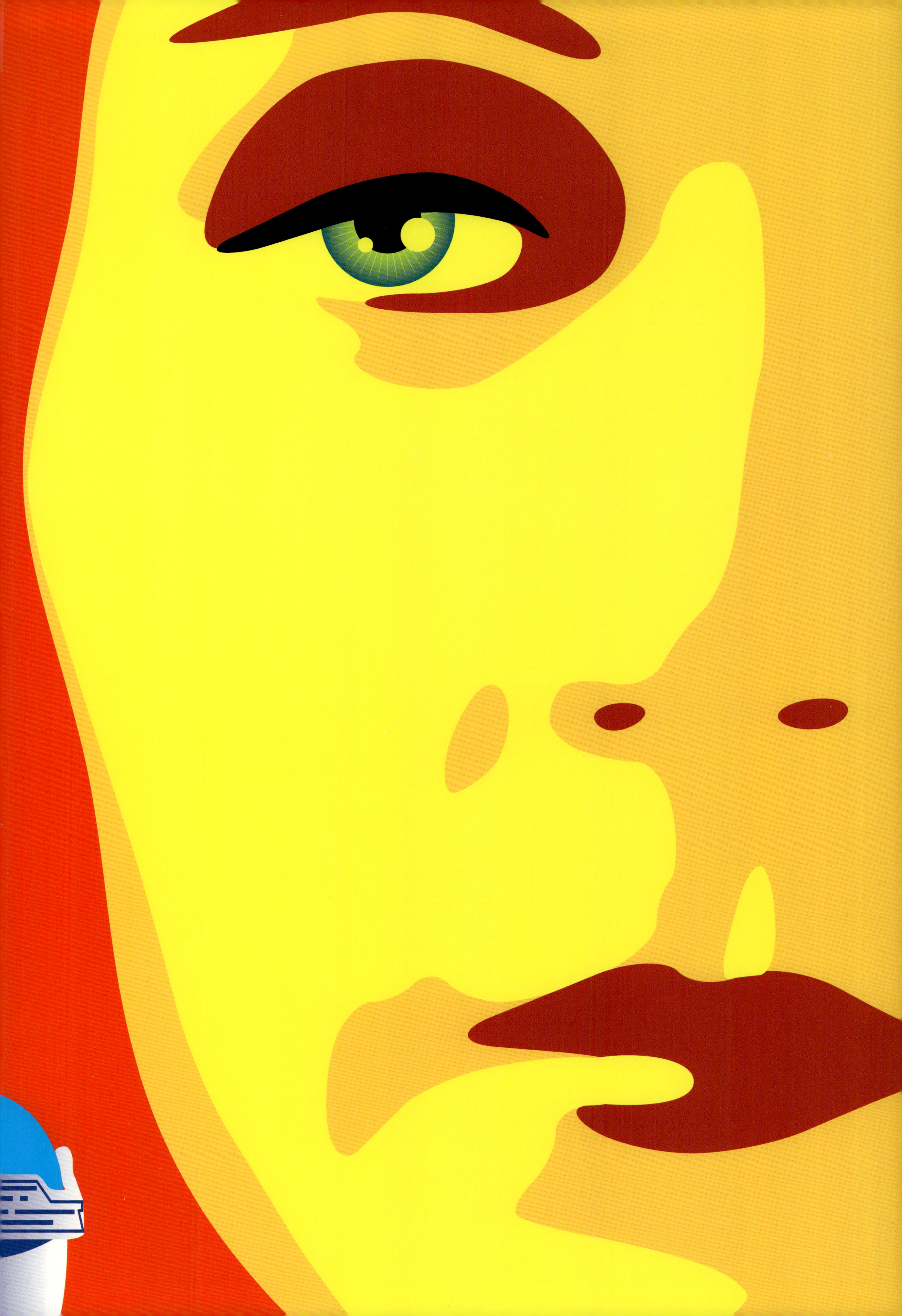

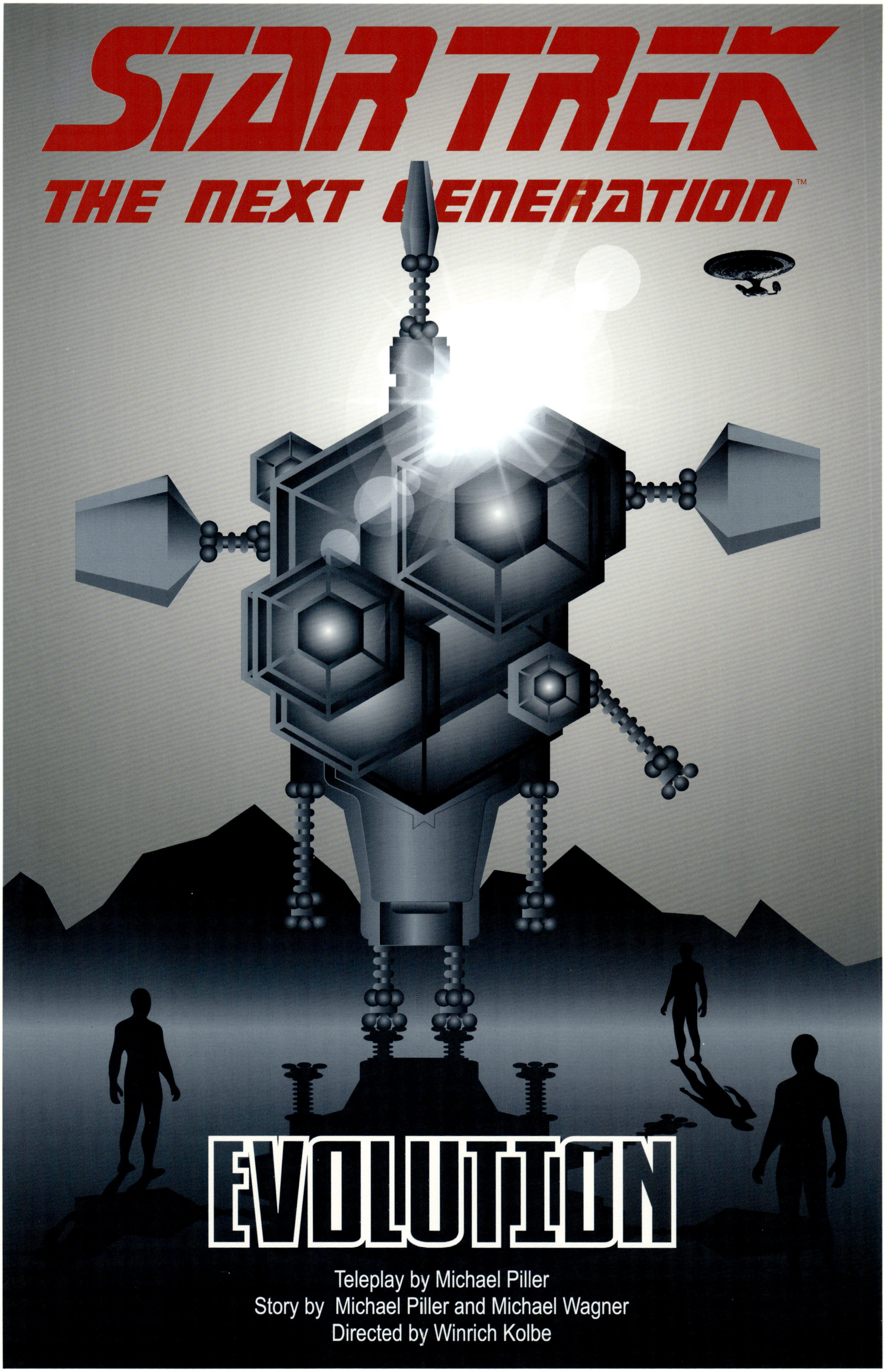
STAR TREK
THE NEXT GENERATION™
EVOLUTION
Teleplay by Michael Piller
Story by Michael Piller and Michael Wagner
Directed by Winrich Kolbe

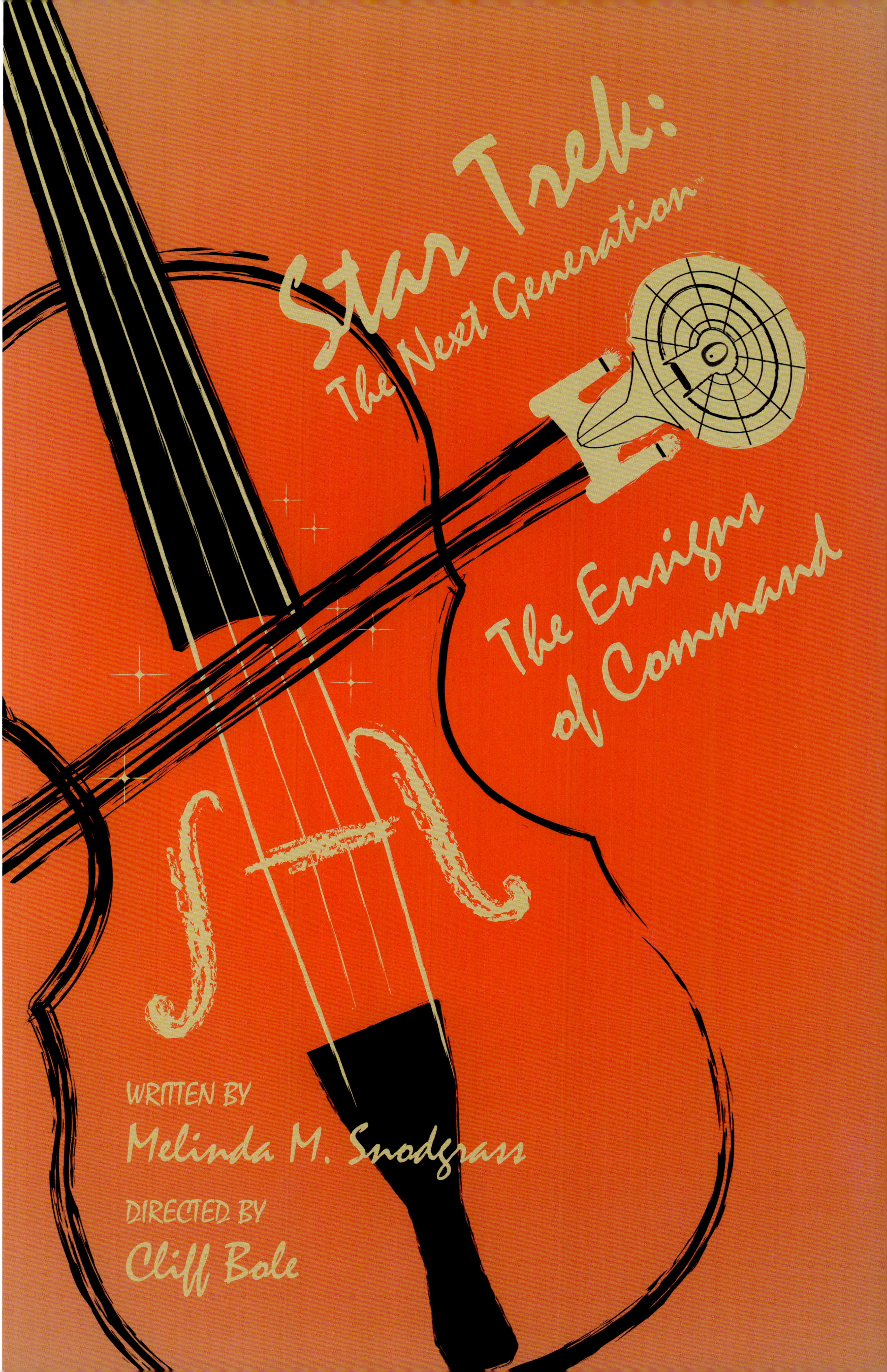
Star Trek:
The Next Generation™
The Ensigns of Command
WRITTEN BY
Melinda M. Snodgrass
DIRECTED BY
Cliff Bole

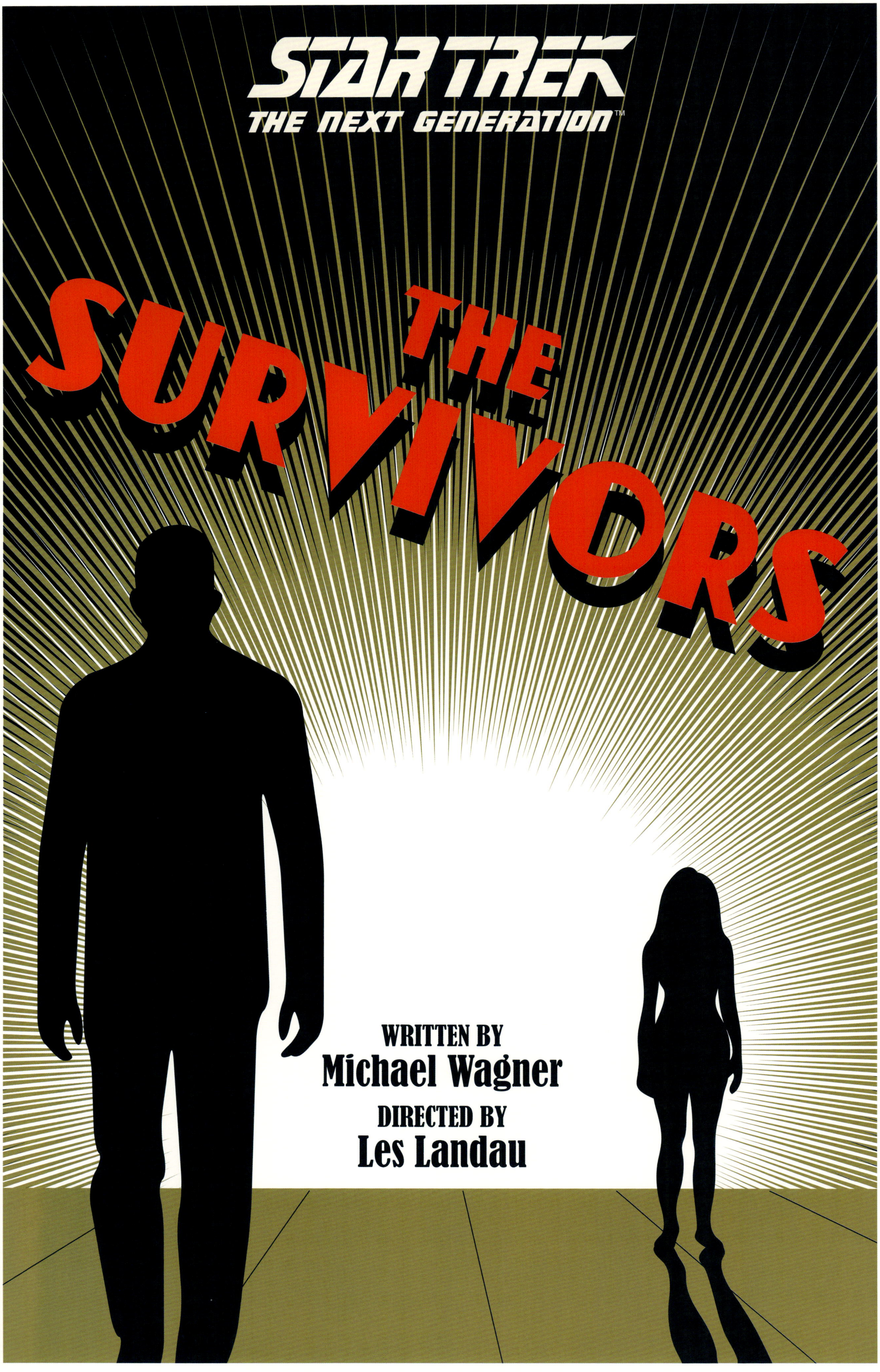
STAR TREK
THE NEXT GENERATION
THE SURVIVORS
WRITTEN BY
Michael Wagner
DIRECTED BY
Les Landau

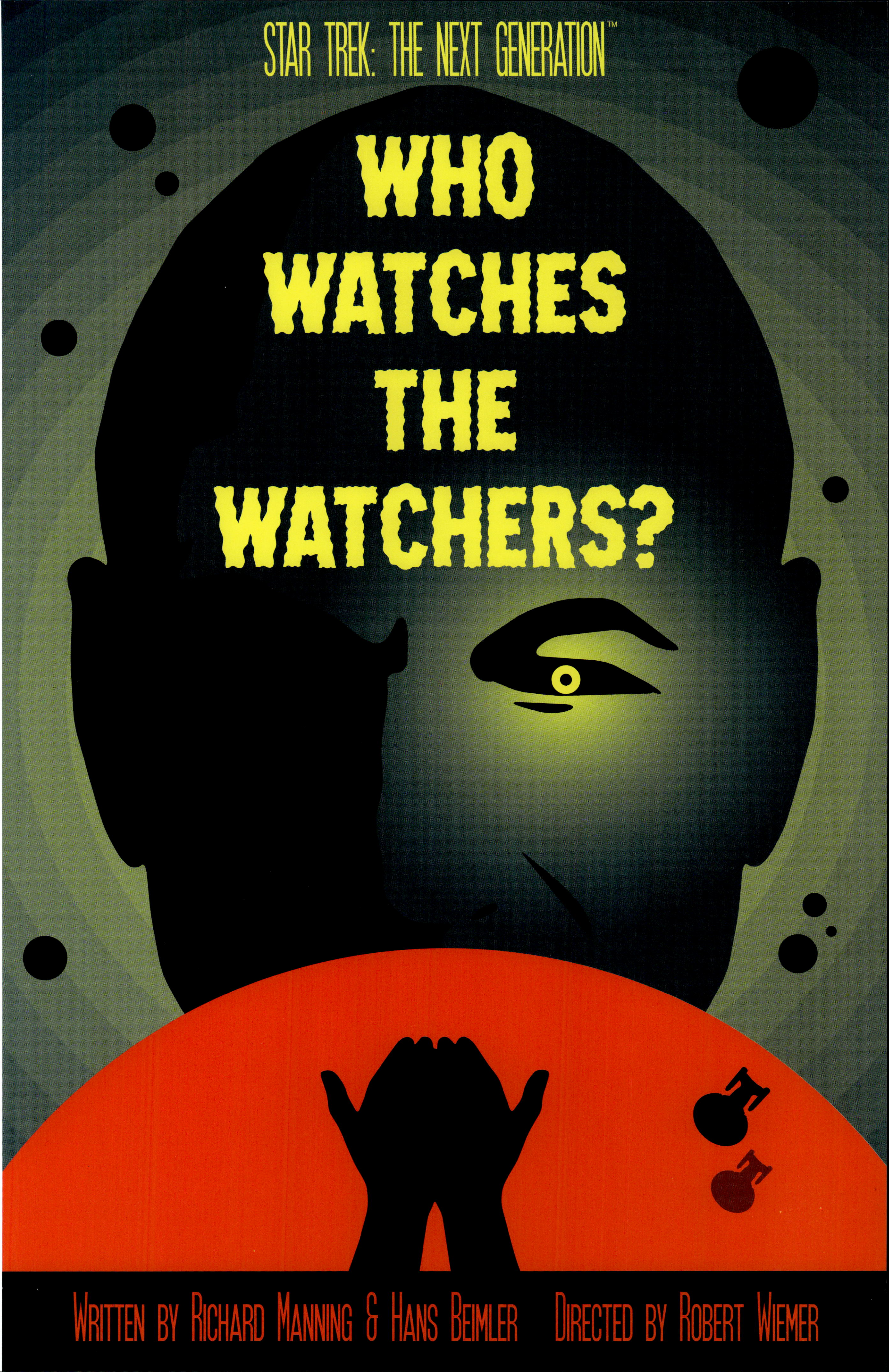
STAR TREK: THE NEXT GENERATION™
WHO WATCHES THE WATCHERS?
WRITTEN BY RICHARD MANNING & HANS BEIMLER DIRECTED BY ROBERT WIEMER

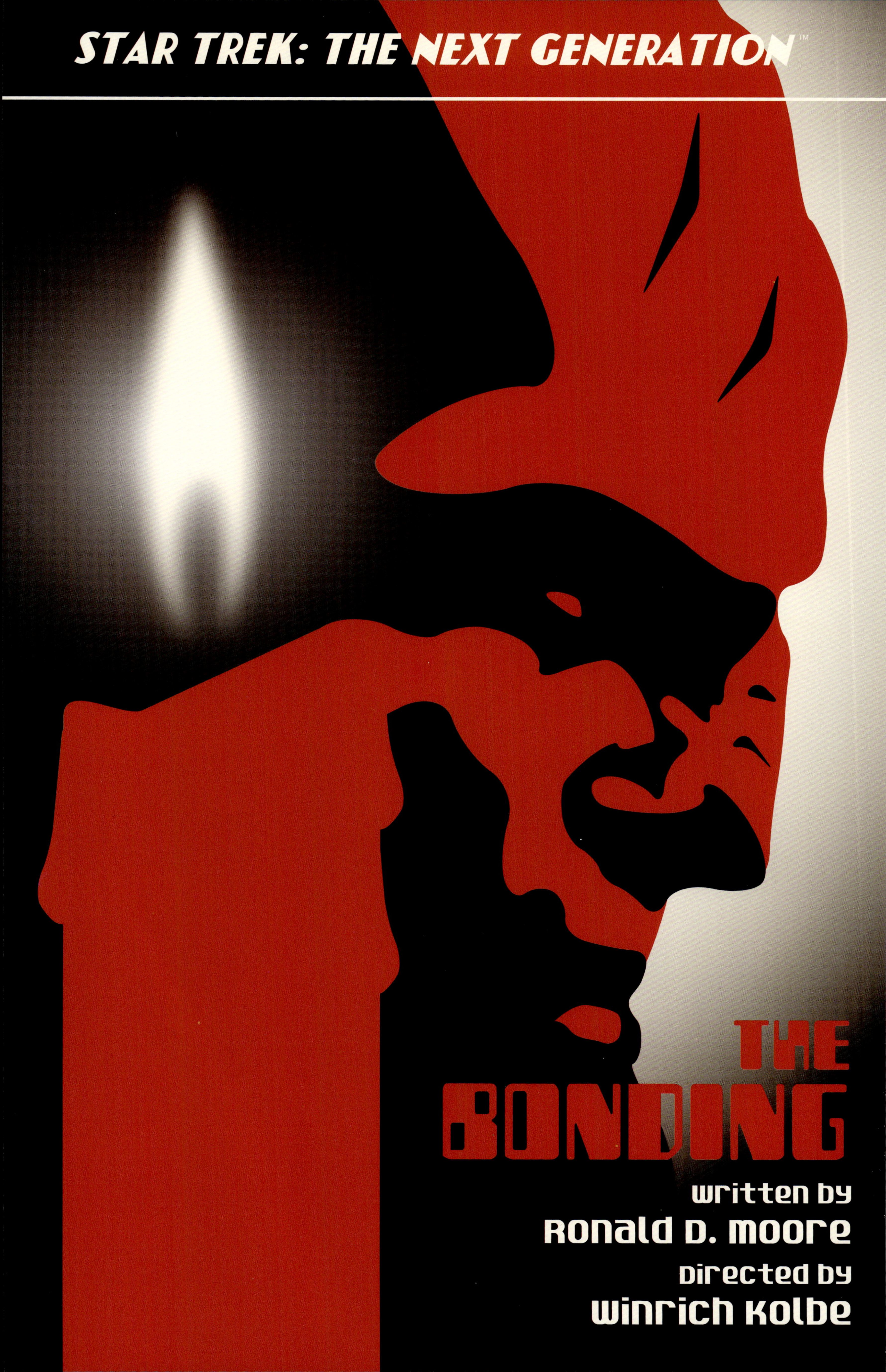
STAR TREK: THE NEXT GENERATION™
THE
BONDING
written by
Ronald D. Moore
Directed by
Winrich Kolbe

STAR TREK: THE NEXT GENERATION™

TELEPLAY BY
RON ROMAN
AND MICHAEL PILLER
& RICHARD DANUS

STORY BY
MICHAEL WAGNER
& RON ROMAN

DIRECTED BY
GABRIELLE BEAUMONT

BOOBY TRAP

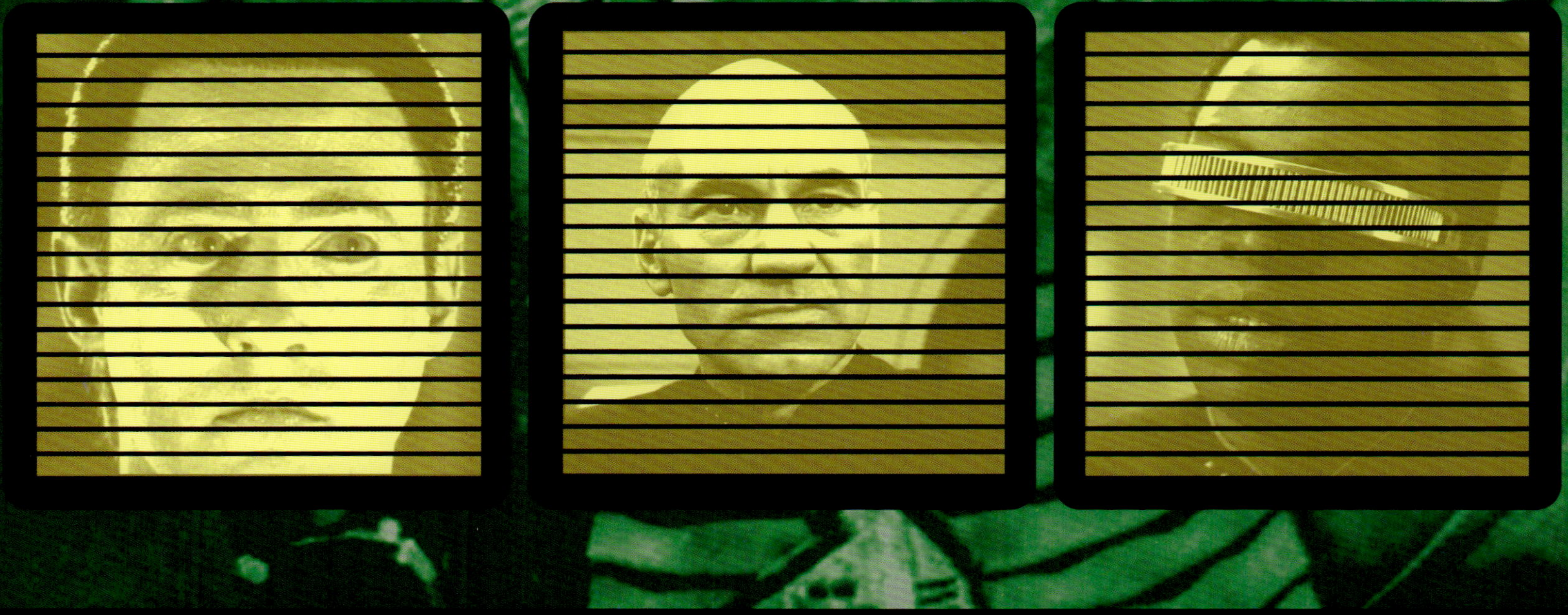

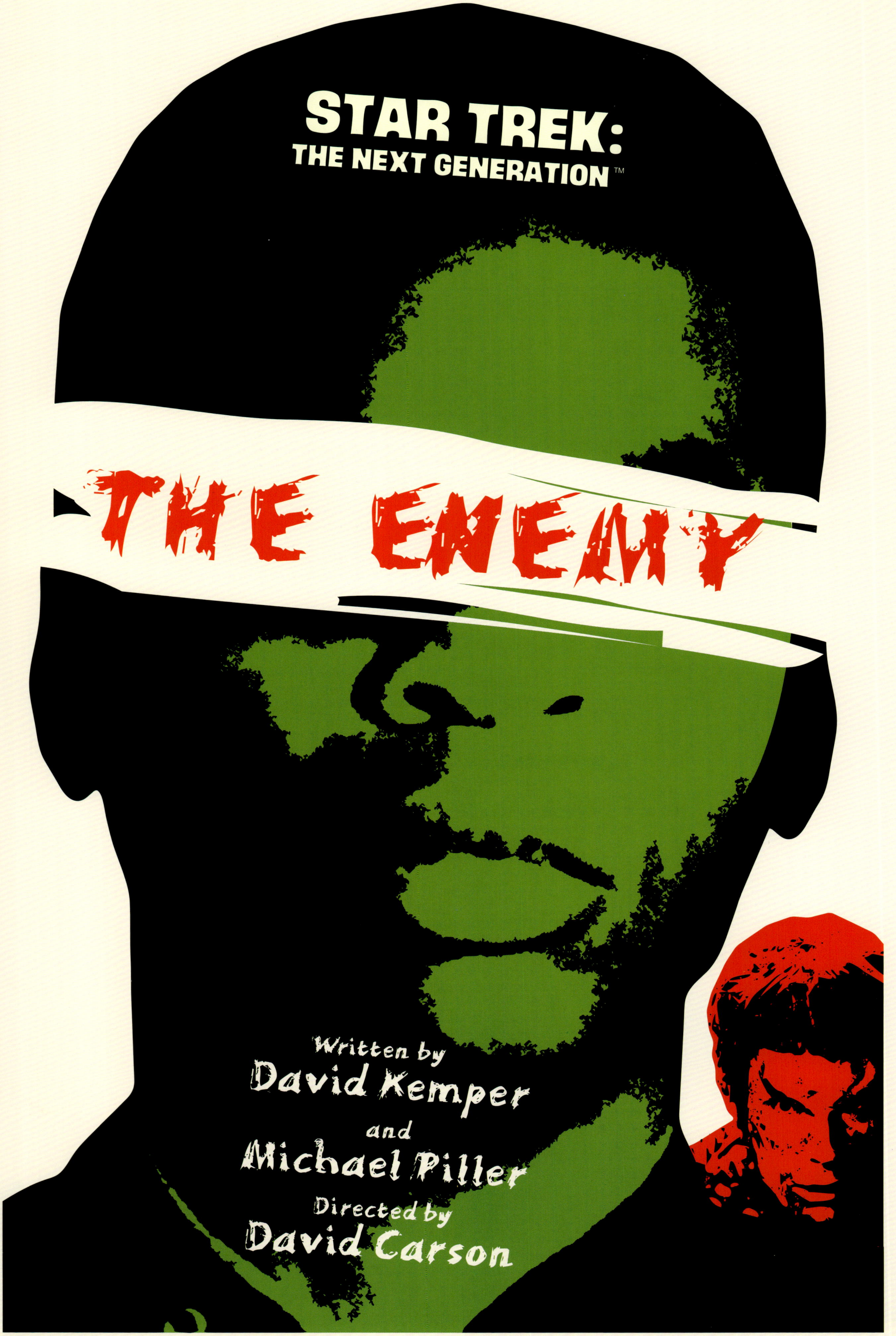

STAR TREK:
THE NEXT GENERATION™
THE ENEMY
Written by
David Kemper
and
Michael Piller
Directed by
David Carson

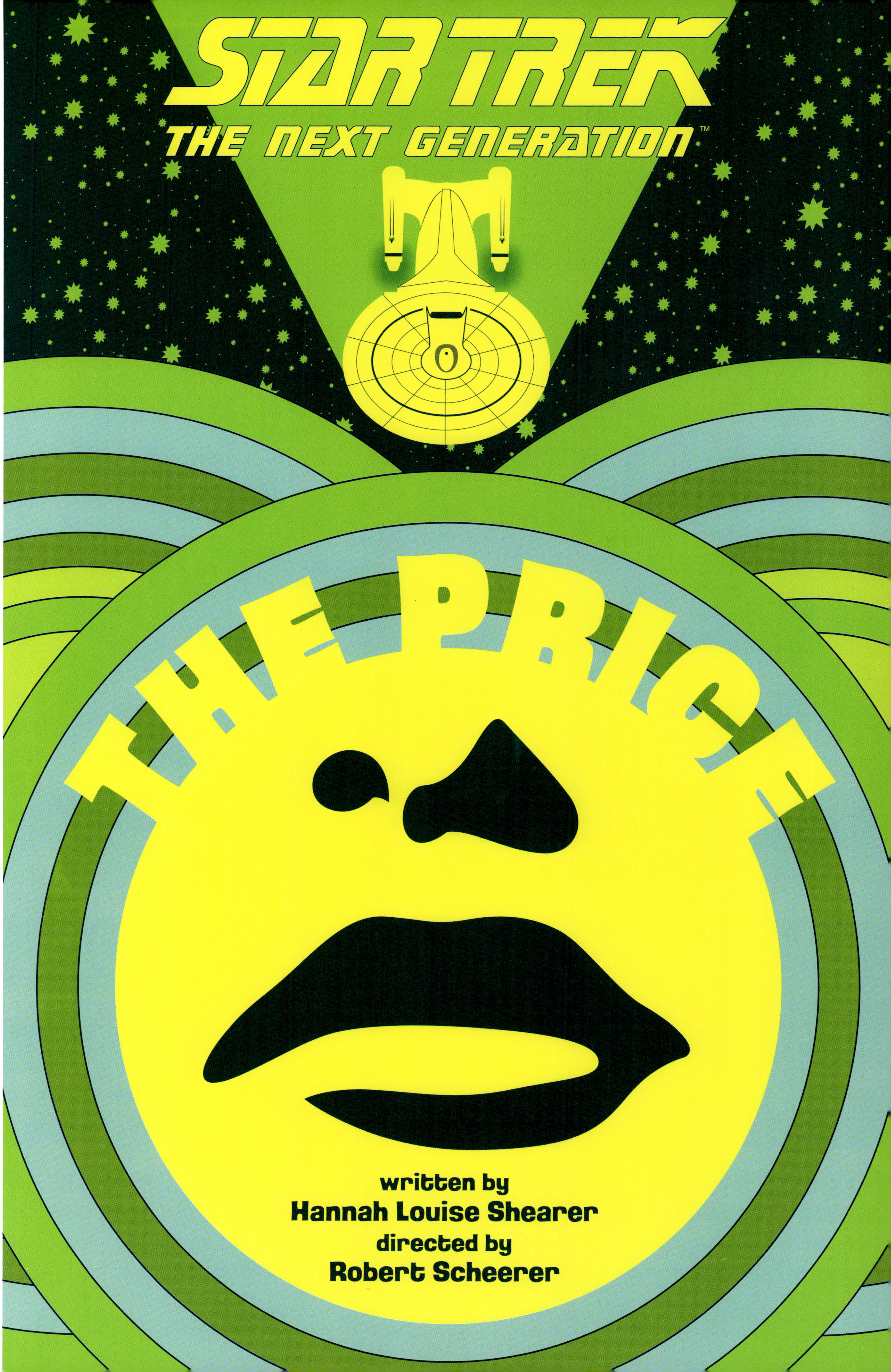
STAR TREK
THE NEXT GENERATION
THE PRICE
written by
Hannah Louise Shearer
directed by
Robert Scheerer

STAR TREK:
THE NEXT GENERATION™

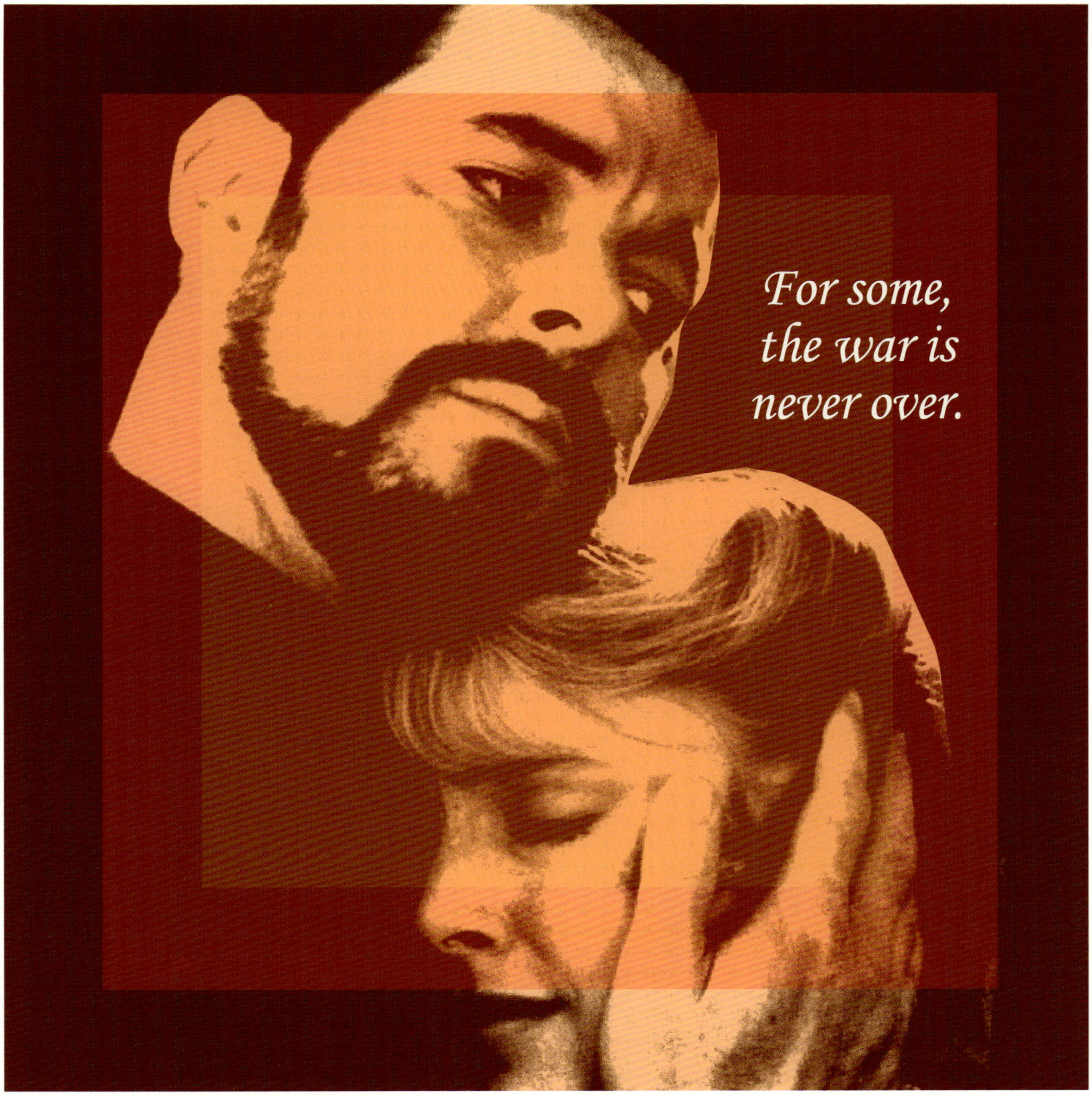

THE VENGEANCE FACTOR

WRITTEN BY
SAM ROLFE

DIRECTED BY
TIMOTHY BOND

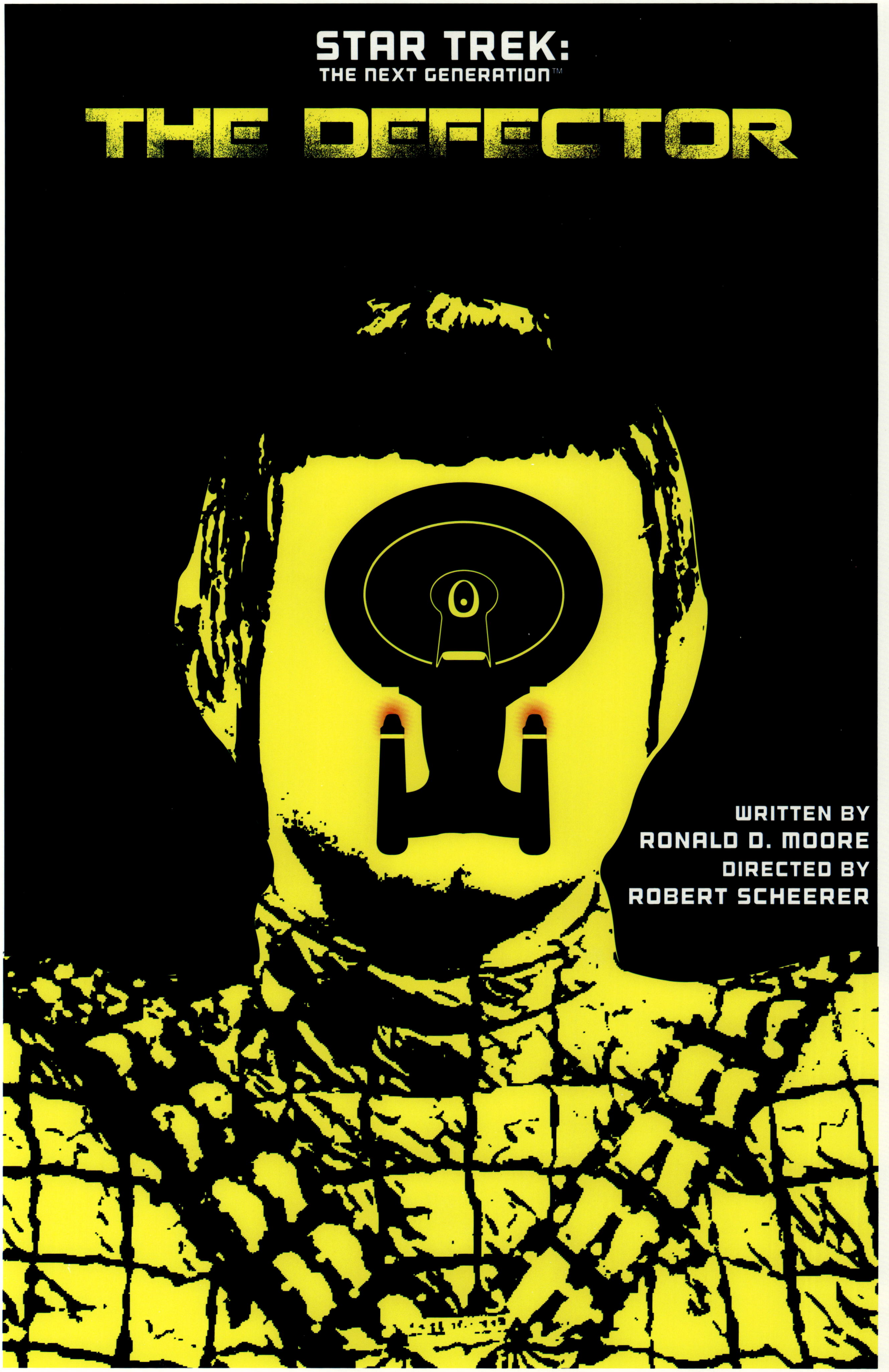
STAR TREK:
THE NEXT GENERATION™
THE DEFECTOR
WRITTEN BY
RONALD D. MOORE
DIRECTED BY
ROBERT SCHEERER

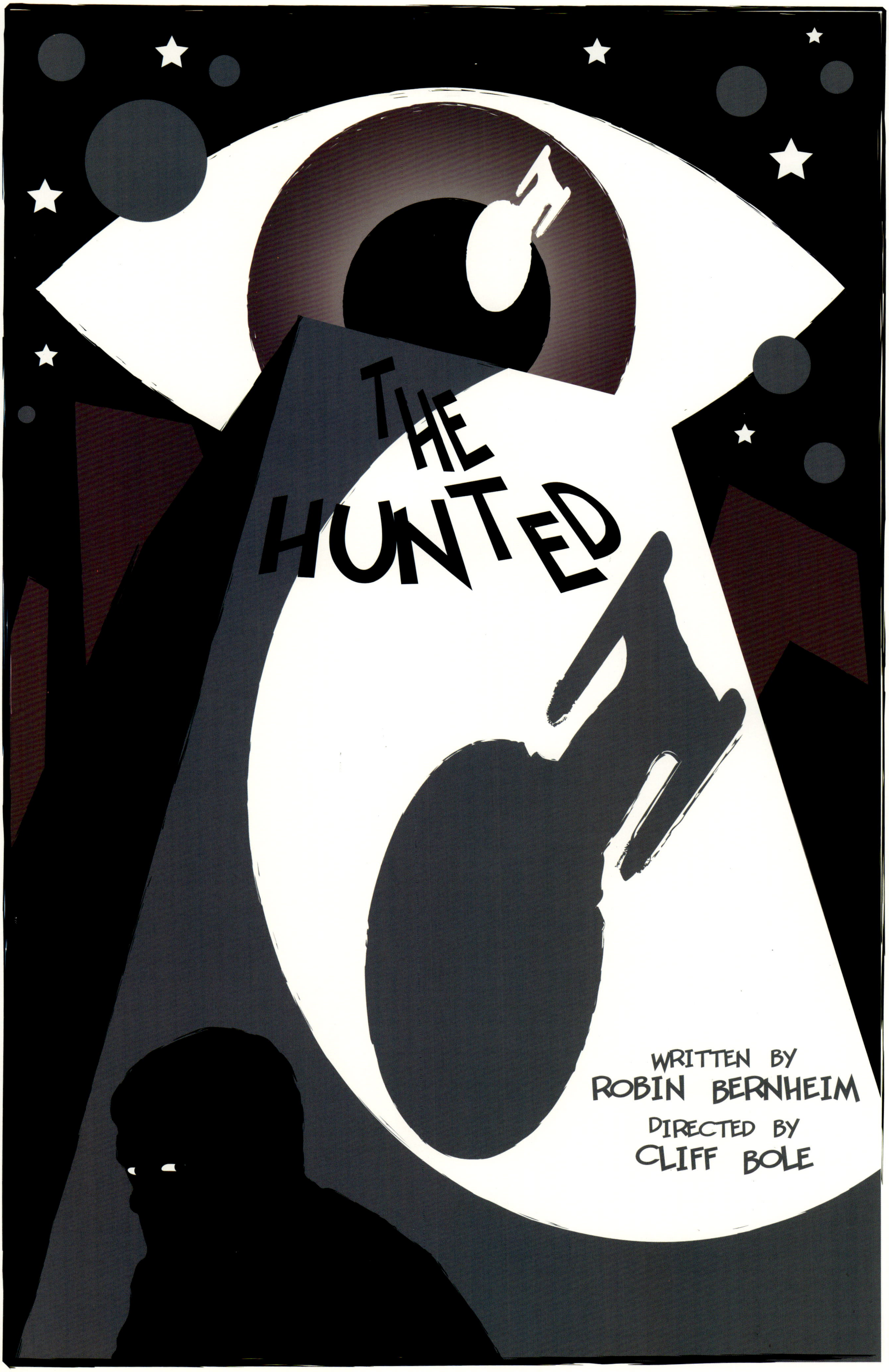
THE HUNTED
WRITTEN BY
ROBIN BERNHEIM
DIRECTED BY
CLIFF BOLE

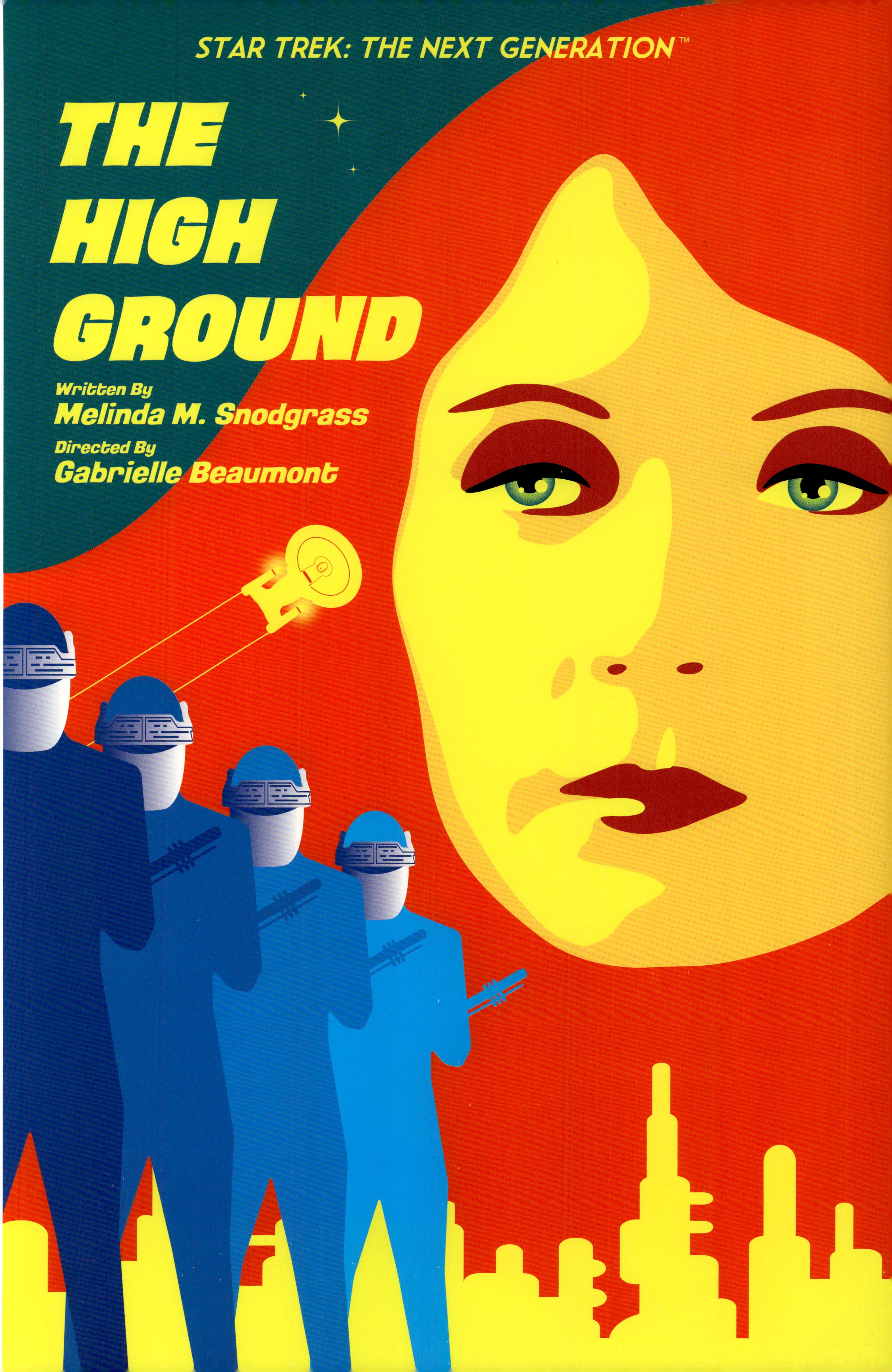
STAR TREK: THE NEXT GENERATION™
THE HIGH GROUND
Written By
Melinda M. Snodgrass
Directed By
Gabrielle Beaumont

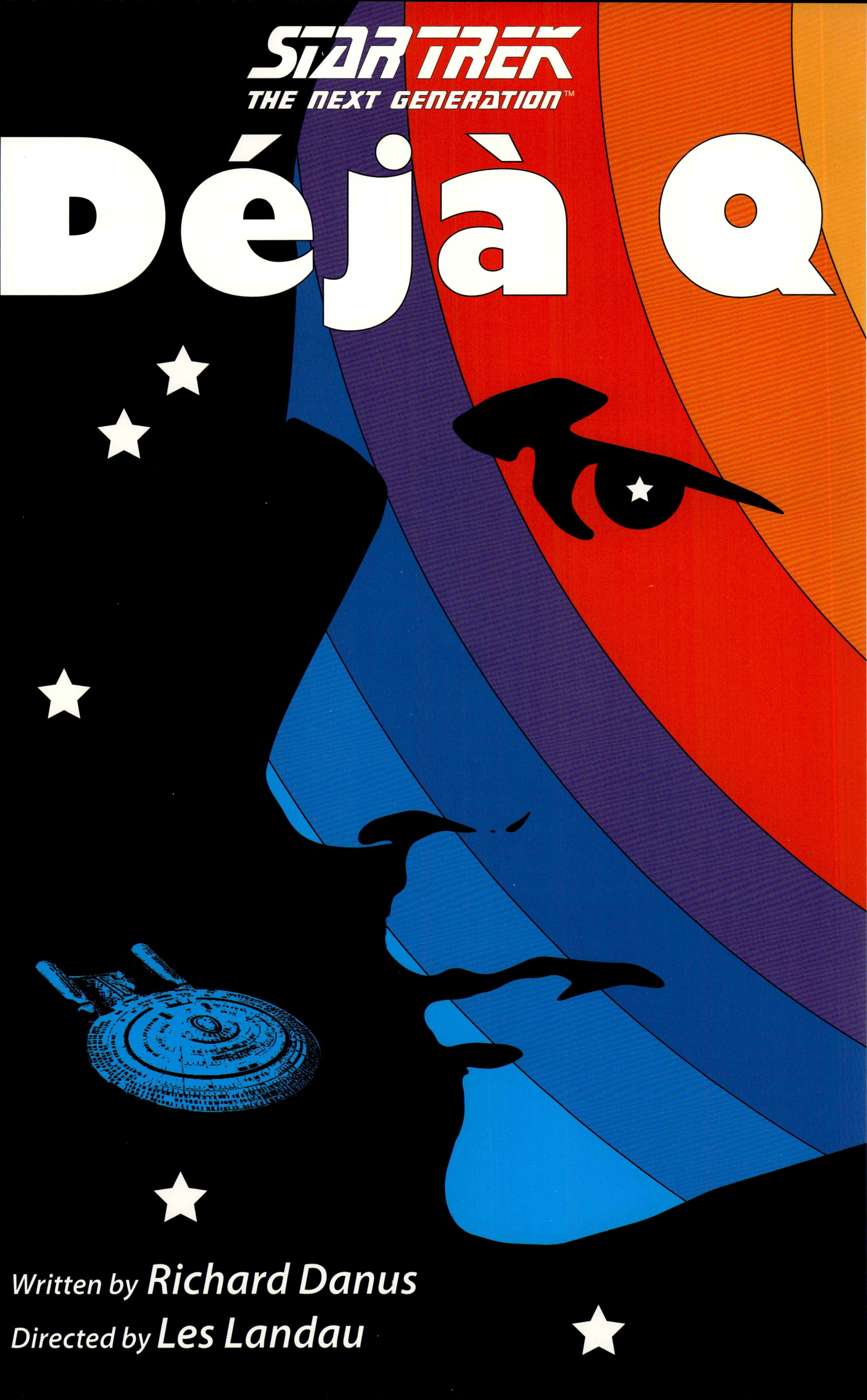
STAR TREK
THE NEXT GENERATION™
Déjà Q
Written by Richard Danus
Directed by Les Landau

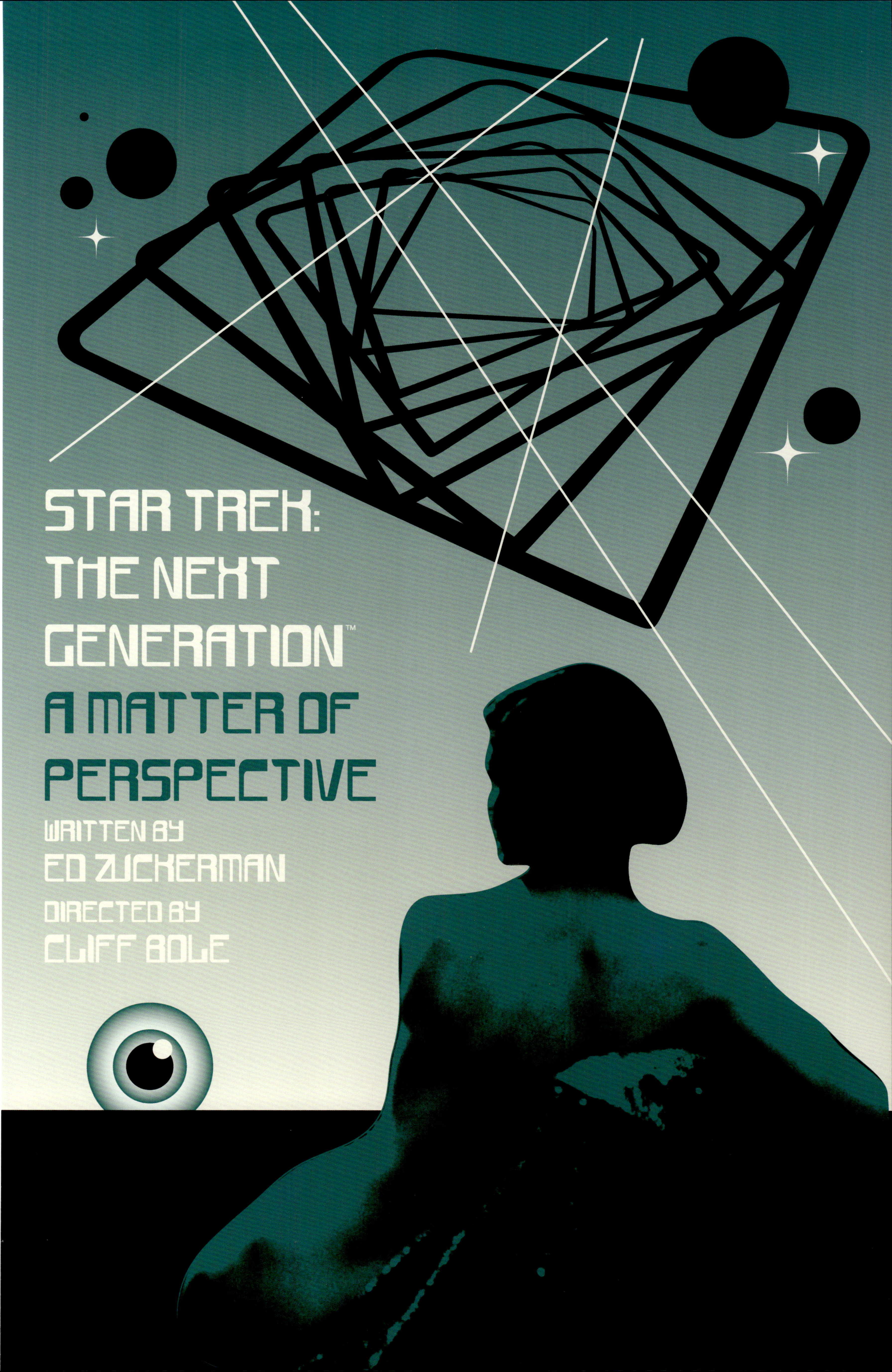

STAR TREK: THE NEXT GENERATION™

A MATTER OF PERSPECTIVE

WRITTEN BY
ED ZUCKERMAN

DIRECTED BY
CLIFF BOLE

STAR TREK
THE NEXT GENERATION™

YESTERDAY'S ENTERPRISE

Teleplay by Ira Steven Behr & Richard Manning & Hans Beimler & Ronald D. Moore

From a Story by Trent Christopher Ganino & Eric A. Stillwell Directed by David Carson

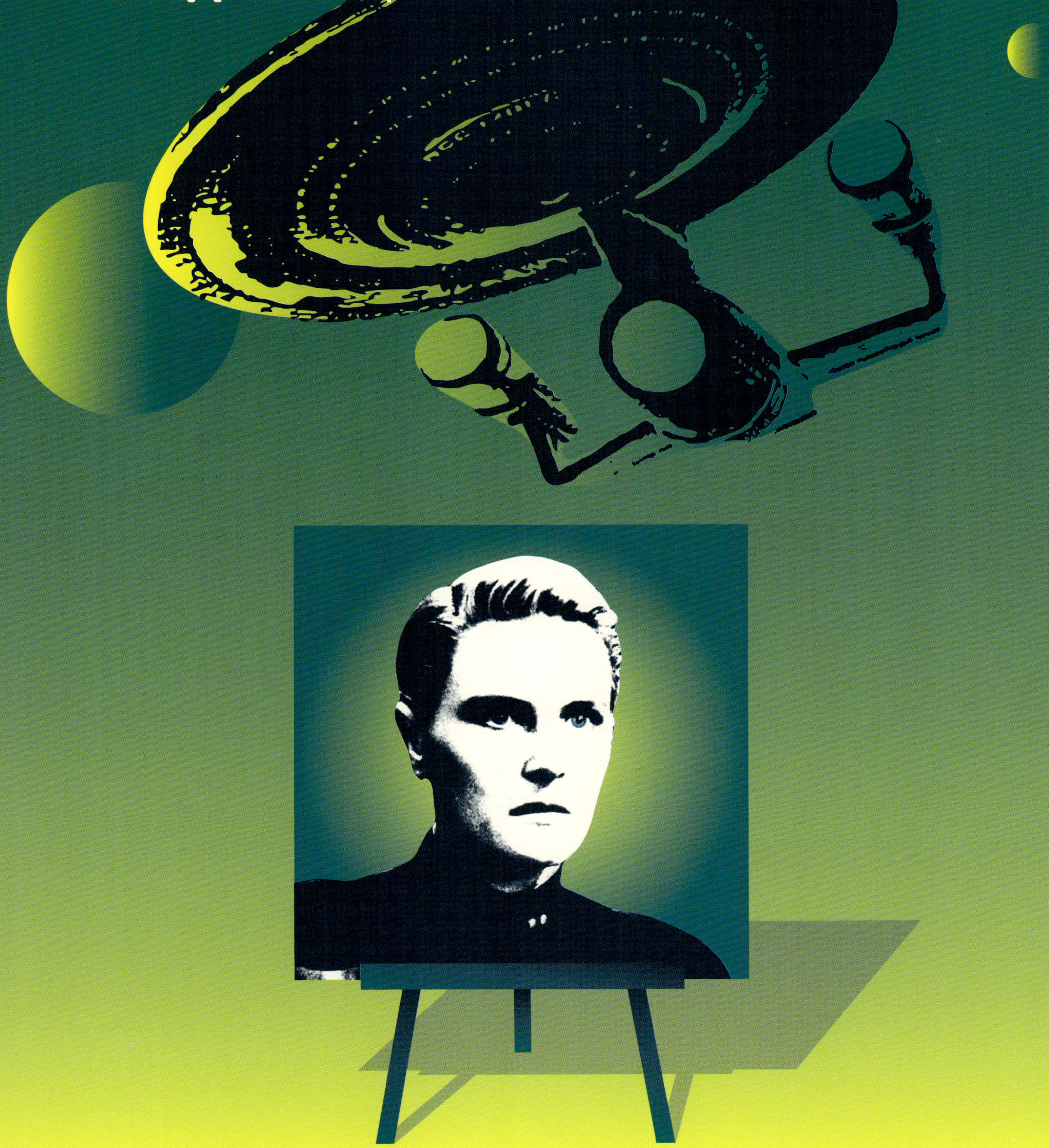

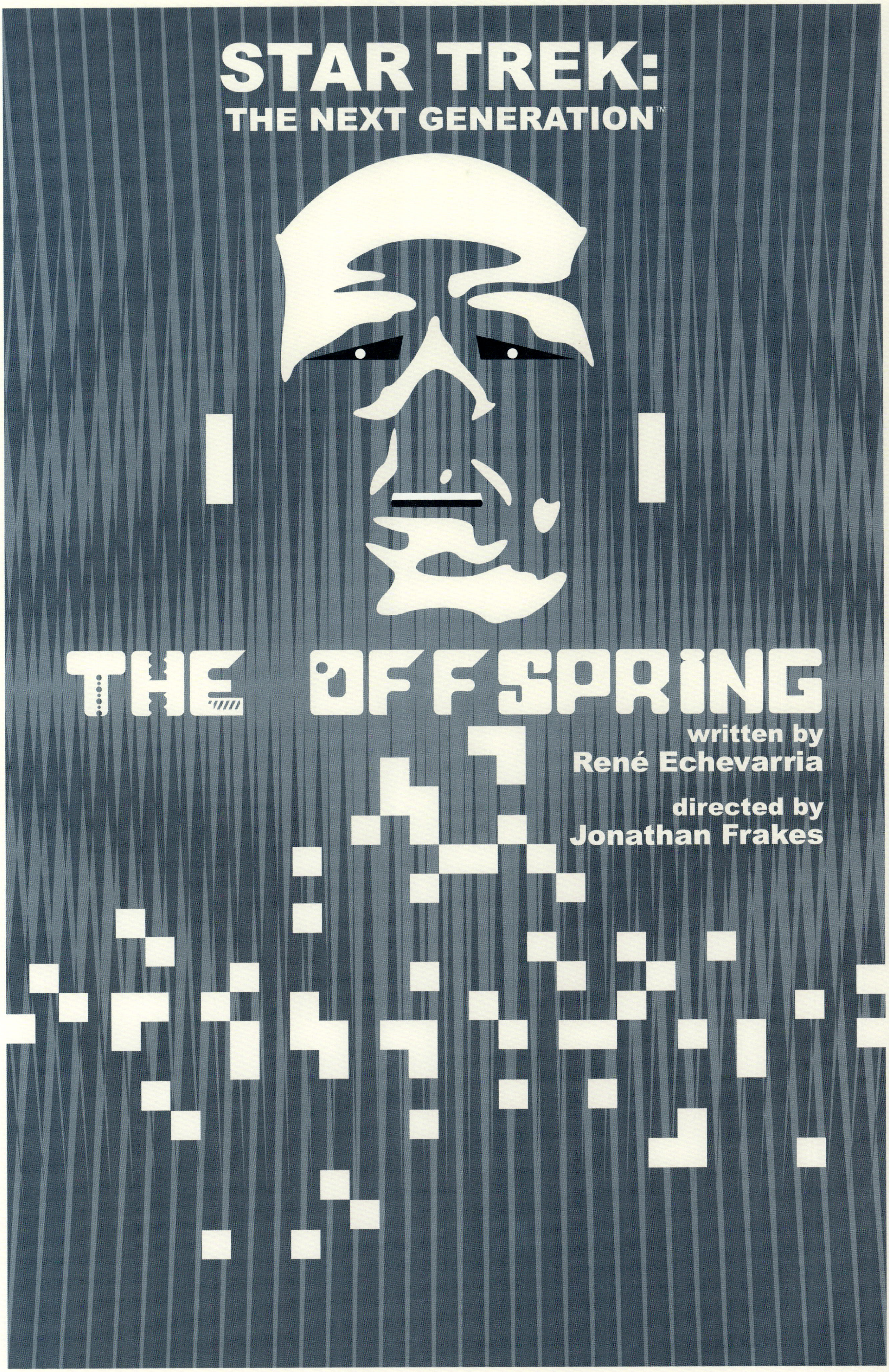
STAR TREK:
THE NEXT GENERATION™
THE OFFSPRING
written by
René Echevarria
directed by
Jonathan Frakes

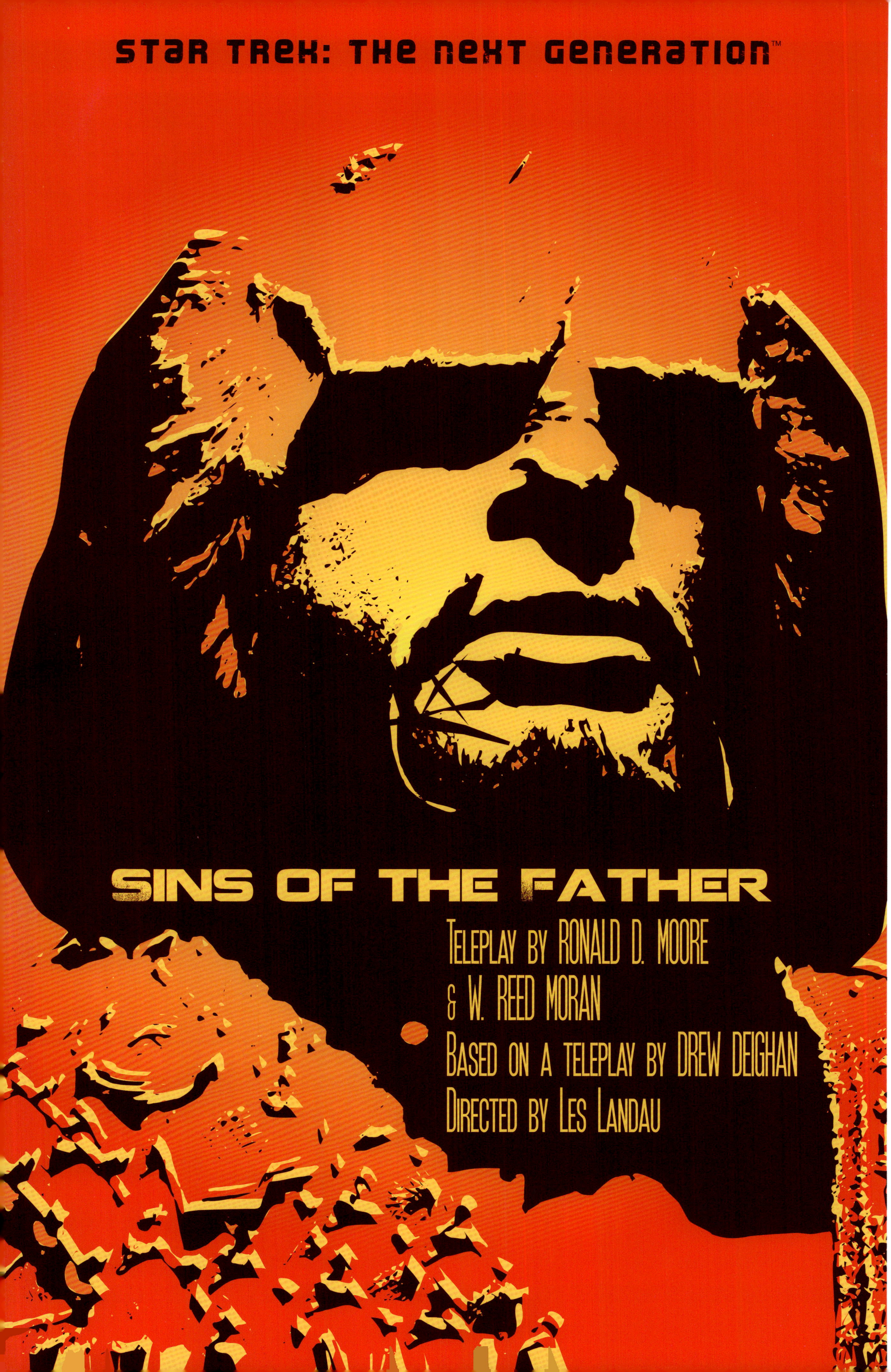
STAR TREK: THE NEXT GENERATION™
SINS OF THE FATHER
TELEPLAY BY RONALD D. MOORE
& W. REED MORAN
BASED ON A TELEPLAY BY DREW DEIGHAN
DIRECTED BY LES LANDAU

STAR TREK
THE NEXT GENERATION™

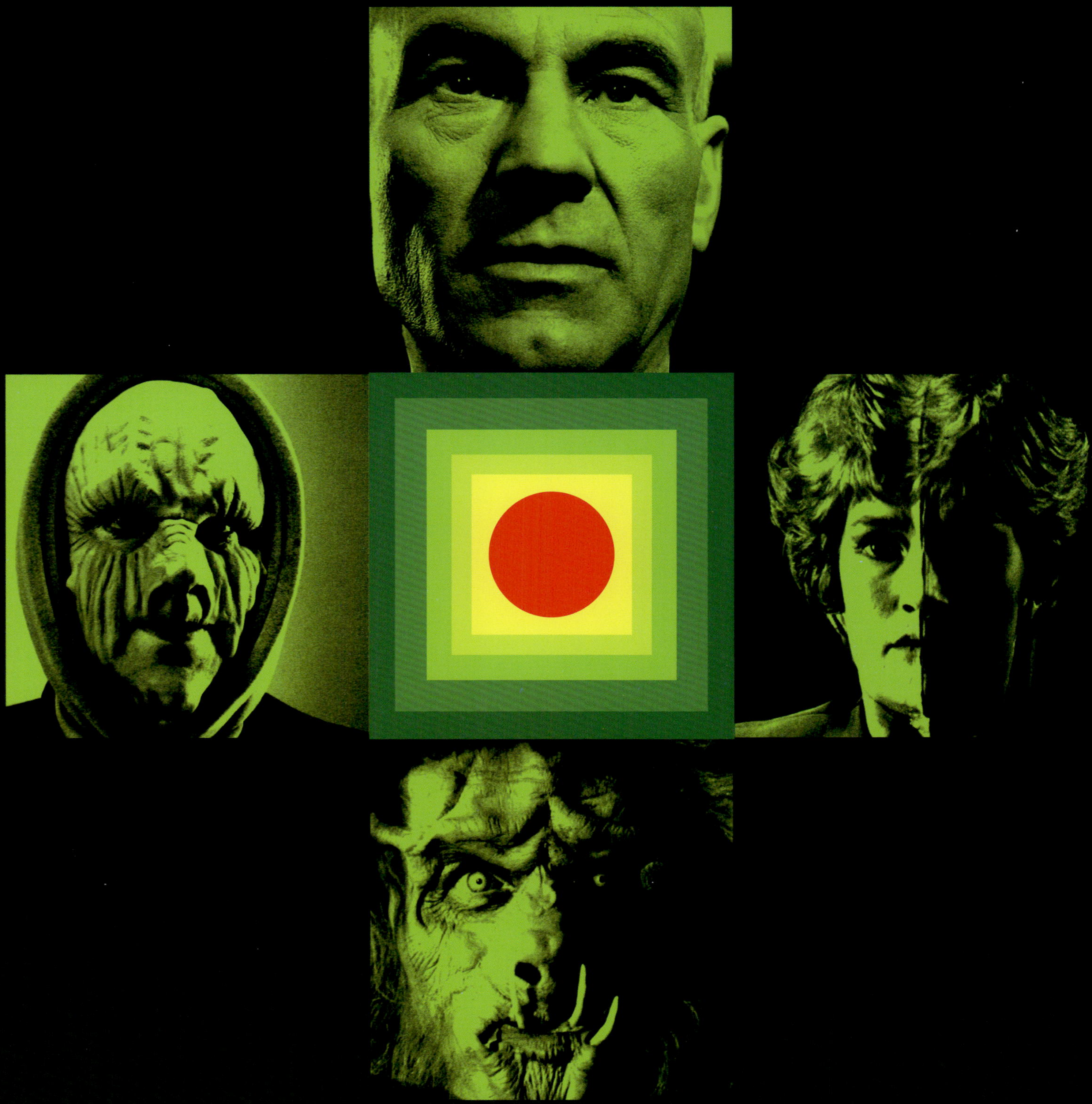

Four strangers. One room. Who can you trust?

ALLEGIANCE

Written by
Richard Manning
&
Hans Beimler
Directed by
Winrich Kolbe

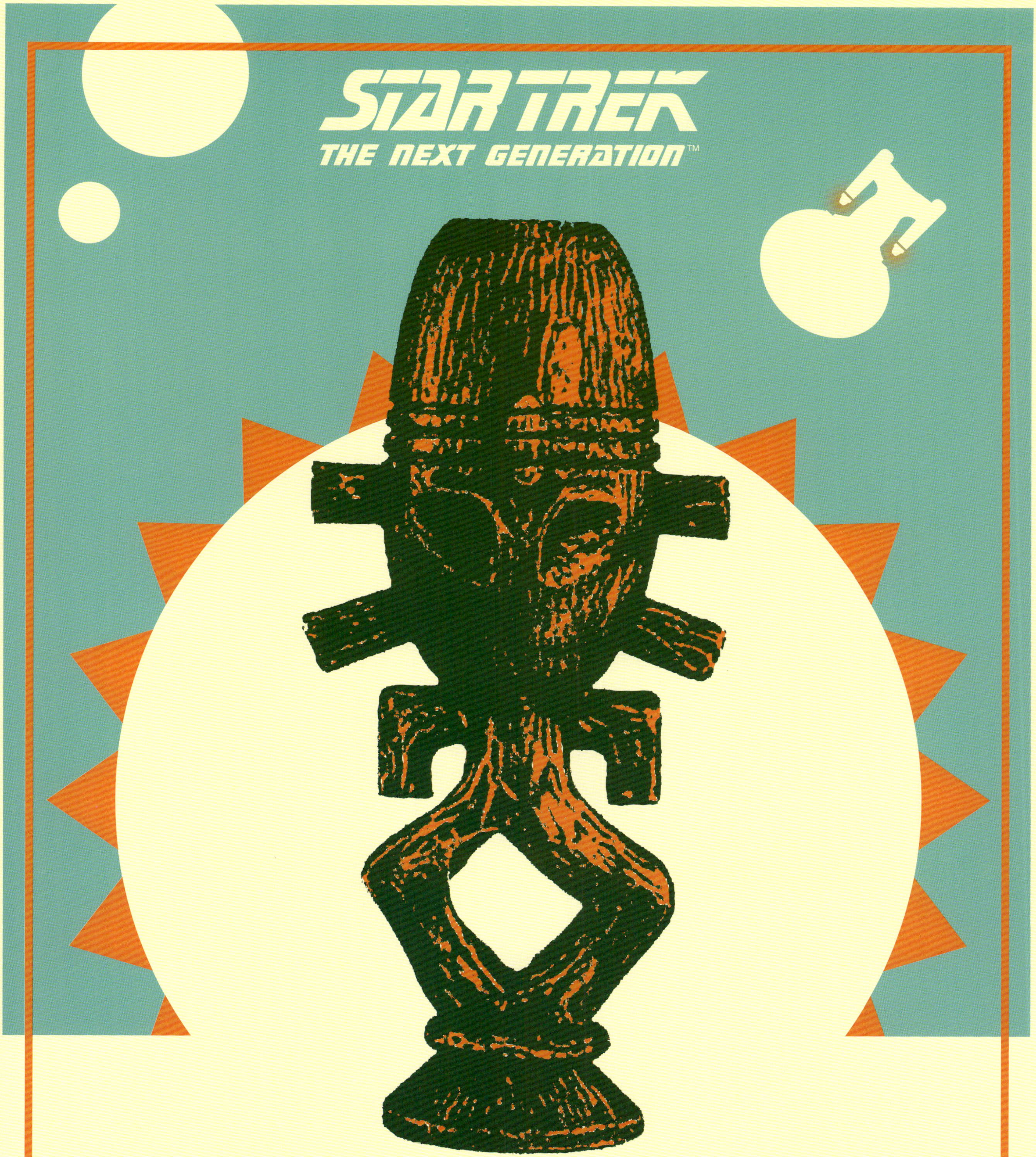

CAPTAIN'S HOLIDAY

Written by **Ira Steven Behr** Directed by **Chip Chalmers**

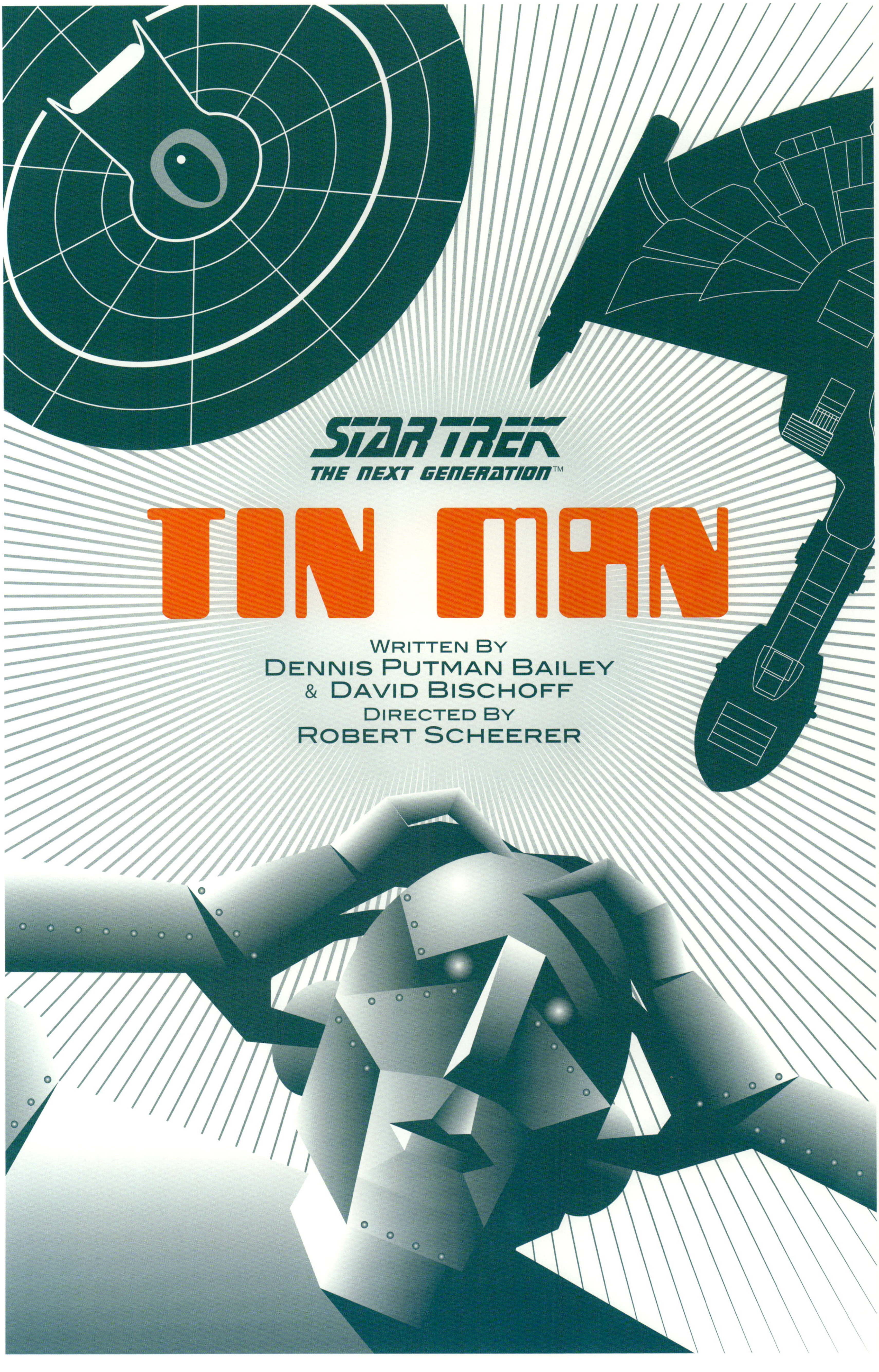
STAR TREK
THE NEXT GENERATION™
TIN MAN
WRITTEN BY
DENNIS PUTMAN BAILEY
& DAVID BISCHOFF
DIRECTED BY
ROBERT SCHEERER

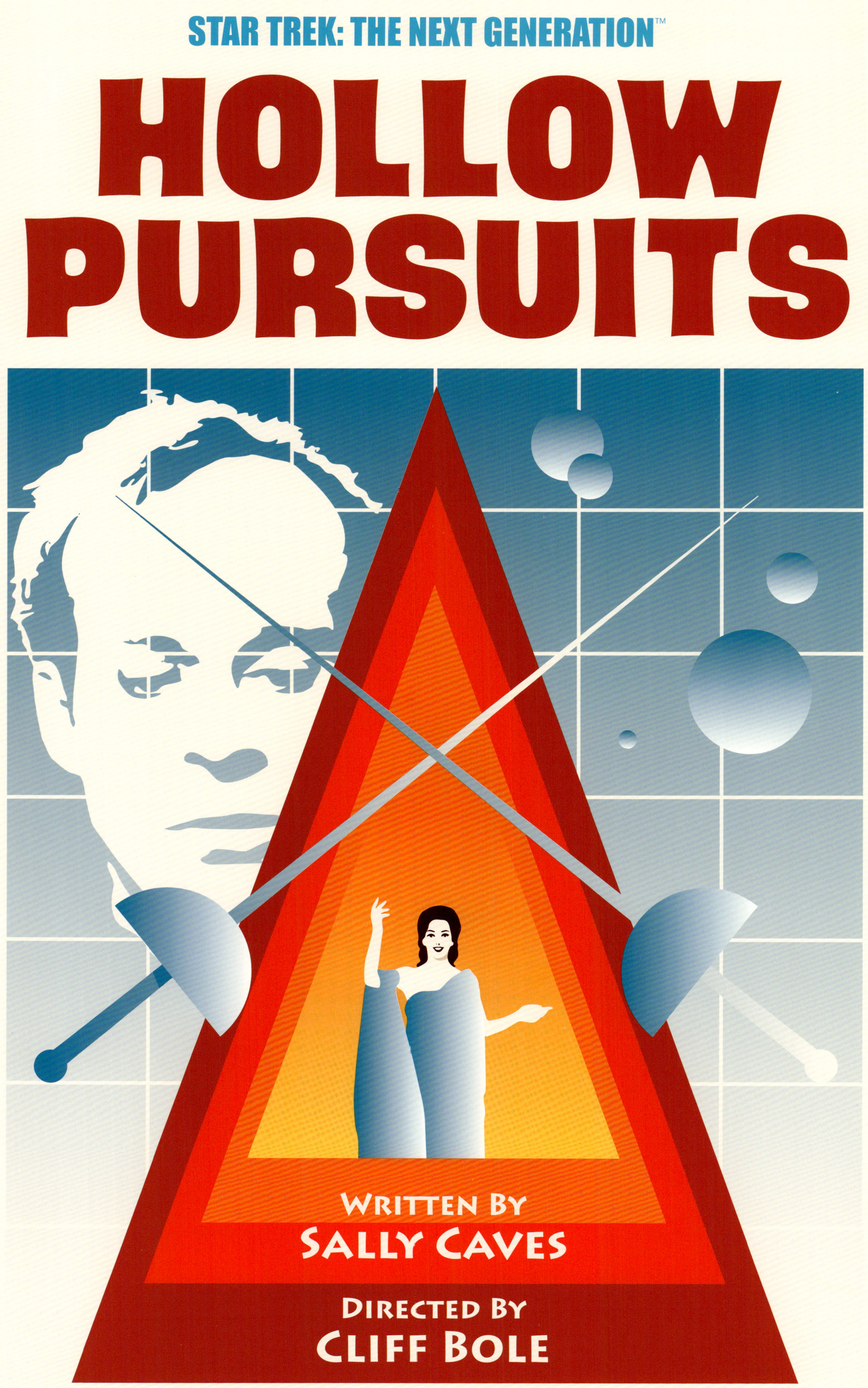
STAR TREK: THE NEXT GENERATION™
HOLLOW PURSUITS
Written By
Sally Caves
Directed By
Cliff Bole

STAR TREK: THE NEXT GENERATION™

The Most Toys

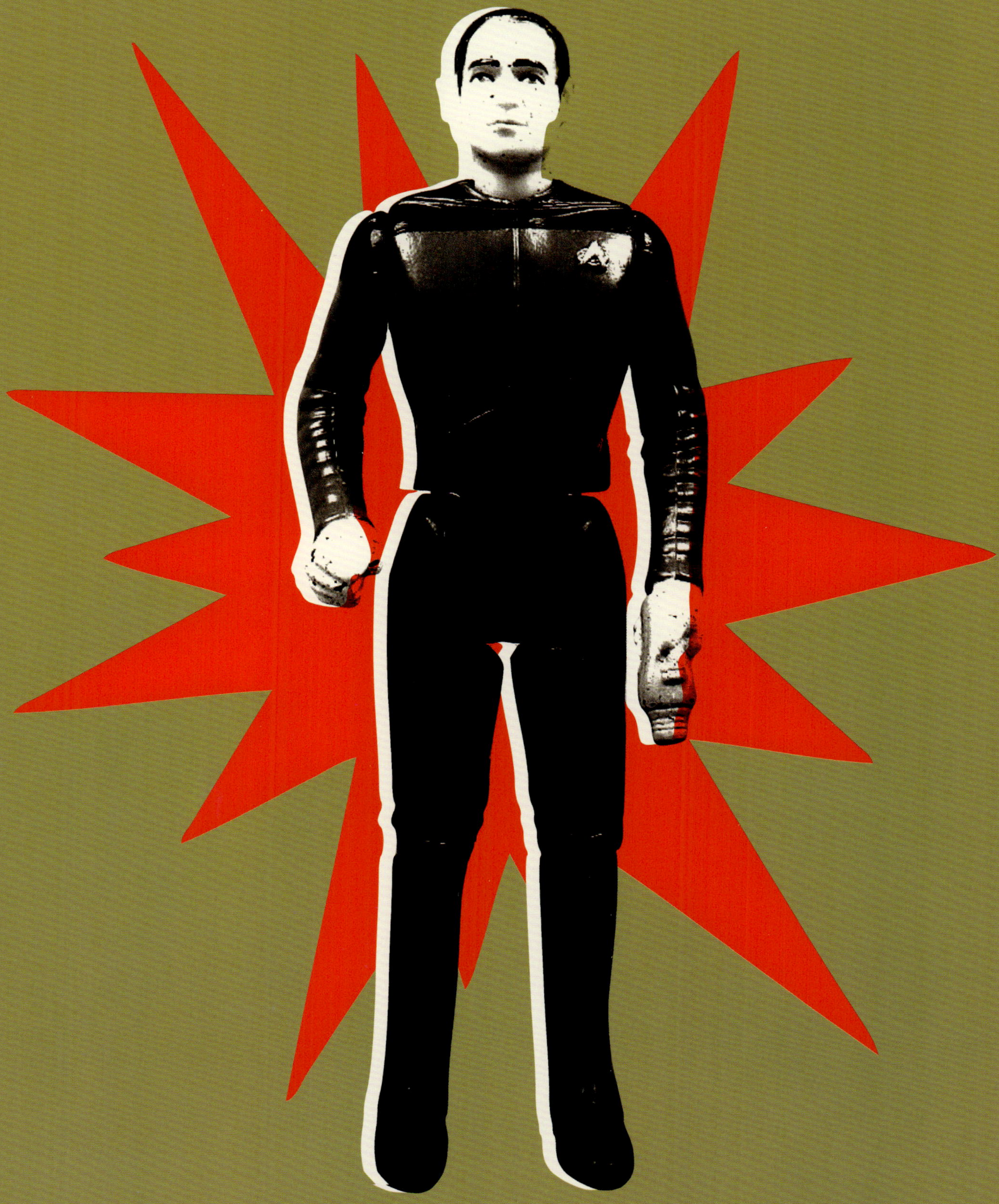

Written by Shari Goodhartz

Directed by Tim Bond

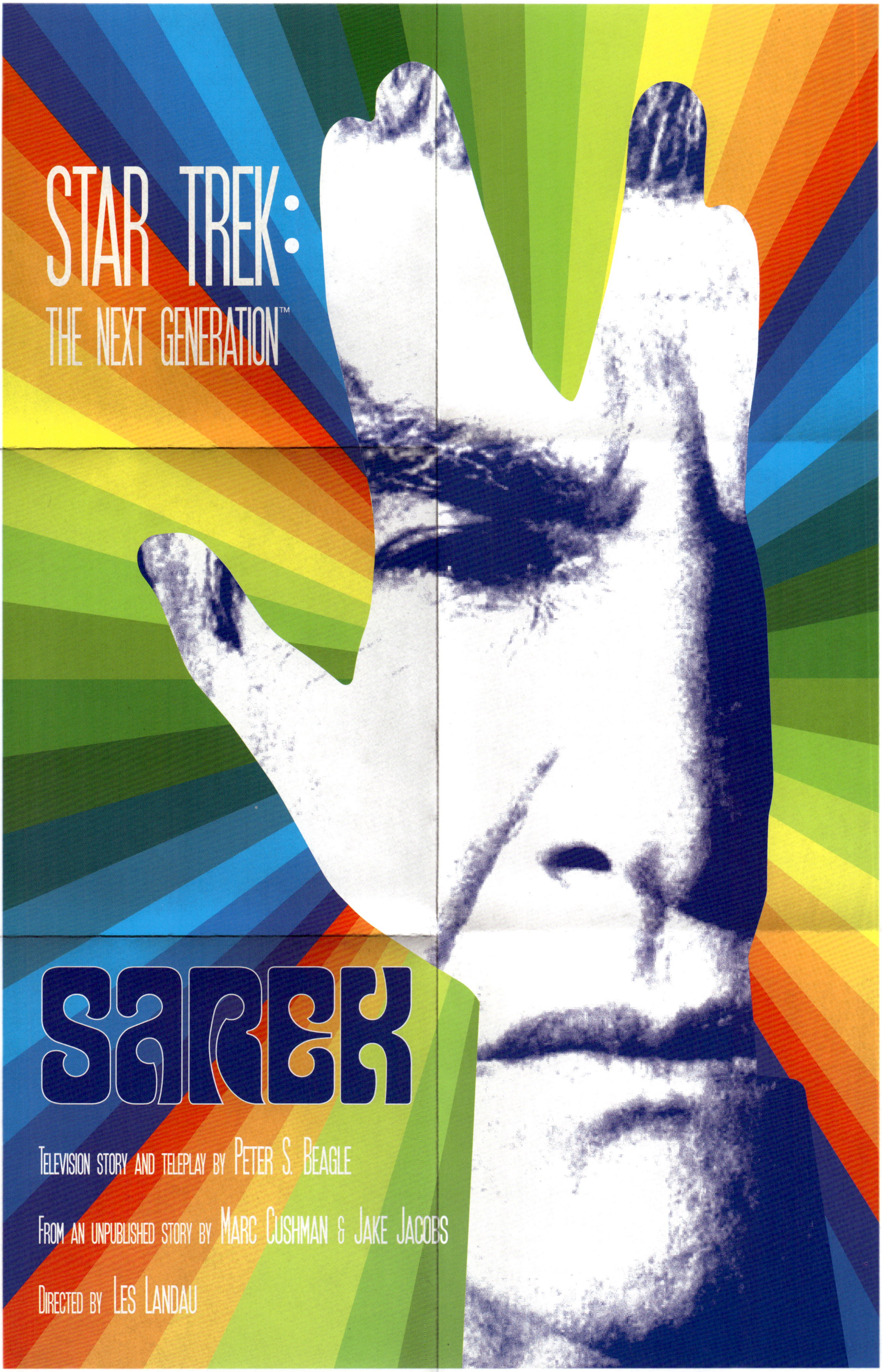
STAR TREK:
THE NEXT GENERATION™
SAREK
Television story and teleplay by Peter S. Beagle
From an unpublished story by Marc Cushman & Jake Jacobs
Directed by Les Landau

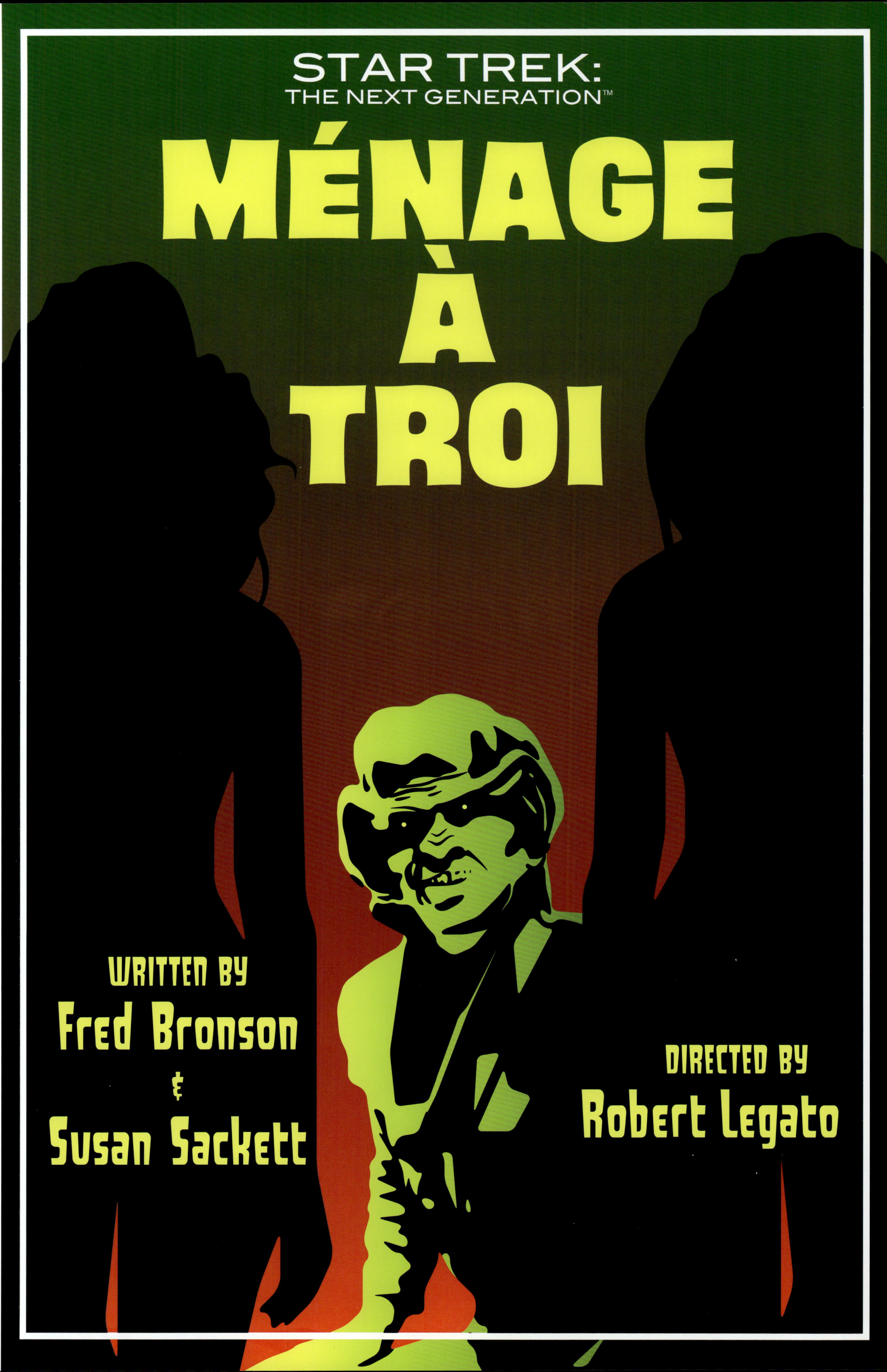
STAR TREK:
THE NEXT GENERATION™
MÉNAGE À TROI
WRITTEN BY
Fred Bronson
&
Susan Sackett
DIRECTED BY
Robert Legato

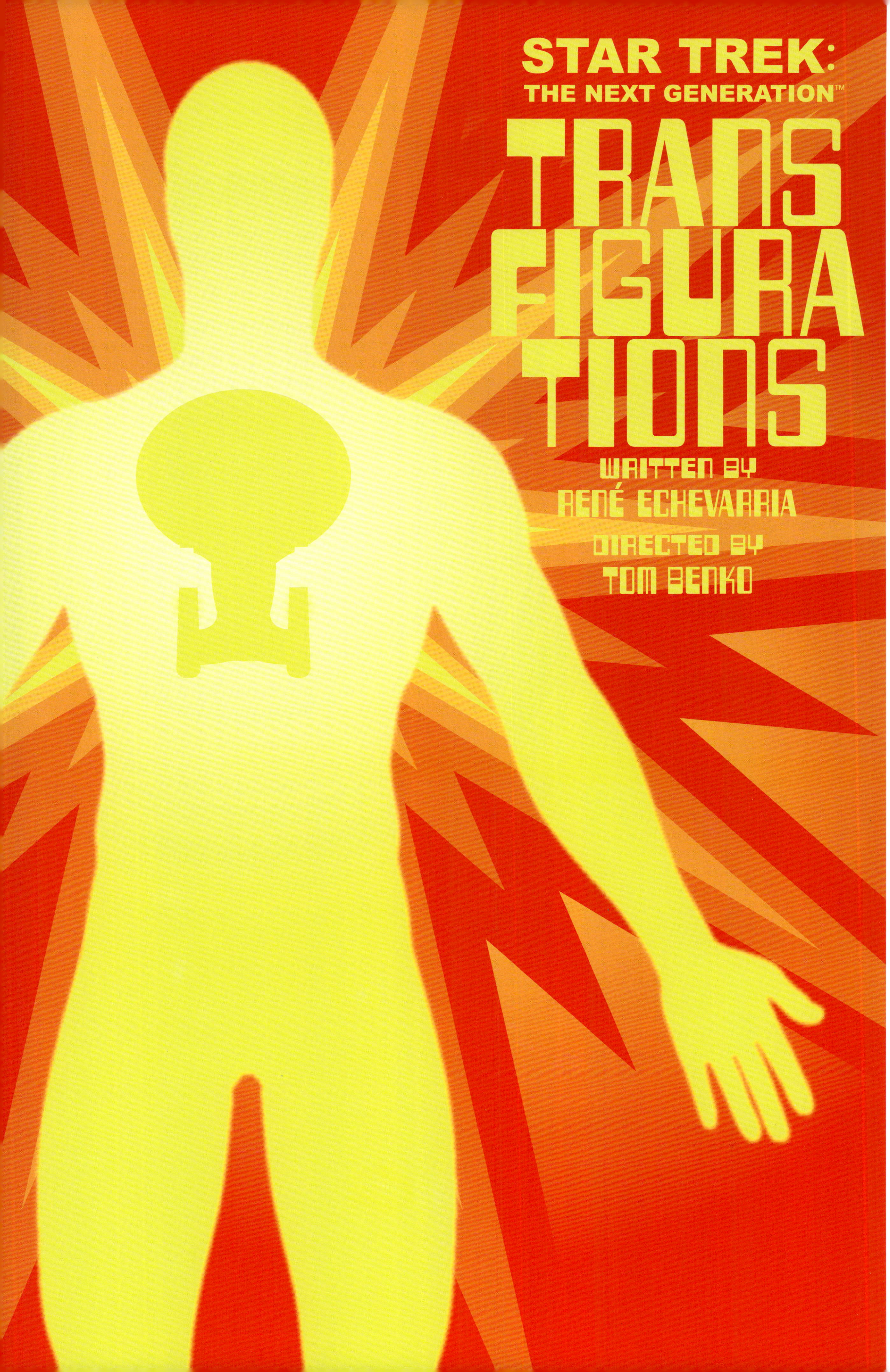
STAR TREK:
THE NEXT GENERATION™
TRANS
FIGURA
TIONS
WRITTEN BY
RENÉ ECHEVARRIA
DIRECTED BY
TOM BENKO

STAR TREK: THE NEXT GENERATION™

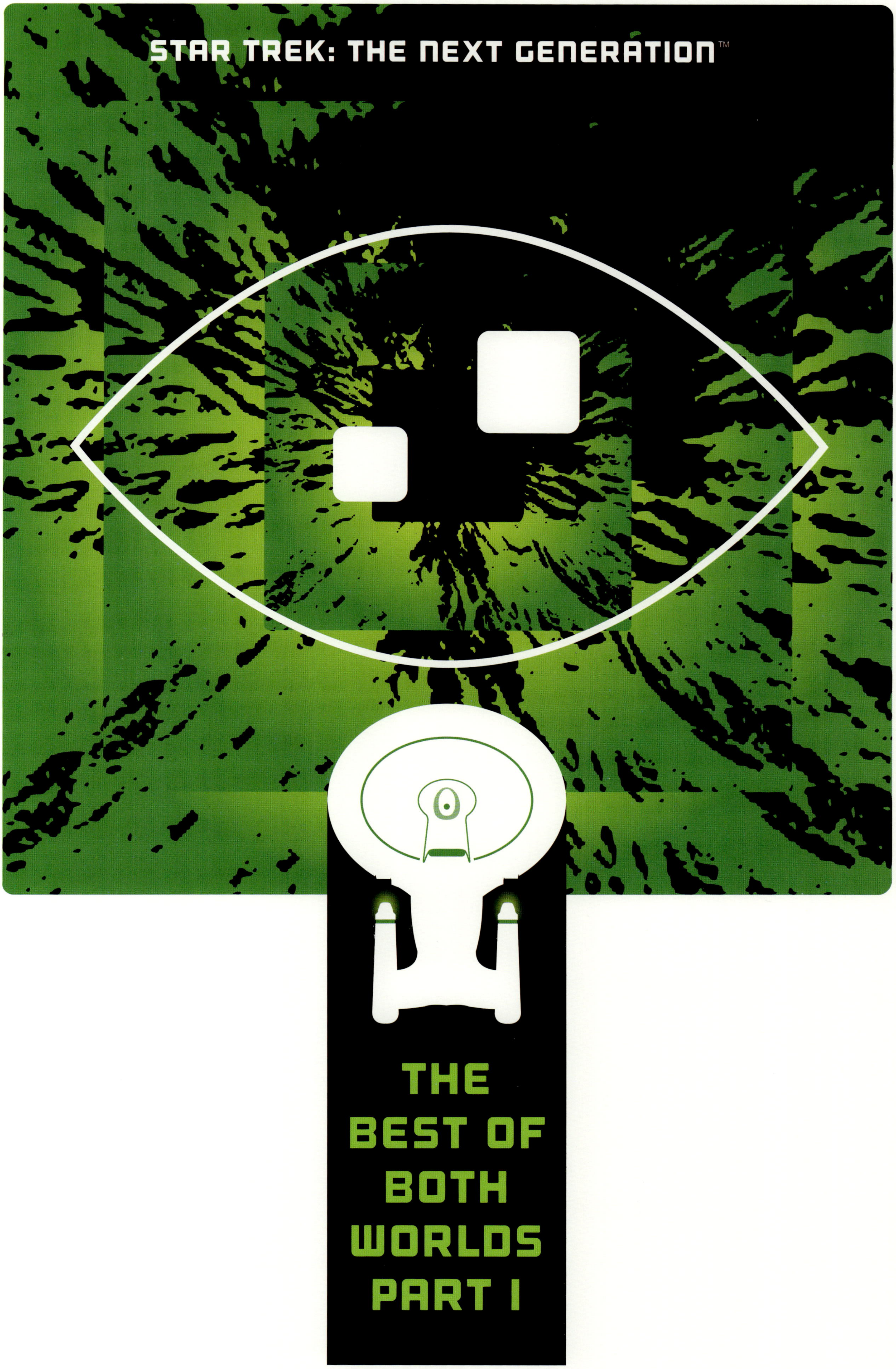

THE BEST OF BOTH WORLDS PART I

WRITTEN BY MICHAEL PILLER DIRECTED BY CLIFF BOLE

Season Four

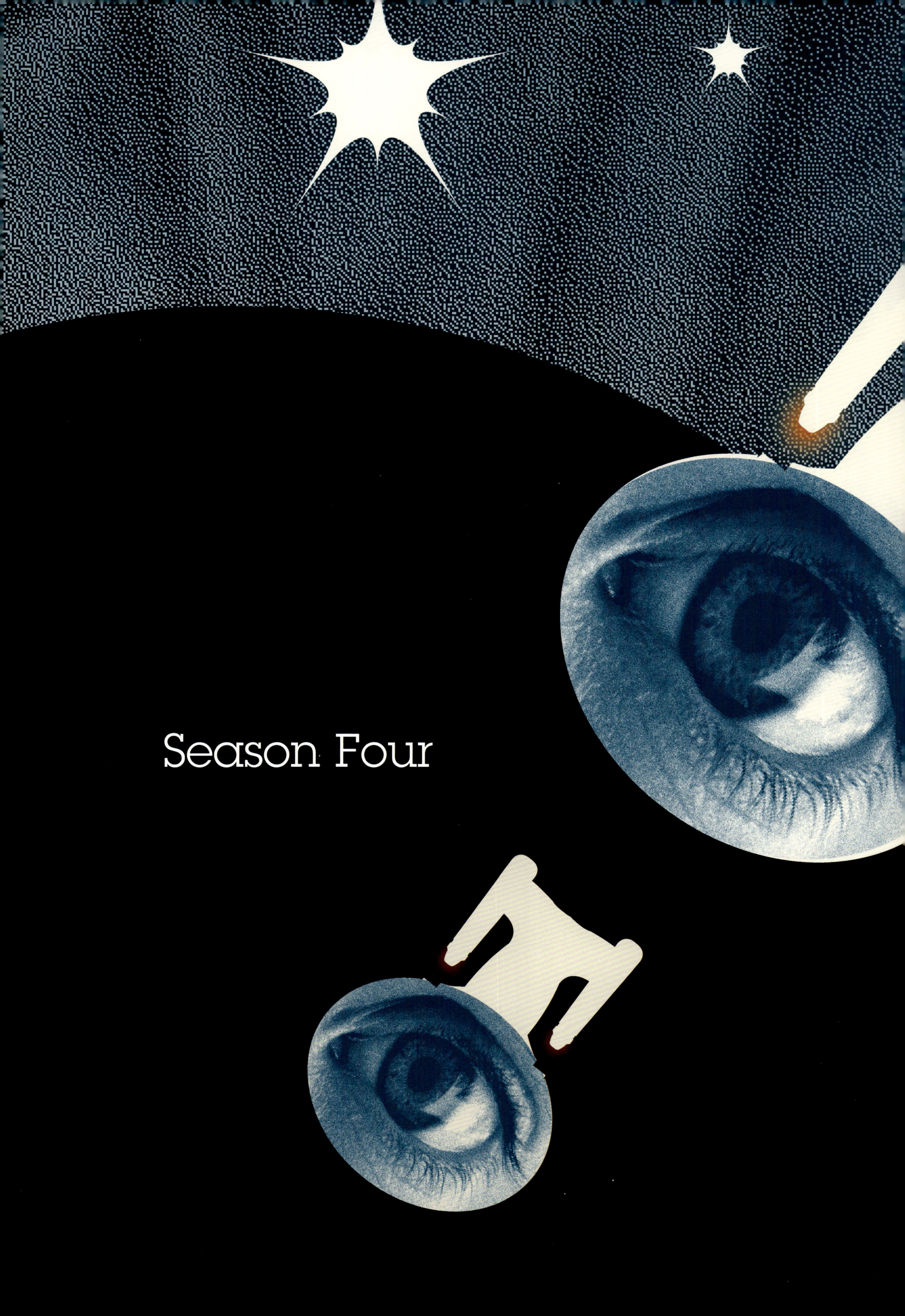

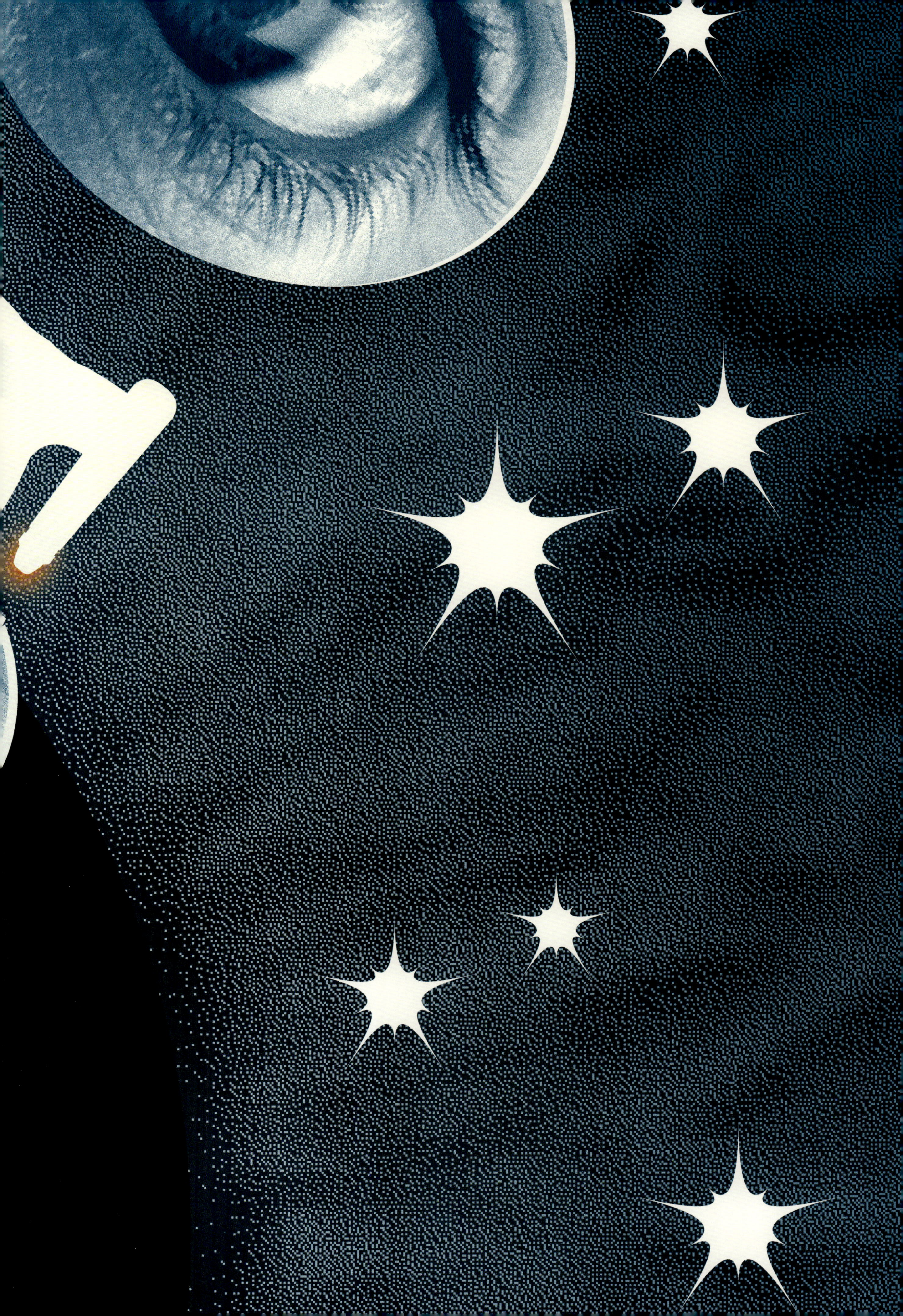

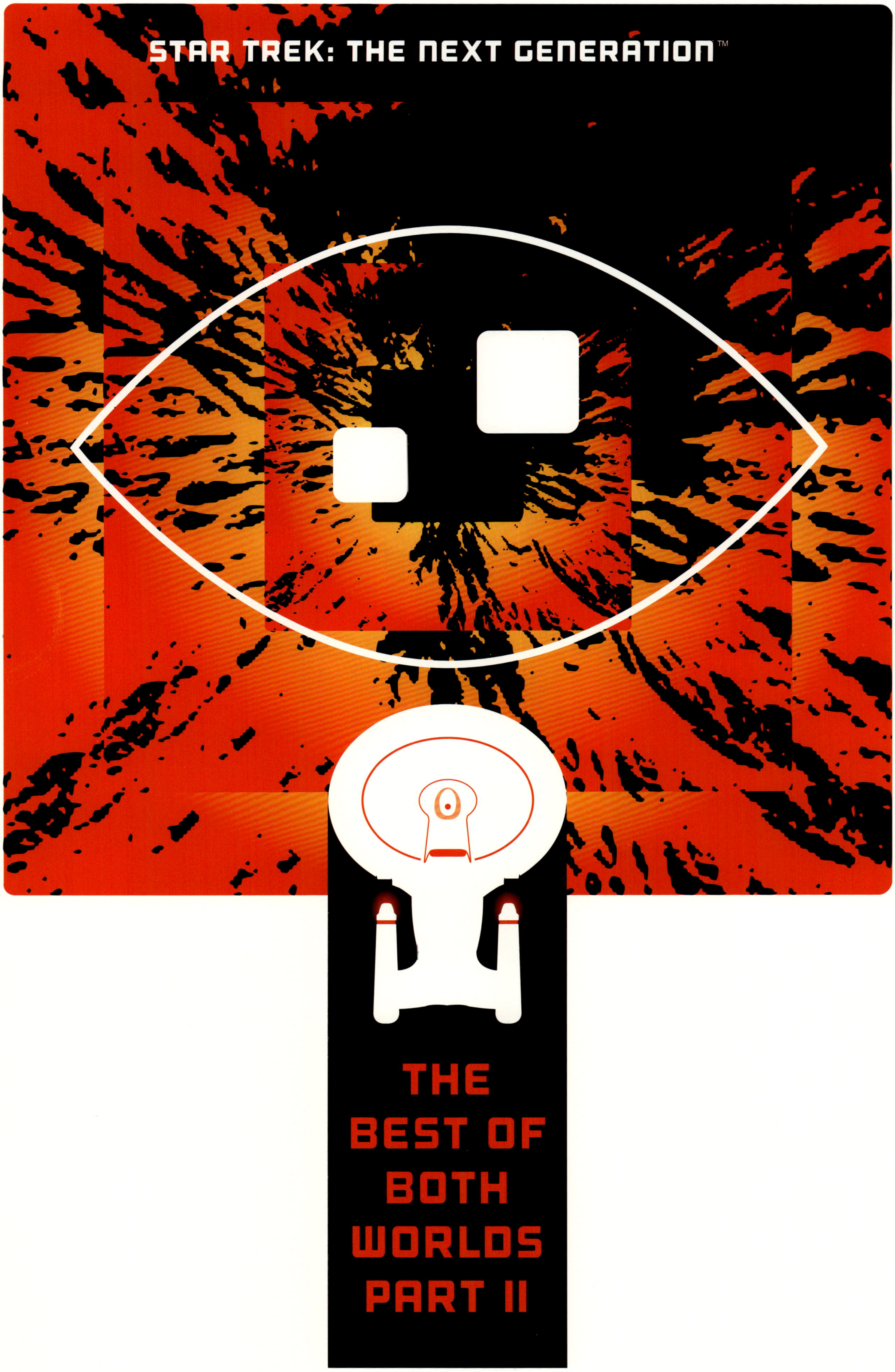

WRITTEN BY MICHAEL PILLER DIRECTED BY CLIFF BOLE

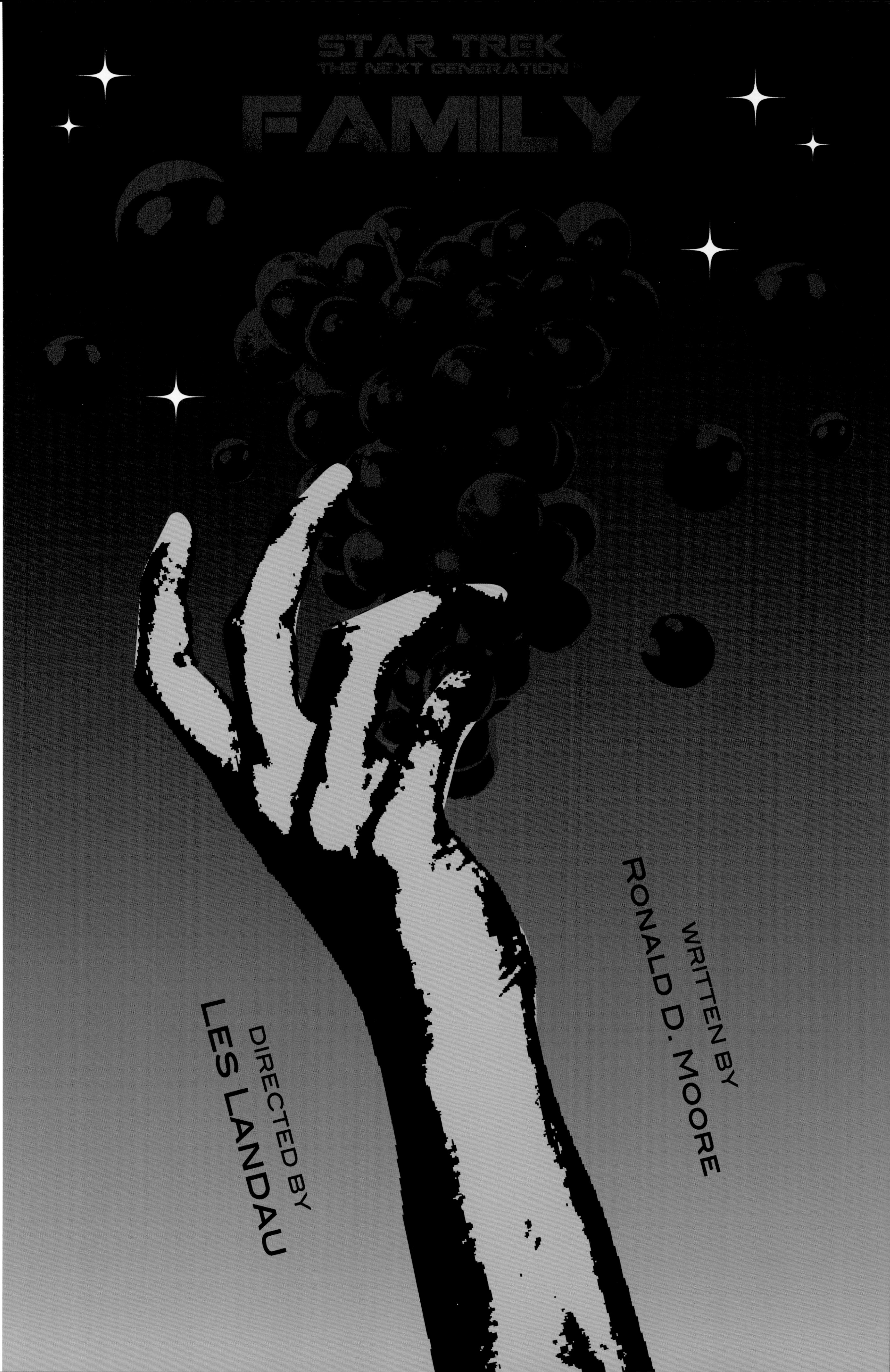
STAR TREK
THE NEXT GENERATION
FAMILY
WRITTEN BY
RONALD D. MOORE
DIRECTED BY
LES LANDAU

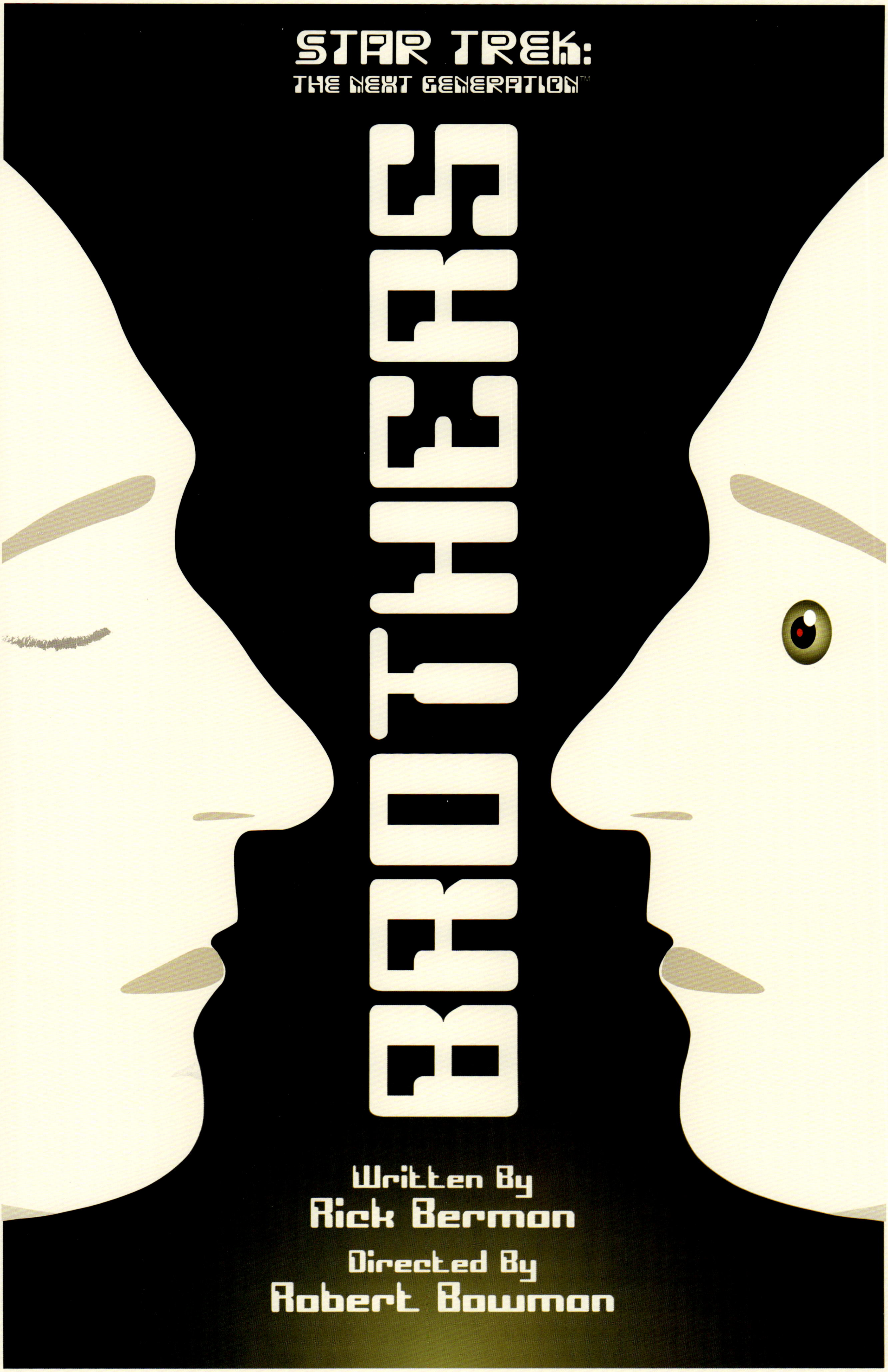

STAR TREK:
THE NEXT GENERATION™
BROTHERS
Written By
Rick Berman
Directed By
Robert Bowman

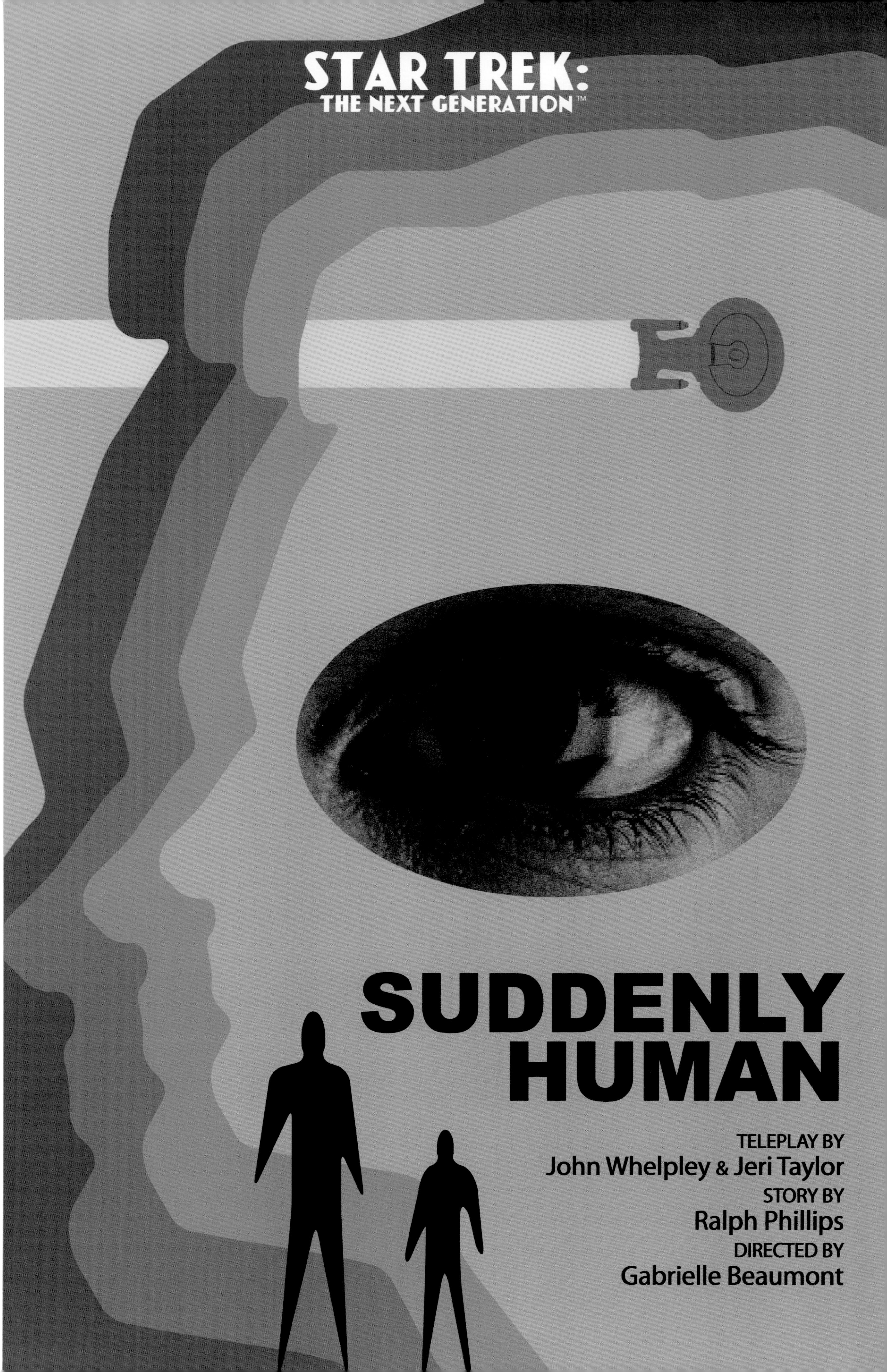
STAR TREK:
THE NEXT GENERATION™
SUDDENLY
HUMAN
TELEPLAY BY
John Whelpley & Jeri Taylor
STORY BY
Ralph Phillips
DIRECTED BY
Gabrielle Beaumont

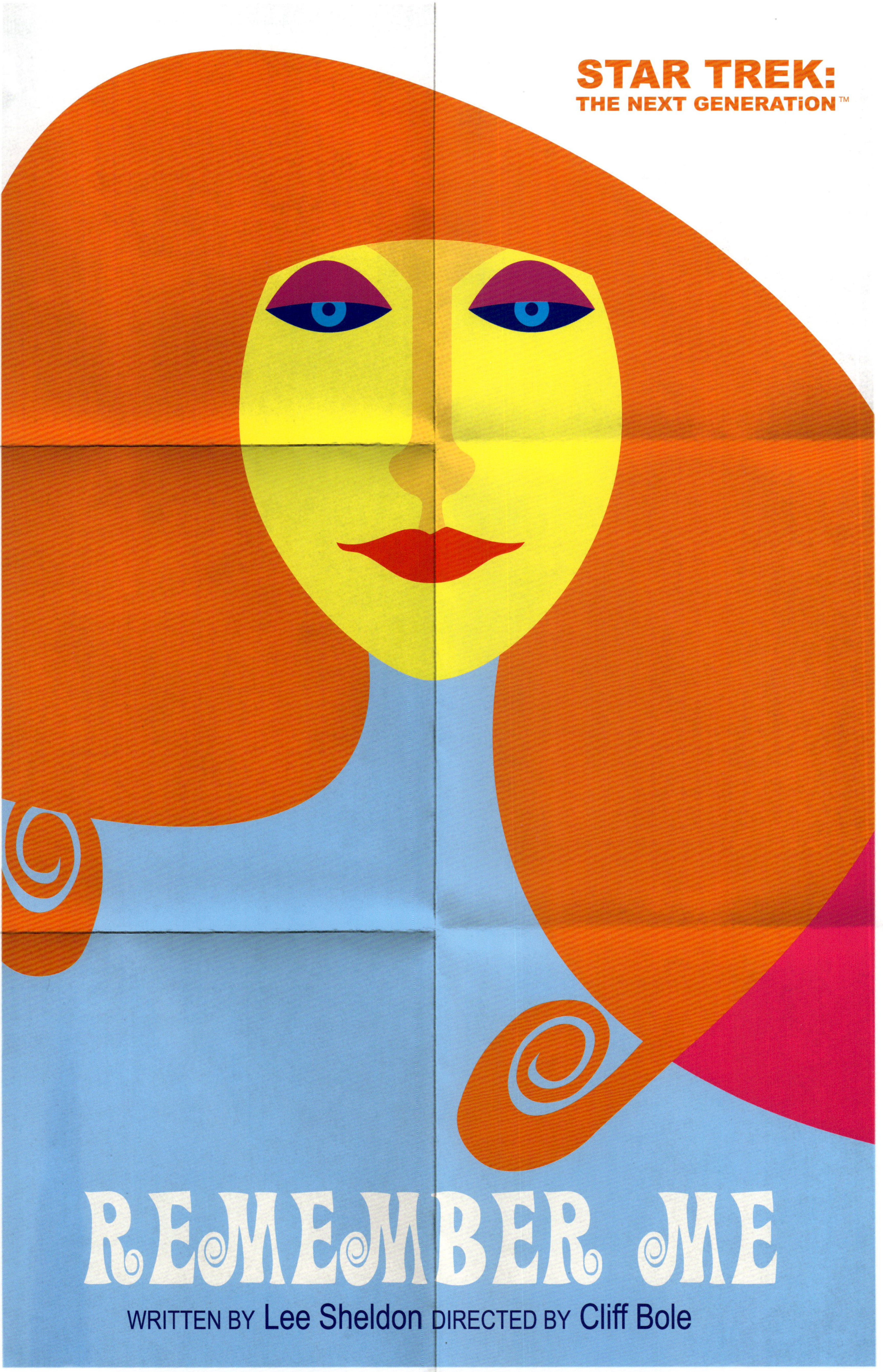
STAR TREK:
THE NEXT GENERATION™
REMEMBER ME
WRITTEN BY Lee Sheldon DIRECTED BY Cliff Bole

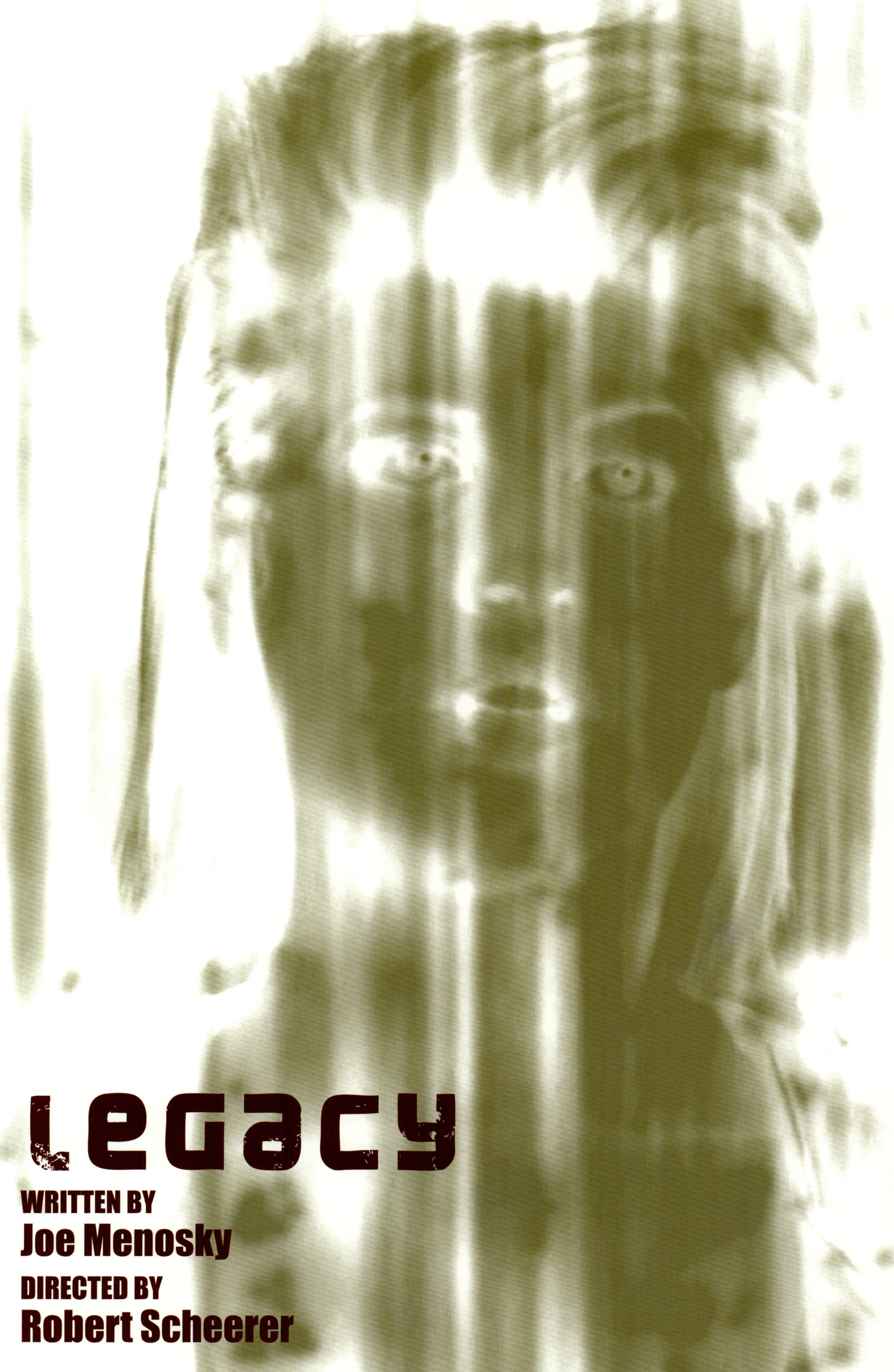

LEGACY

WRITTEN BY
Joe Menosky

DIRECTED BY
Robert Scheerer

STAR TREK:
THE NEXT GENERATION™

REUNION

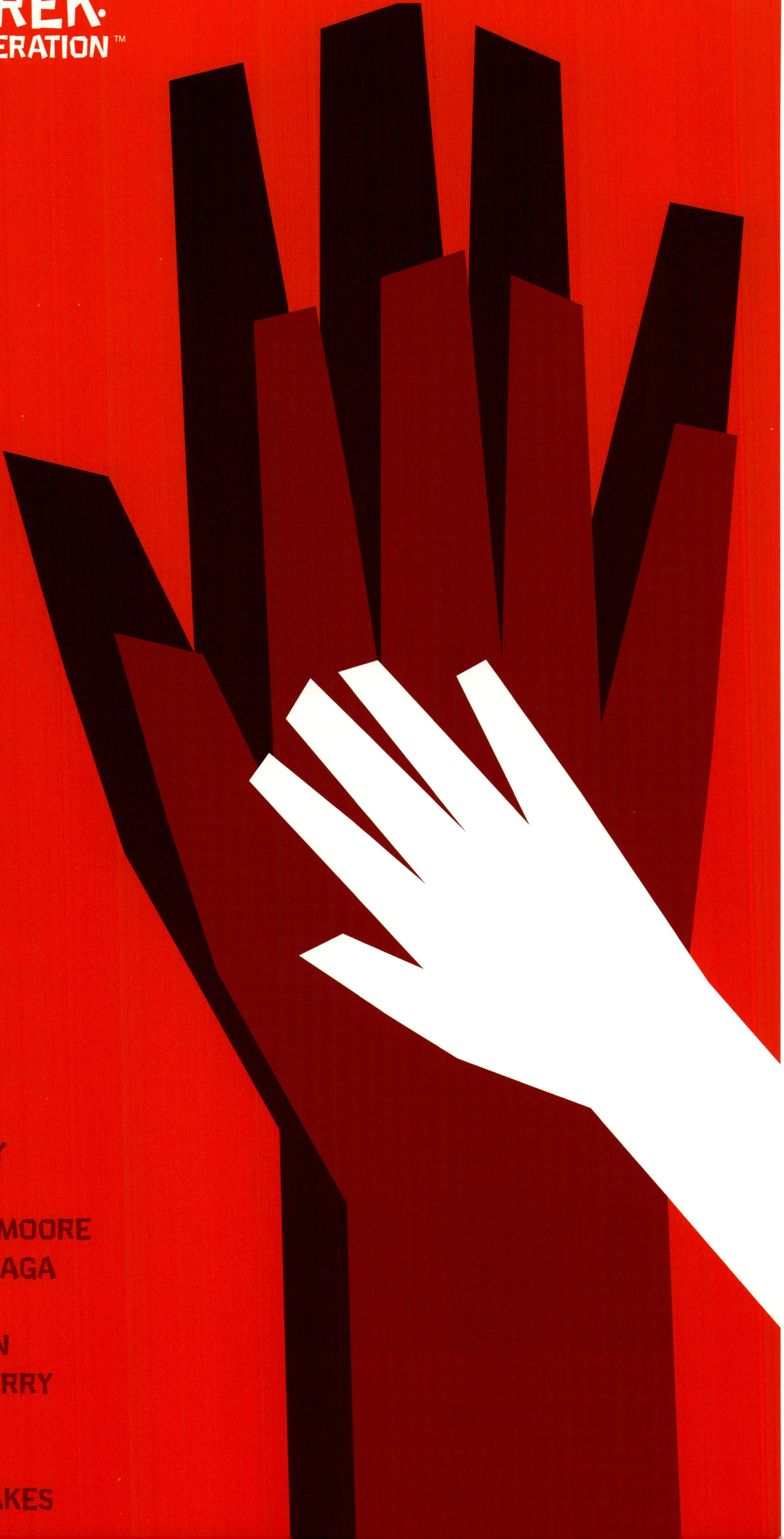

TELEPLAY BY
THOMAS PERRY
& JO PERRY
AND RONALD D. MOORE
& BRANNON BRAGA

STORY BY
DREW DEIGHAN
AND THOMAS PERRY
& JO PERRY

DIRECTED BY
JONATHAN FRAKES

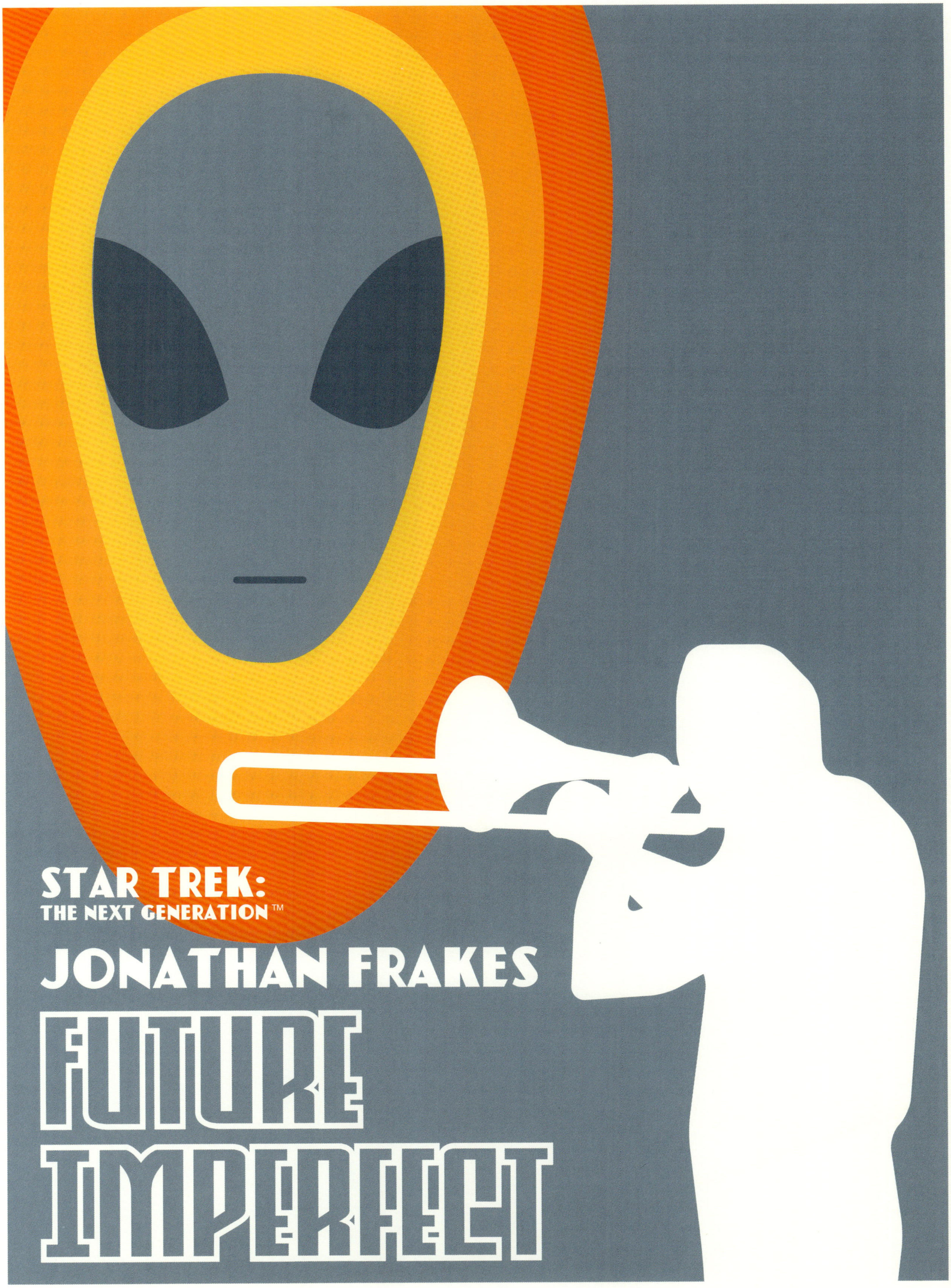

Written By
J. Larry Carroll
&
David Bennett Carren
Directed By
Les Landau

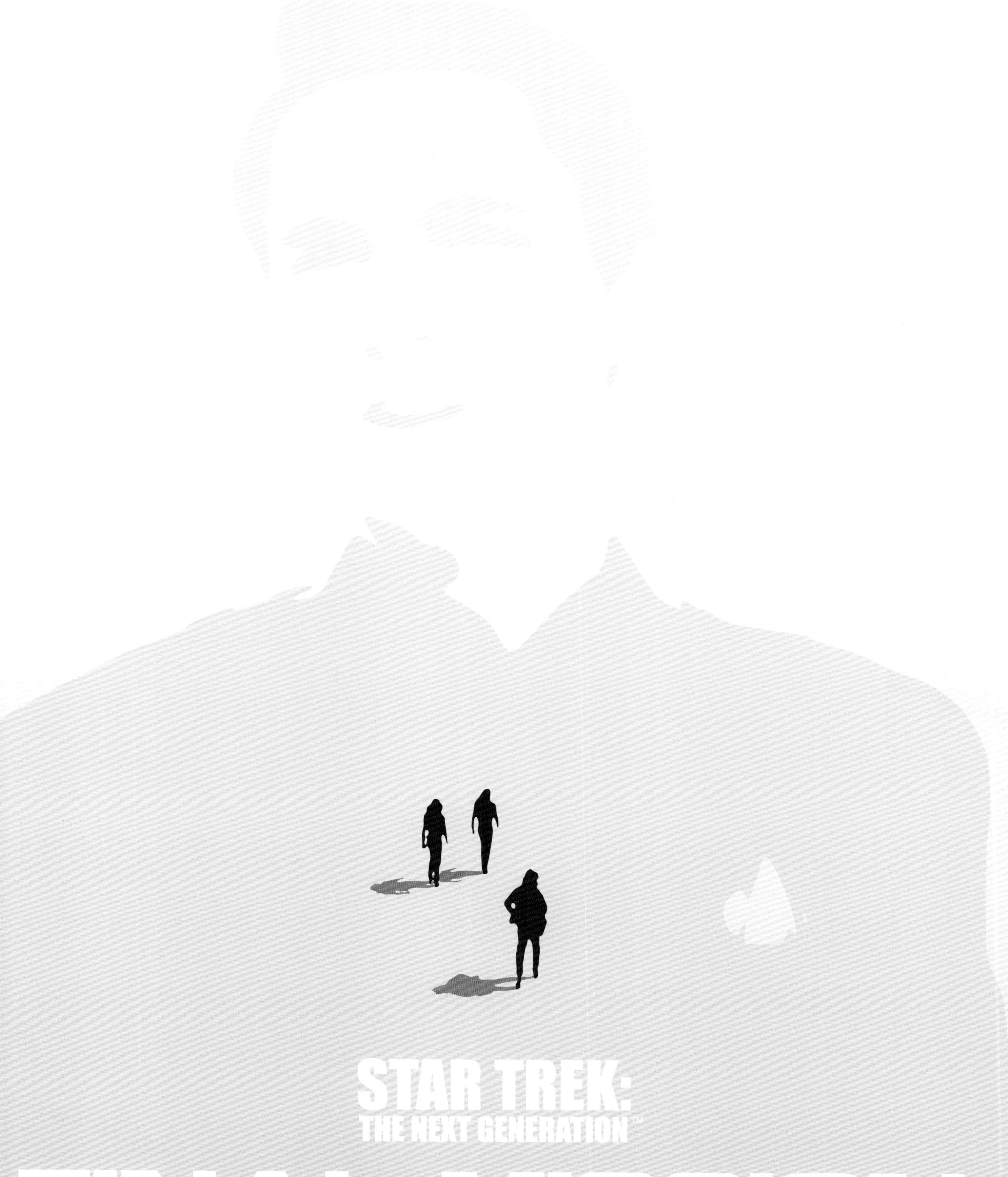

STAR TREK: THE NEXT GENERATION™

FINAL MISSION

TELEPLAY BY
Kasey Arnold-Ince and Jeri Taylor

STORY BY
Kasey Arnold-Ince

DIRECTED BY
Corey Allen

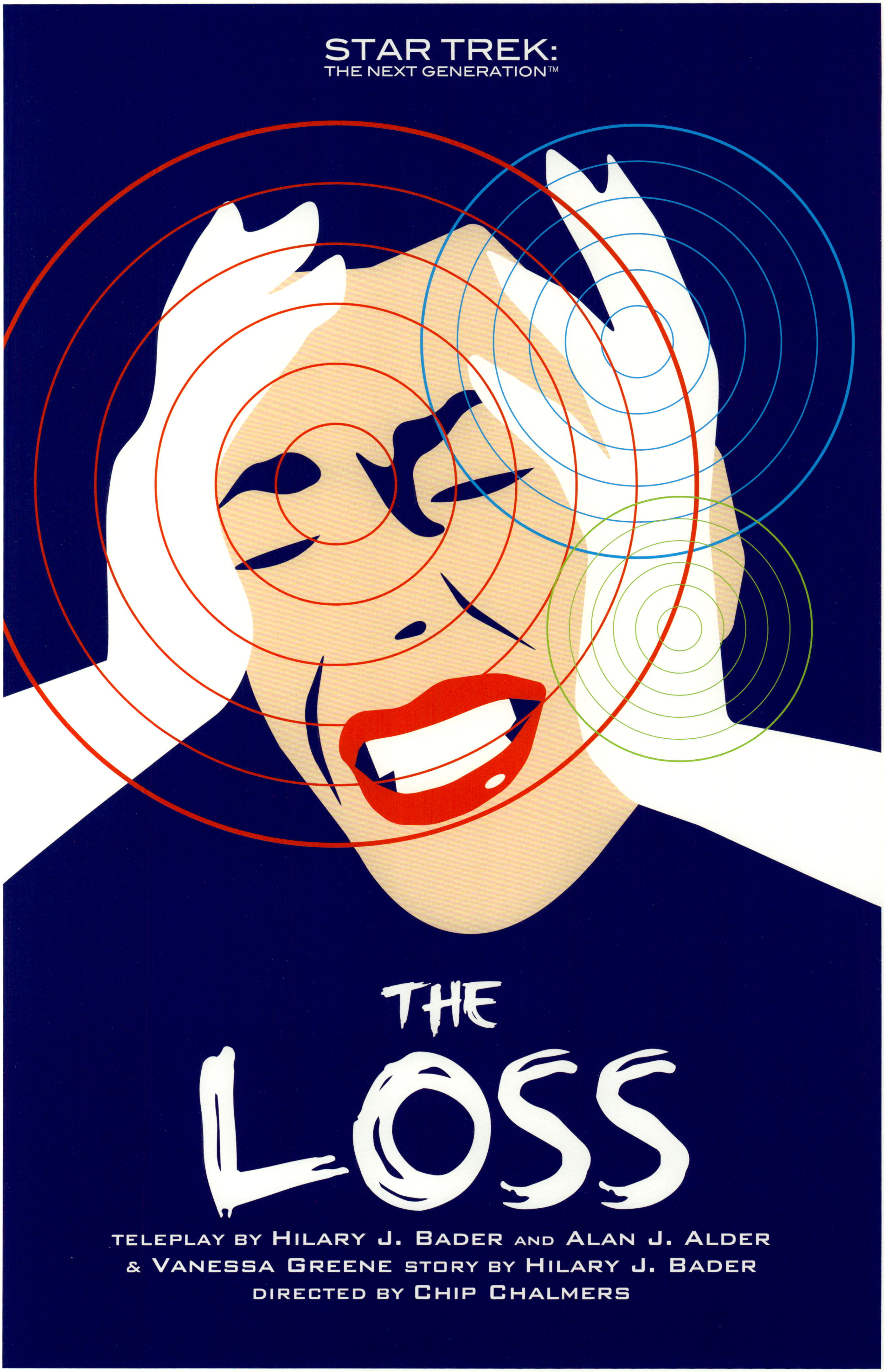
STAR TREK:
THE NEXT GENERATION™
THE
LOSS
TELEPLAY BY HILARY J. BADER AND ALAN J. ALDER
& VANESSA GREENE STORY BY HILARY J. BADER
DIRECTED BY CHIP CHALMERS

STAR TREK
THE NEXT GENERATION™

Data's Day

Teleplay By
Harold Apter
and
Ronald D. Moore
Story By
Harold Apter
Directed By
Robert Wiemer

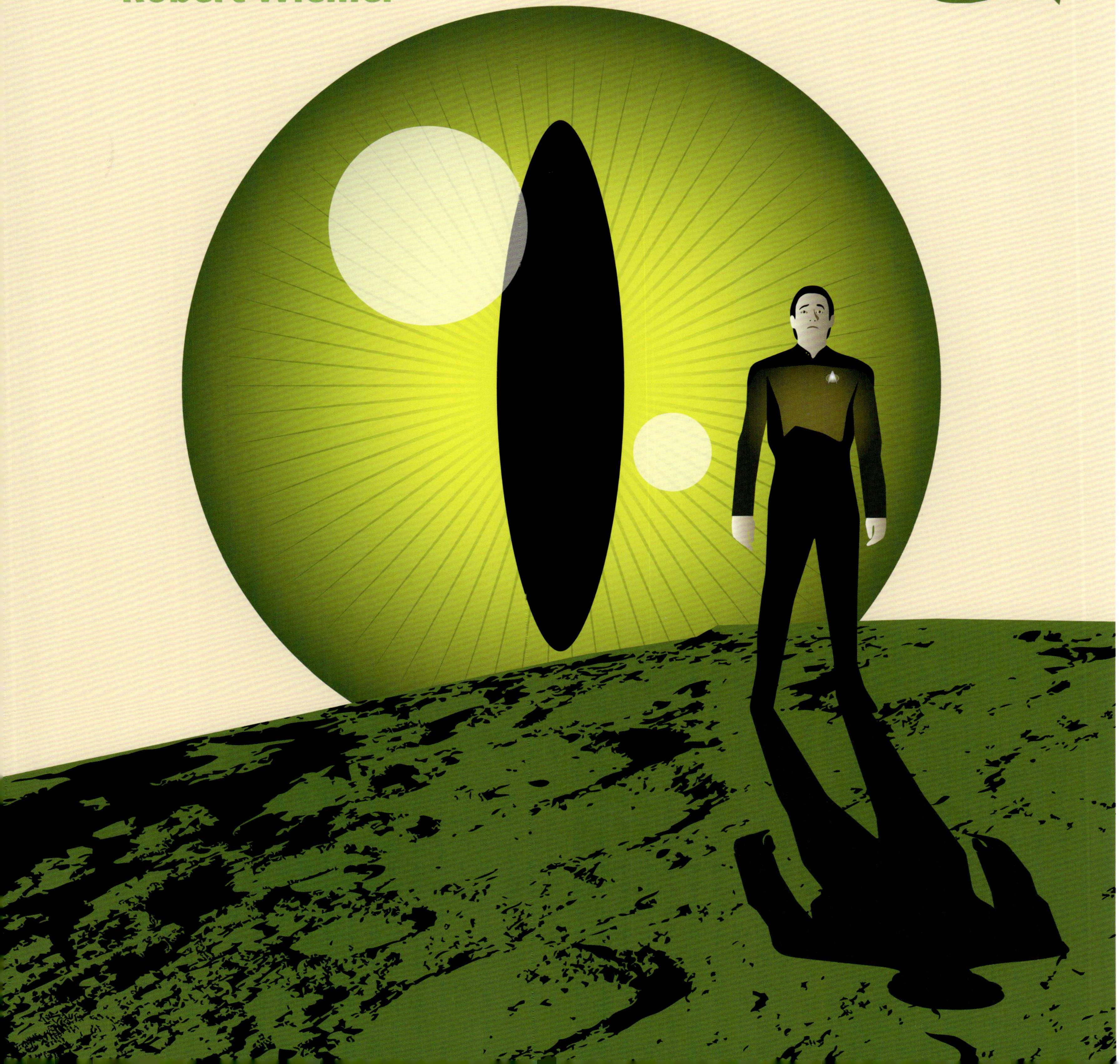

STAR TREK:
THE NEXT GENERATION™

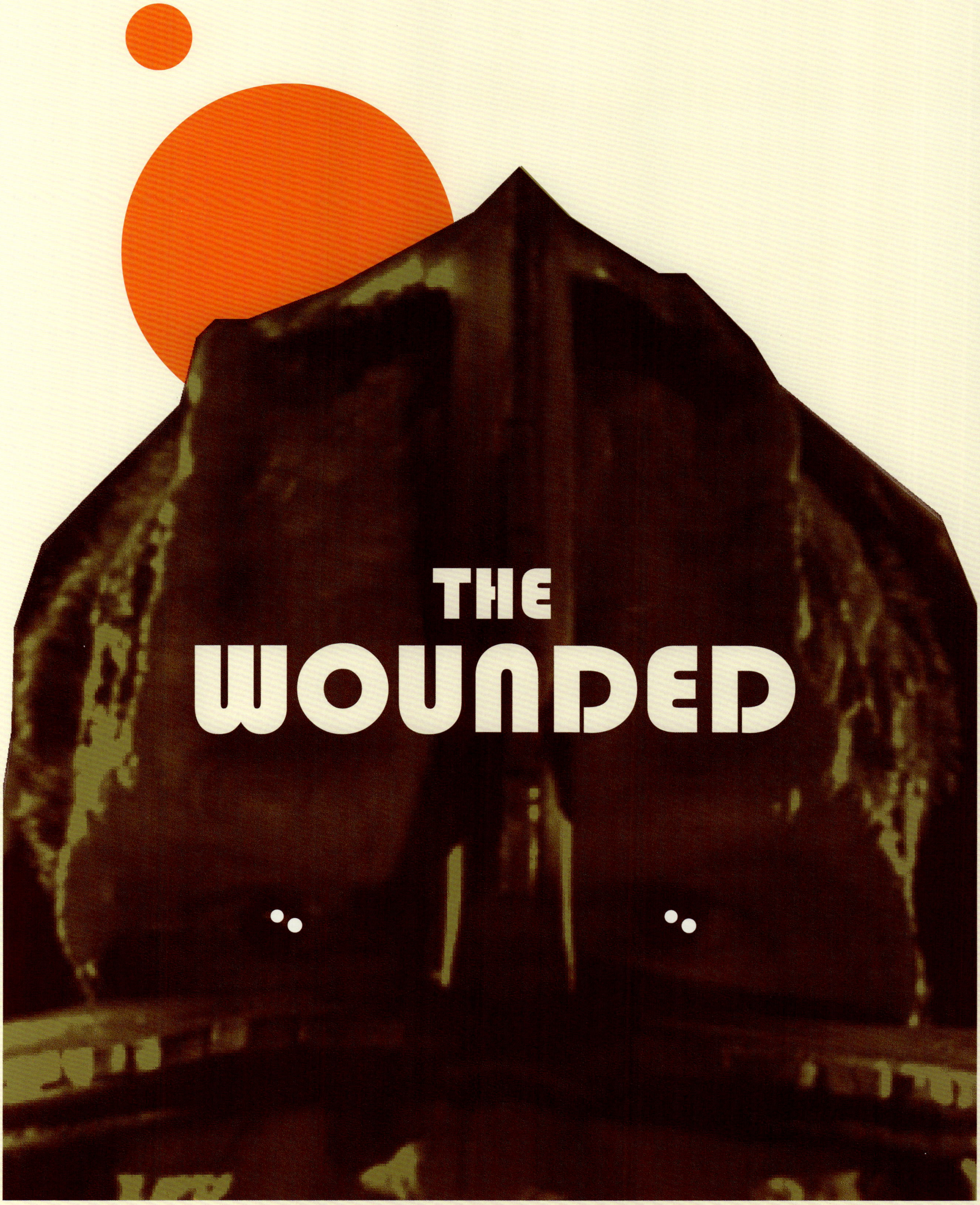

TELEPLAY BY JERI TAYLOR

STORY BY STUART CHARNO & SARA CHARNO AND CY CHERMAK

DIRECTED BY CHIP CHALMERS

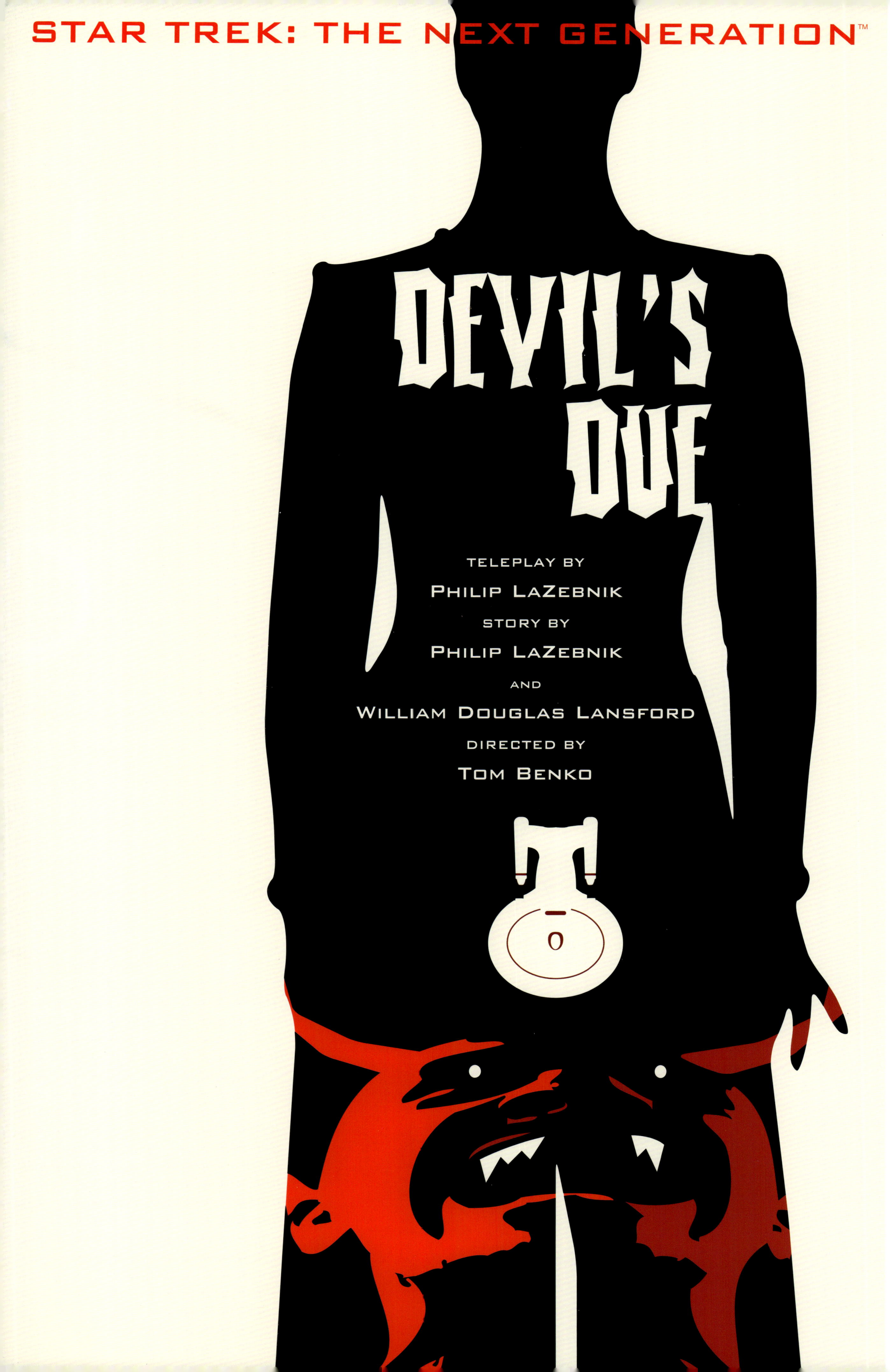
STAR TREK: THE NEXT GENERATION™
DEVIL'S DUE
TELEPLAY BY
PHILIP LAZEBNIK
STORY BY
PHILIP LAZEBNIK
AND
WILLIAM DOUGLAS LANSFORD
DIRECTED BY
TOM BENKO

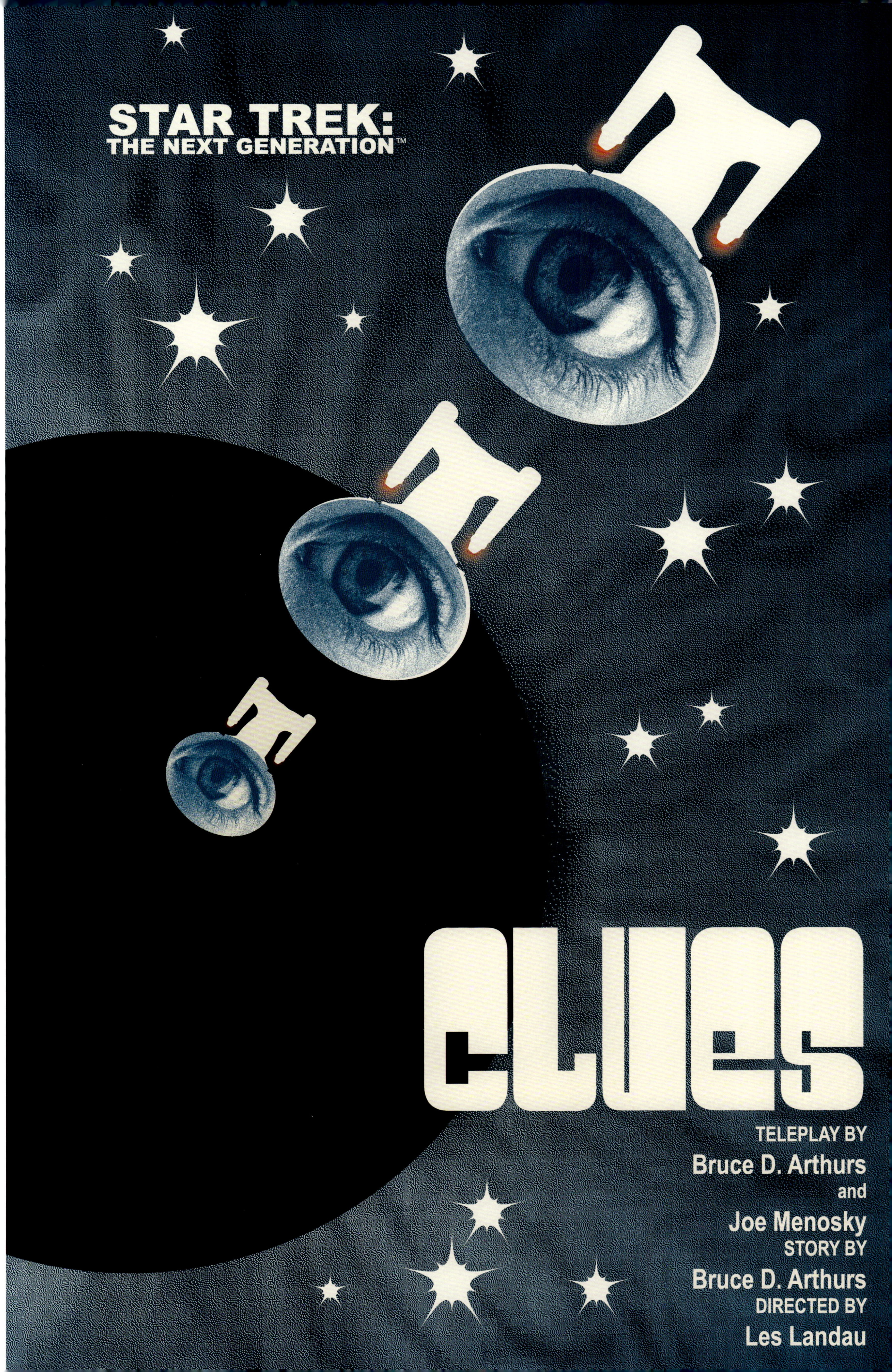
STAR TREK:
THE NEXT GENERATION™
CLUES
TELEPLAY BY
Bruce D. Arthurs
and
Joe Menosky
STORY BY
Bruce D. Arthurs
DIRECTED BY
Les Landau

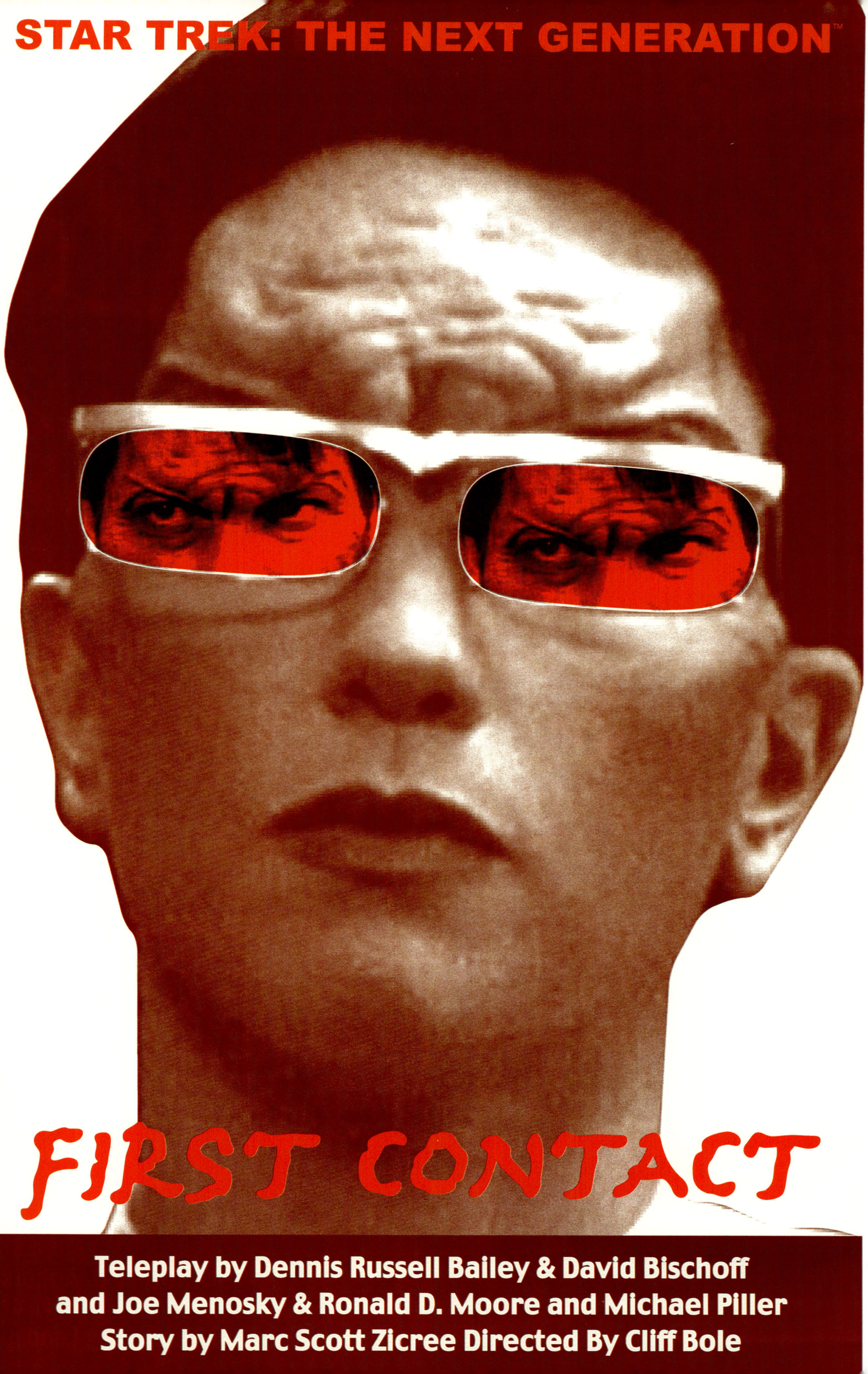
STAR TREK: THE NEXT GENERATION™
FIRST CONTACT
Teleplay by Dennis Russell Bailey & David Bischoff
and Joe Menosky & Ronald D. Moore and Michael Piller
Story by Marc Scott Zicree Directed By Cliff Bole

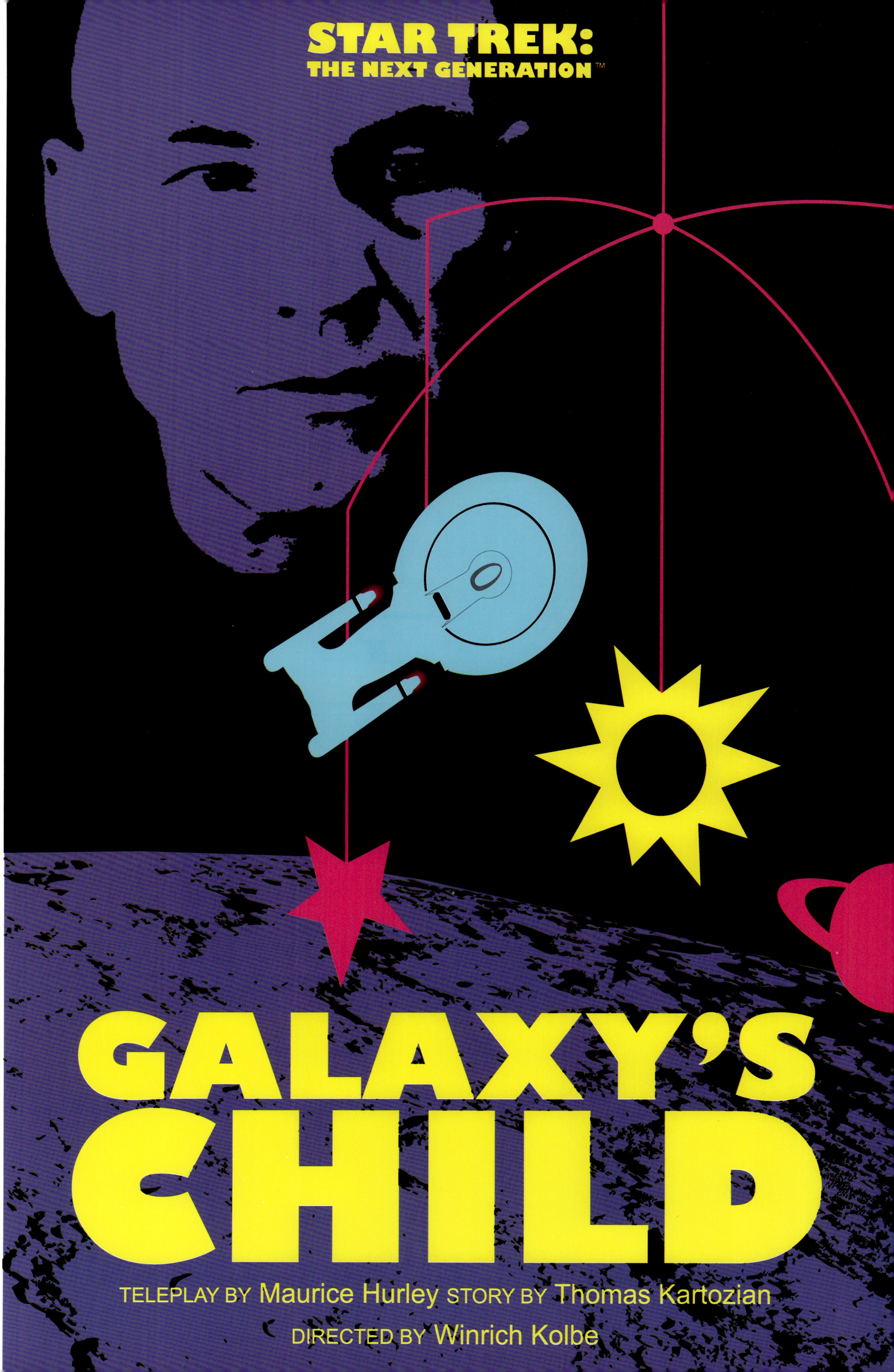
STAR TREK:
THE NEXT GENERATION™
GALAXY'S CHILD
TELEPLAY BY Maurice Hurley STORY BY Thomas Kartozian
DIRECTED BY Winrich Kolbe

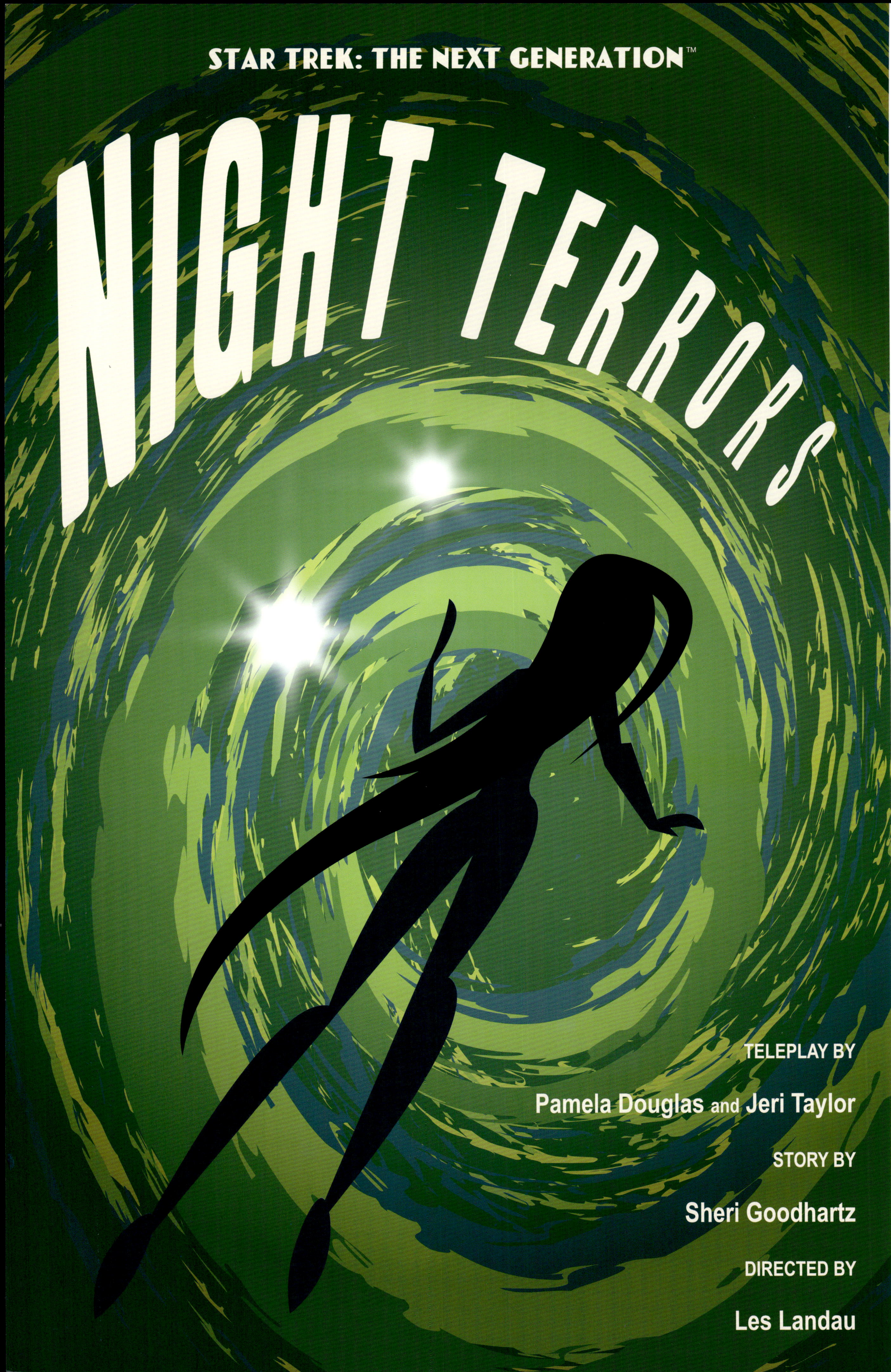
STAR TREK: THE NEXT GENERATION™
NIGHT TERRORS
TELEPLAY BY
Pamela Douglas and Jeri Taylor
STORY BY
Sheri Goodhartz
DIRECTED BY
Les Landau

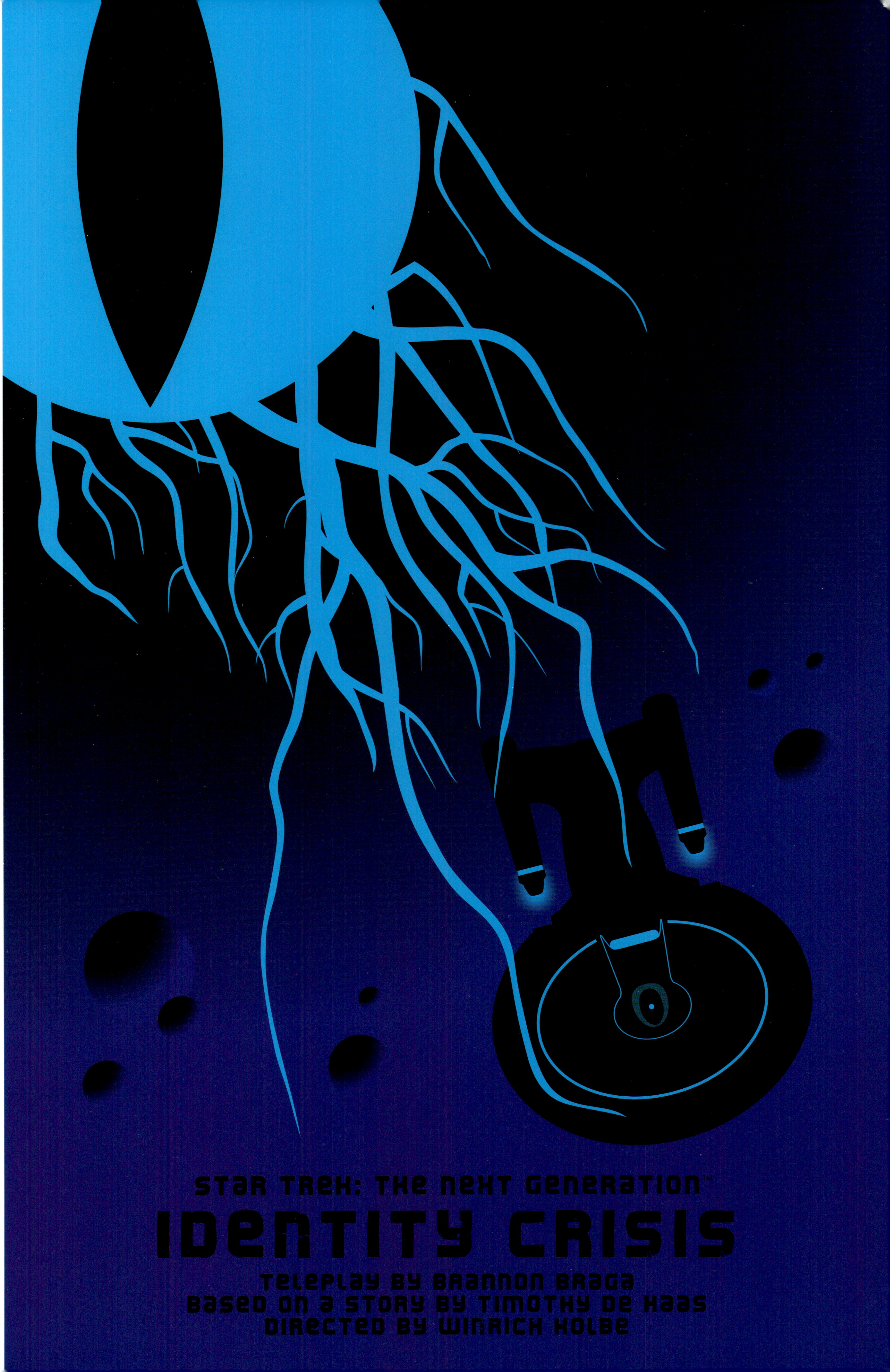
STAR TREK: THE NEXT GENERATION™
IDENTITY CRISIS
TELEPLAY BY BRANNON BRAGA
BASED ON A STORY BY TIMOTHY DE HAAS
DIRECTED BY WINRICH KOLBE

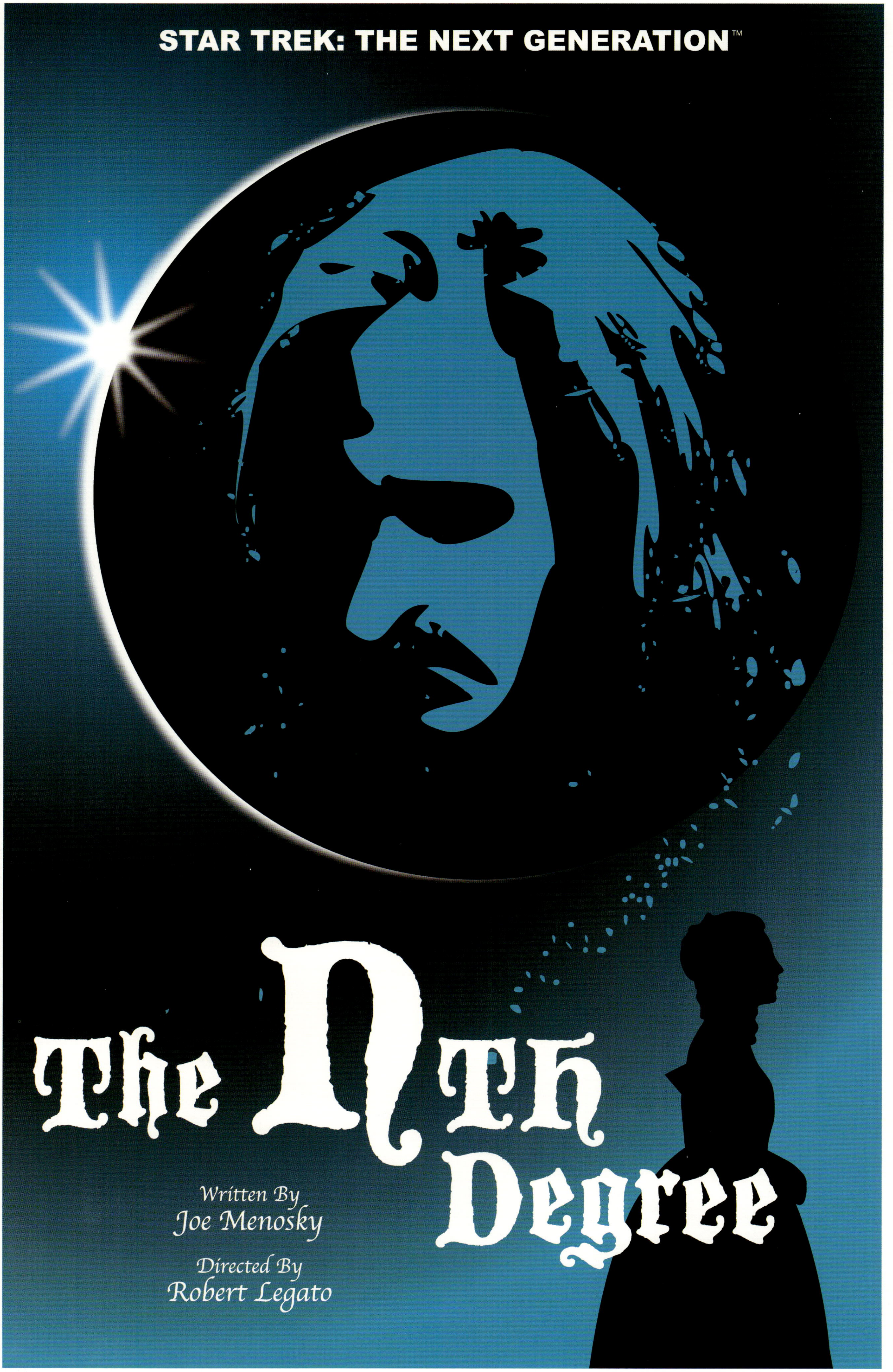
STAR TREK: THE NEXT GENERATION™
The Nth Degree
Written By
Joe Menosky
Directed By
Robert Legato

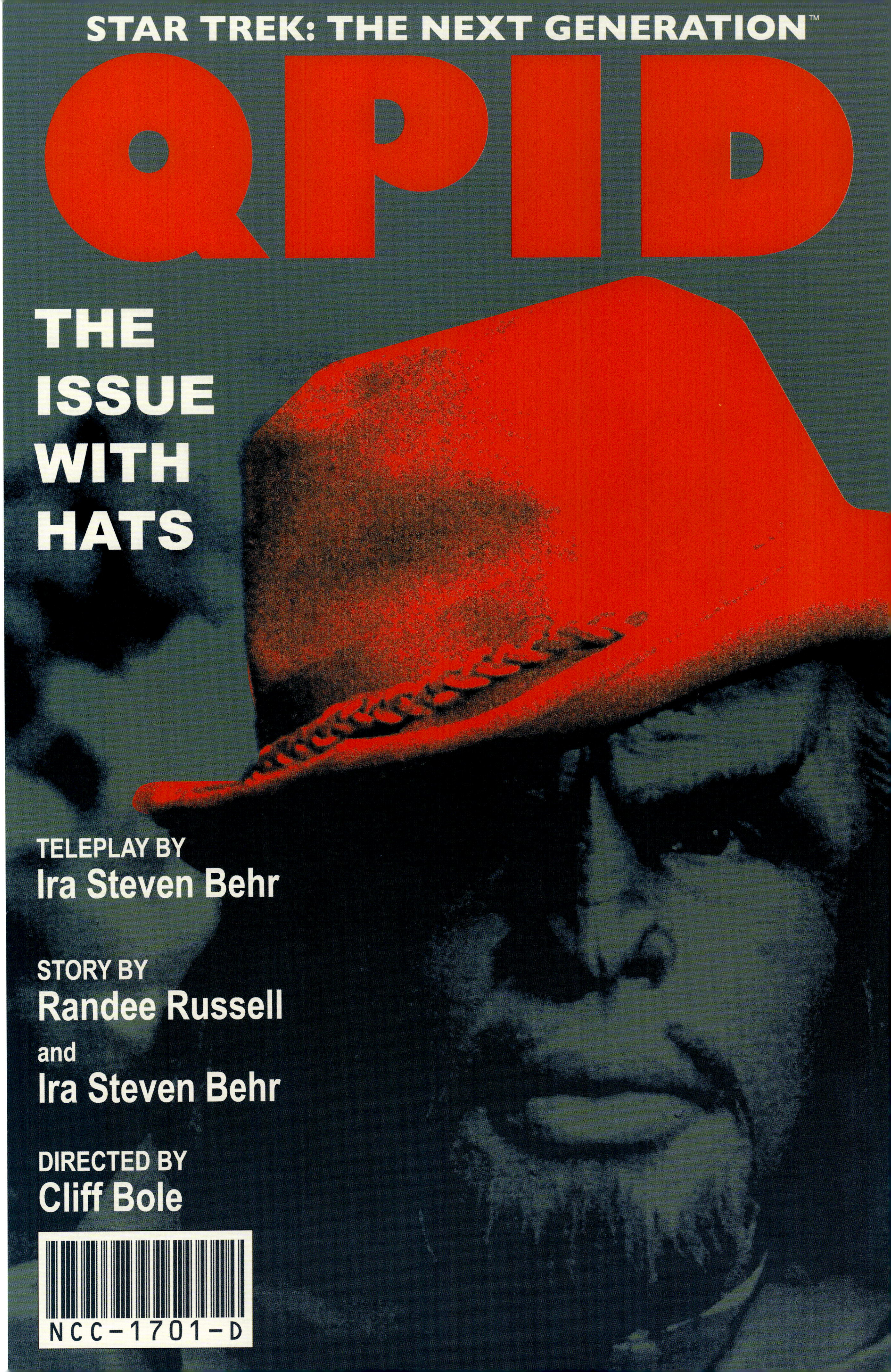
STAR TREK: THE NEXT GENERATION™
QPID
THE ISSUE WITH HATS
TELEPLAY BY
Ira Steven Behr
STORY BY
Randee Russell
and
Ira Steven Behr
DIRECTED BY
Cliff Bole
NCC-1701-D

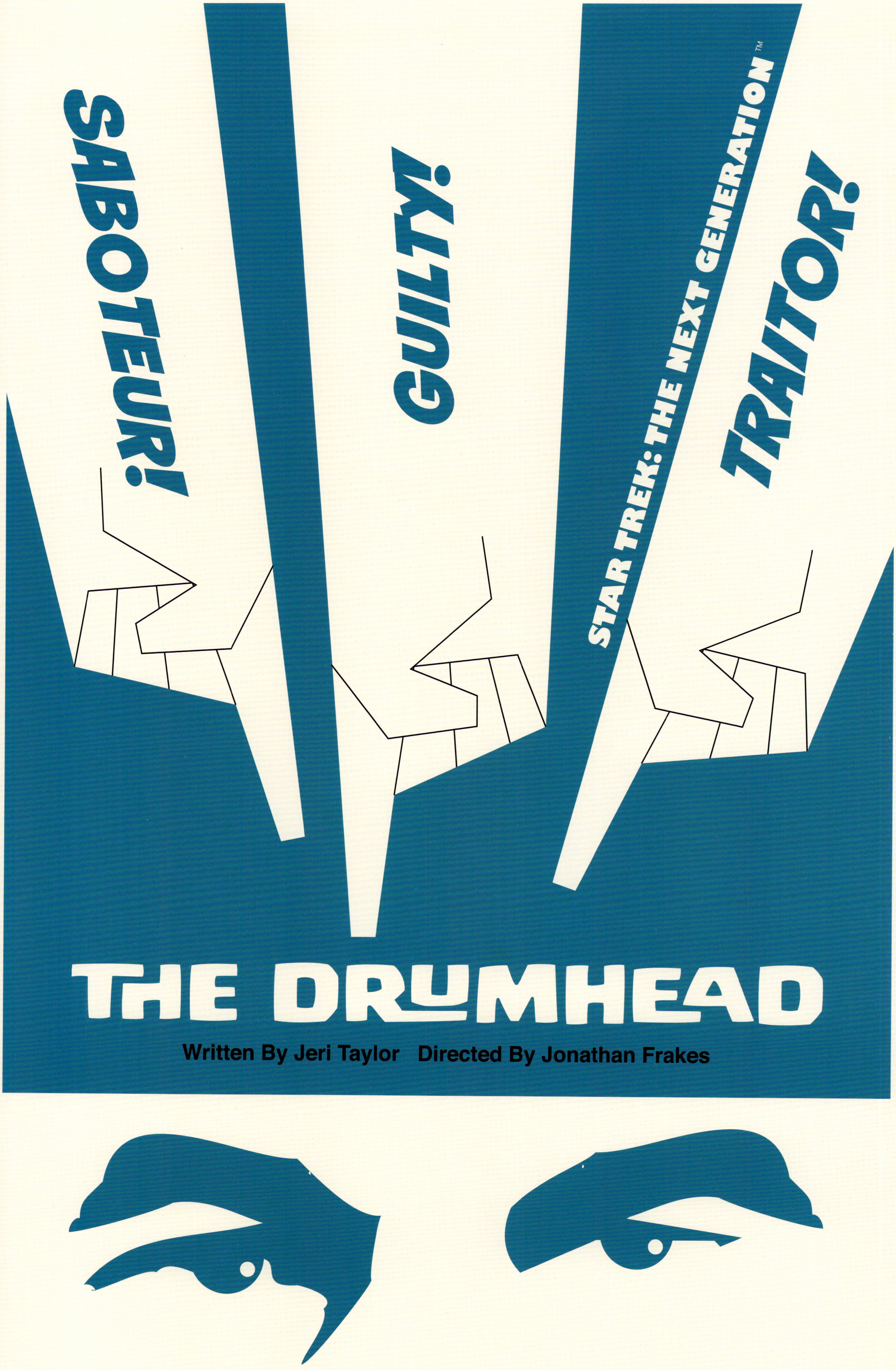
SABOTEUR!
GUILTY!
STAR TREK: THE NEXT GENERATION™
TRAITOR!
THE DRUMHEAD
Written By Jeri Taylor Directed By Jonathan Frakes

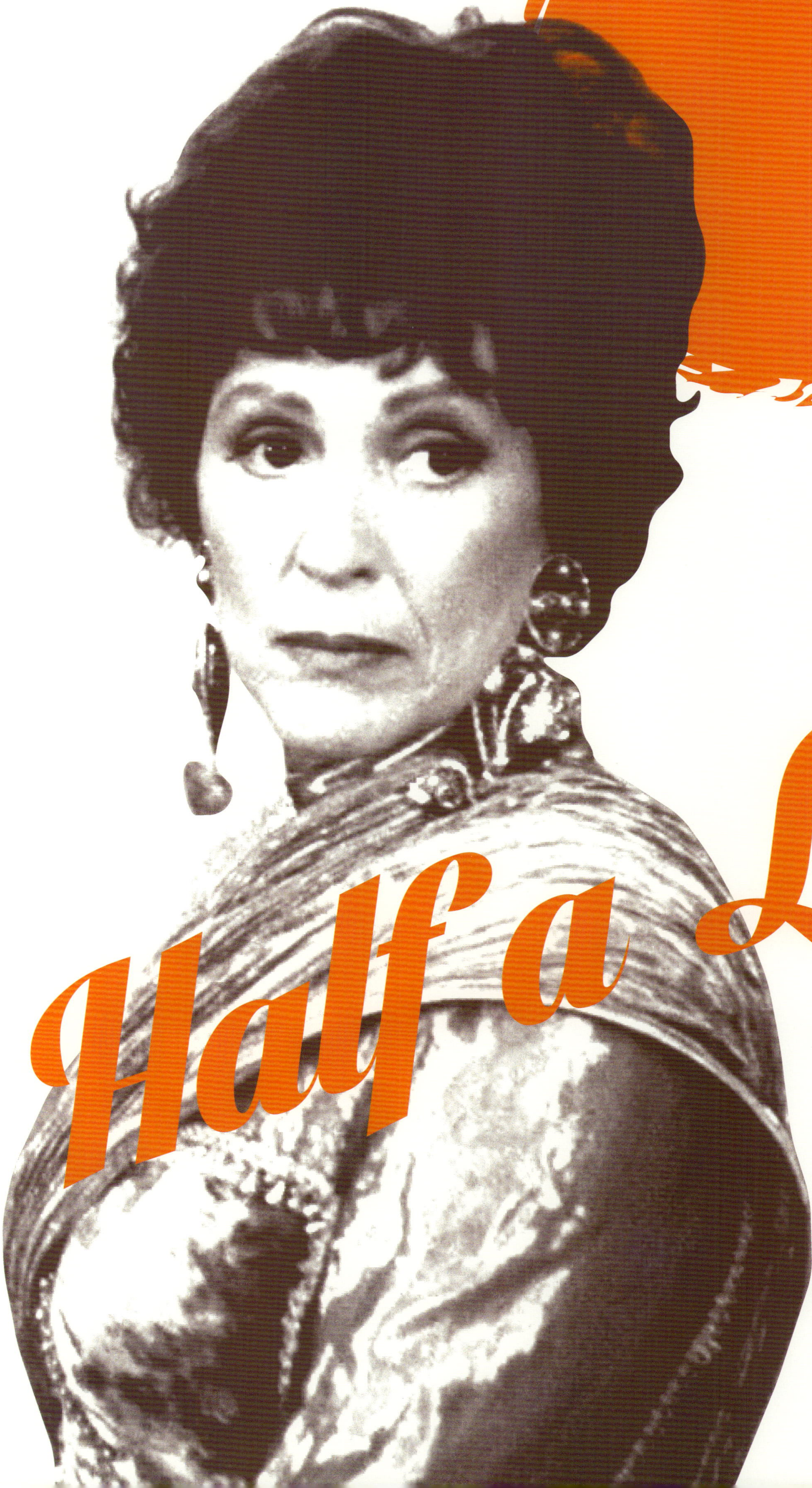

STAR TREK: THE NEXT GENERATION™

Half a Life

TELEPLAY BY

Peter Allan Fields

STORY BY

Ted Roberts

and

Peter Allan Fields

DIRECTED BY

Les Landau

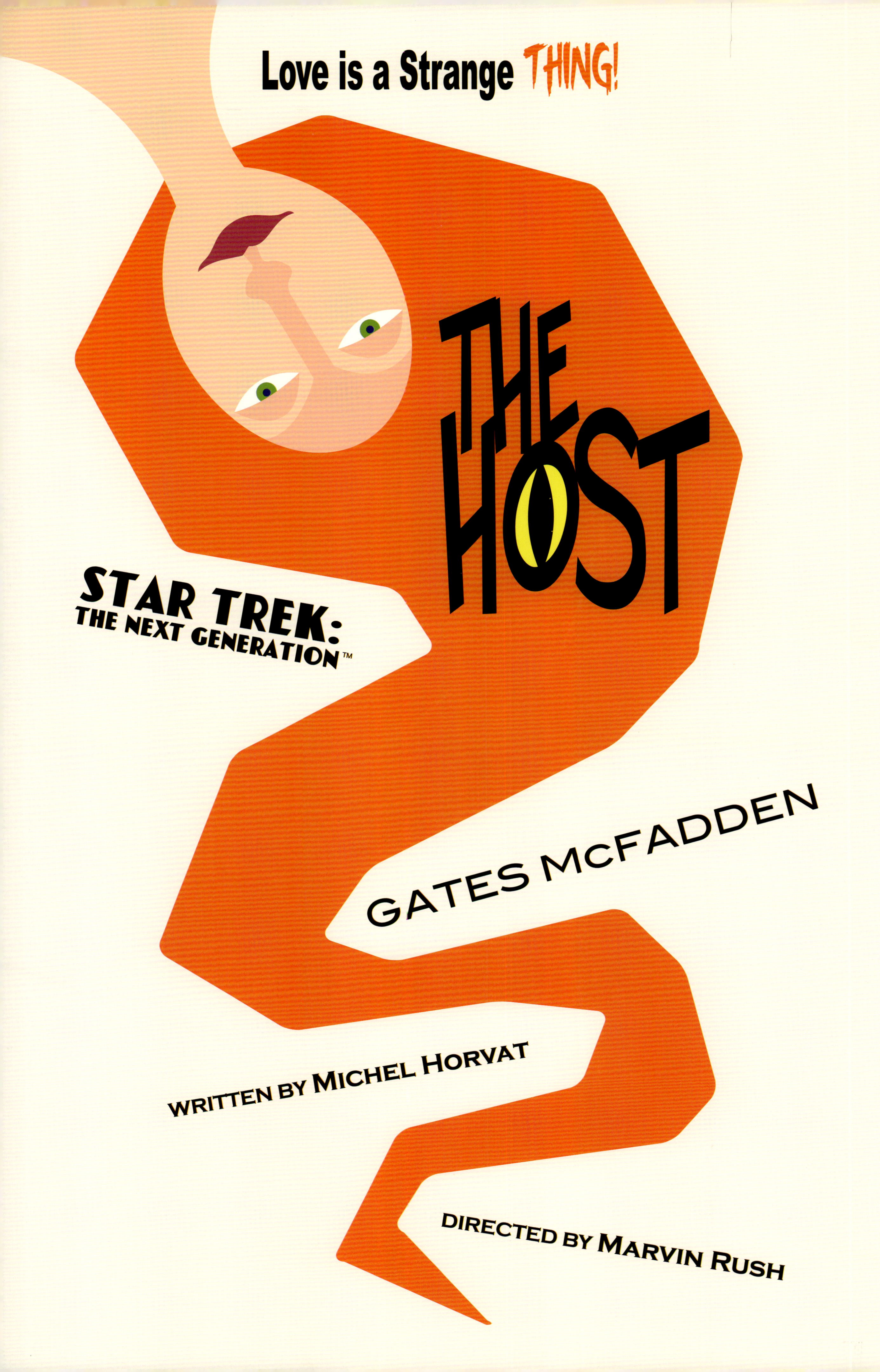
Love is a Strange THING!
THE HOST
STAR TREK:
THE NEXT GENERATION™
GATES McFADDEN
WRITTEN BY MICHEL HORVAT
DIRECTED BY MARVIN RUSH

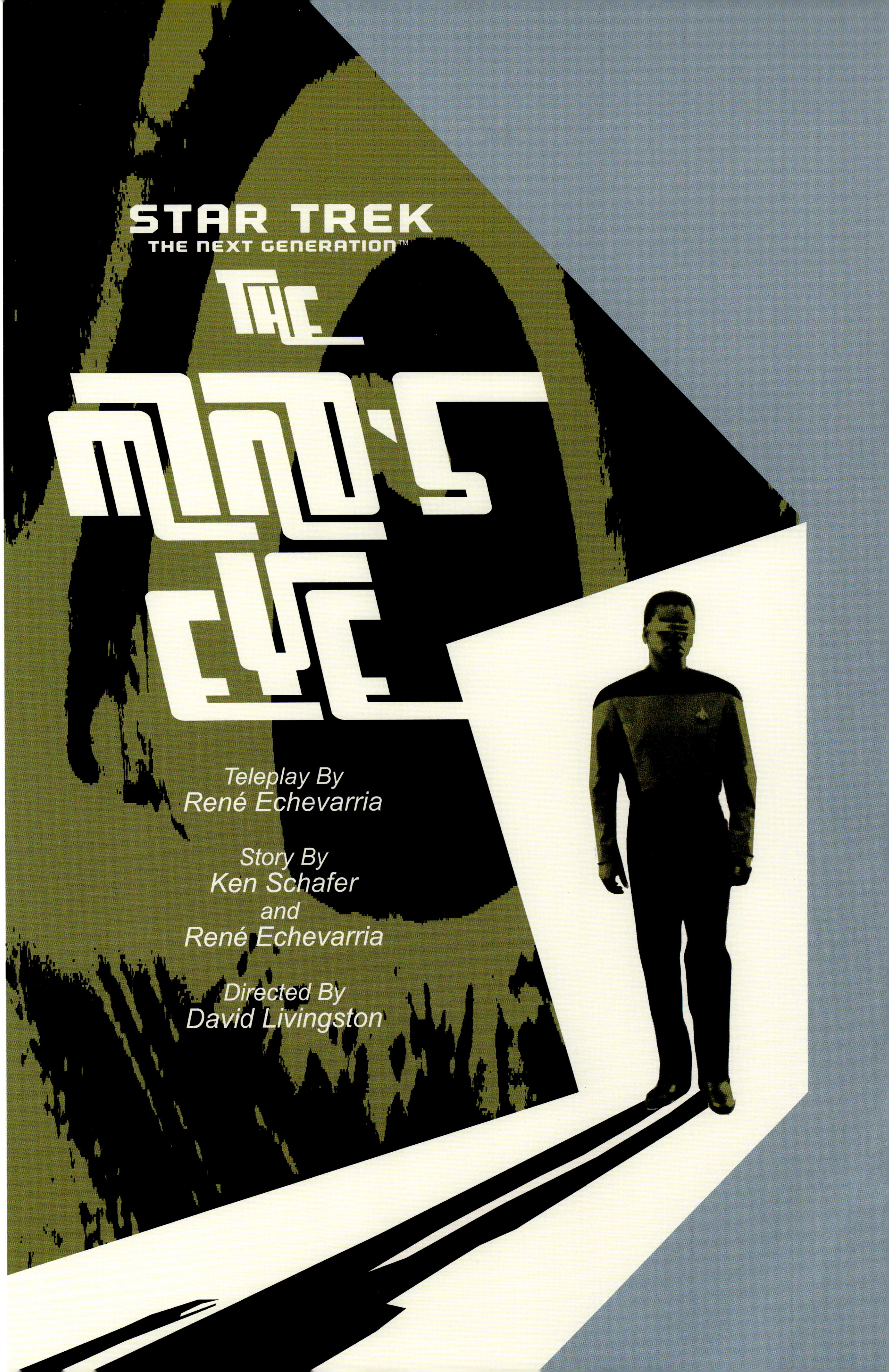
STAR TREK
THE NEXT GENERATION™
THE
MIND'S
EYE
Teleplay By
René Echevarria
Story By
Ken Schafer
and
René Echevarria
Directed By
David Livingston

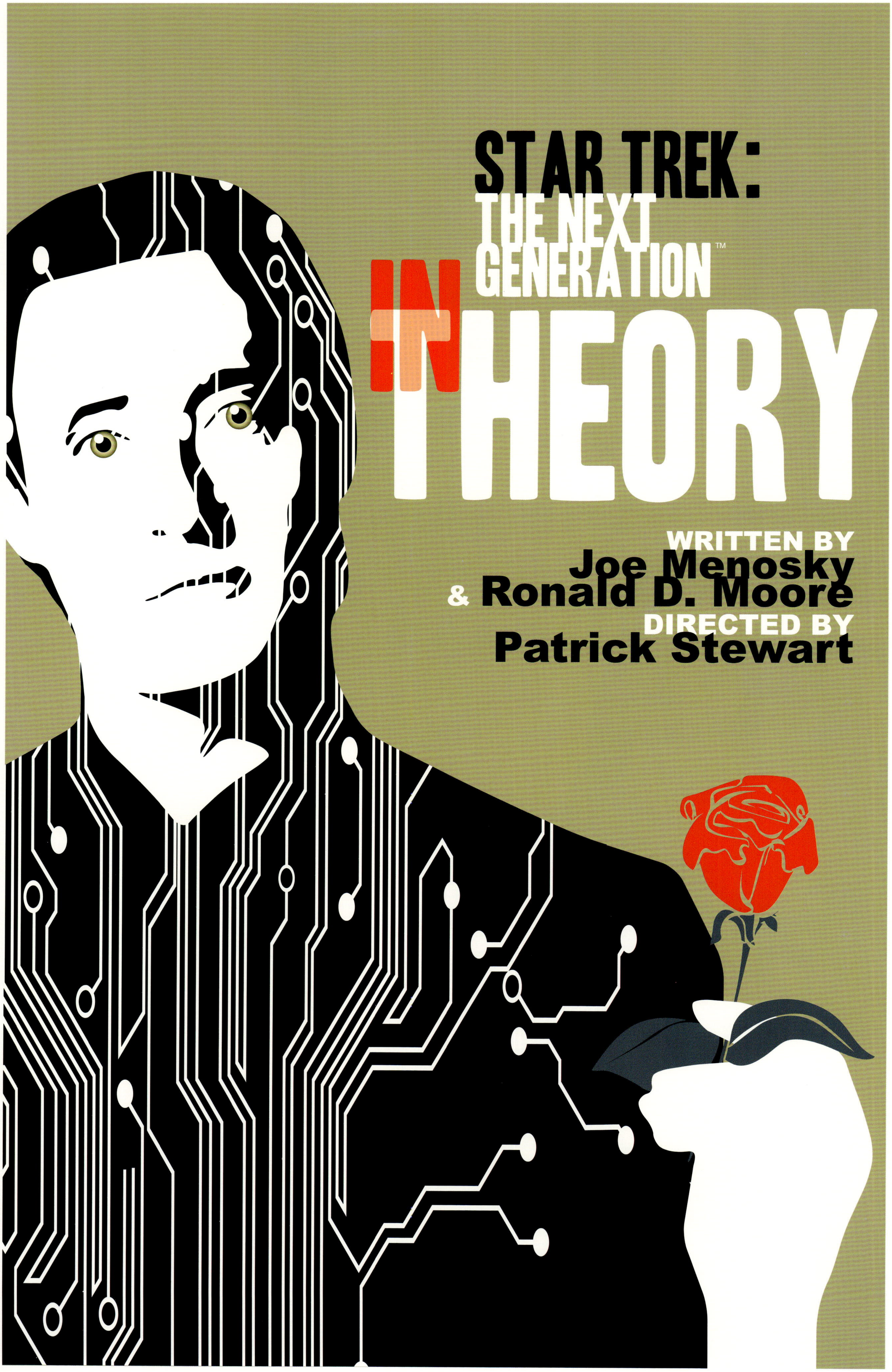
STAR TREK:
THE NEXT GENERATION™
IN THEORY
WRITTEN BY
Joe Menosky
& Ronald D. Moore
DIRECTED BY
Patrick Stewart

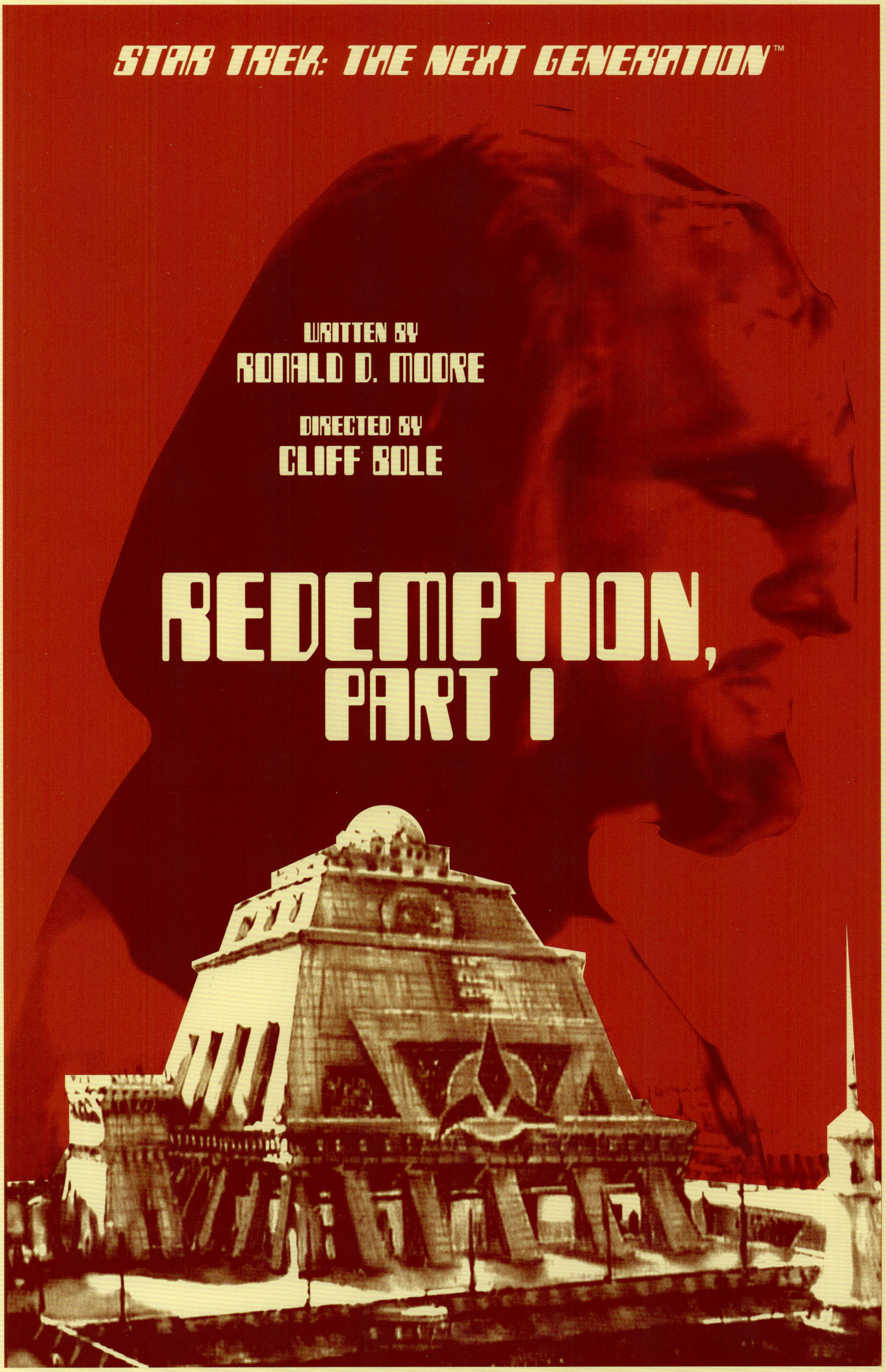
STAR TREK: THE NEXT GENERATION™
WRITTEN BY
RONALD D. MOORE
DIRECTED BY
CLIFF BOLE
REDEMPTION, PART I

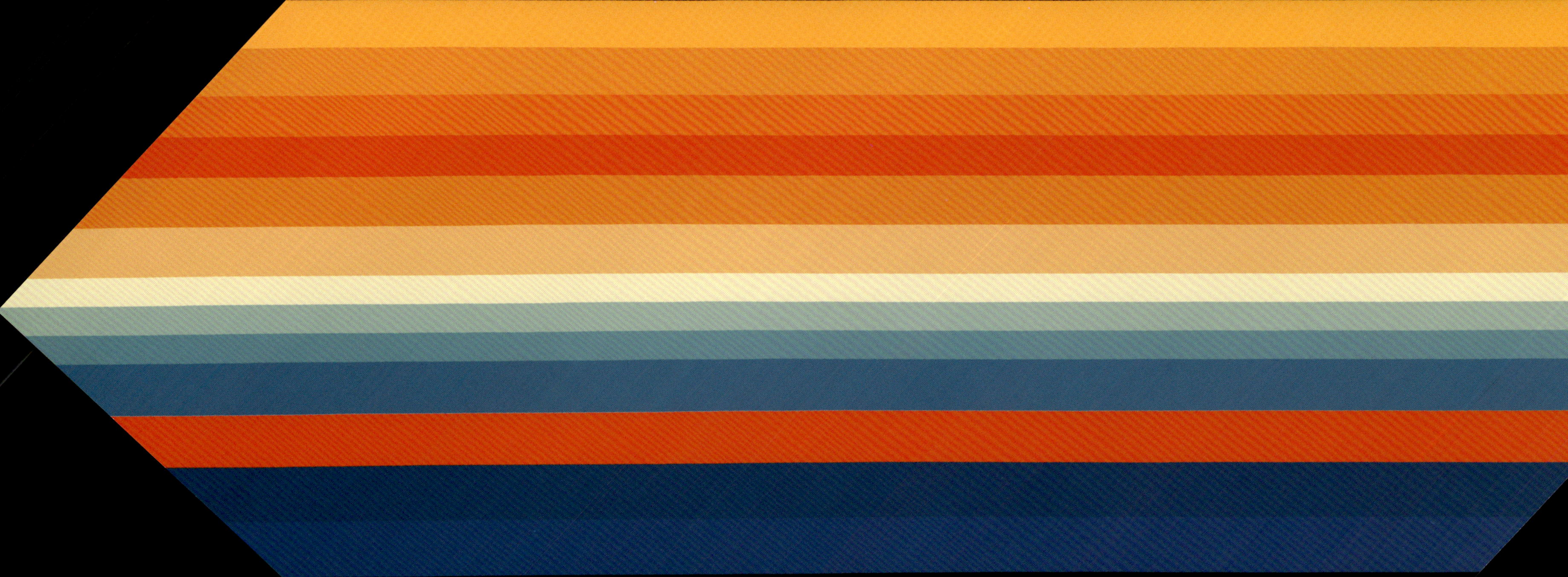

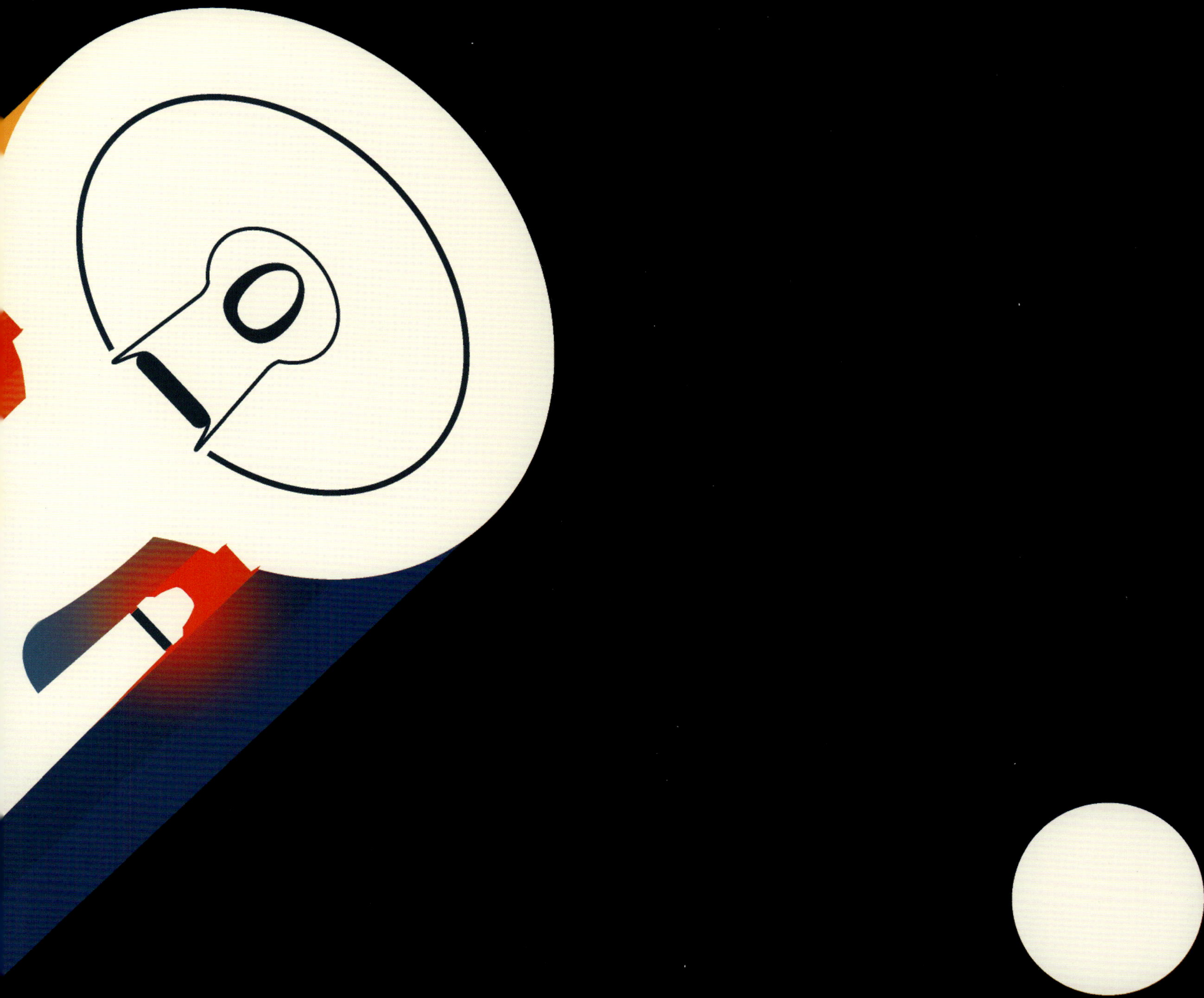

Season Five

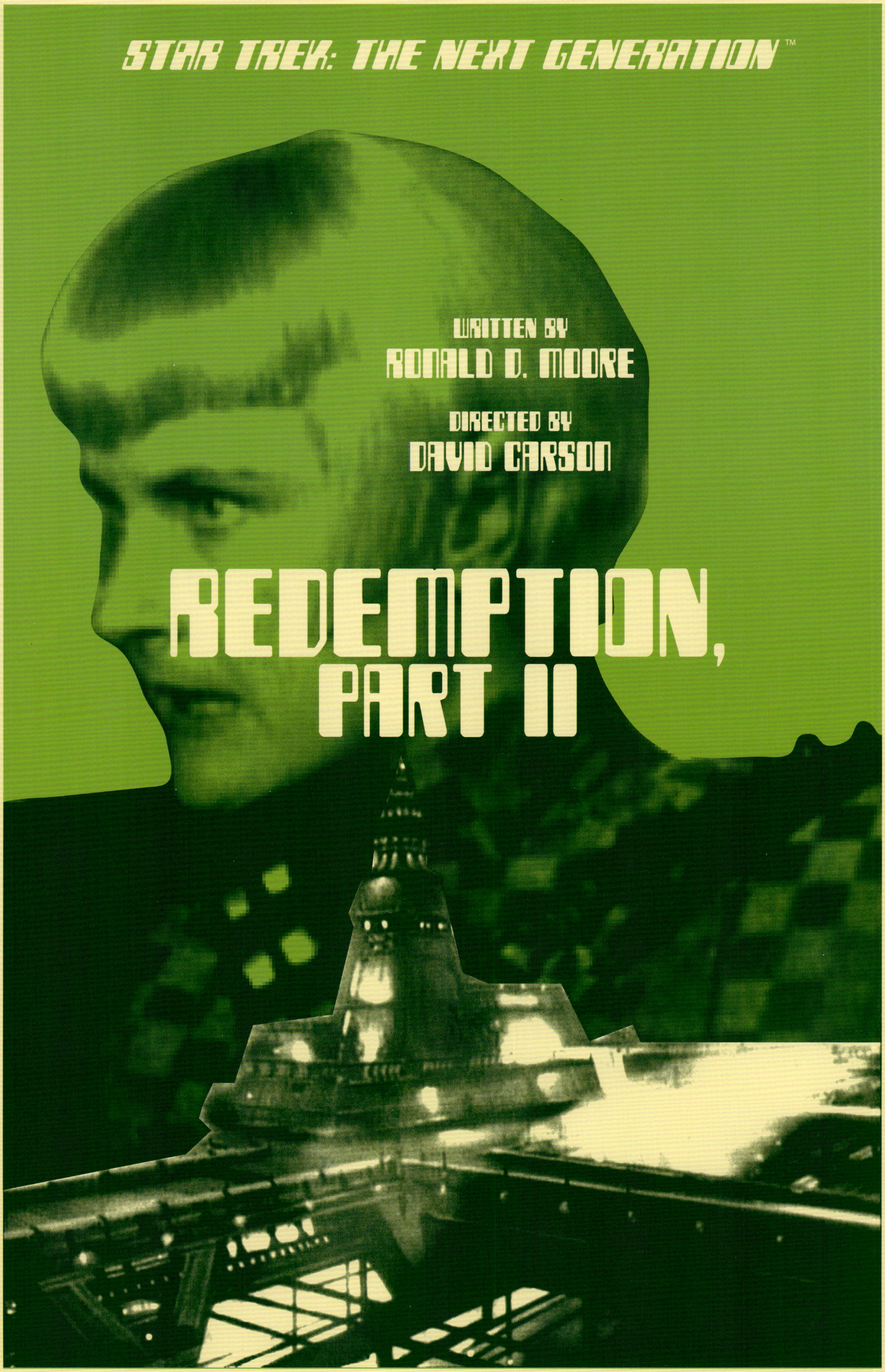
STAR TREK: THE NEXT GENERATION™
WRITTEN BY
RONALD D. MOORE
DIRECTED BY
DAVID CARSON
REDEMPTION,
PART II

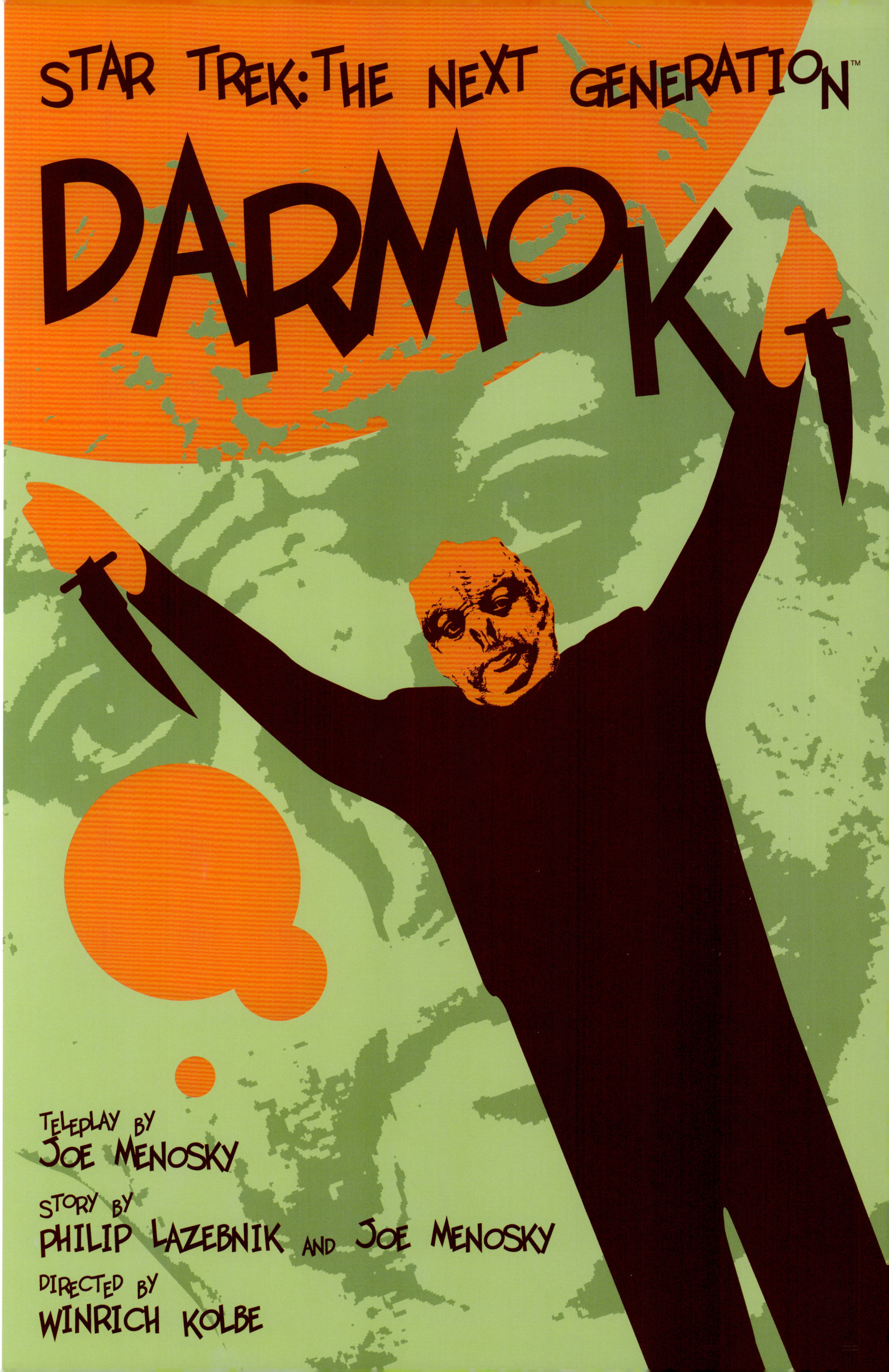
STAR TREK: THE NEXT GENERATION™
DARMOK
TELEPLAY BY
JOE MENOSKY
STORY BY
PHILIP LAZEBNIK AND JOE MENOSKY
DIRECTED BY
WINRICH KOLBE

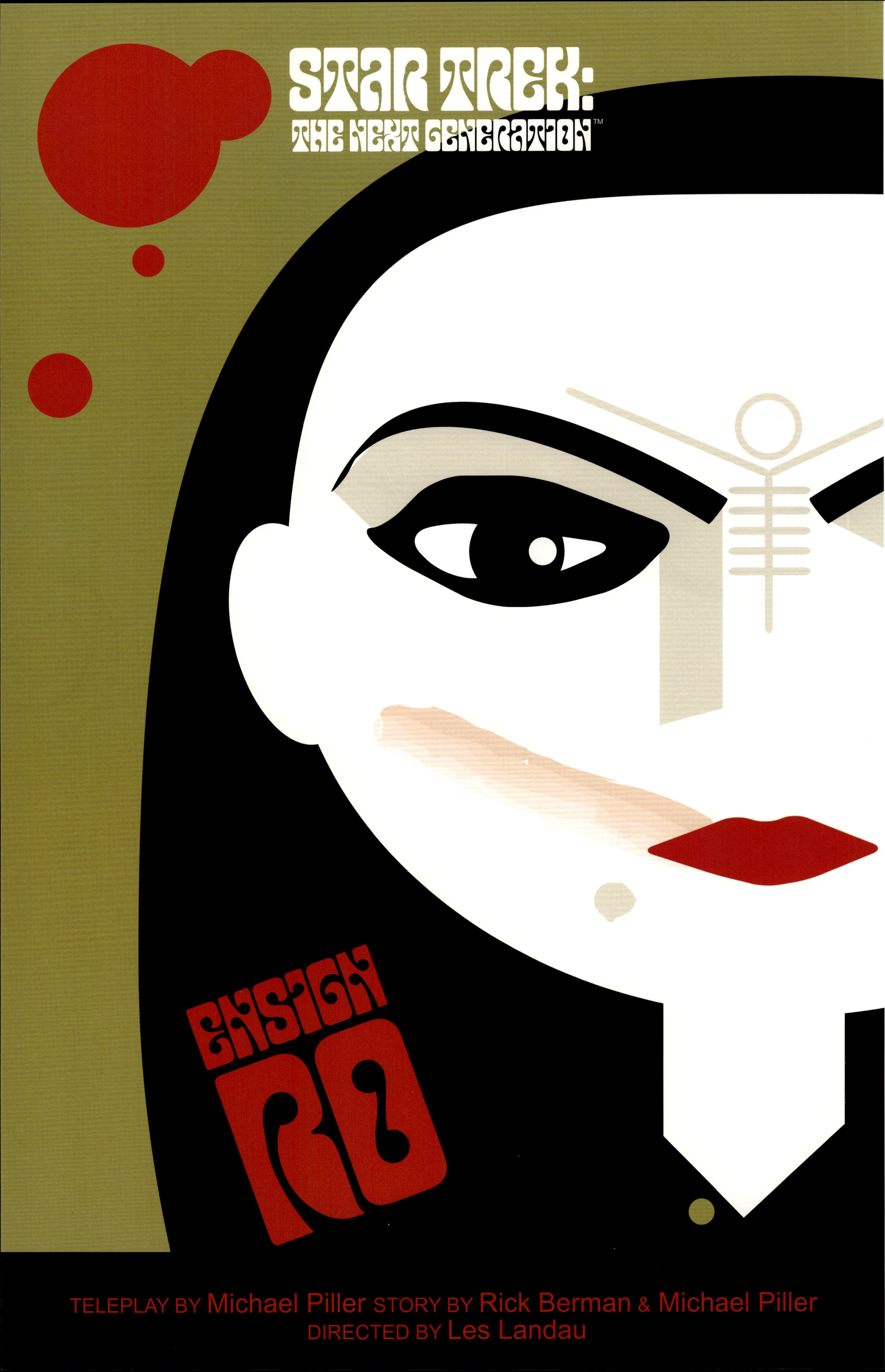
STAR TREK:
THE NEXT GENERATION™
ENSIGN RO
TELEPLAY BY Michael Piller STORY BY Rick Berman & Michael Piller
DIRECTED BY Les Landau

STAR TREK: THE NEXT GENERATION™

SILICON AVATAR

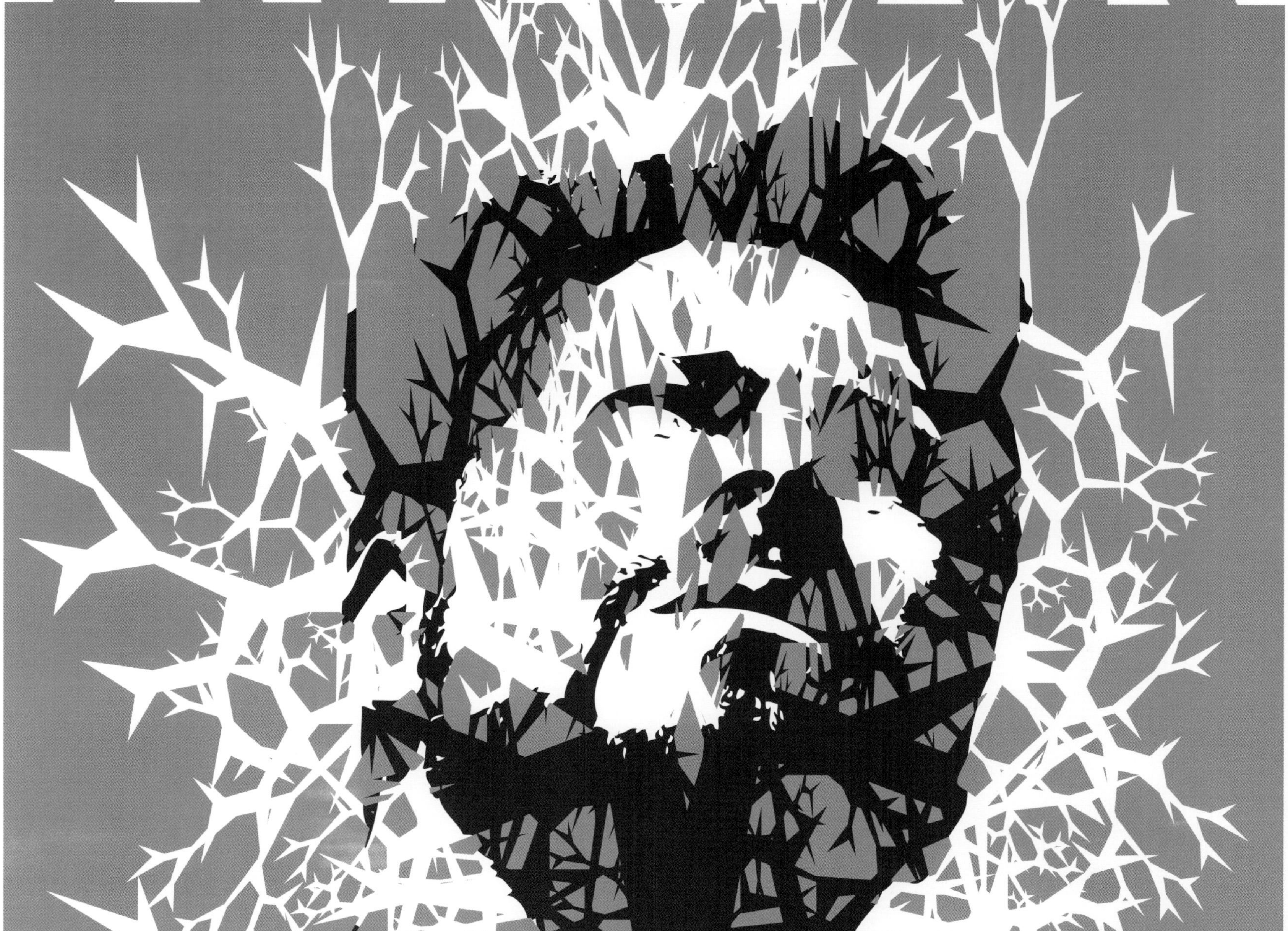

TELEPLAY BY Jeri Taylor STORY BY Lawrence V. Conley DIRECTED BY Cliff Bole

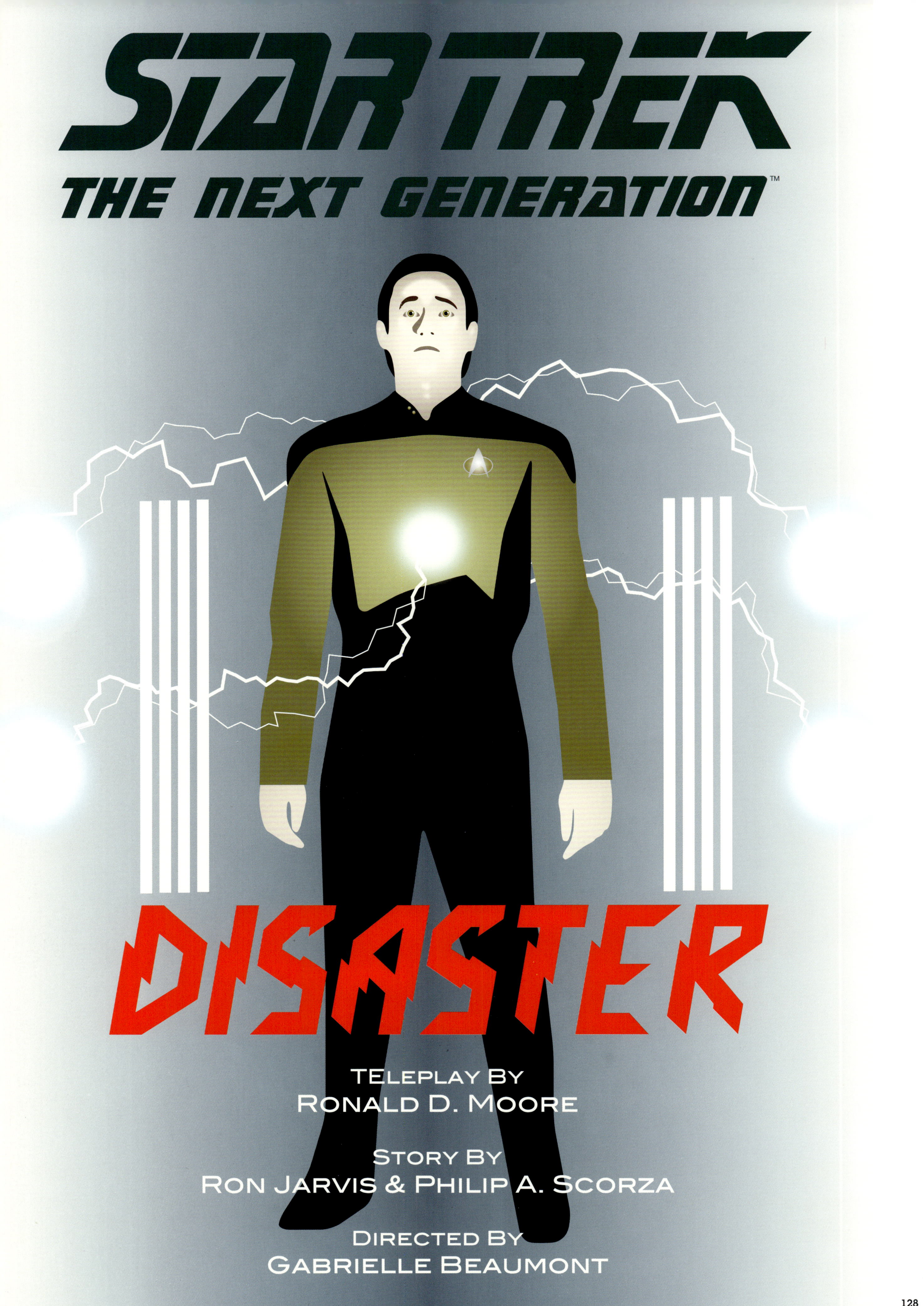
STAR TREK
THE NEXT GENERATION™
DISASTER
TELEPLAY BY
RONALD D. MOORE
STORY BY
RON JARVIS & PHILIP A. SCORZA
DIRECTED BY
GABRIELLE BEAUMONT

STAR TREK: THE NEXT GENERATION™

THE GAME

TELEPLAY BY BRANNON BRAGA

STORY BY SUSAN SACKETT & FRED BRONSON AND BRANNON BRAGA

DIRECTED BY COREY ALLEN

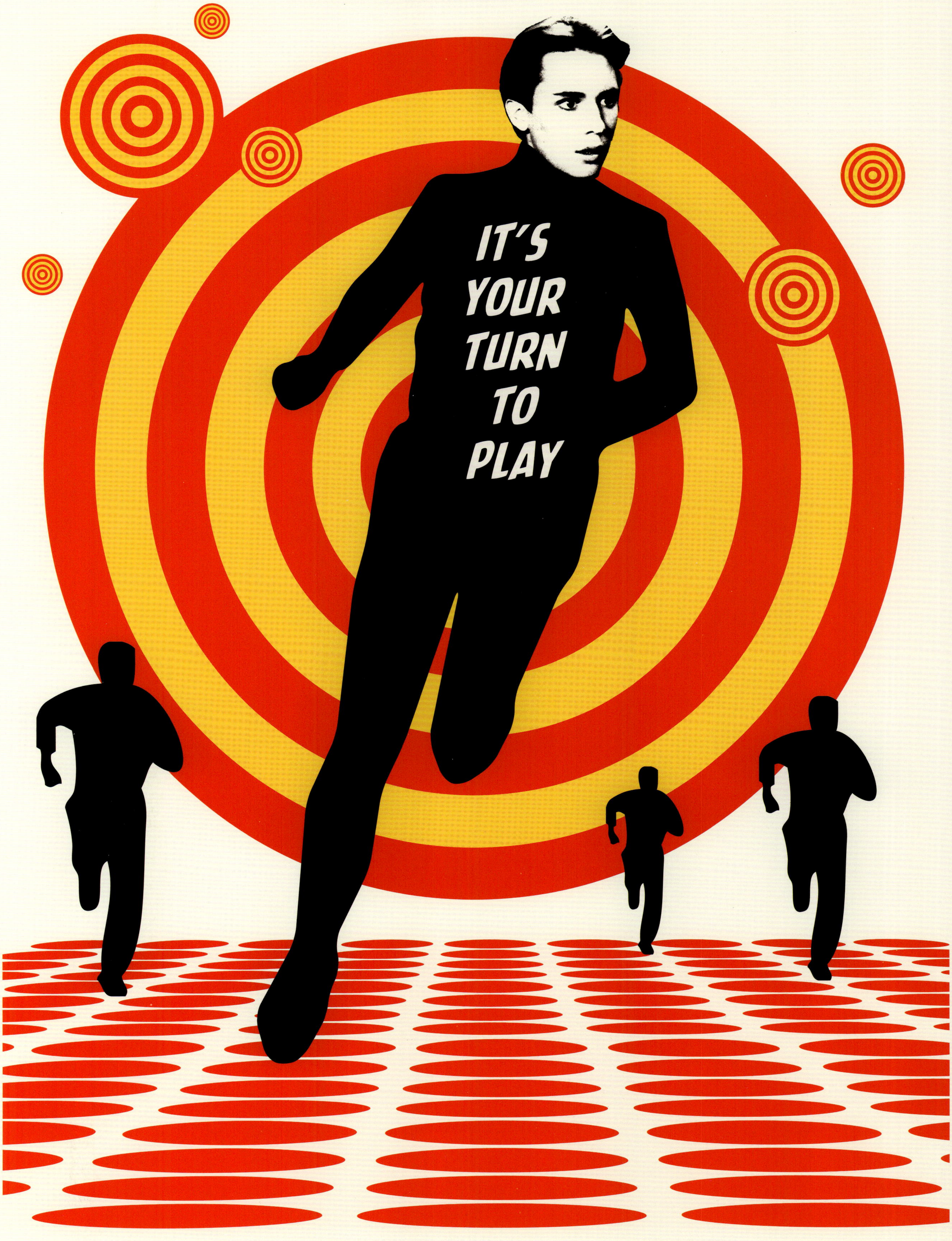

STAR TREK:
THE NEXT GENERATION™

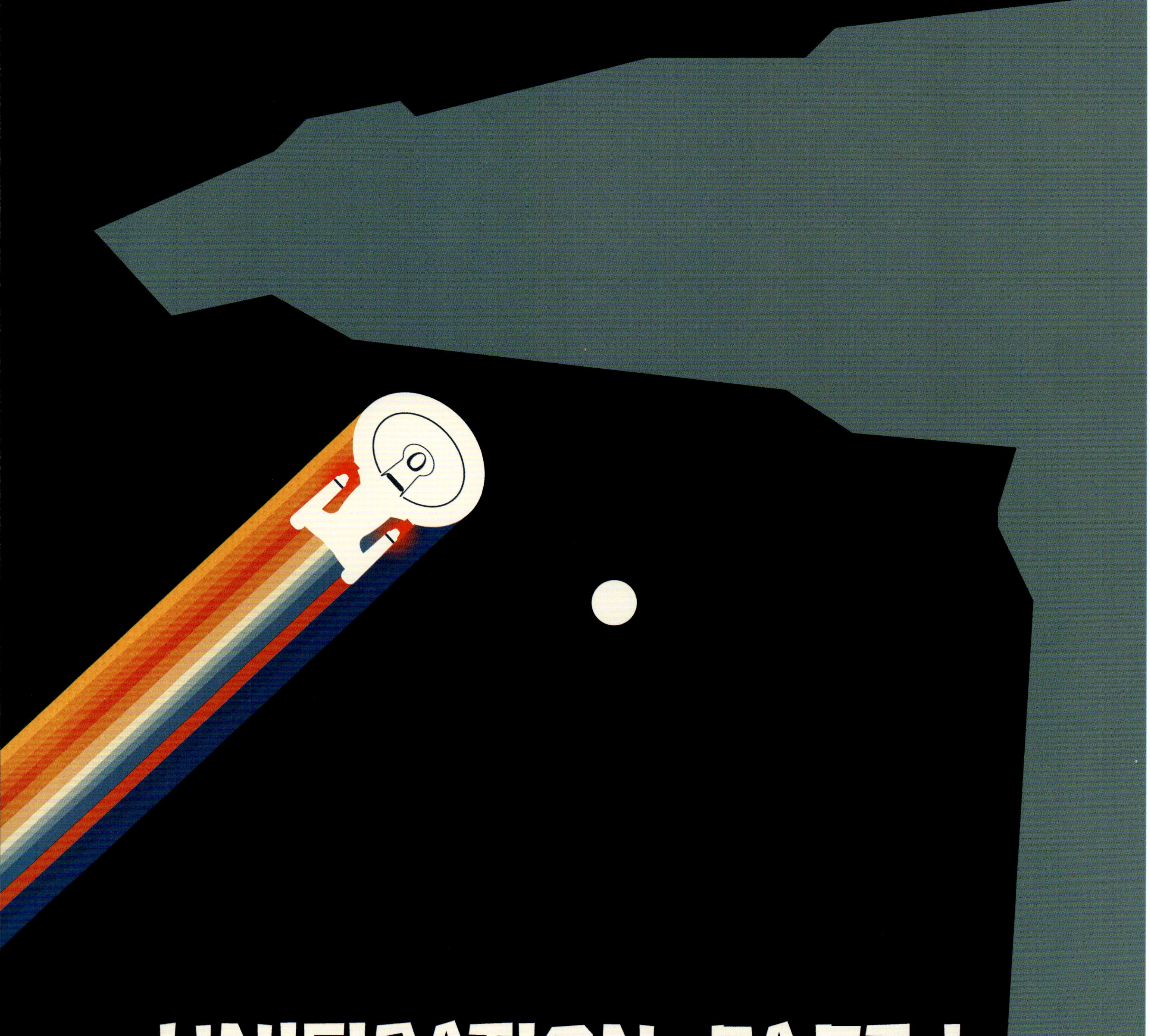

UNIFICATION, PART I

TELEPLAY BY
JERI TAYLOR

STORY BY
RICK BERMAN AND MICHAEL PILLER

DIRECTED BY
LES LANDAU

STAR TREK:
THE NEXT GENERATION™

UNIFICATION, PART II

TELEPLAY BY
MICHAEL PILLER

STORY BY
RICK BERMAN AND MICHAEL PILLER

DIRECTED BY
CLIFF BOLE

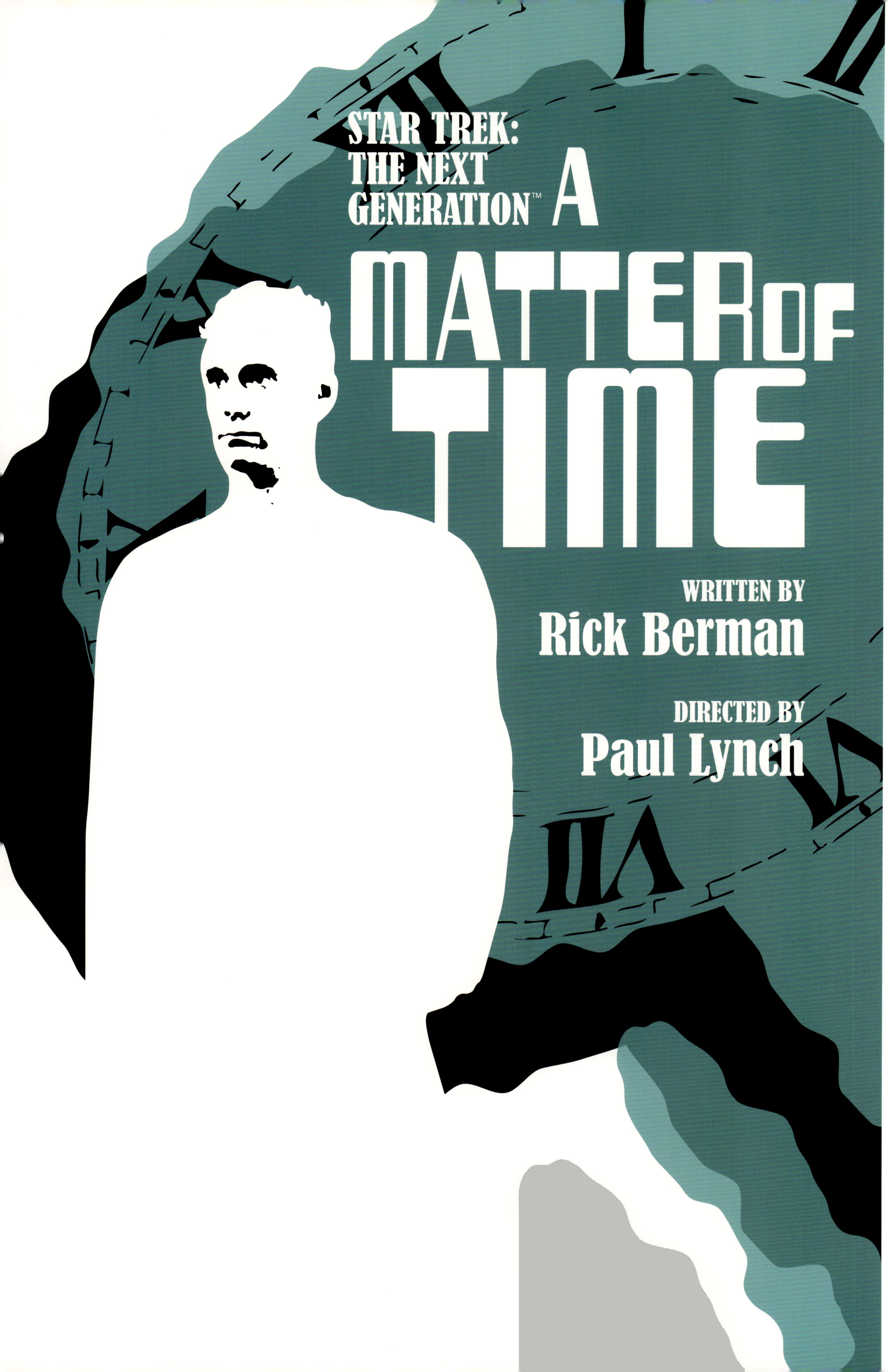
STAR TREK:
THE NEXT
GENERATION™
A
MATTER OF
TIME
WRITTEN BY
Rick Berman
DIRECTED BY
Paul Lynch

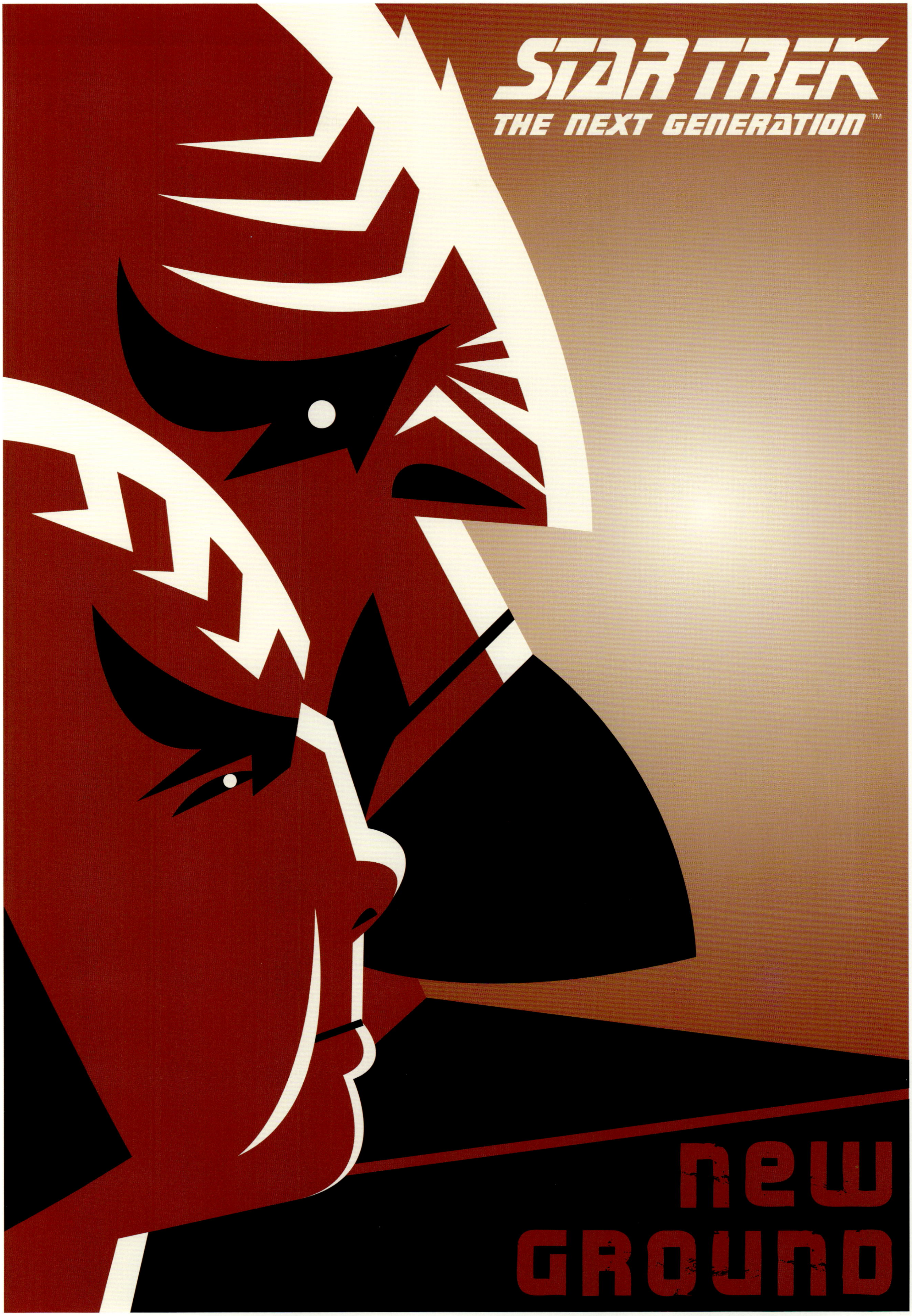

TELEPLAY BY GRANT ROSENBERG STORY BY SARA CHARNO AND STUART CHARNO
DIRECTED BY ROBERT SCHEERER

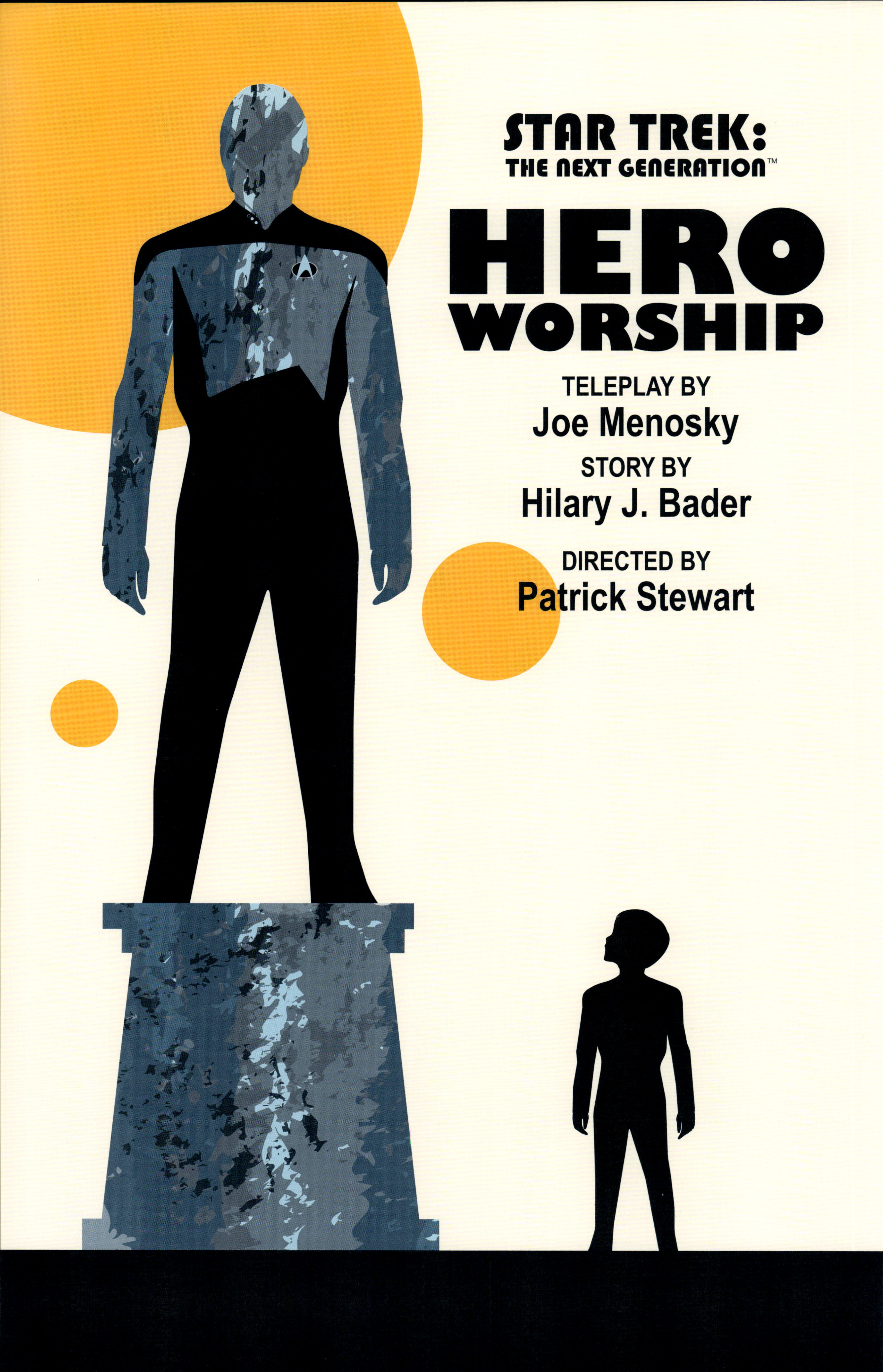

STAR TREK: THE NEXT GENERATION™

HERO WORSHIP

TELEPLAY BY
Joe Menosky

STORY BY
Hilary J. Bader

DIRECTED BY
Patrick Stewart

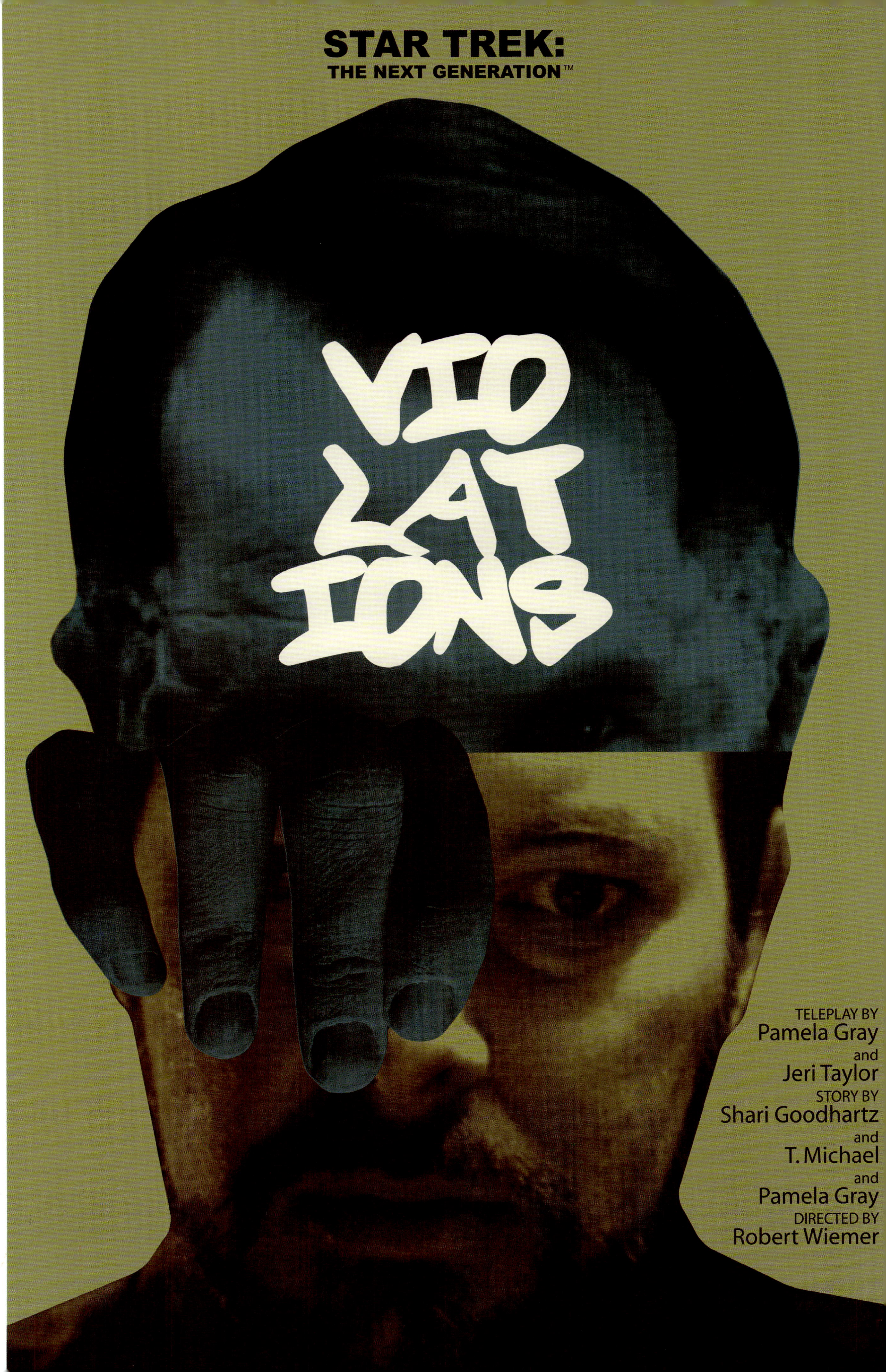
STAR TREK:
THE NEXT GENERATION™
VIO
LAT
IONS
TELEPLAY BY
Pamela Gray
and
Jeri Taylor
STORY BY
Shari Goodhartz
and
T. Michael
and
Pamela Gray
DIRECTED BY
Robert Wiemer

STAR TREK: THE NEXT GENERATION™

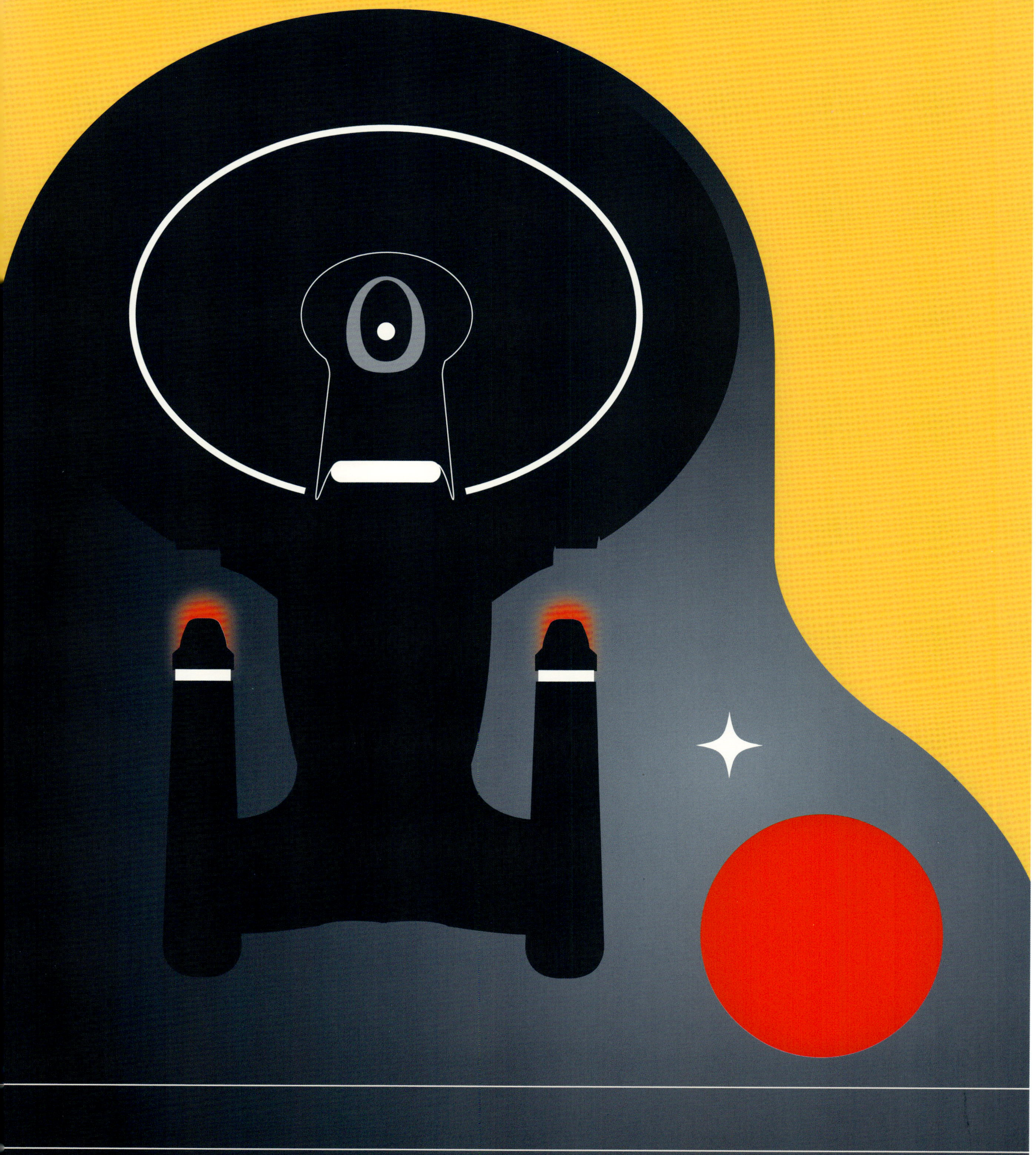

THE MASTERPIECE SOCIETY

Teleplay By **Adam Belanoff** and **Michael Piller**
Story By **James Kahn** and **Adam Belanoff**
Directed By **Winrich Kolbe**

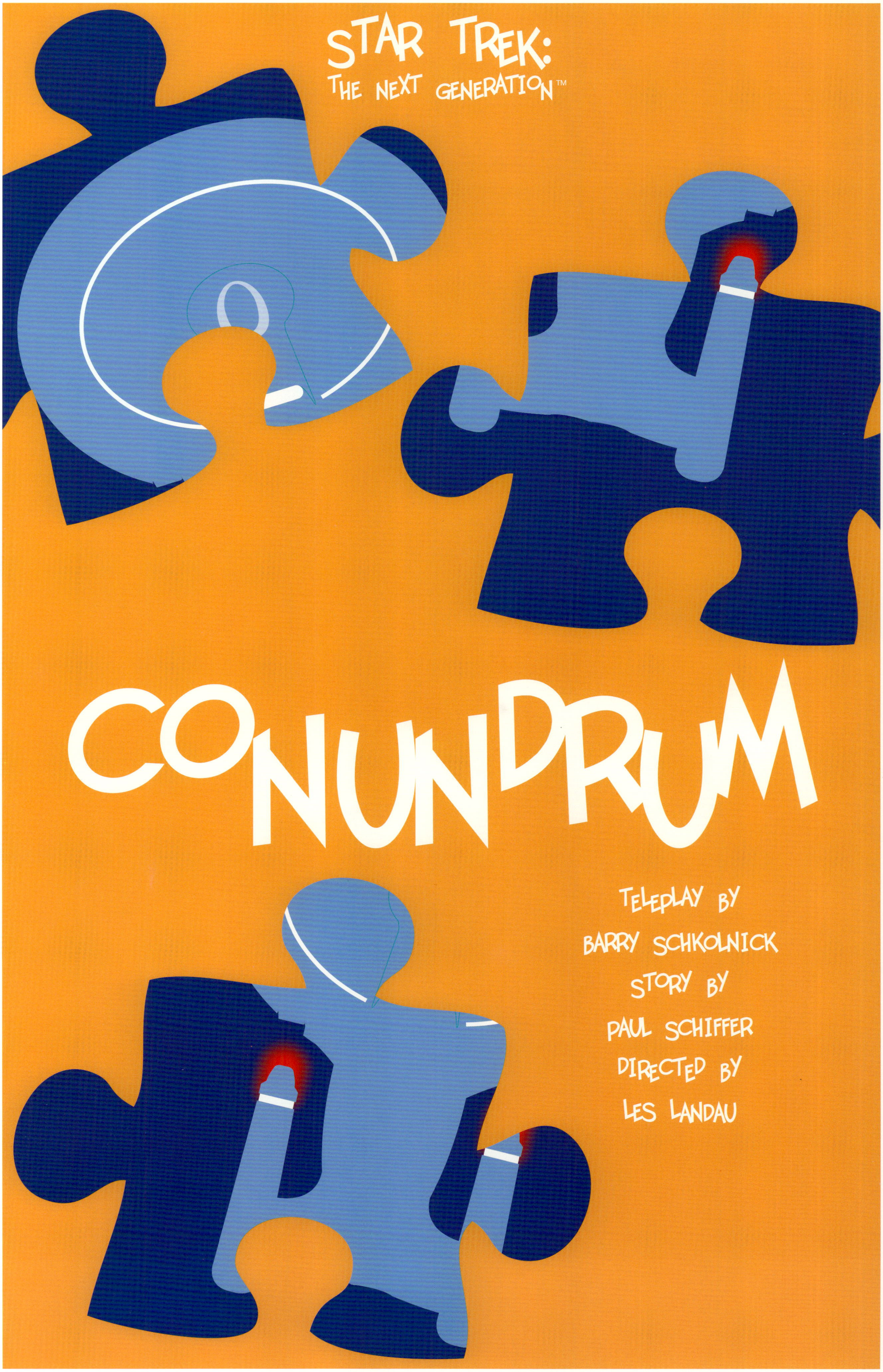
STAR TREK:
THE NEXT GENERATION™
CONUNDRUM
TELEPLAY BY
BARRY SCHKOLNICK
STORY BY
PAUL SCHIFFER
DIRECTED BY
LES LANDAU

STAR TREK: THE NEXT GENERATION™

POWER PLAY

TELEPLAY BY

RENE BALCER

AND

HERBERT J. WRIGHT

&

BRANNON BRAGA

STORY BY

PAUL REUBEN

AND

MAURICE HURLEY

DIRECTED BY

DAVID LIVINGSTON

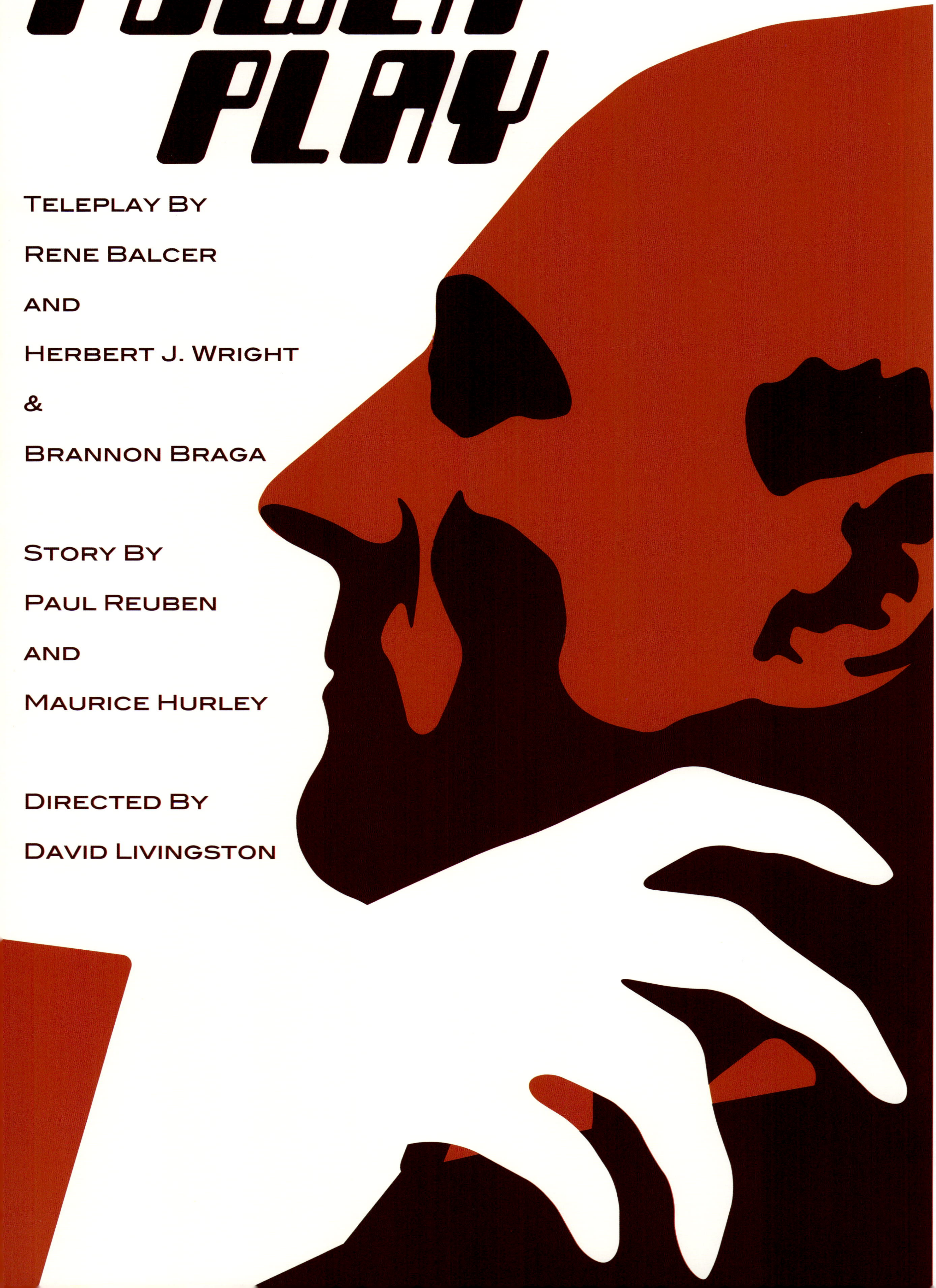

STAR TREK: THE NEXT GENERATION™

ETHICS

TELEPLAY BY

Ronald D. Moore

STORY BY

Sara Charno and Stuart Charno

DIRECTED BY

Chip Chalmers

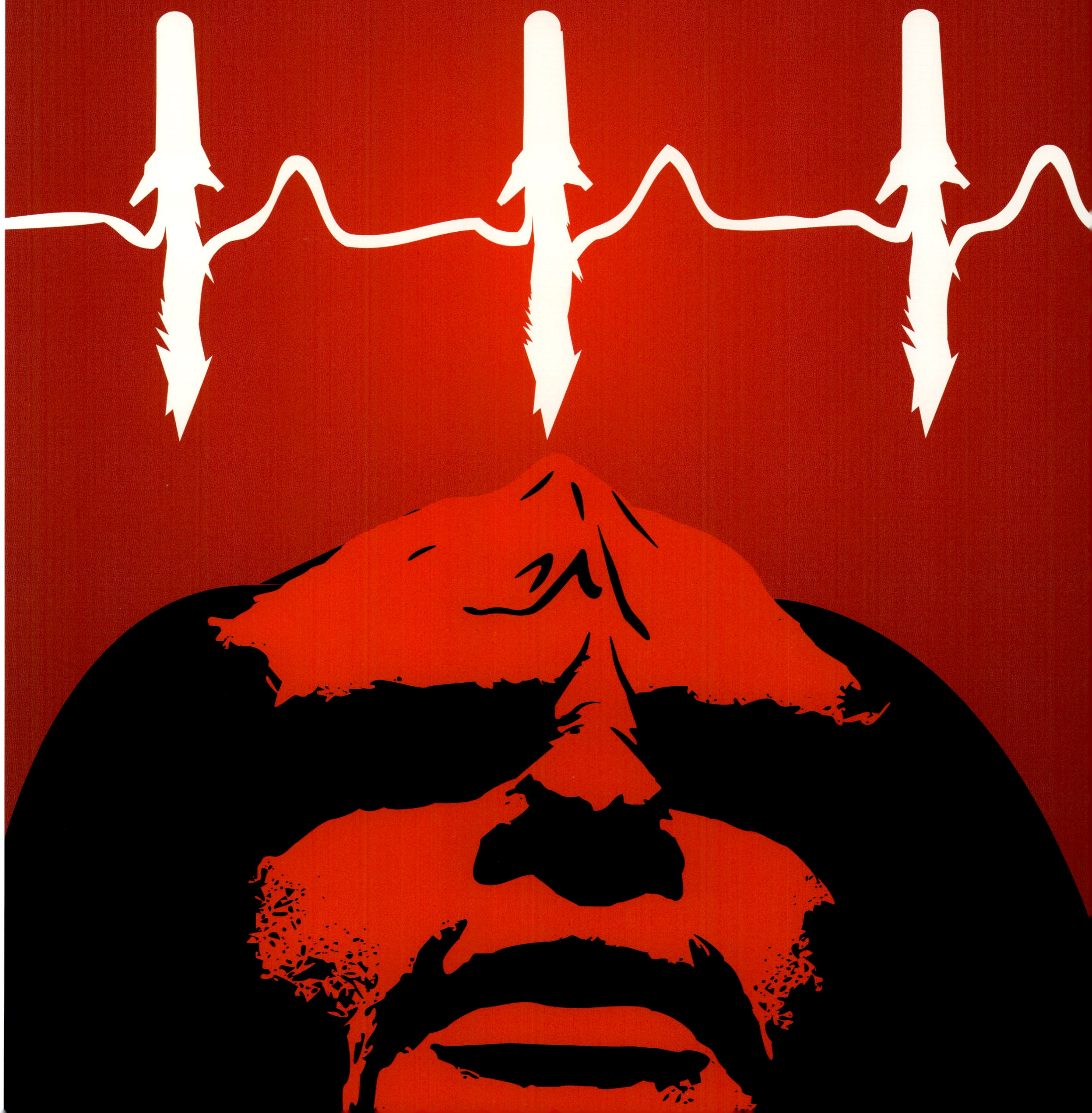

"You see Commander, on this world, everyone wants to be normal."

"She is!"

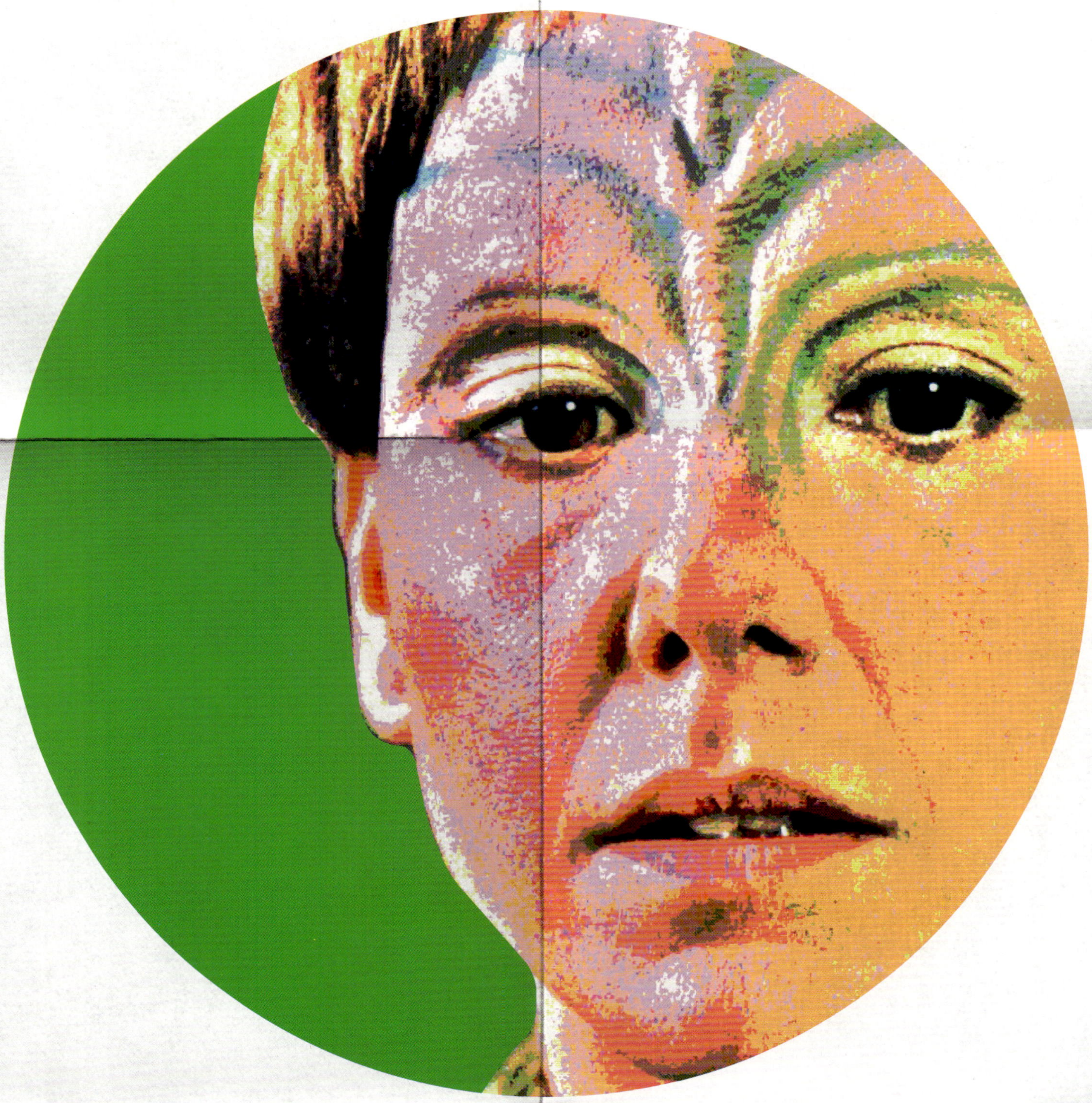

Star Trek: The Next Generation™

The Outcast

Written by
Jeri Taylor

Directed by
Robert Scheerer

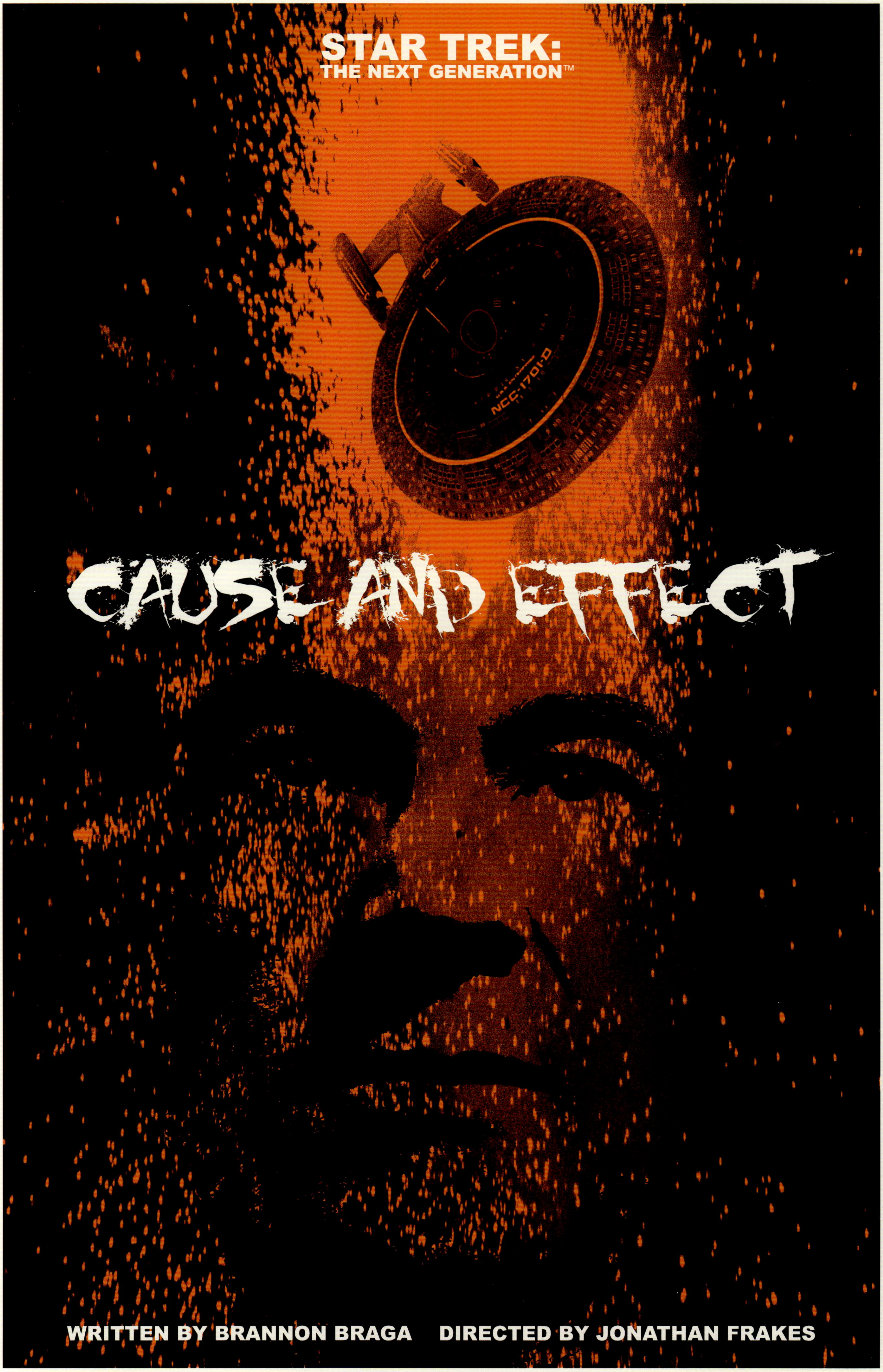
STAR TREK:
THE NEXT GENERATION™
NCC-1701-D
CAUSE AND EFFECT
WRITTEN BY BRANNON BRAGA DIRECTED BY JONATHAN FRAKES

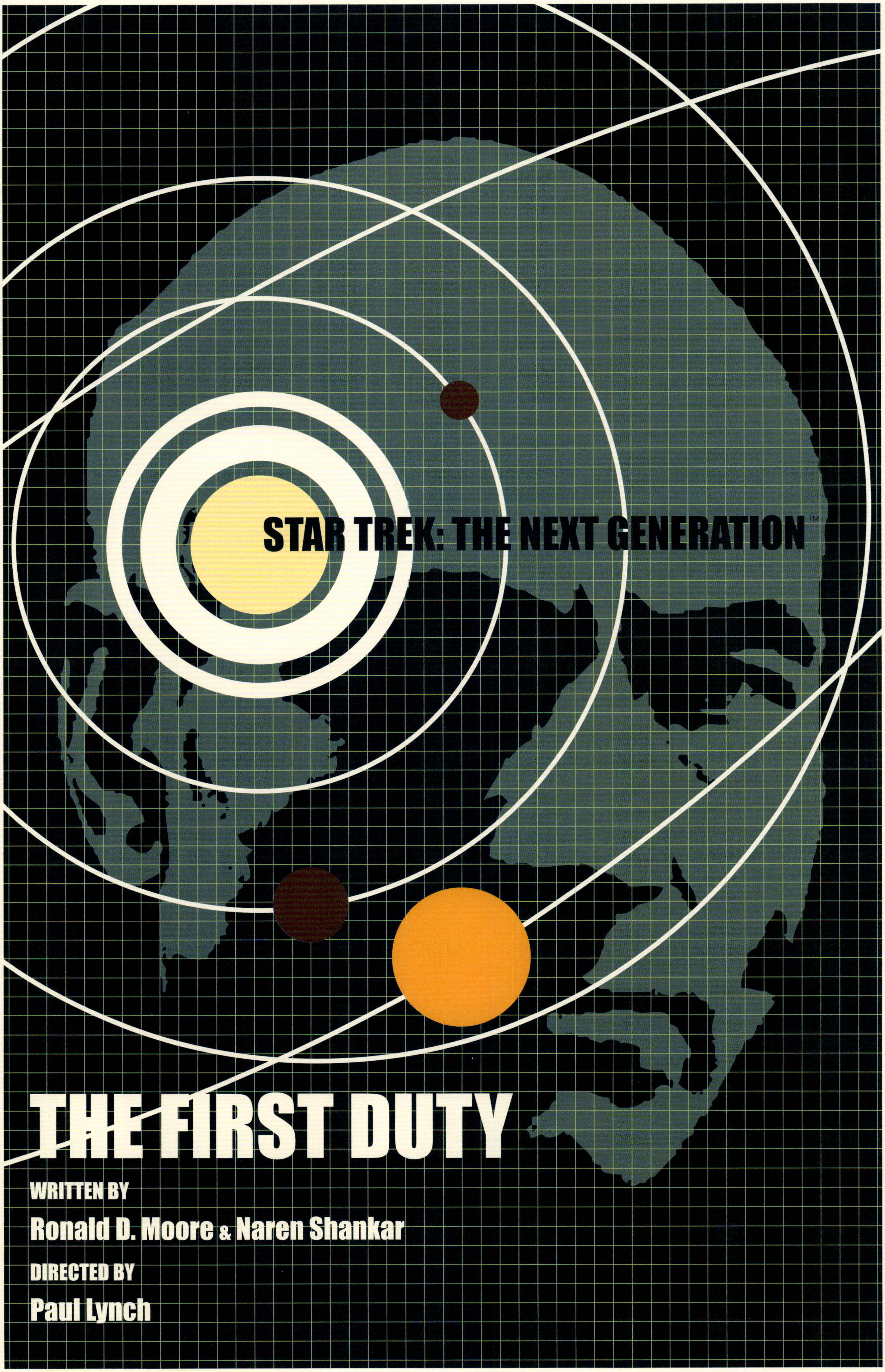
STAR TREK: THE NEXT GENERATION™
THE FIRST DUTY
WRITTEN BY
Ronald D. Moore & Naren Shankar
DIRECTED BY
Paul Lynch

STAR TREK: THE NEXT GENERATION™

COST OF LIVING

WRITTEN BY

Peter Allan Fields

DIRECTED BY

Winrich Kolbe

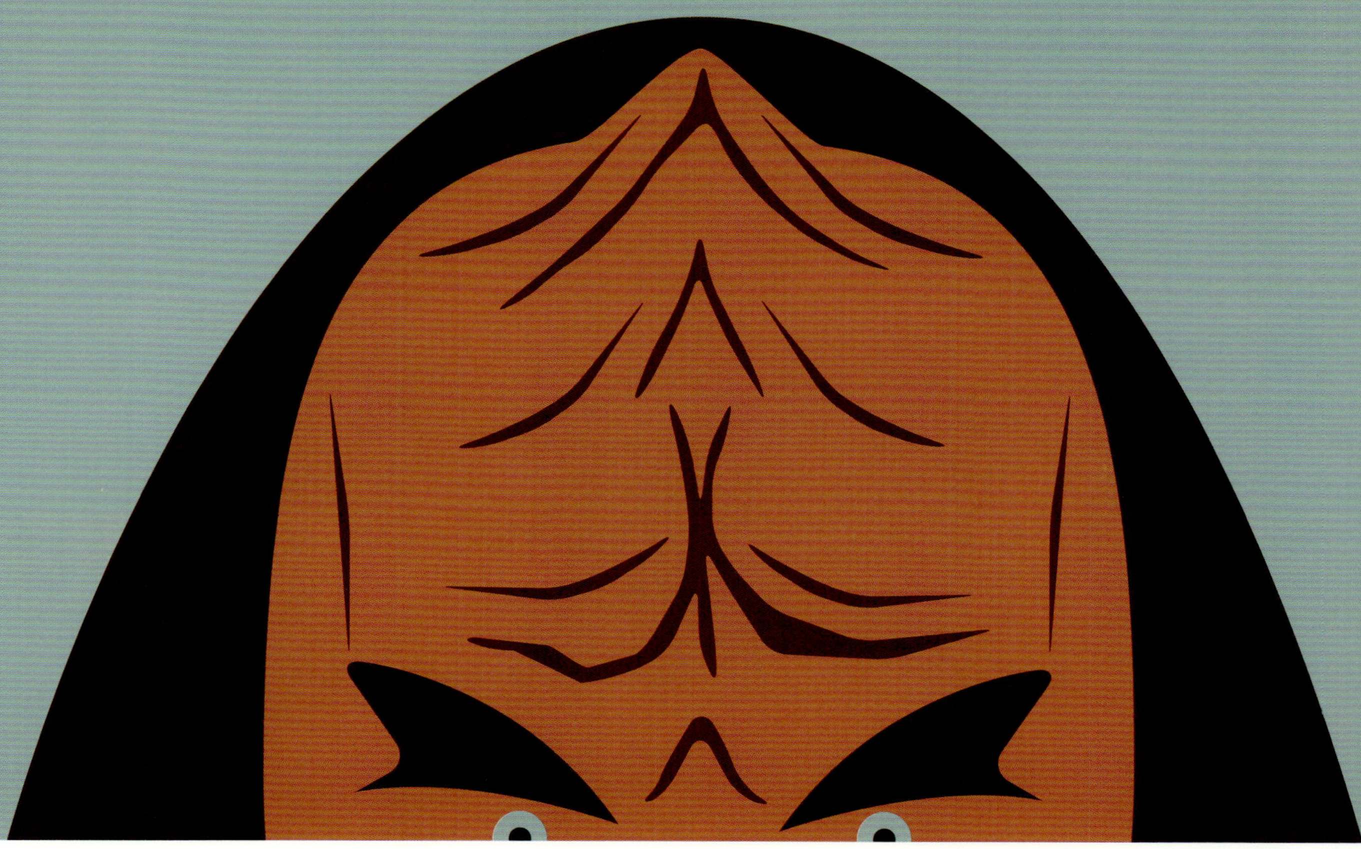

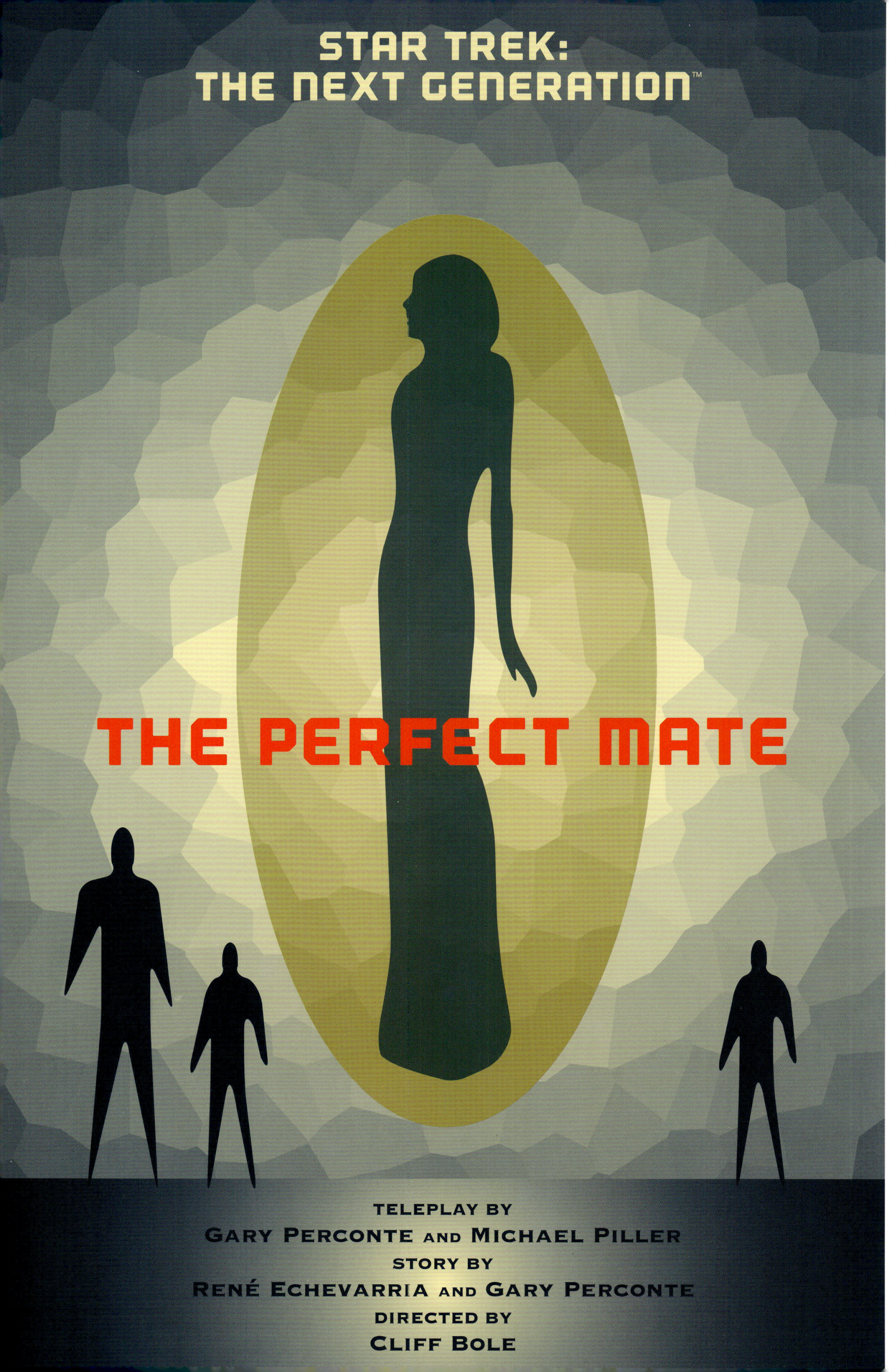
STAR TREK:
THE NEXT GENERATION™
THE PERFECT MATE
TELEPLAY BY
GARY PERCONTE AND MICHAEL PILLER
STORY BY
RENÉ ECHEVARRIA AND GARY PERCONTE
DIRECTED BY
CLIFF BOLE

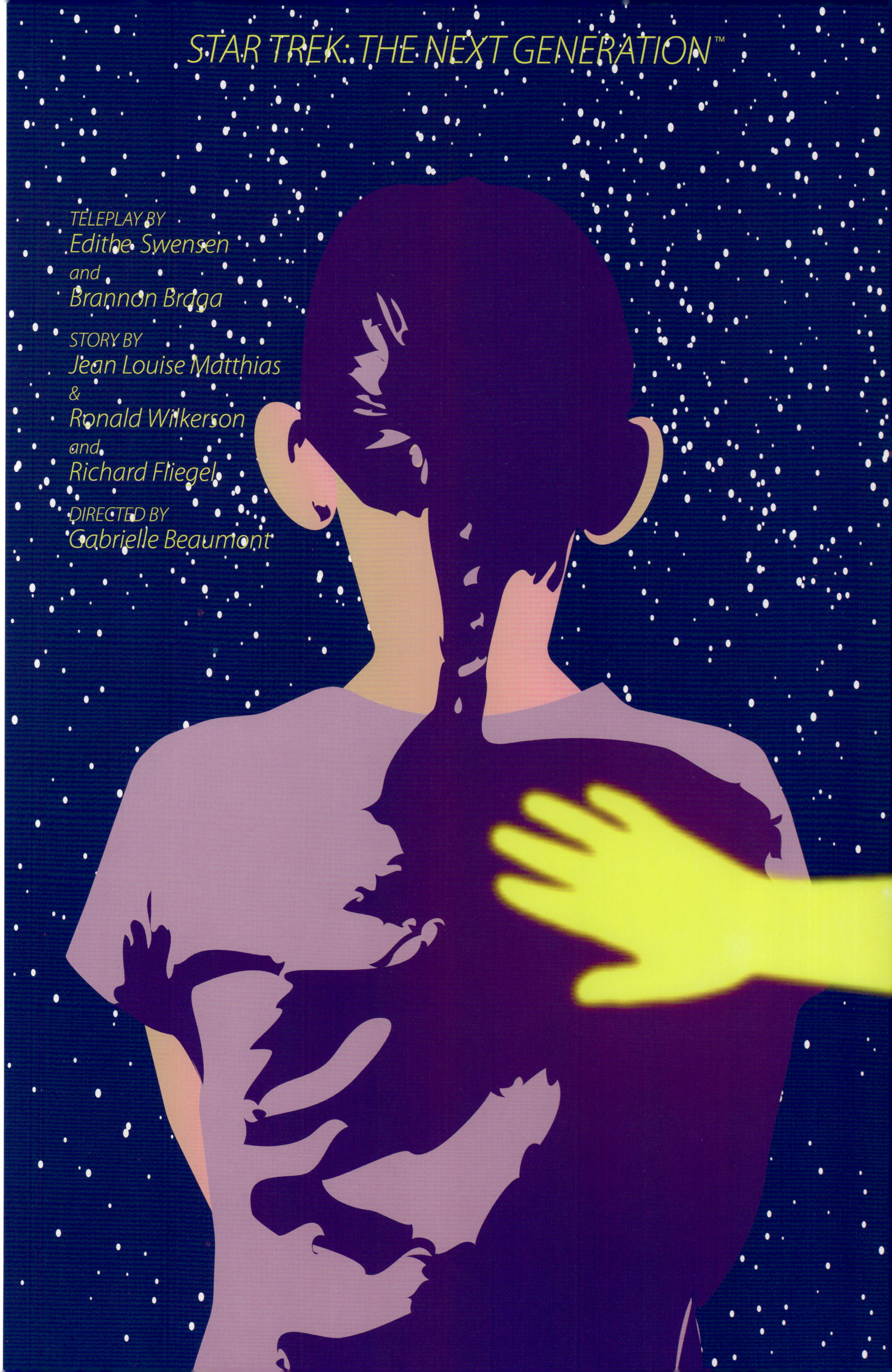
STAR TREK: THE NEXT GENERATION™
TELEPLAY BY
Edithe Swensen
and
Brannon Braga
STORY BY
Jean Louise Matthias
&
Ronald Wilkerson
and
Richard Fliegel
DIRECTED BY
Gabrielle Beaumont

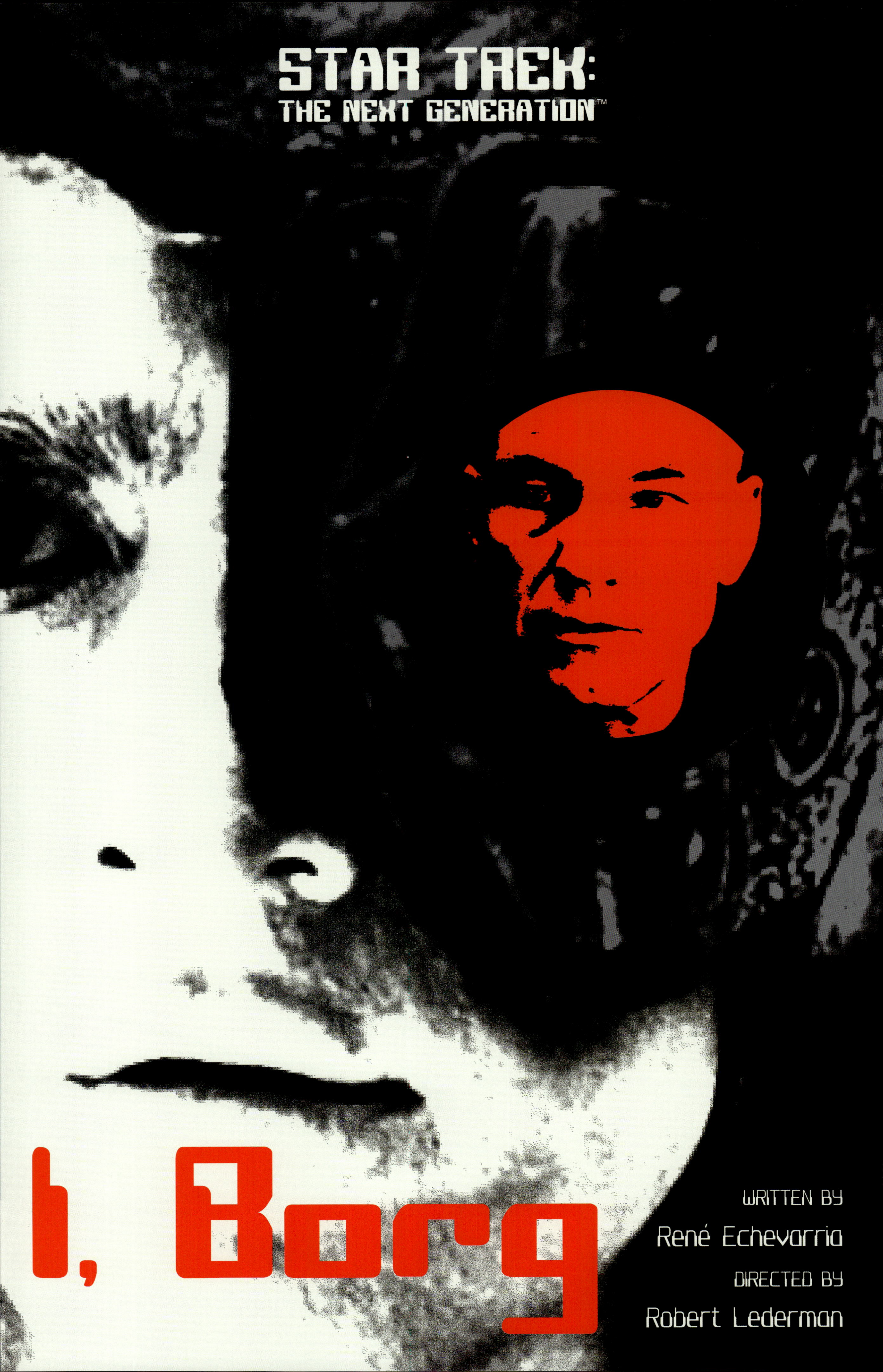
STAR TREK:
THE NEXT GENERATION™
I, Borg
WRITTEN BY
René Echevarria
DIRECTED BY
Robert Lederman

STAR TREK: THE NEXT GENERATION™

THE NEXT PHASE

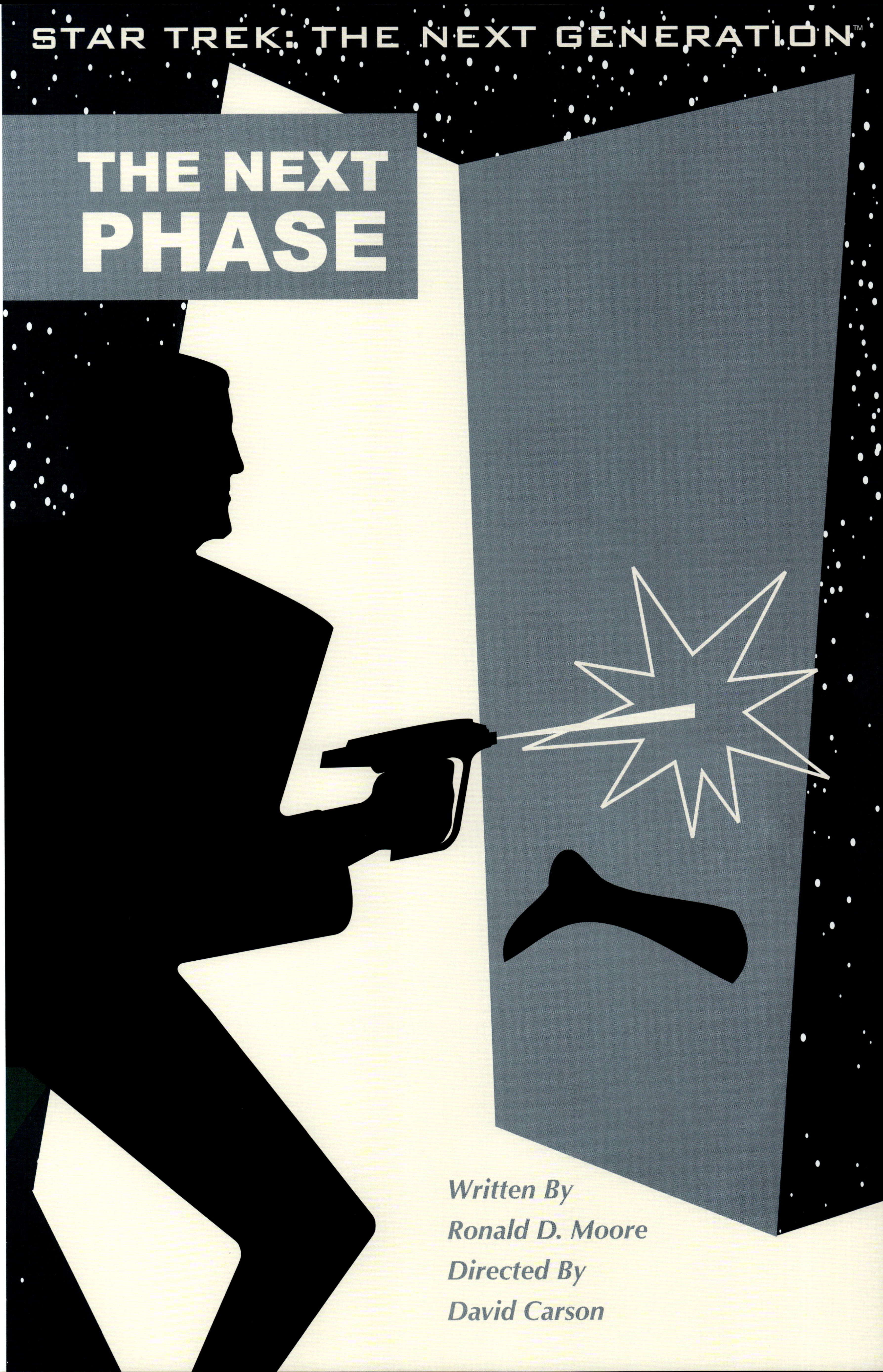

Written By
Ronald D. Moore
Directed By
David Carson

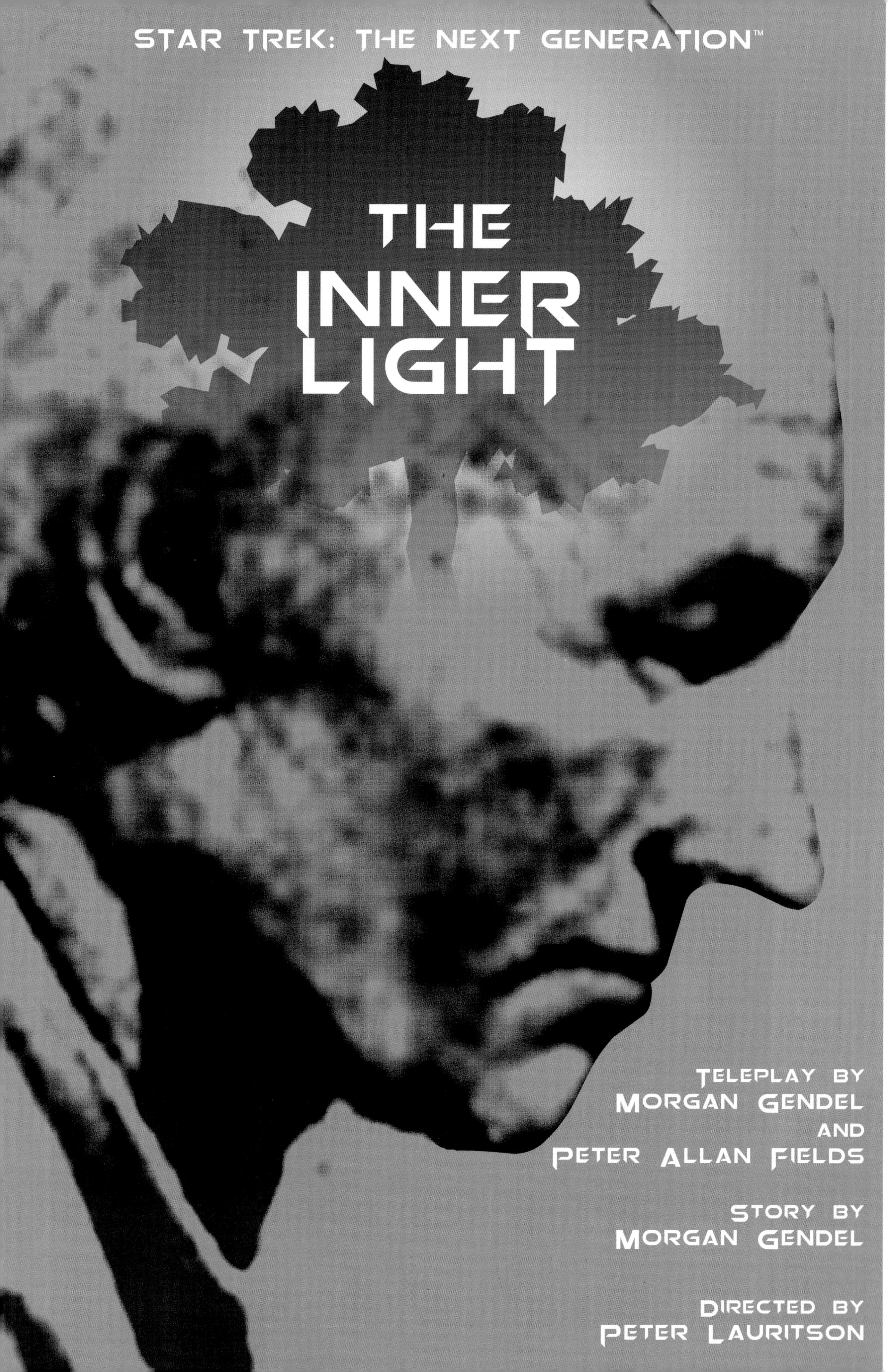

STAR TREK: THE NEXT GENERATION™

THE INNER LIGHT

TELEPLAY BY
MORGAN GENDEL
AND
PETER ALLAN FIELDS

STORY BY
MORGAN GENDEL

DIRECTED BY
PETER LAURITSON

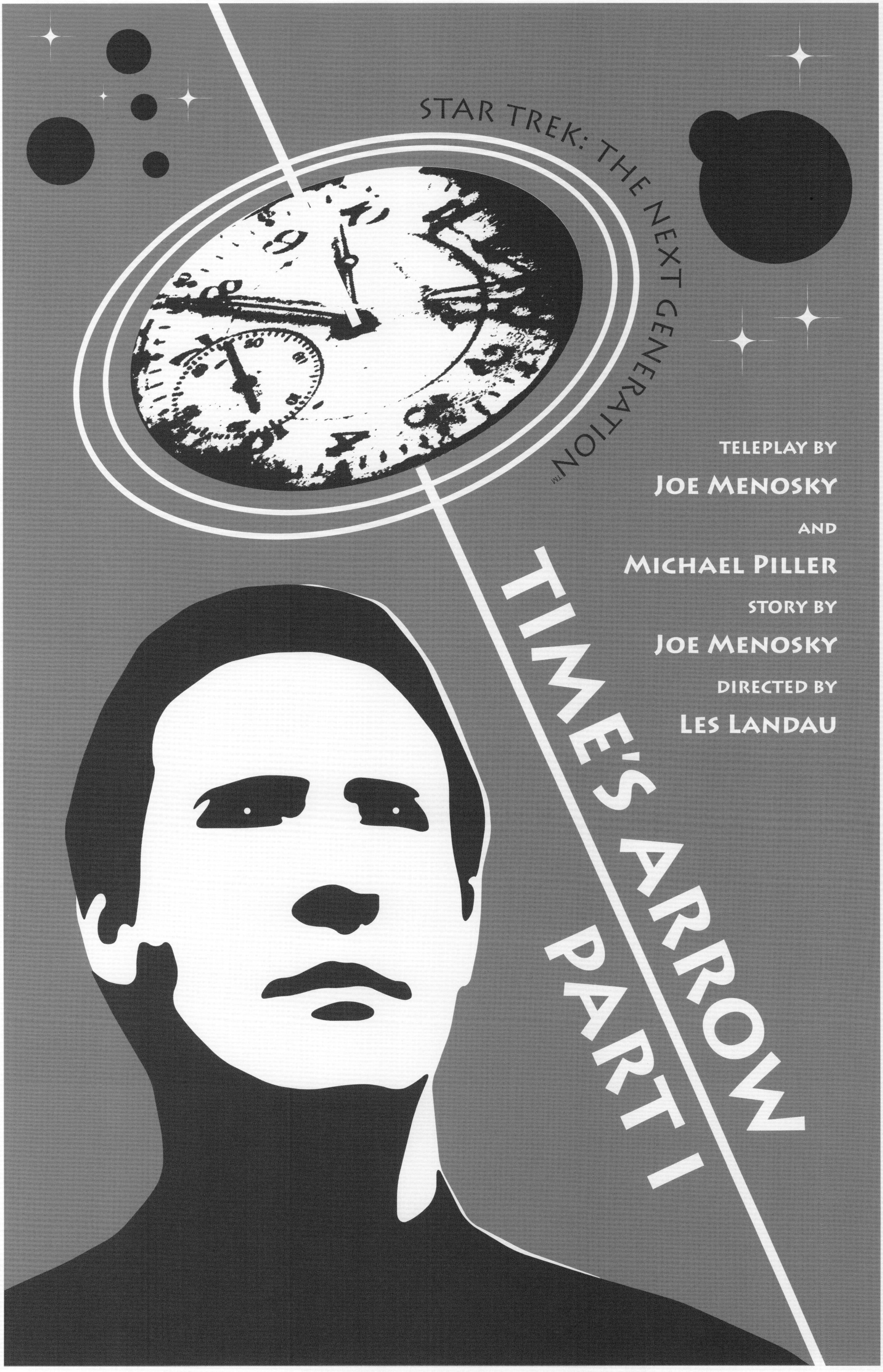
STAR TREK: THE NEXT GENERATION™
TELEPLAY BY
JOE MENOSKY
AND
MICHAEL PILLER
STORY BY
JOE MENOSKY
DIRECTED BY
LES LANDAU
TIME'S ARROW PART I

Season Six

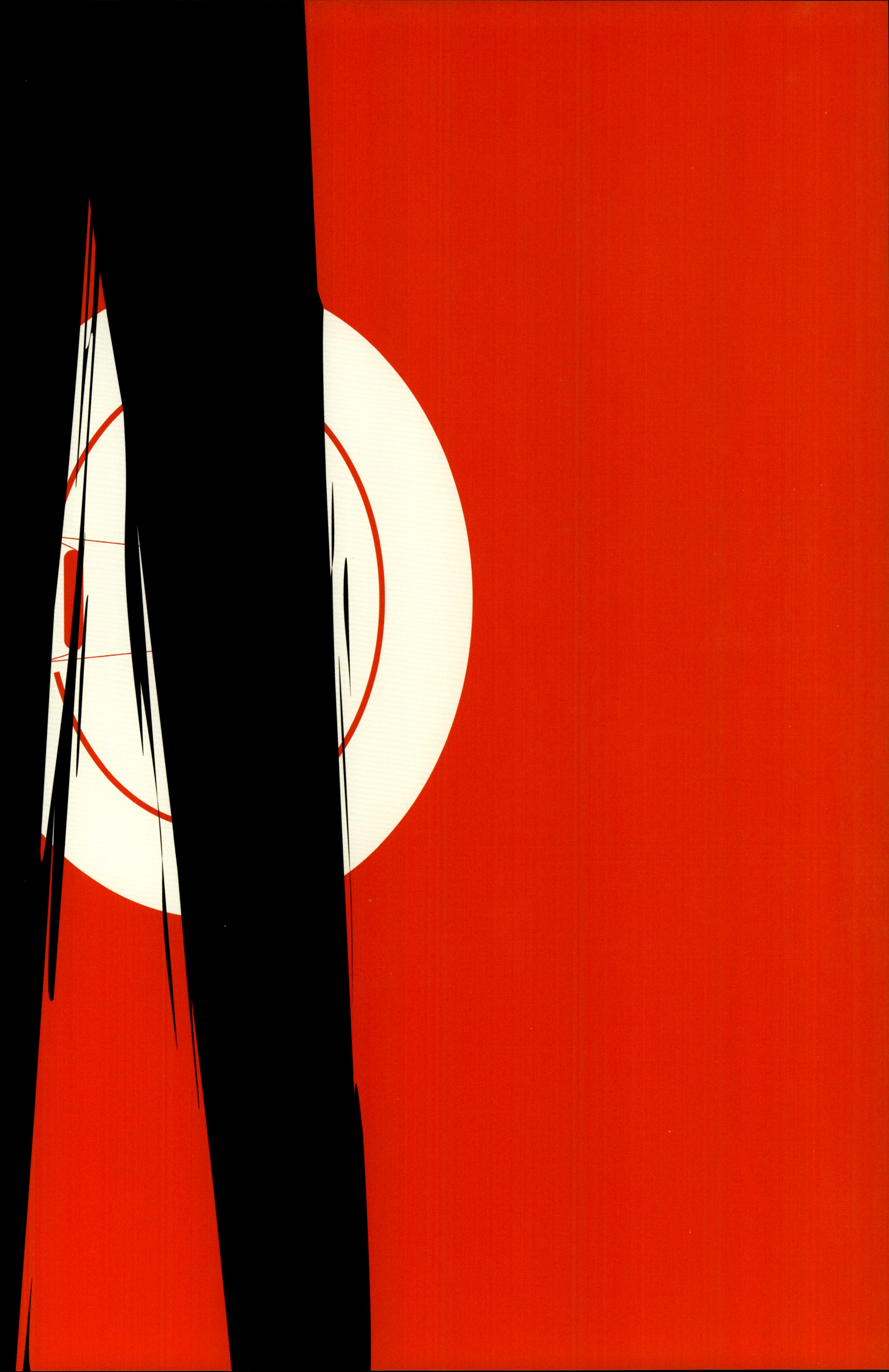

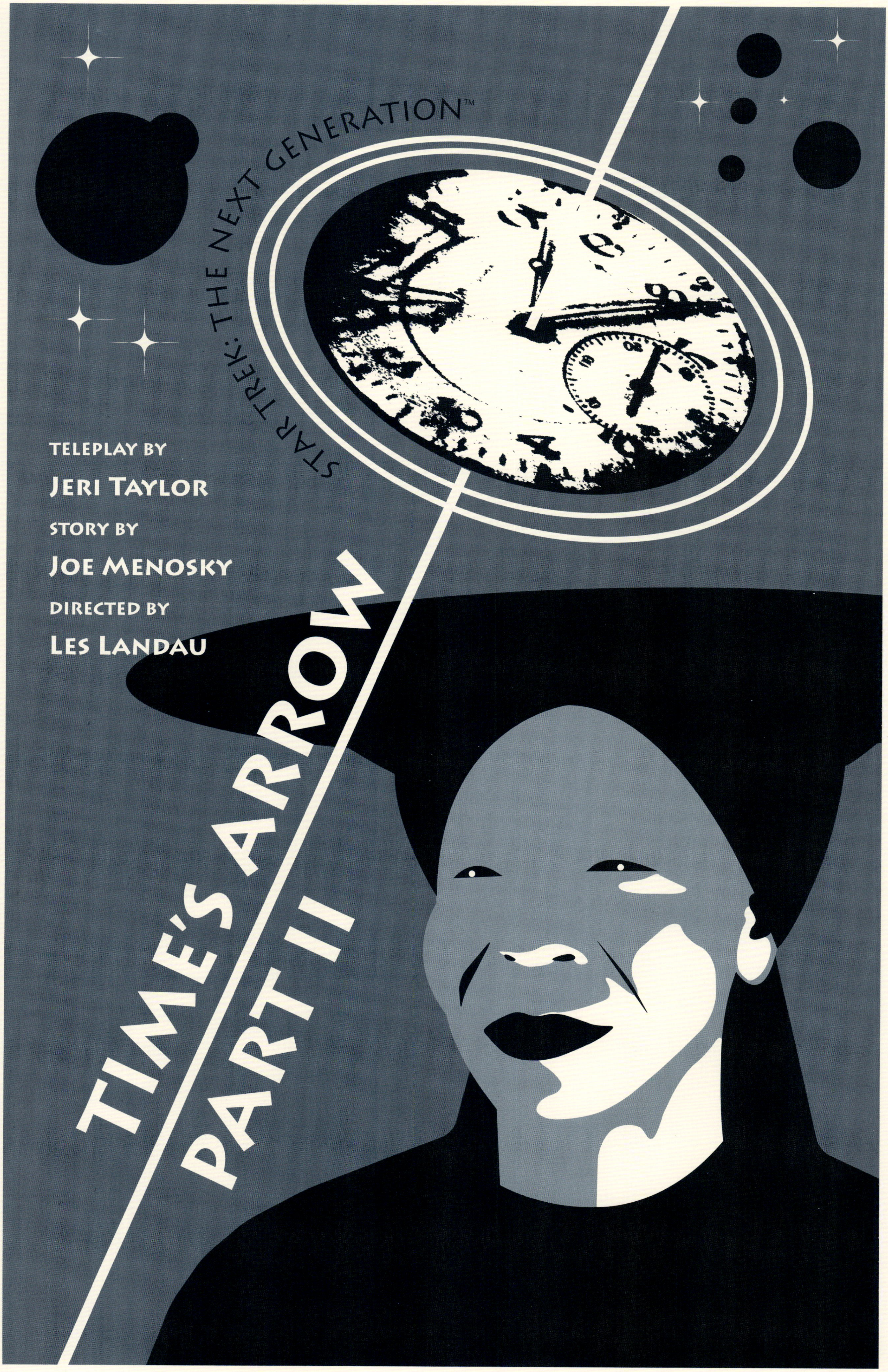
STAR TREK: THE NEXT GENERATION™
TELEPLAY BY
JERI TAYLOR
STORY BY
JOE MENOSKY
DIRECTED BY
LES LANDAU
TIME'S ARROW
PART II

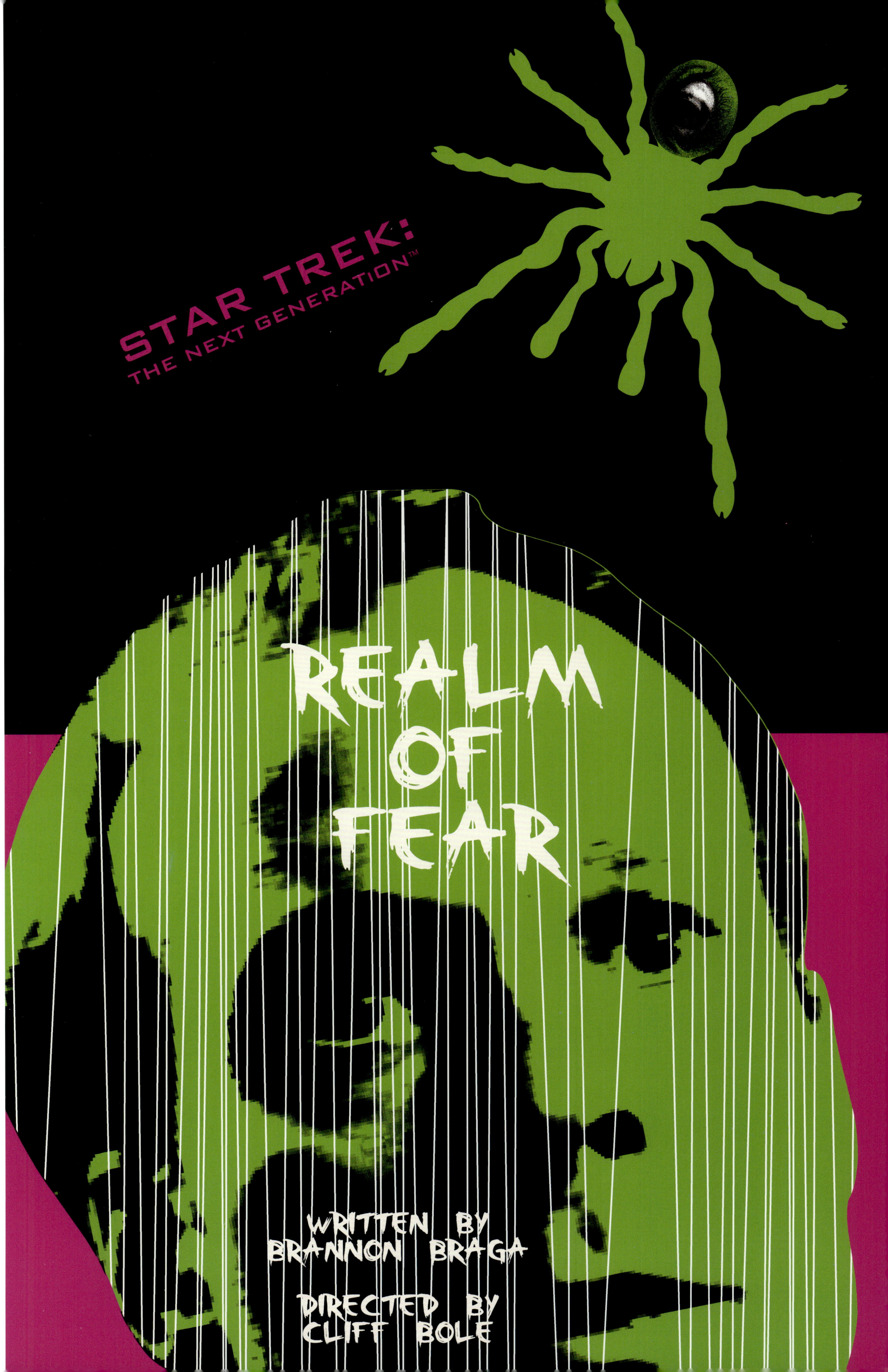
STAR TREK:
THE NEXT GENERATION™
REALM OF FEAR
WRITTEN BY
BRANNON BRAGA
DIRECTED BY
CLIFF BOLE

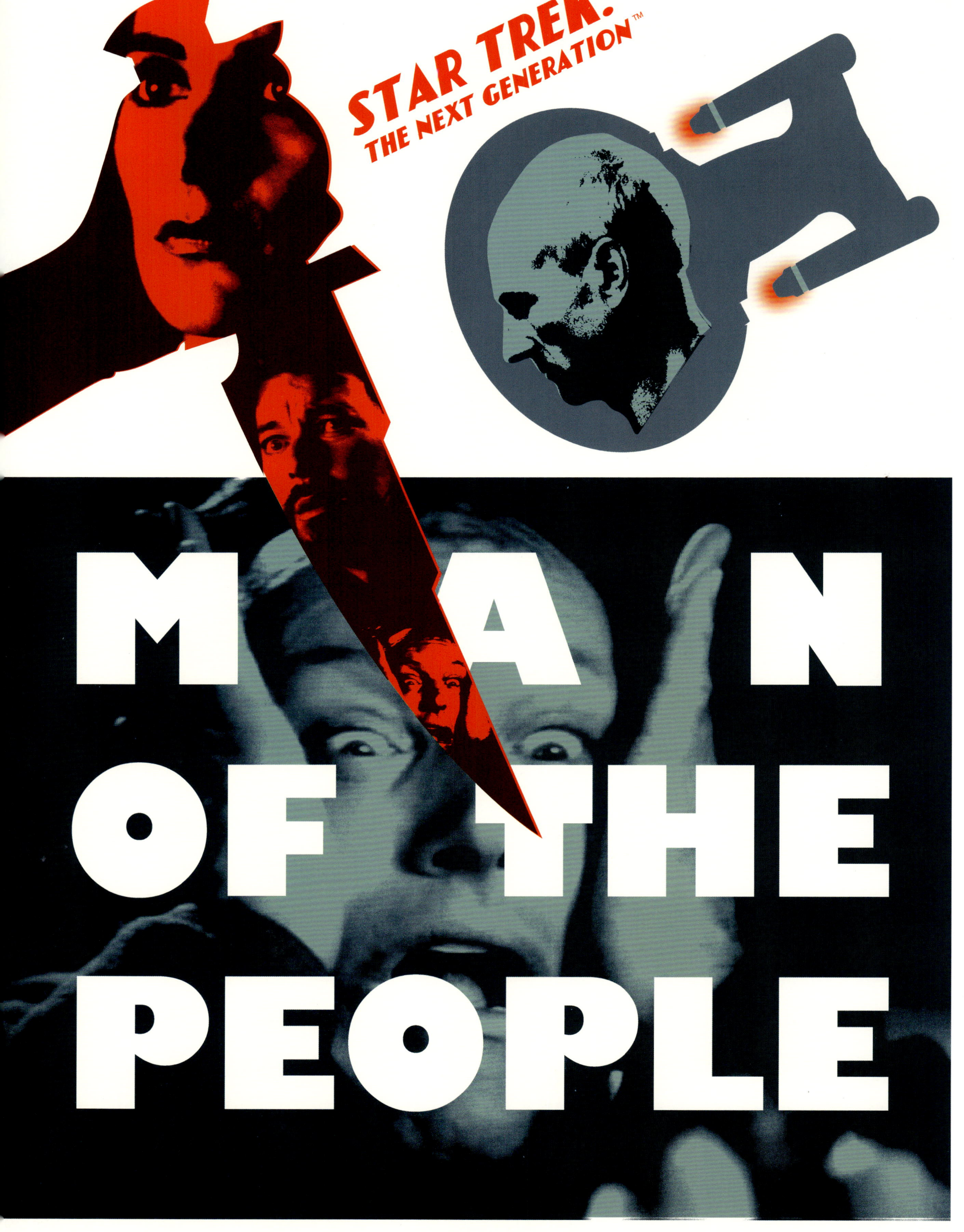

WRITTEN BY
Frank Abatemarco
DIRECTED BY
Winrich Kolbe

RELICS

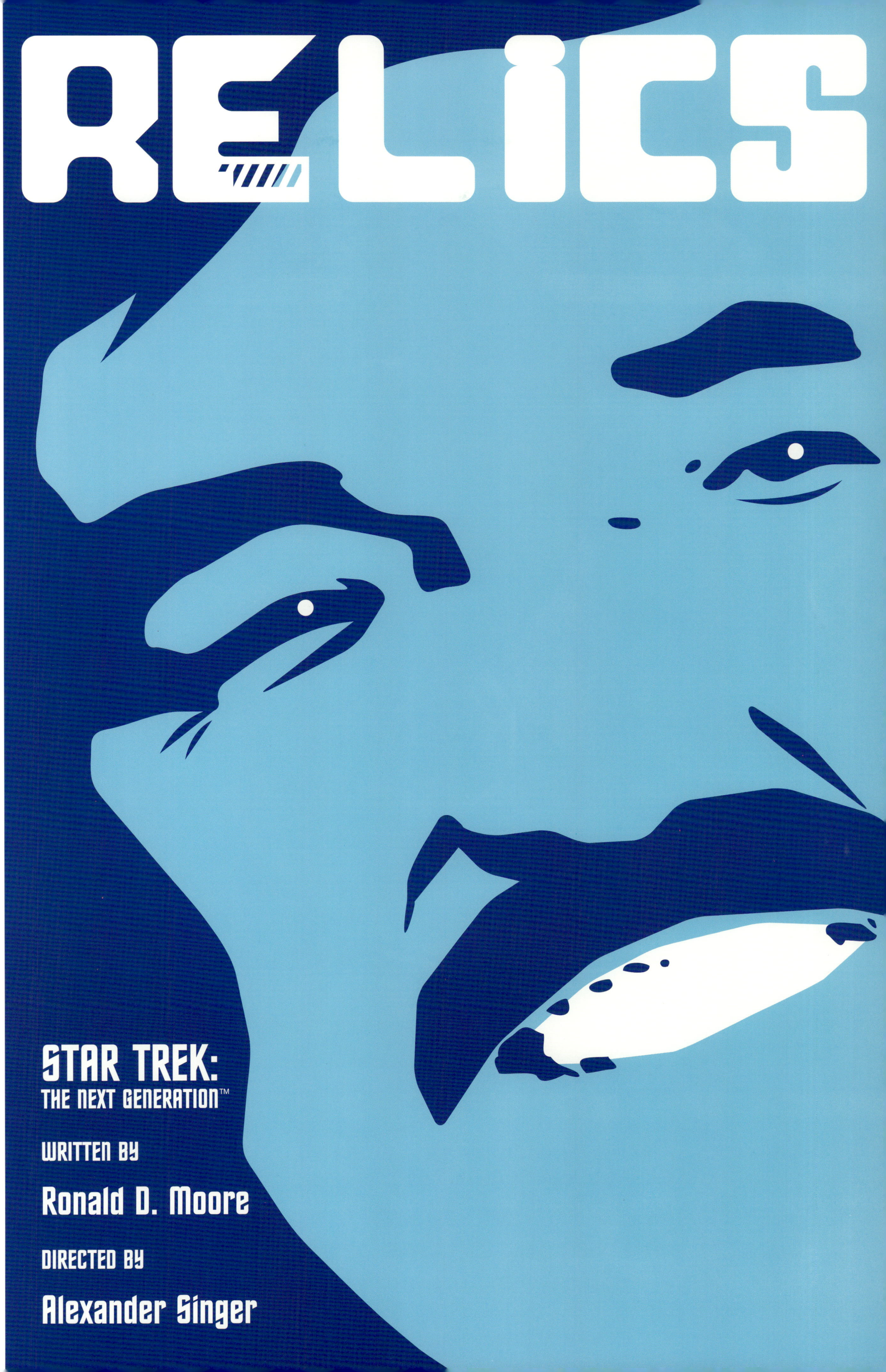

STAR TREK:
THE NEXT GENERATION™

WRITTEN BY
Ronald D. Moore

DIRECTED BY
Alexander Singer

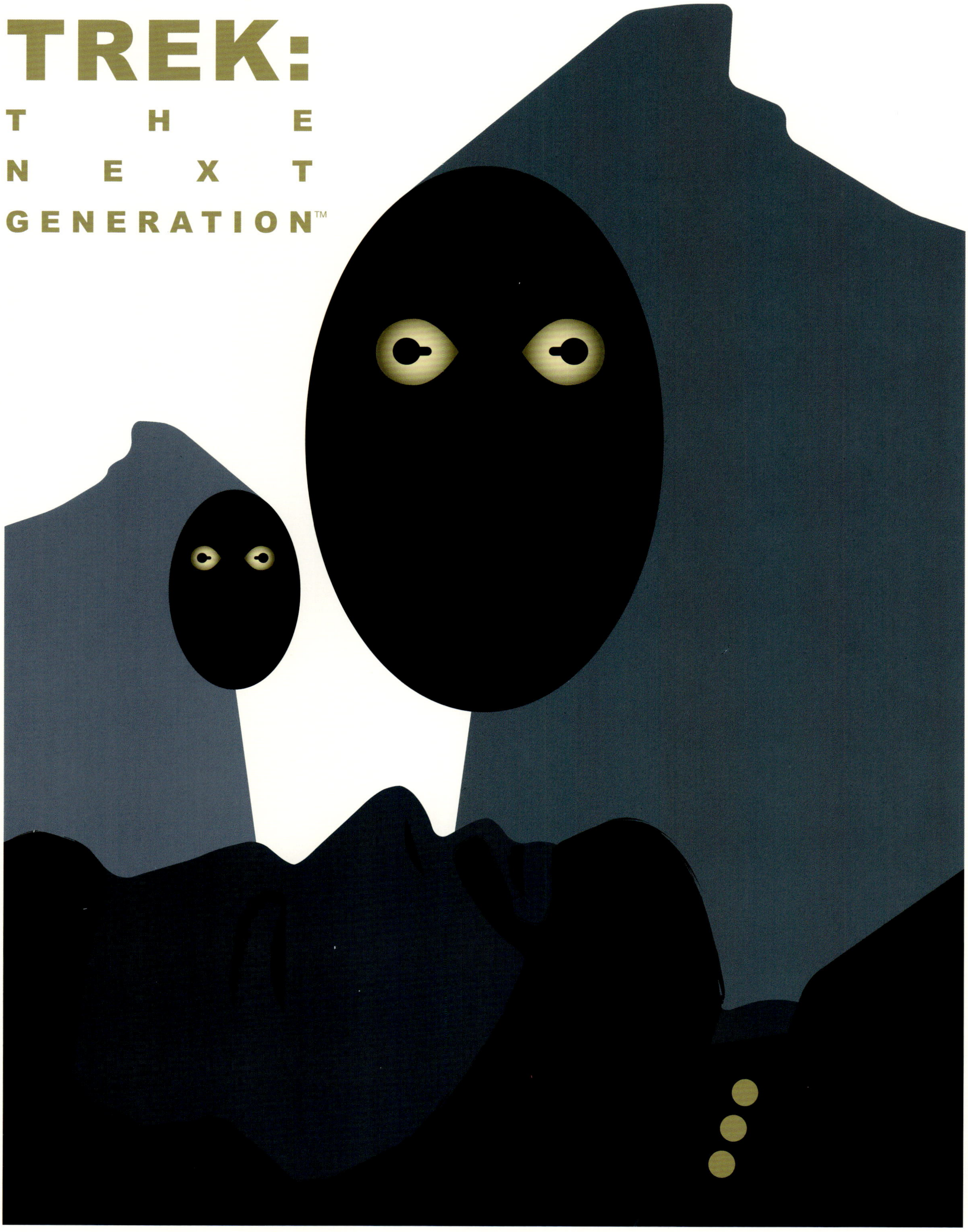

STAR TREK: THE NEXT GENERATION™

SCHISMS

TELEPLAY BY BRANNON BRAGA
STORY BY JEAN LOUISE MATTHIAS & RONALD WILKERSON
DIRECTED BY ROBERT WIEMER

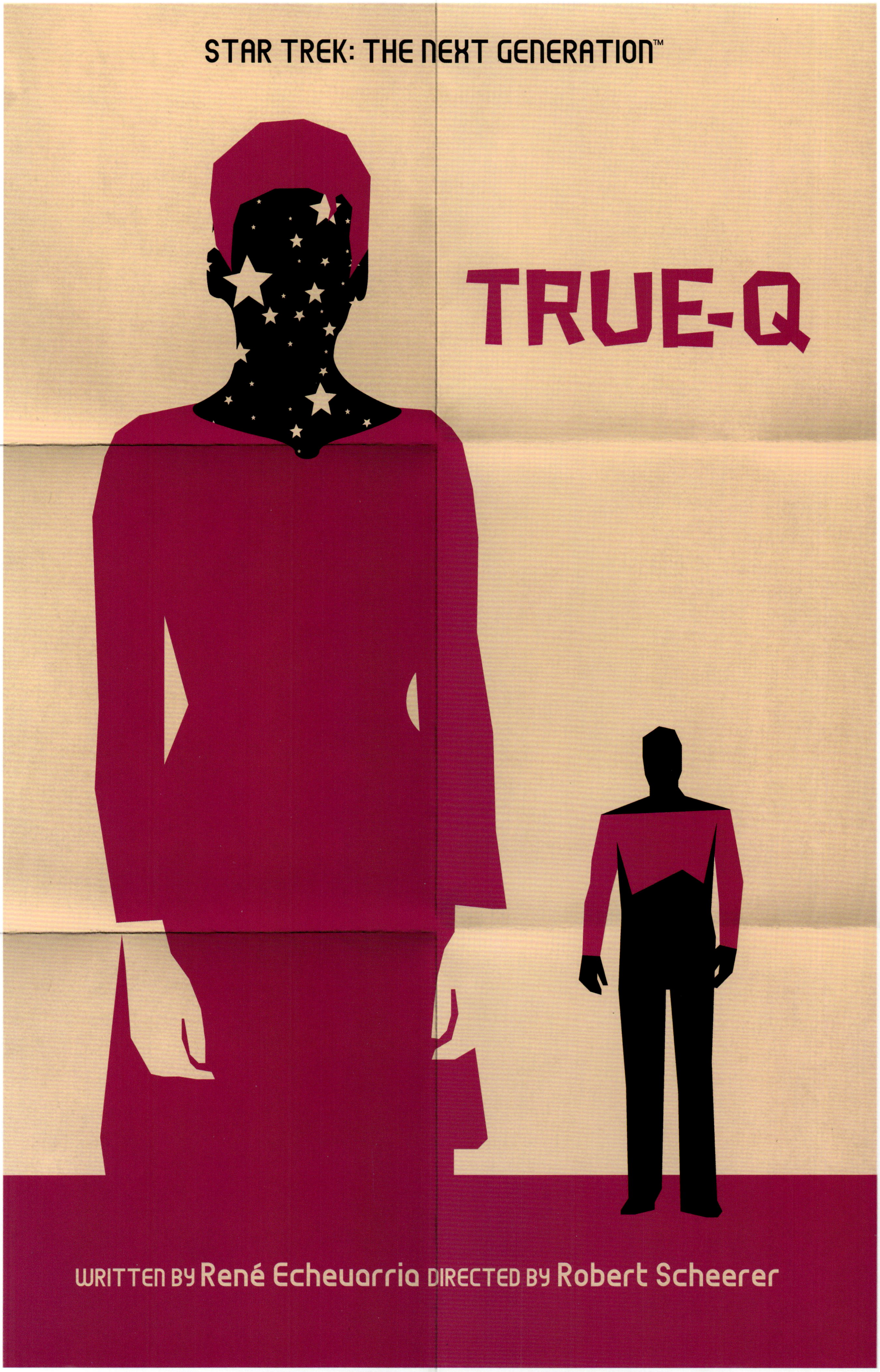
STAR TREK: THE NEXT GENERATION™
TRUE-Q
WRITTEN BY René Echevarria DIRECTED BY Robert Scheerer

RASCALS

STAR TREK: THE NEXT GENERATION™

TELEPLAY BY
Allison Hock

STORY BY
Ward Botsford
&
Diana Dru Botsford
and
Michael Piller

DIRECTED BY
Adam Nimoy

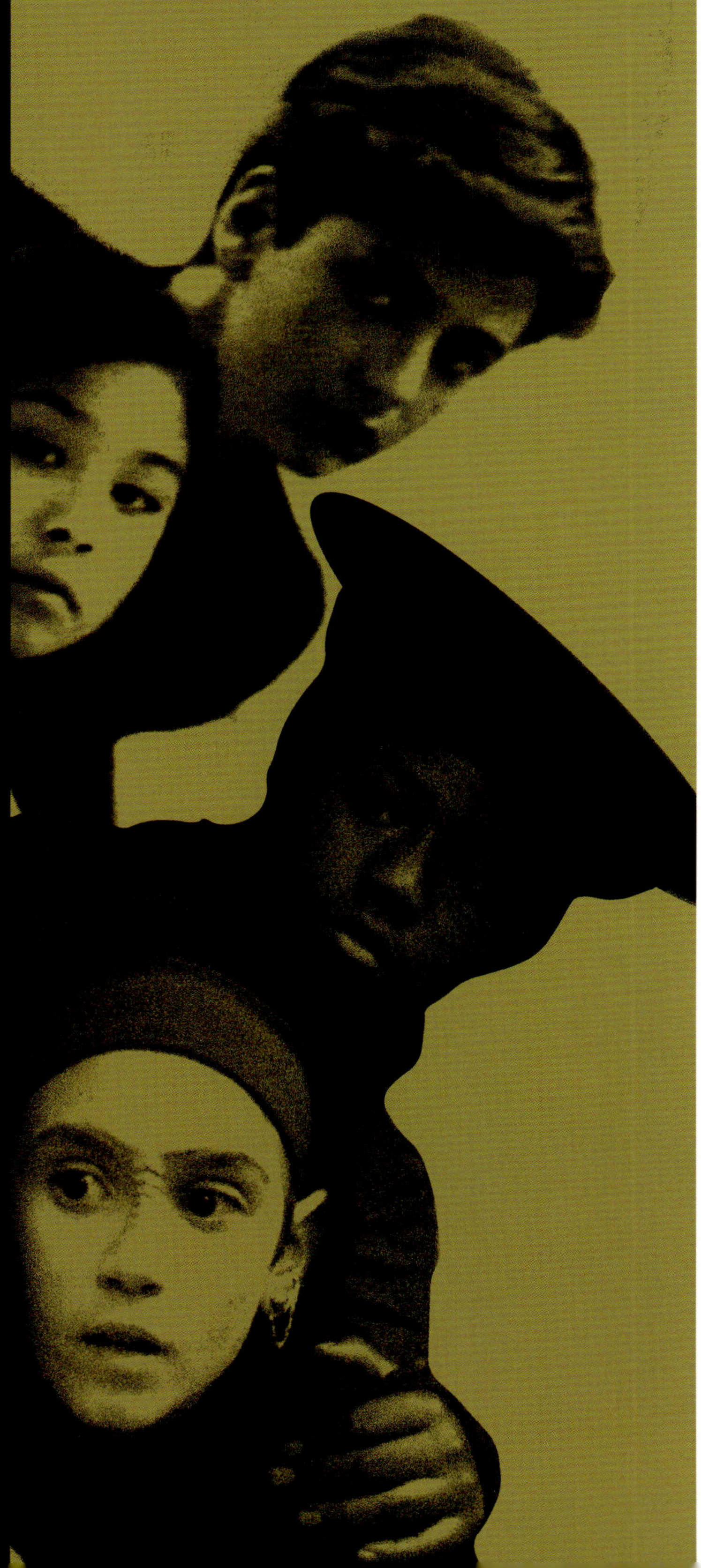

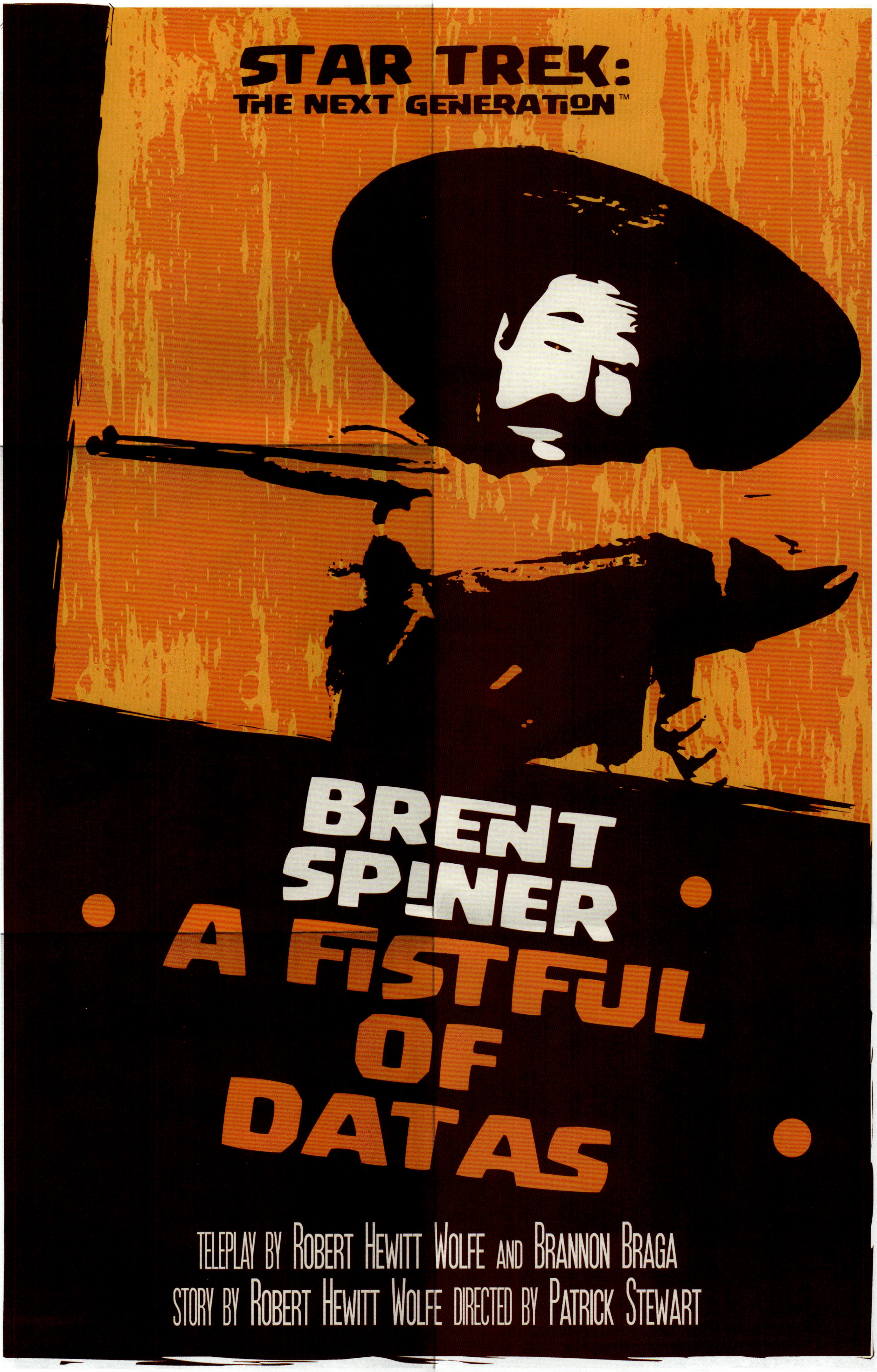
STAR TREK:
THE NEXT GENERATION™
BRENT SPINER
A FISTFUL OF DATAS
TELEPLAY BY ROBERT HEWITT WOLFE AND BRANNON BRAGA
STORY BY ROBERT HEWITT WOLFE DIRECTED BY PATRICK STEWART

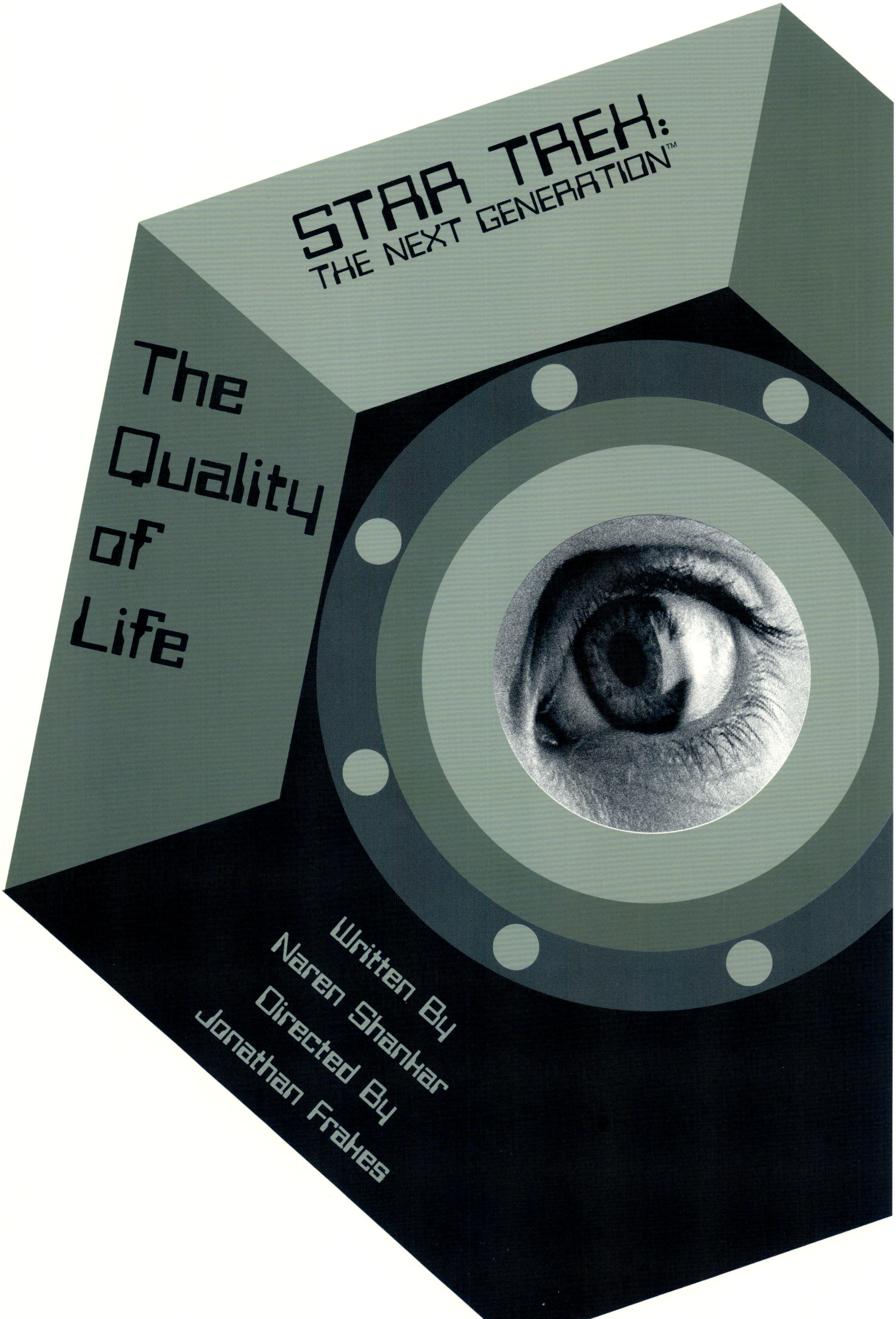
STAR TREK:
THE NEXT GENERATION™
The Quality of Life
Written By
Naren Shankar
Directed By
Jonathan Frakes

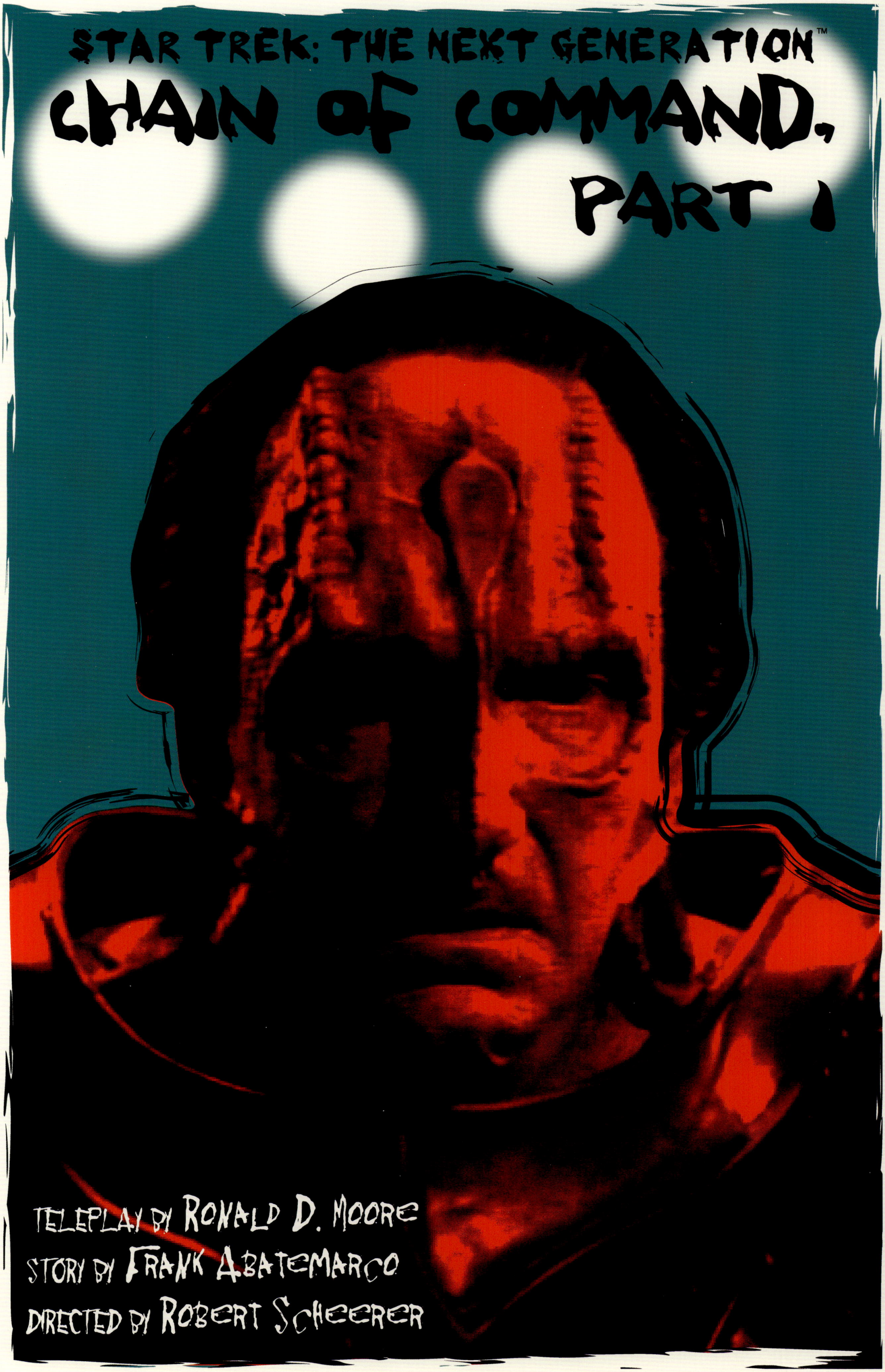
STAR TREK: THE NEXT GENERATION™
CHAIN OF COMMAND, PART I
TELEPLAY BY RONALD D. MOORE
STORY BY FRANK ABATEMARCO
DIRECTED BY ROBERT SCHEERER

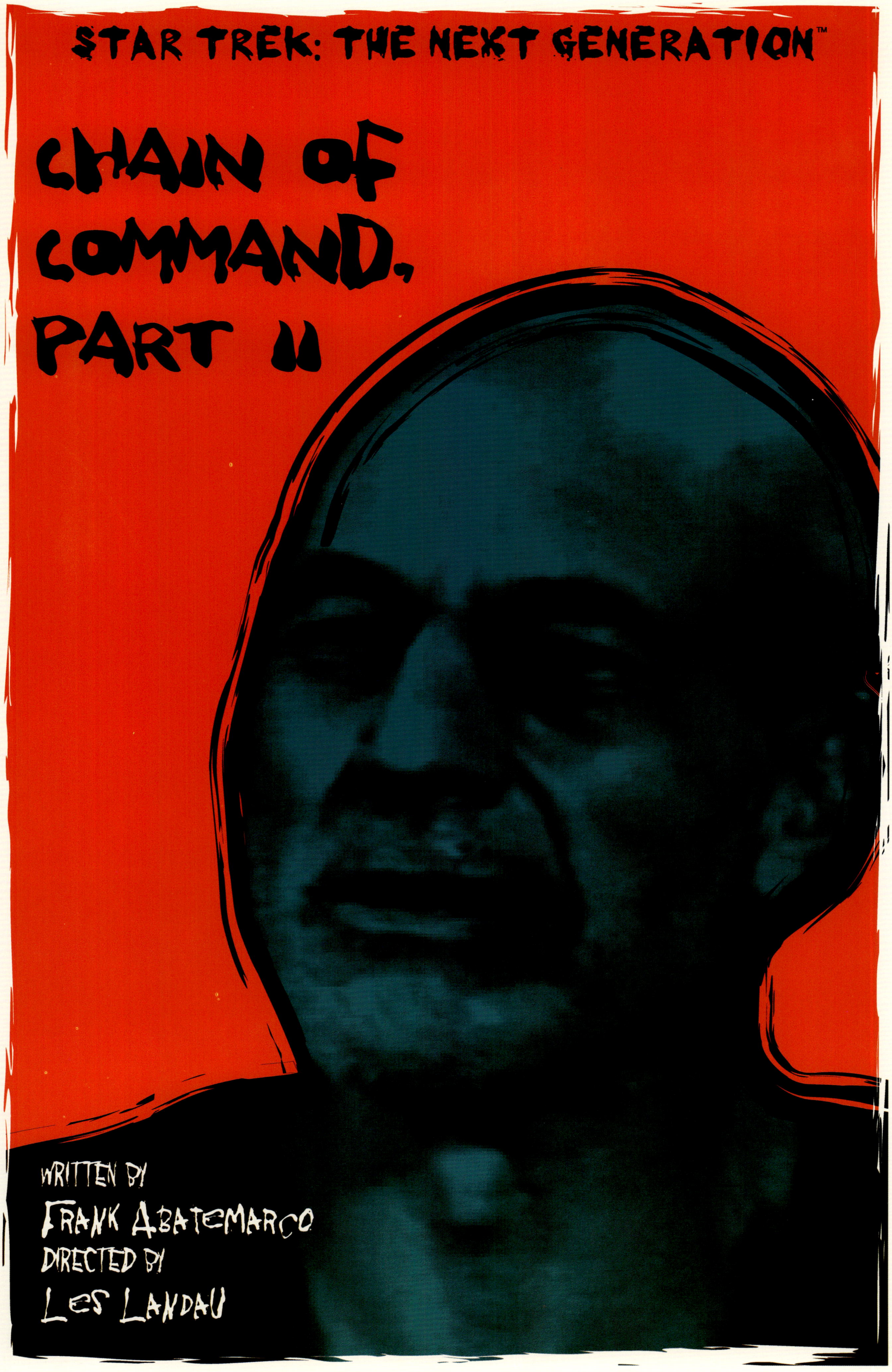
STAR TREK: THE NEXT GENERATION™
CHAIN OF COMMAND, PART II
WRITTEN BY
FRANK ABATEMARCO
DIRECTED BY
LES LANDAU

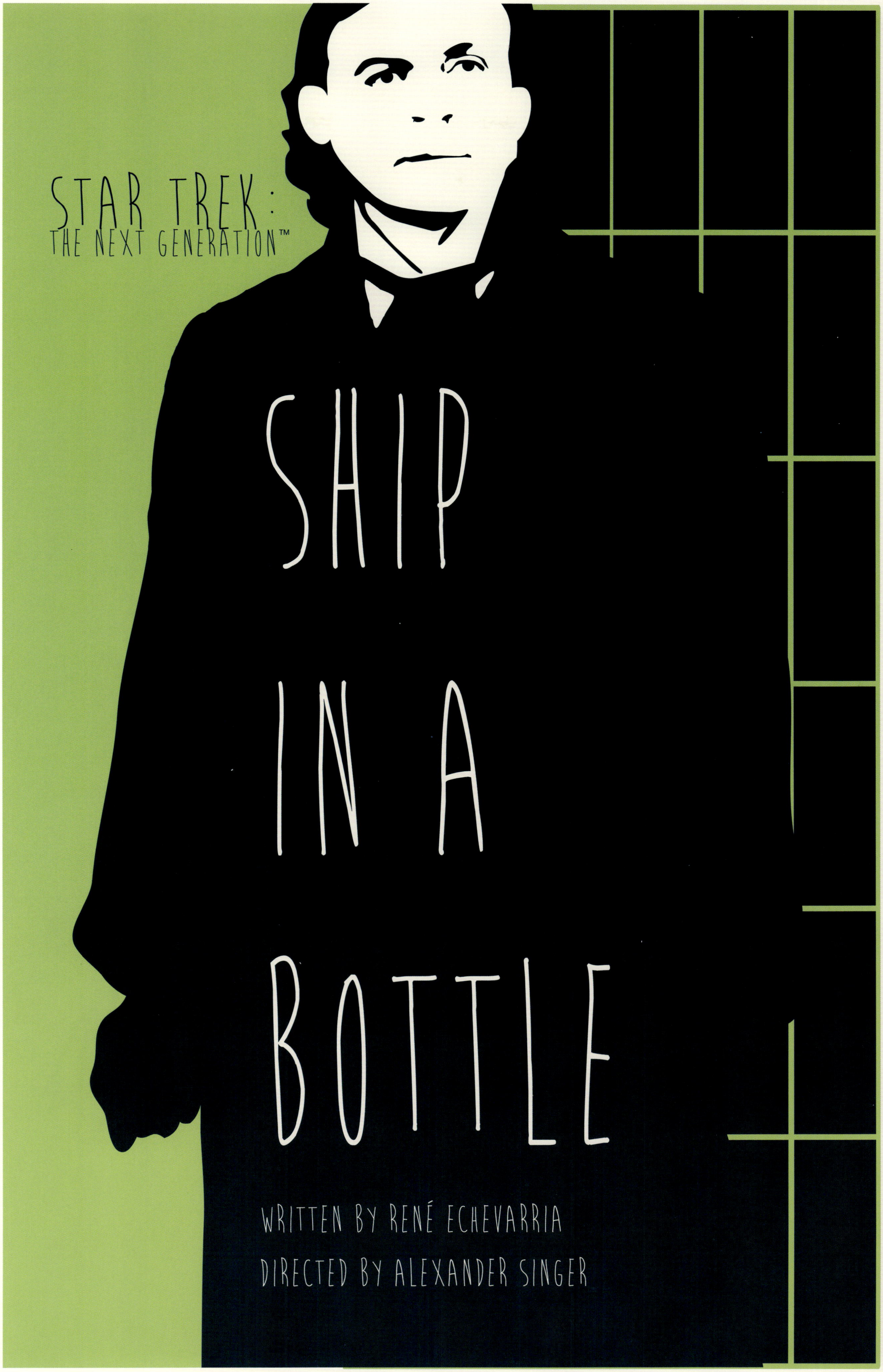
STAR TREK:
THE NEXT GENERATION™
SHIP
IN A
BOTTLE
WRITTEN BY RENÉ ECHEVARRIA
DIRECTED BY ALEXANDER SINGER

STAR TREK:
THE NEXT GENERATION™

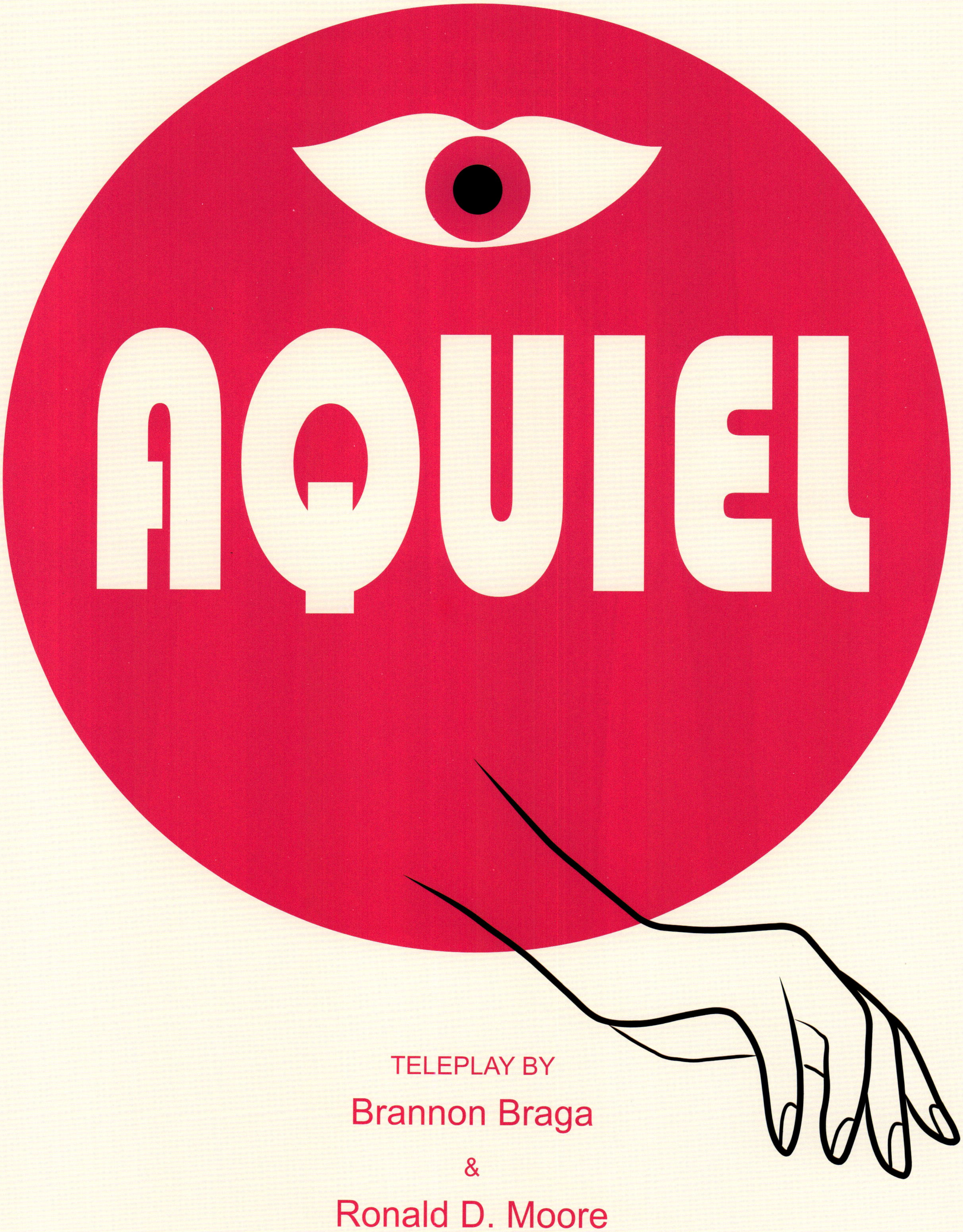

TELEPLAY BY

Brannon Braga

&

Ronald D. Moore

STORY BY

Jeri Taylor

DIRECTED BY

Cliff Bole

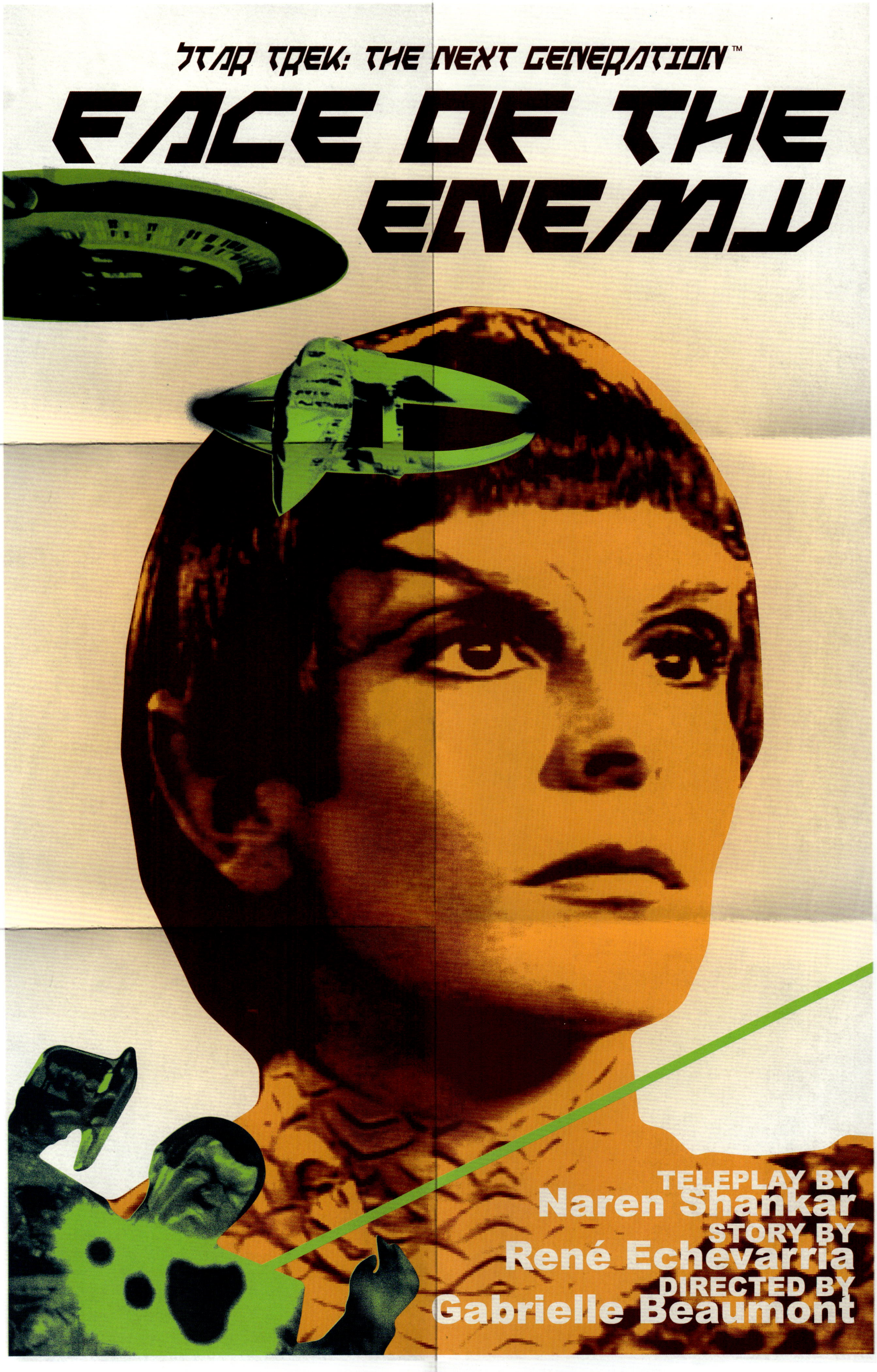
STAR TREK: THE NEXT GENERATION™
FACE OF THE ENEMY
TELEPLAY BY
Naren Shankar
STORY BY
René Echevarria
DIRECTED BY
Gabrielle Beaumont

STAR TREK: THE NEXT GENERATION™

TAPESTRY

WRITTEN BY

RONALD D. MOORE

DIRECTED BY

LES LANDAU

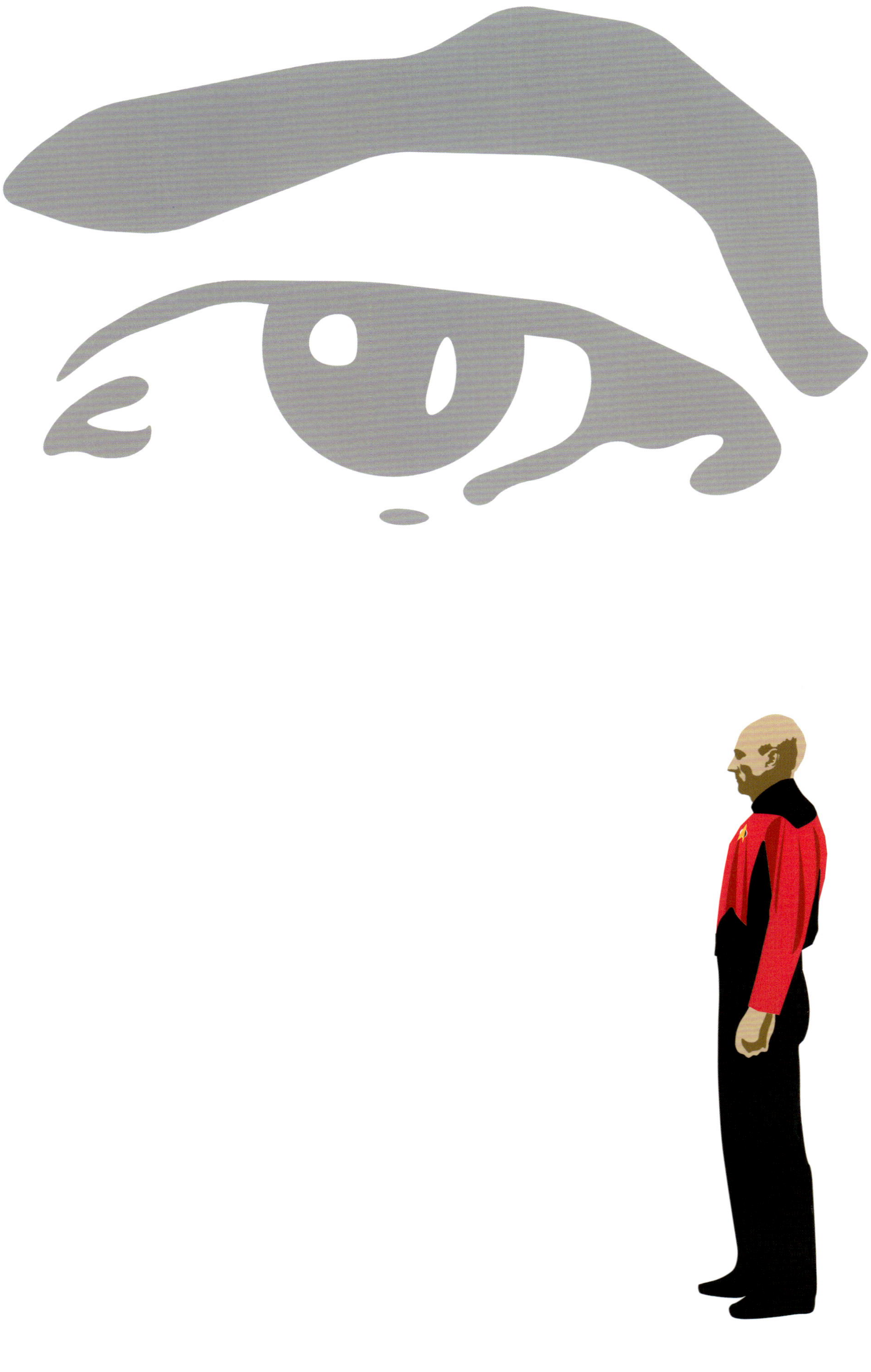

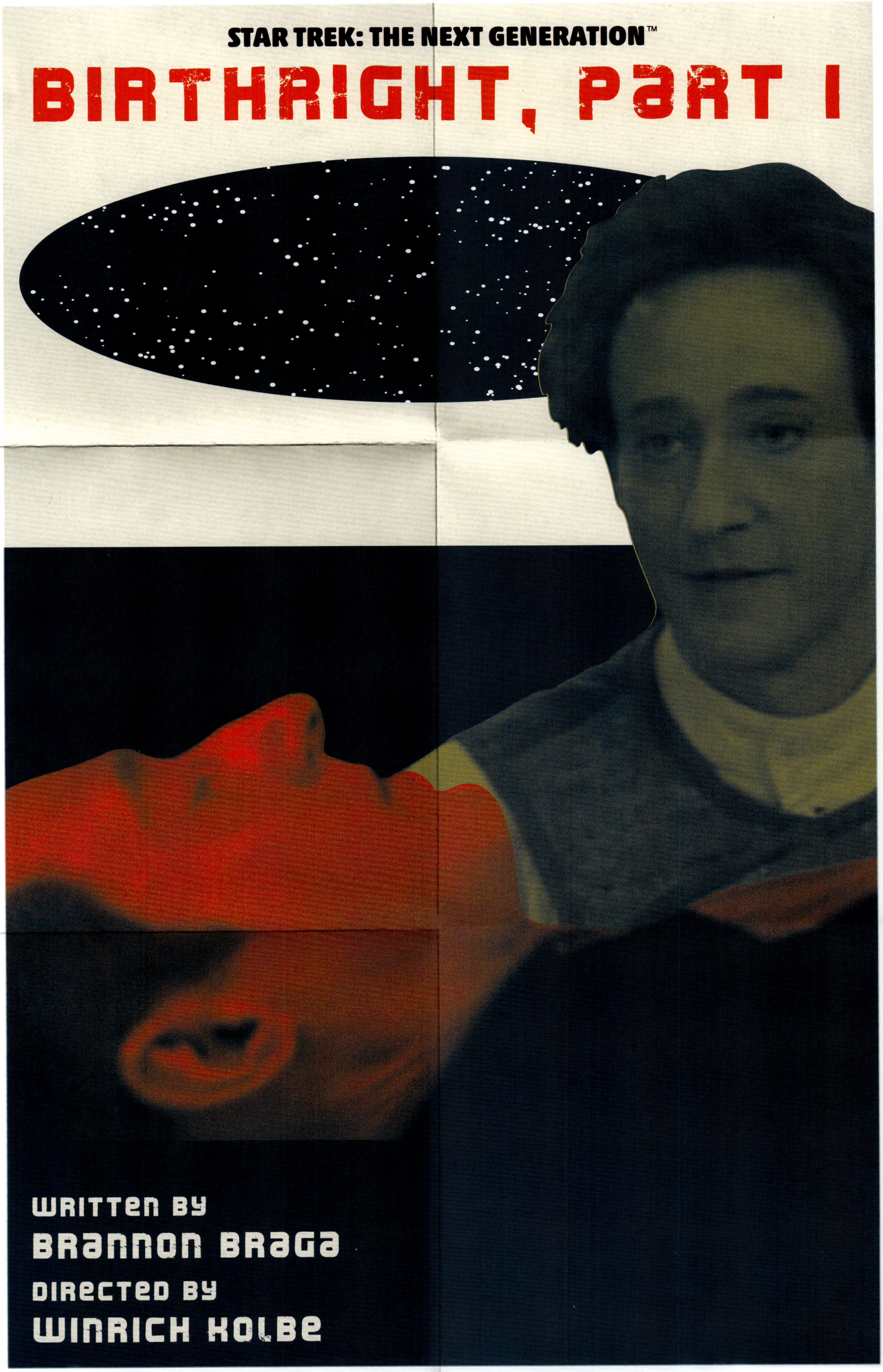
STAR TREK: THE NEXT GENERATION™
BIRTHRIGHT, PART I
WRITTEN BY
BRANNON BRAGA
DIRECTED BY
WINRICH KOLBE

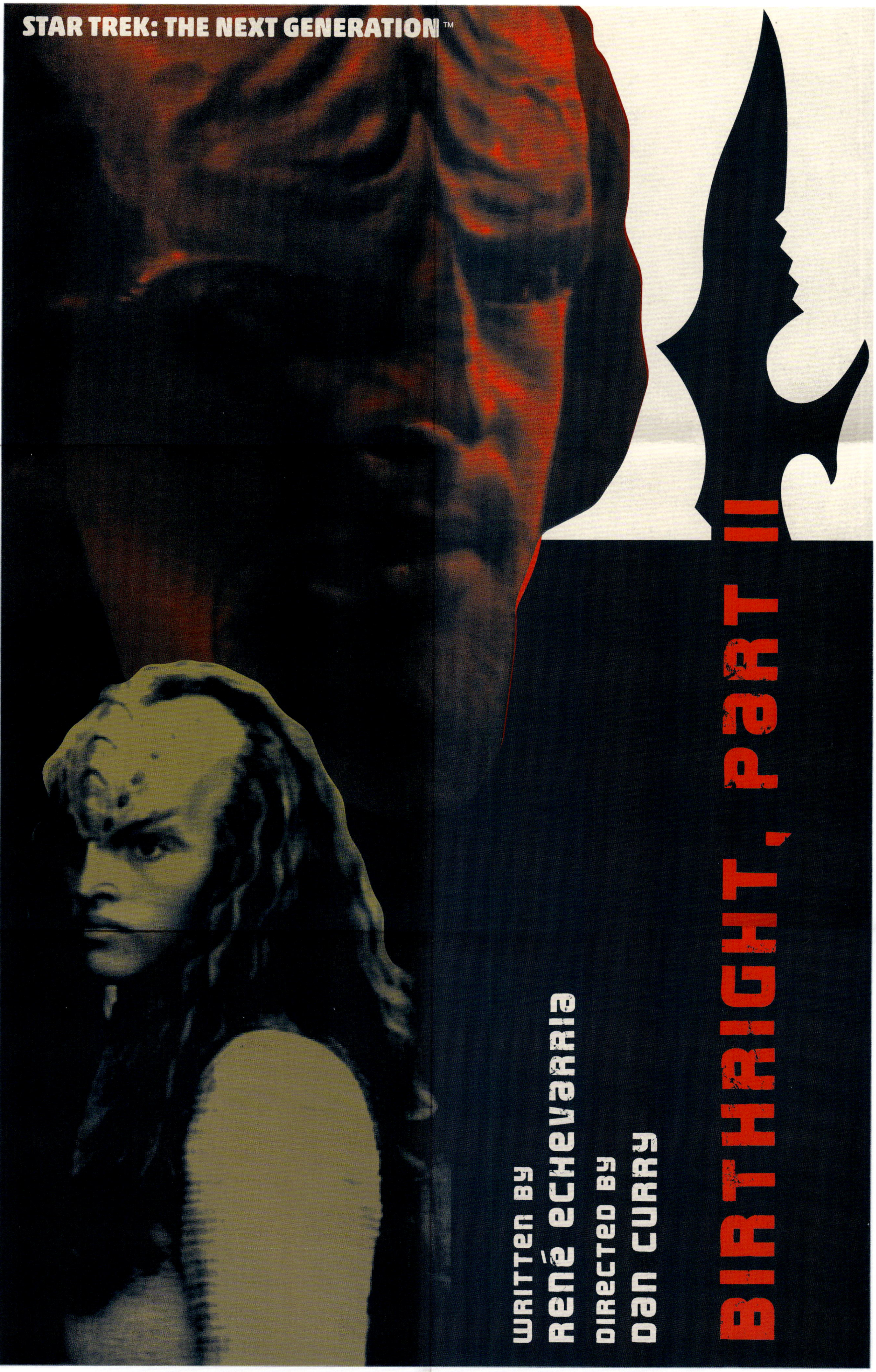
STAR TREK: THE NEXT GENERATION™
BIRTHRIGHT, PART II
WRITTEN BY
RENÉ ECHEVARRIA
DIRECTED BY
DAN CURRY

STAR TREK: THE NEXT GENERATION™

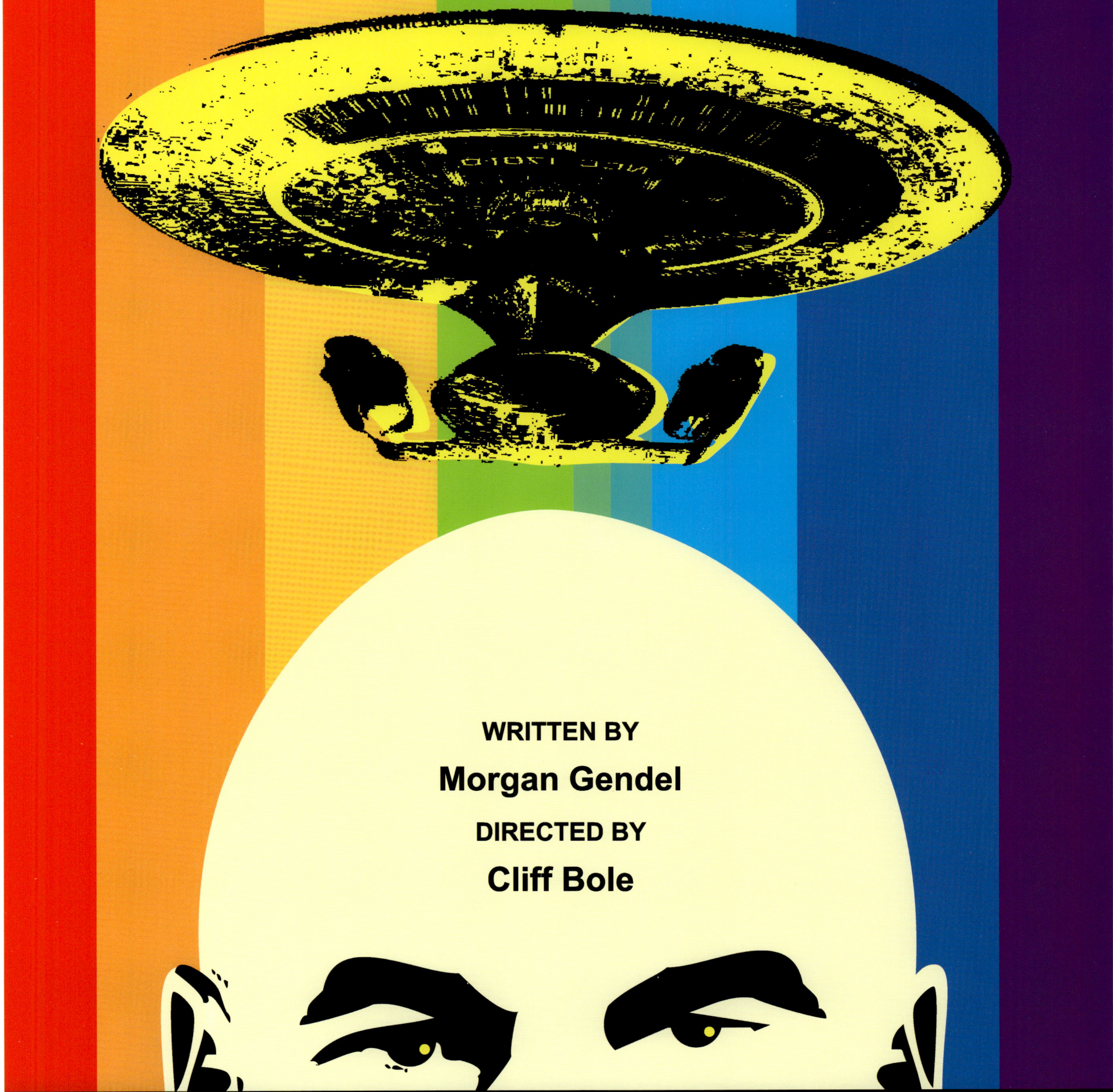

WRITTEN BY

Morgan Gendel

DIRECTED BY

Cliff Bole

STARSHIP MINE

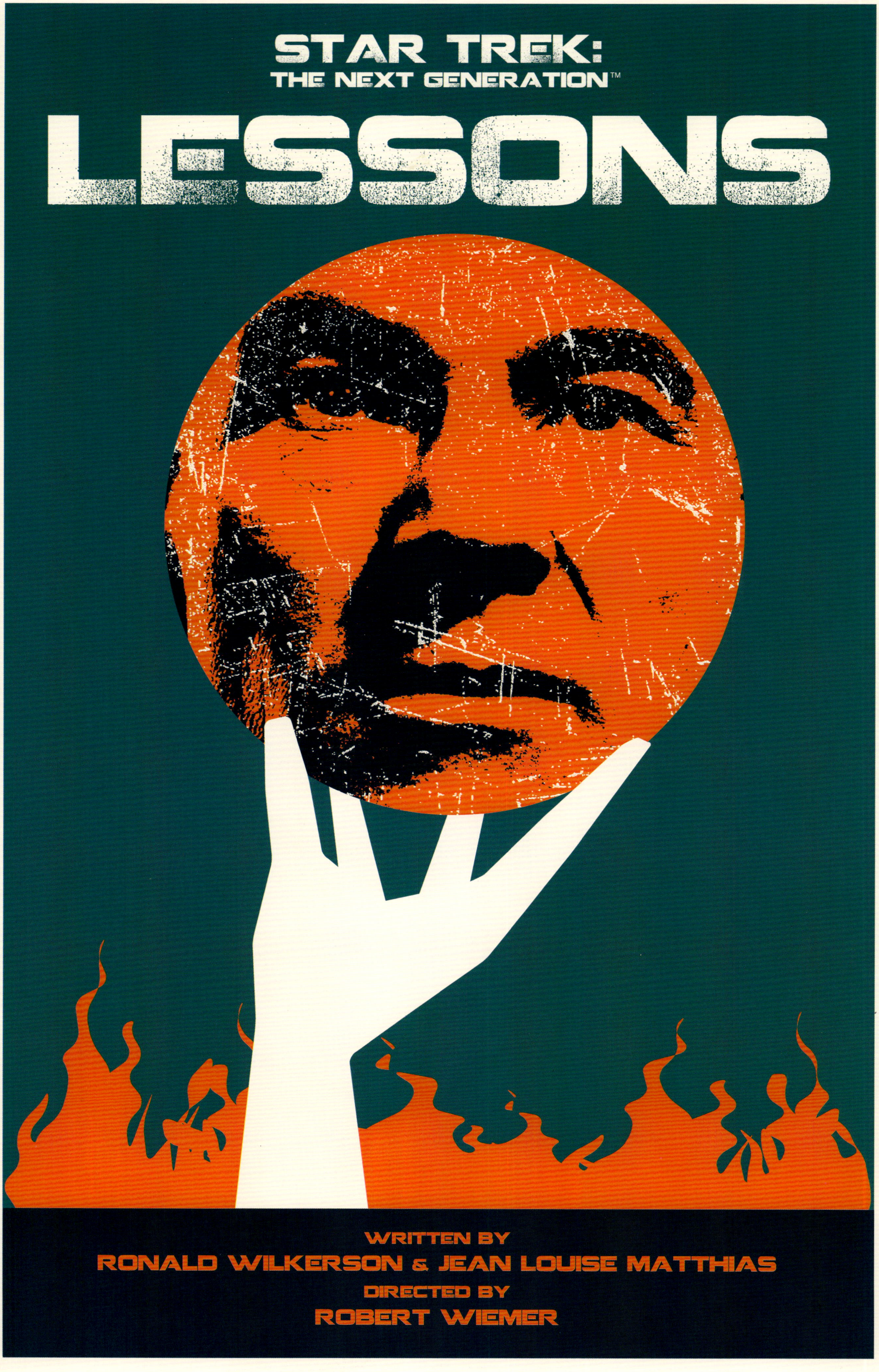
STAR TREK:
THE NEXT GENERATION™
LESSONS
WRITTEN BY
RONALD WILKERSON & JEAN LOUISE MATTHIAS
DIRECTED BY
ROBERT WIEMER

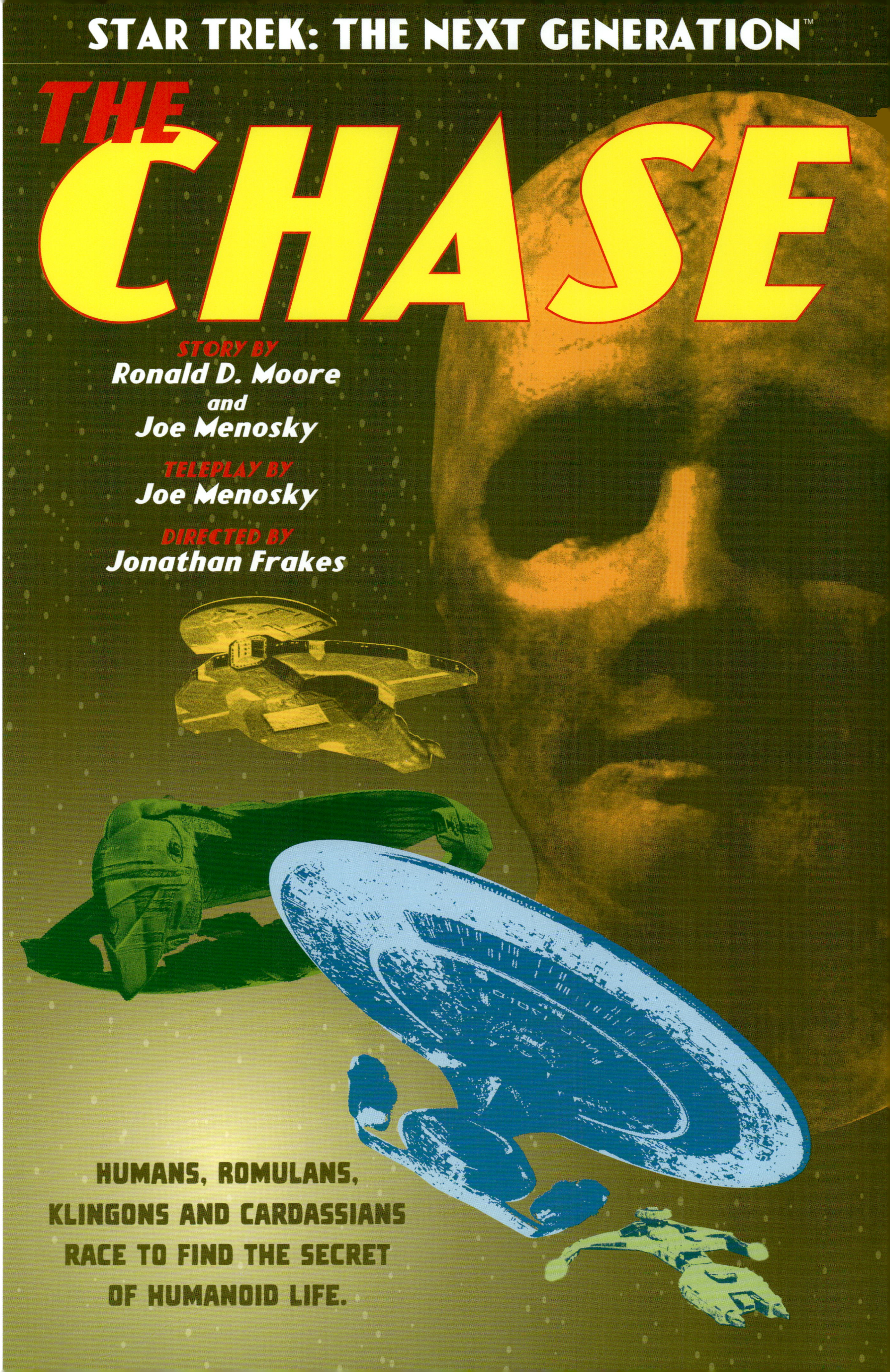
STAR TREK: THE NEXT GENERATION™
THE CHASE
STORY BY
Ronald D. Moore
and
Joe Menosky
TELEPLAY BY
Joe Menosky
DIRECTED BY
Jonathan Frakes
HUMANS, ROMULANS, KLINGONS AND CARDASSIANS RACE TO FIND THE SECRET OF HUMANOID LIFE.

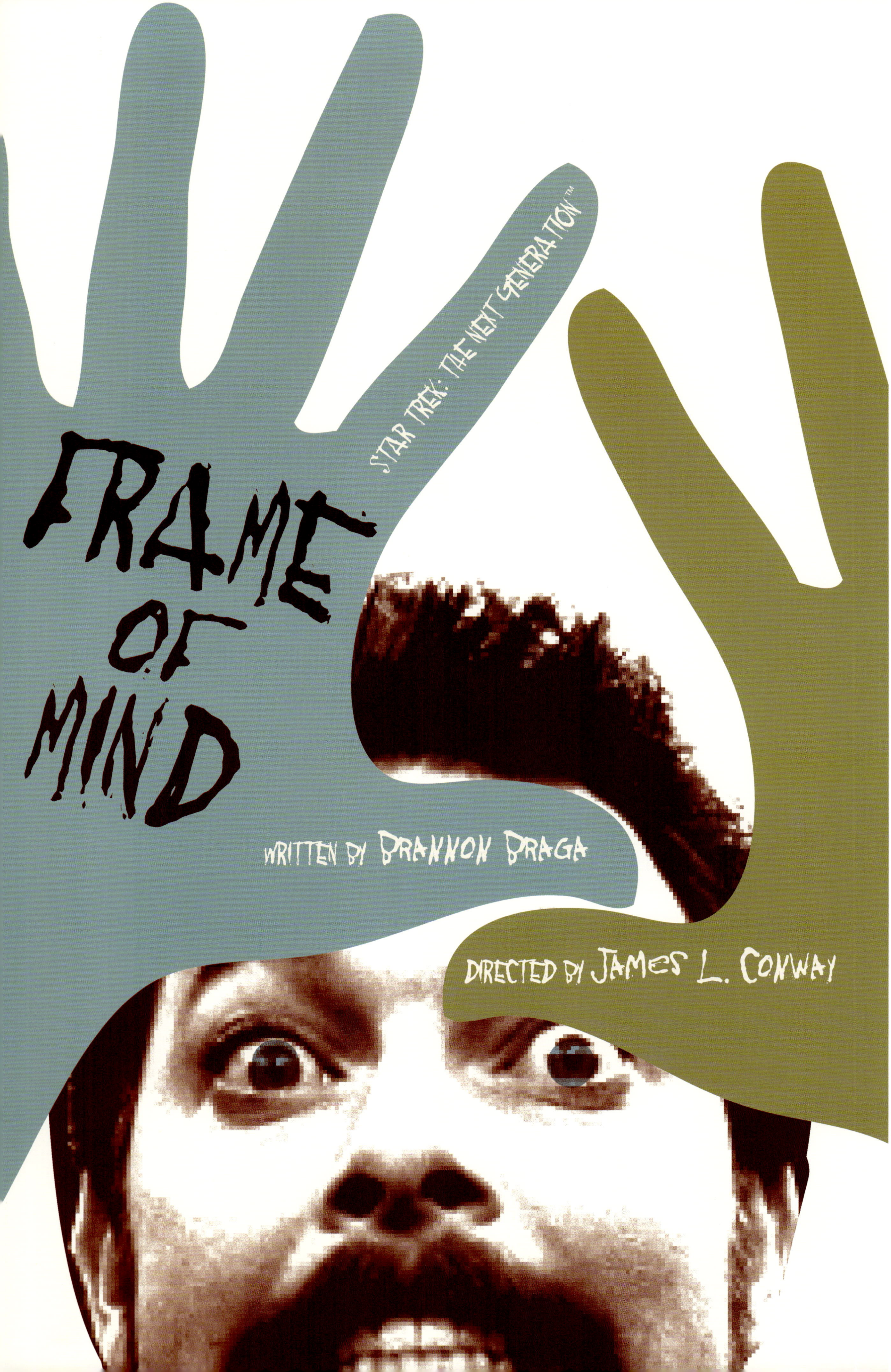
STAR TREK: THE NEXT GENERATION™
FRAME OF MIND
WRITTEN BY BRANNON BRAGA
DIRECTED BY JAMES L. CONWAY

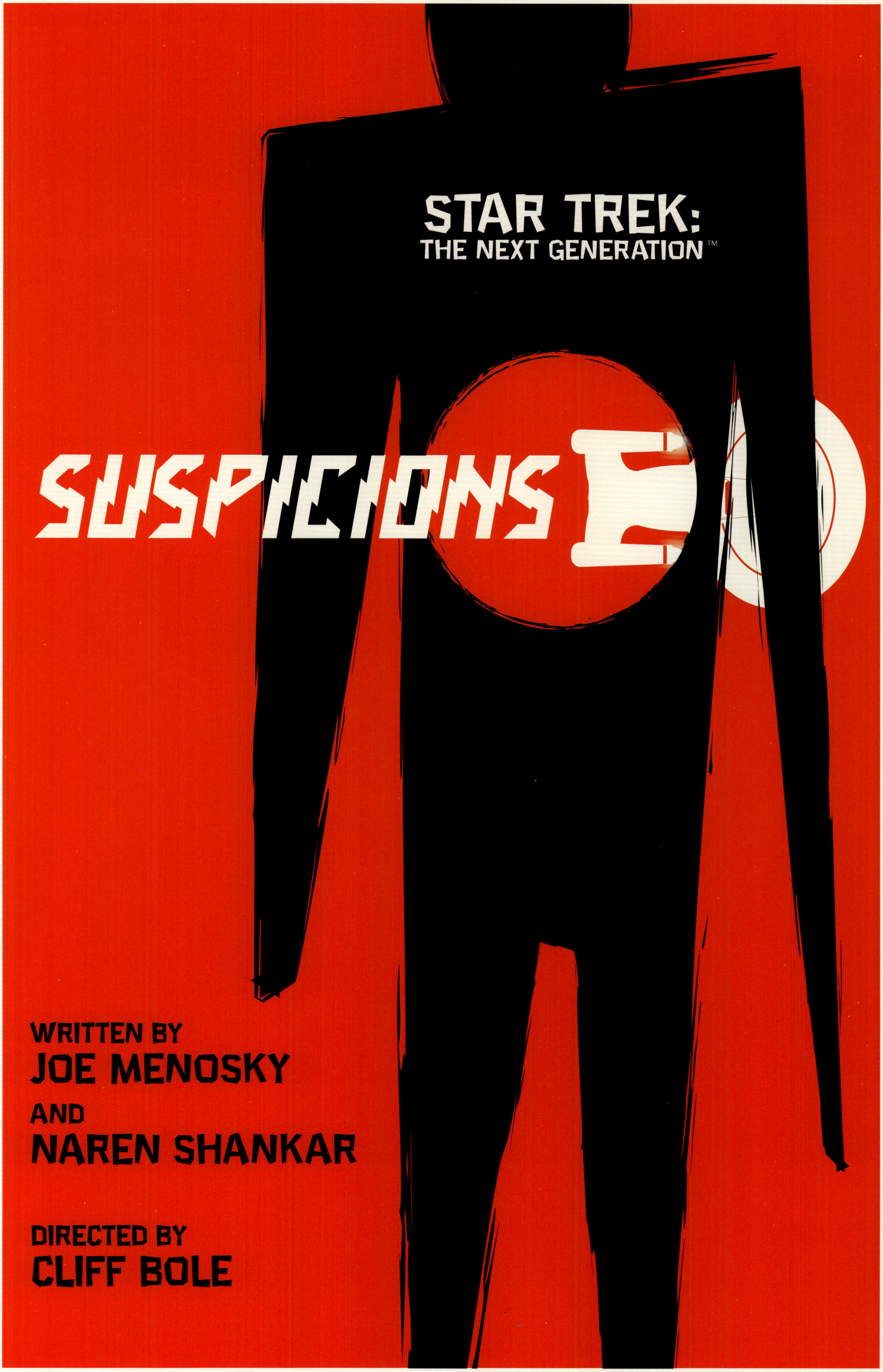
STAR TREK:
THE NEXT GENERATION™
SUSPICIONS
WRITTEN BY
JOE MENOSKY
AND
NAREN SHANKAR
DIRECTED BY
CLIFF BOLE

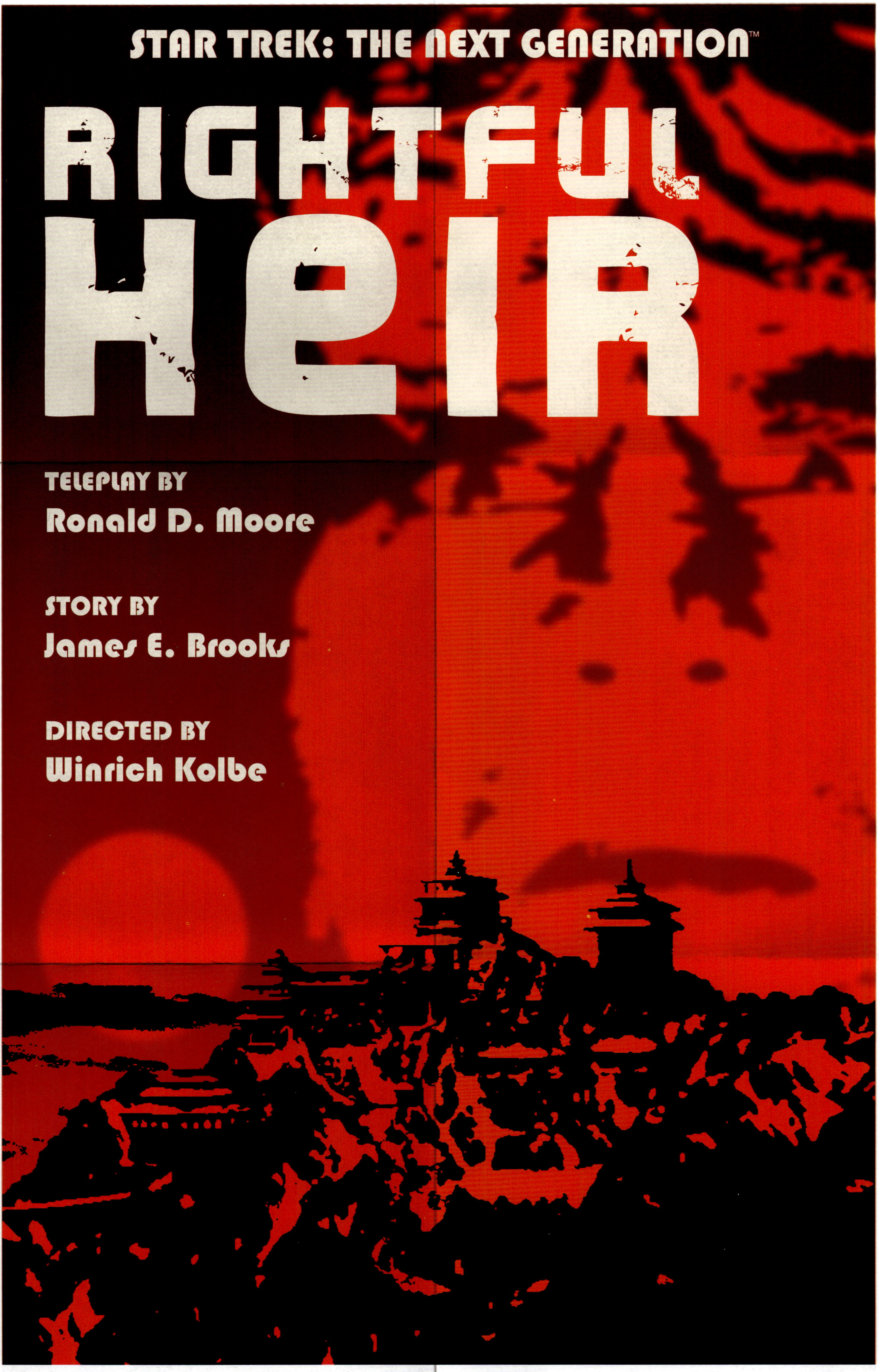
STAR TREK: THE NEXT GENERATION™
RIGHTFUL HEIR
TELEPLAY BY
Ronald D. Moore
STORY BY
James E. Brooks
DIRECTED BY
Winrich Kolbe

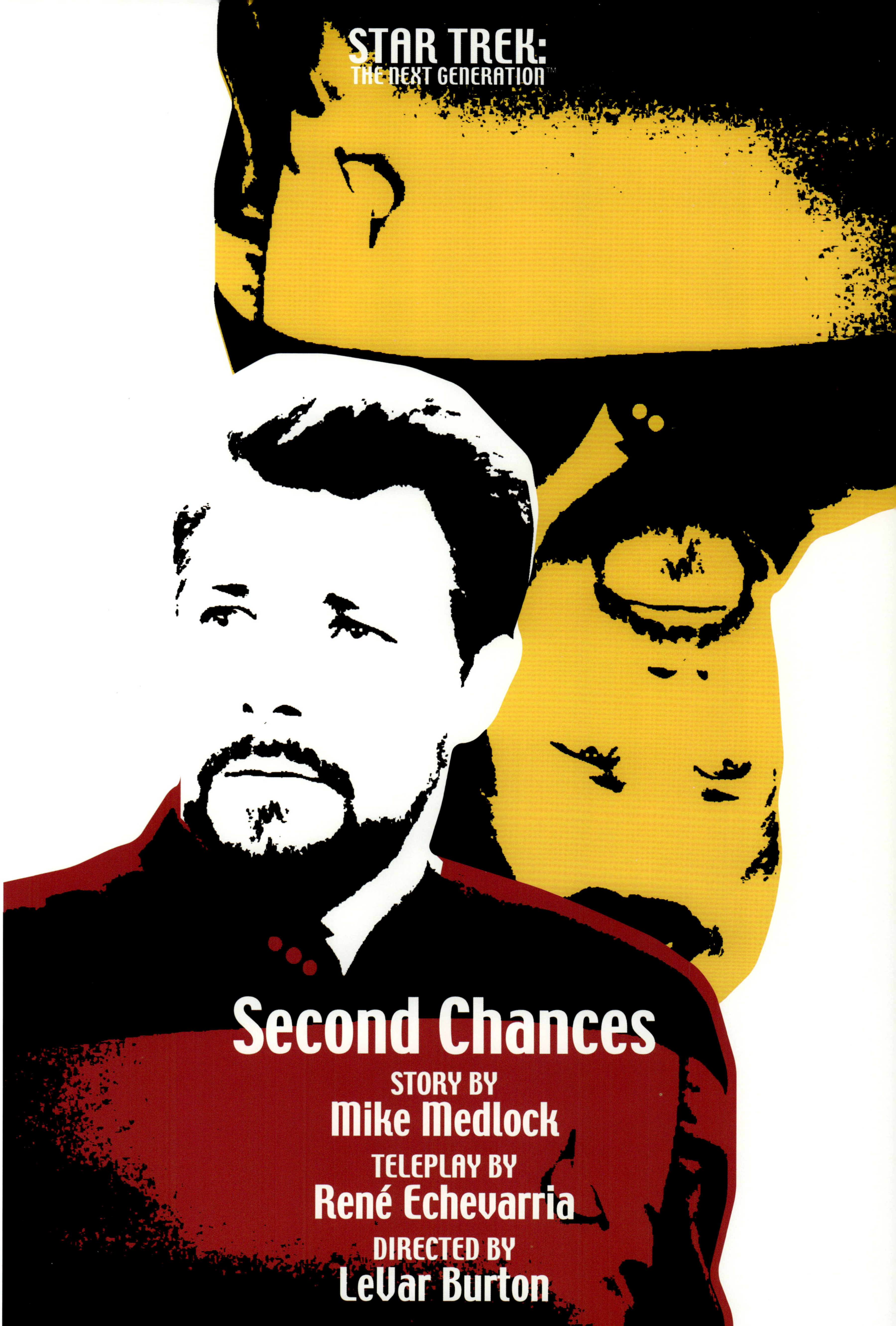
STAR TREK:
THE NEXT GENERATION™
Second Chances
STORY BY
Mike Medlock
TELEPLAY BY
René Echevarria
DIRECTED BY
LeVar Burton

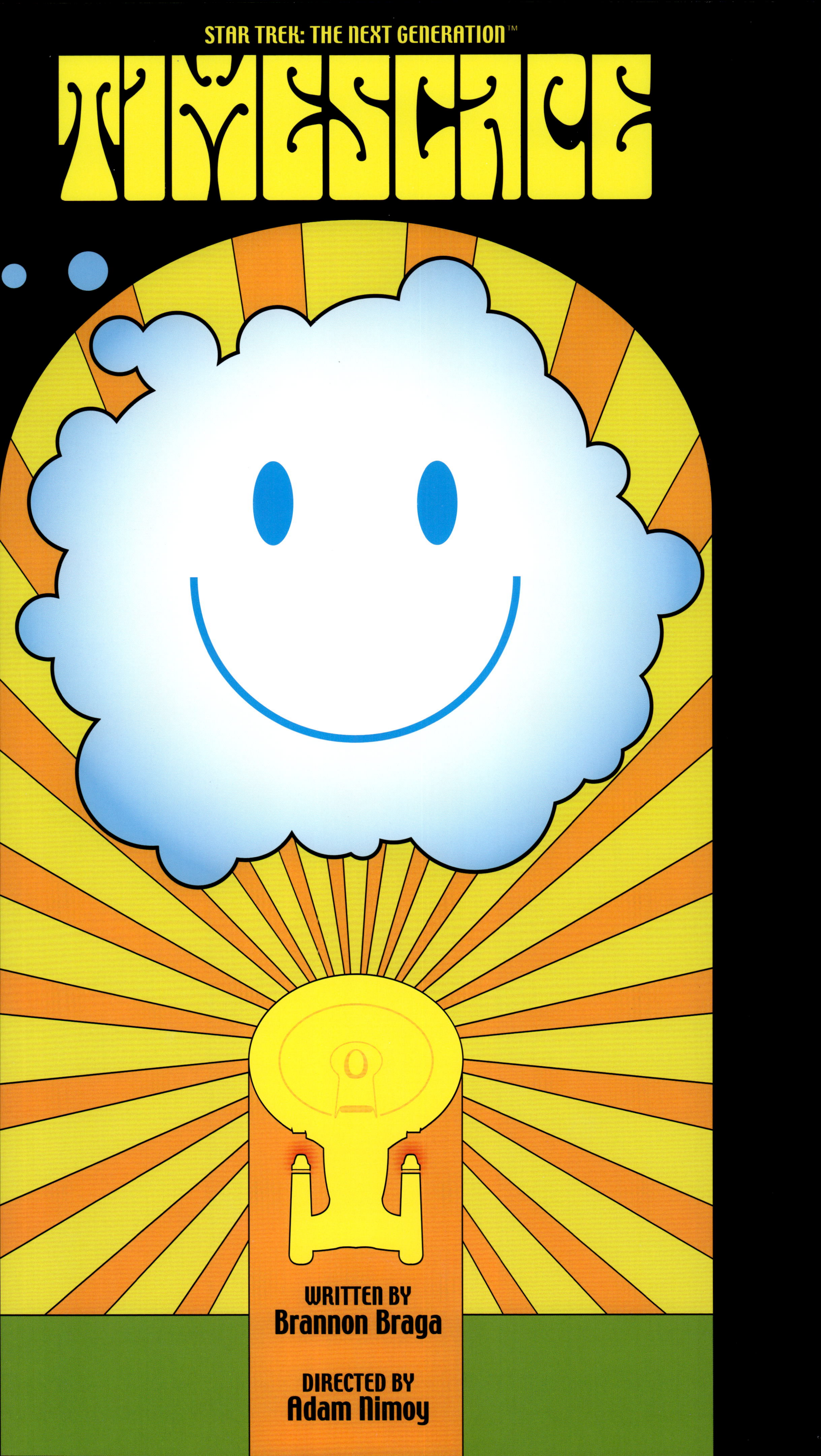
STAR TREK: THE NEXT GENERATION™
TIMESCAPE
WRITTEN BY
Brannon Braga
DIRECTED BY
Adam Nimoy

STAR TREK:

THE NEXT GENERATION™

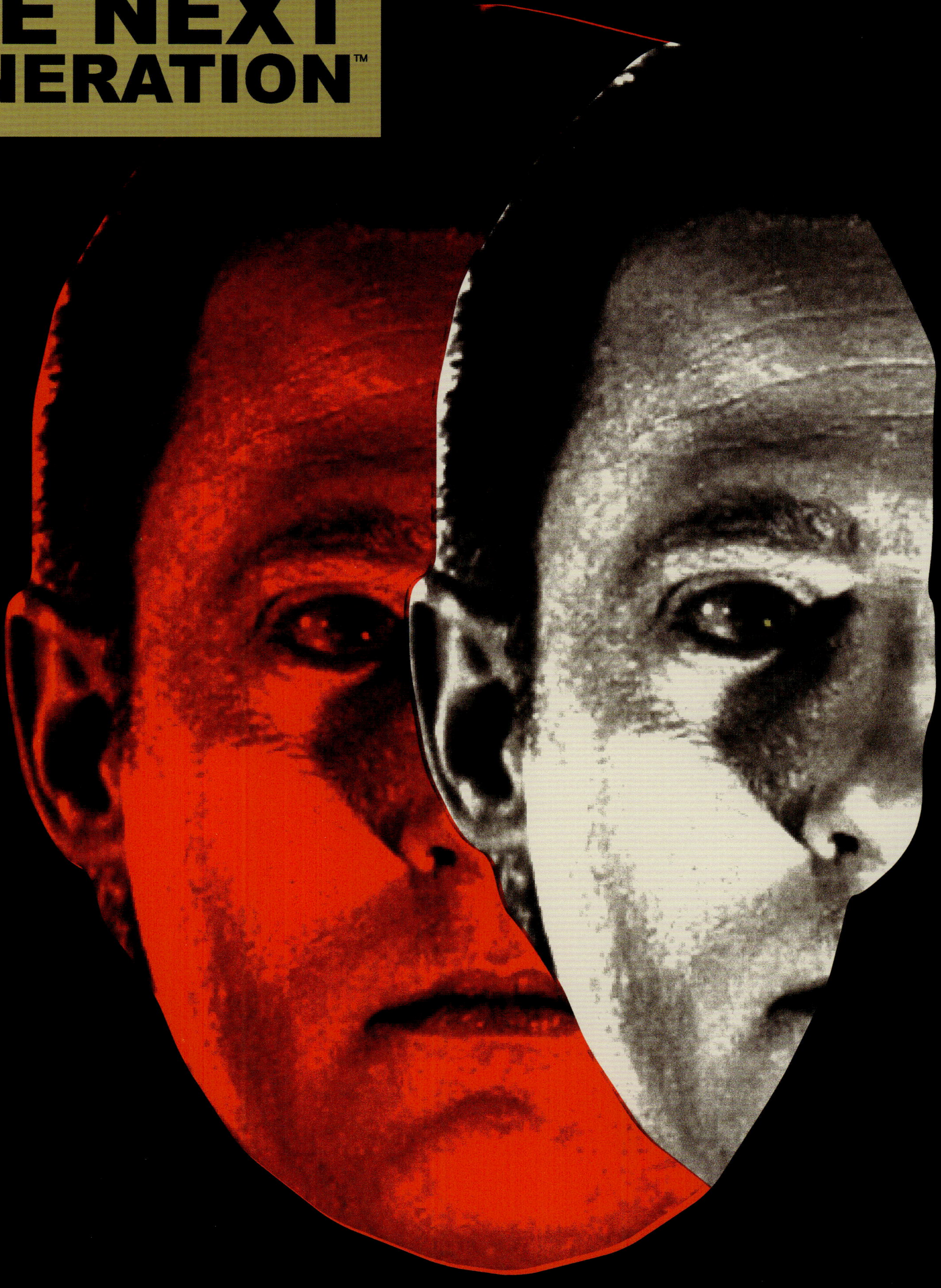

DESCENT, PART I

STORY BY Jeri Taylor TELEPLAY BY Ronald D. Moore DIRECTED BY Alexander Singer

Season Seven

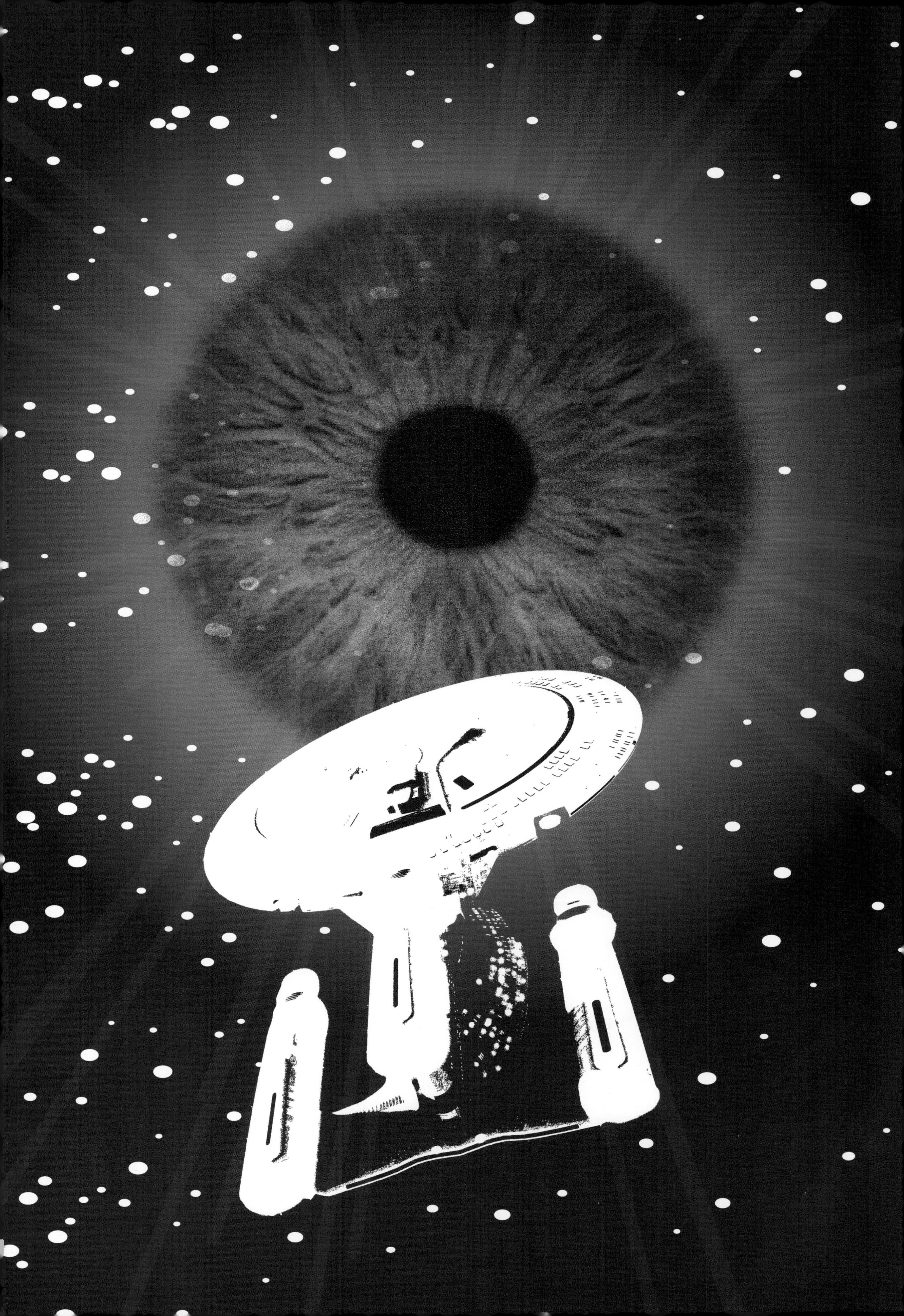

STAR TREK: THE NEXT GENERATION™

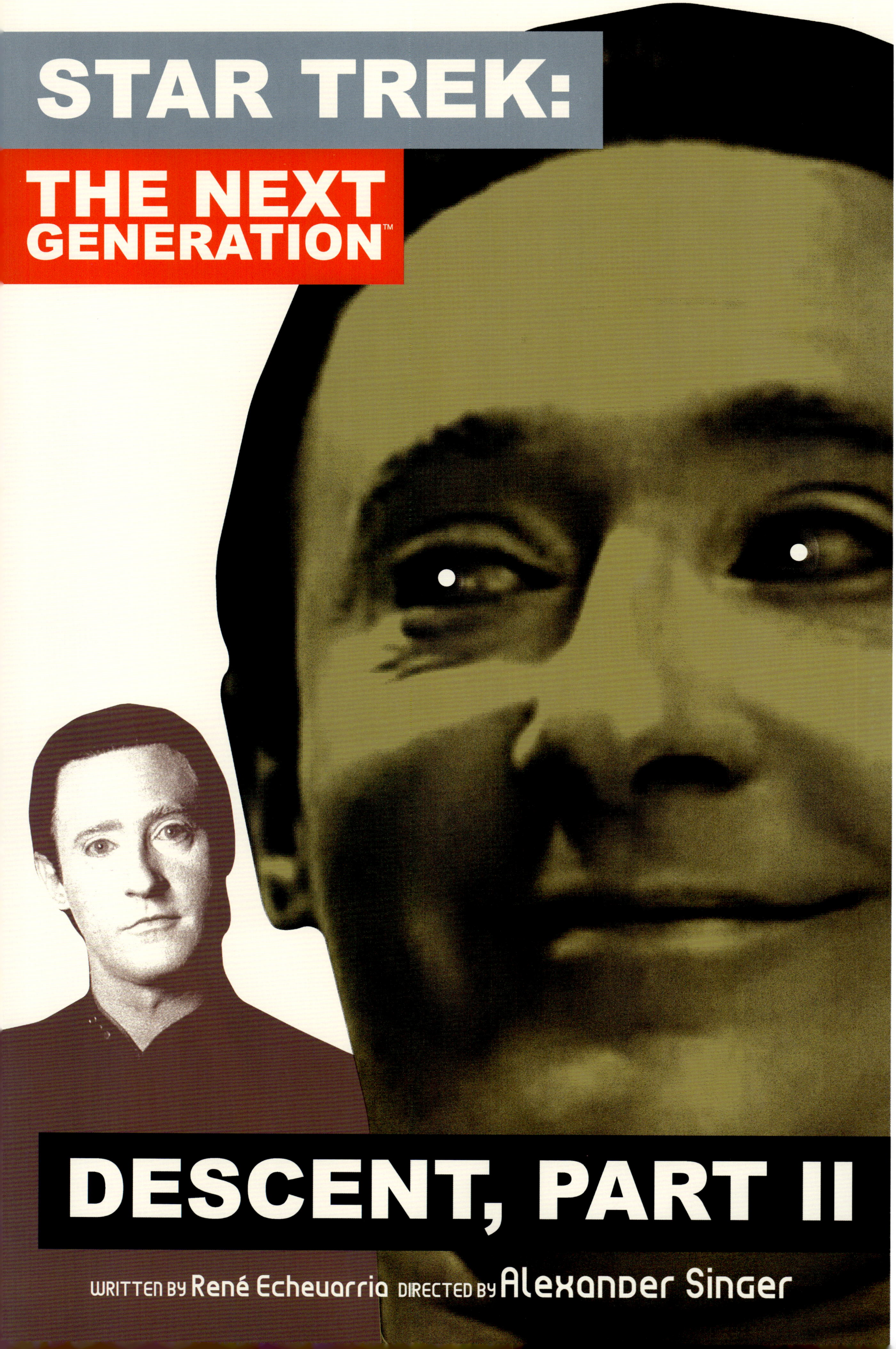

DESCENT, PART II

WRITTEN BY René Echevarria DIRECTED BY Alexander Singer

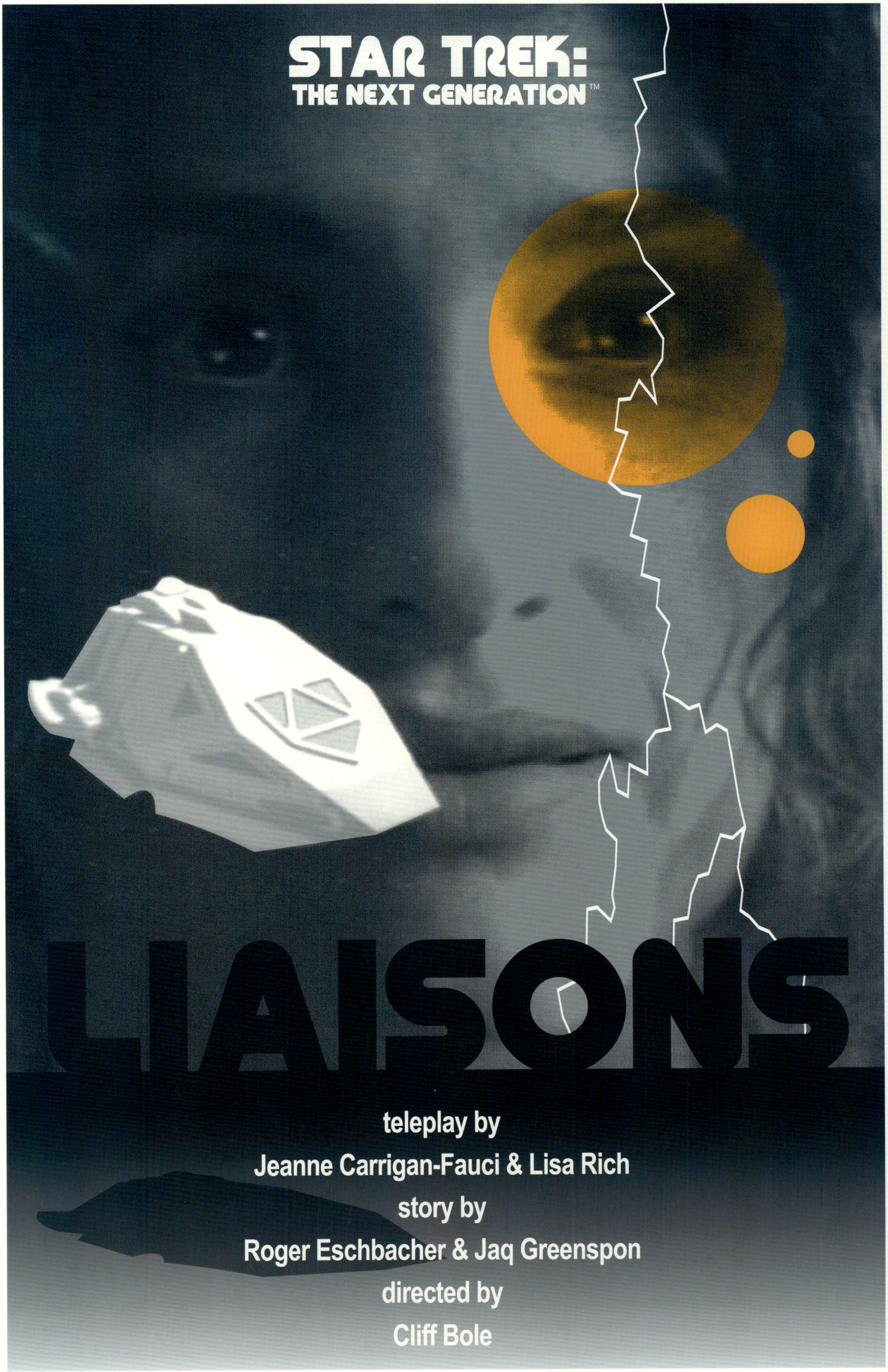
STAR TREK:
THE NEXT GENERATION™
LIAISONS
teleplay by
Jeanne Carrigan-Fauci & Lisa Rich
story by
Roger Eschbacher & Jaq Greenspon
directed by
Cliff Bole

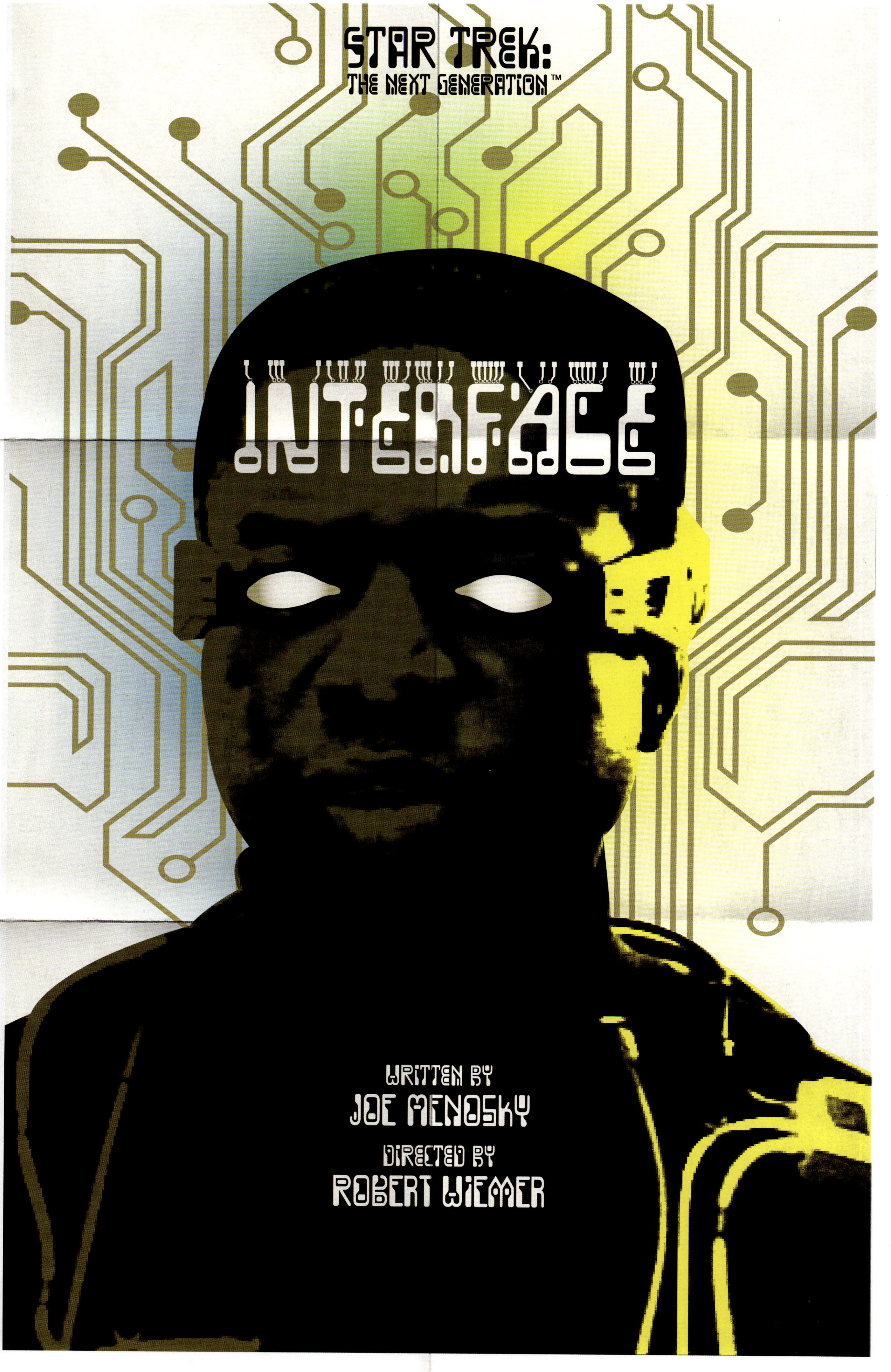
STAR TREK:
THE NEXT GENERATION™
INTERFACE
WRITTEN BY
JOE MENOSKY
DIRECTED BY
ROBERT WIEMER

STAR TREK:
THE NEXT GENERATION™

GAMBIT PART I

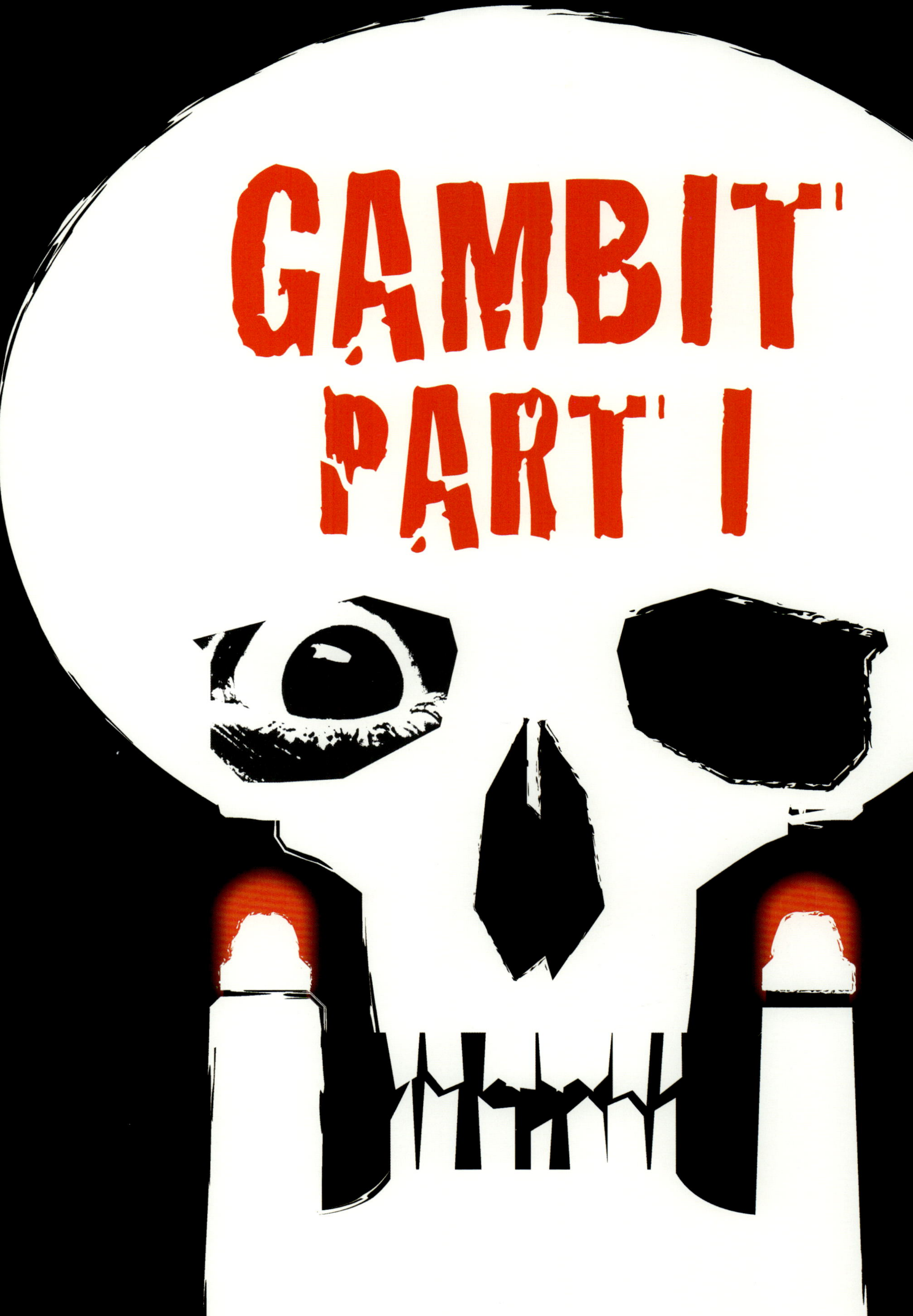

TELEPLAY BY NAREN SHANKAR

STORY BY CHRISTOPHER HATTON and NAREN SHA

DIRECTED BY PETER LAURITSON

STAR TREK:
THE NEXT GENERATION™

GAMBIT PART II

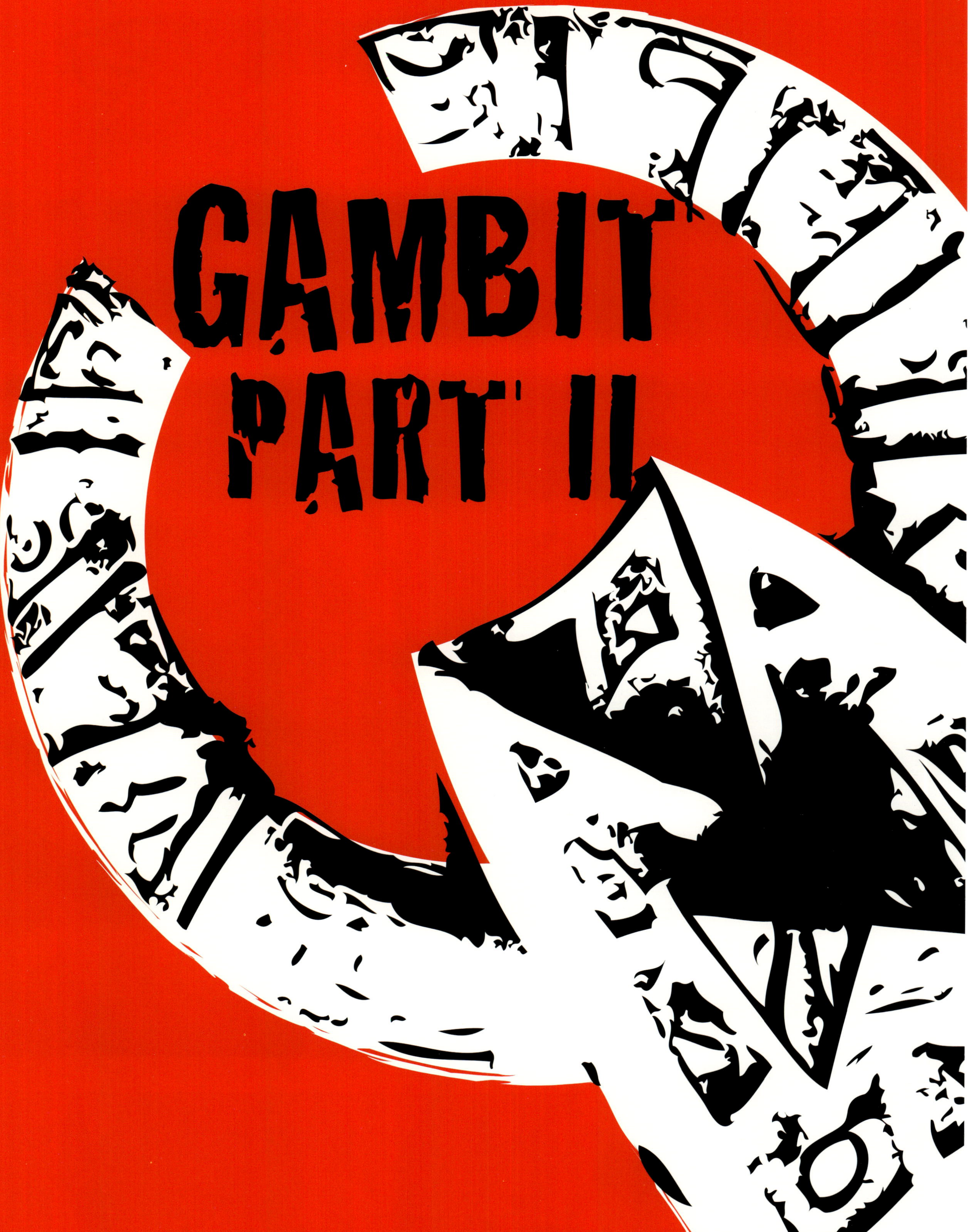

TELEPLAY BY RONALD D. MOORE

STORY BY NAREN SHANKAR

DIRECTED BY ALEXANDER SINGER

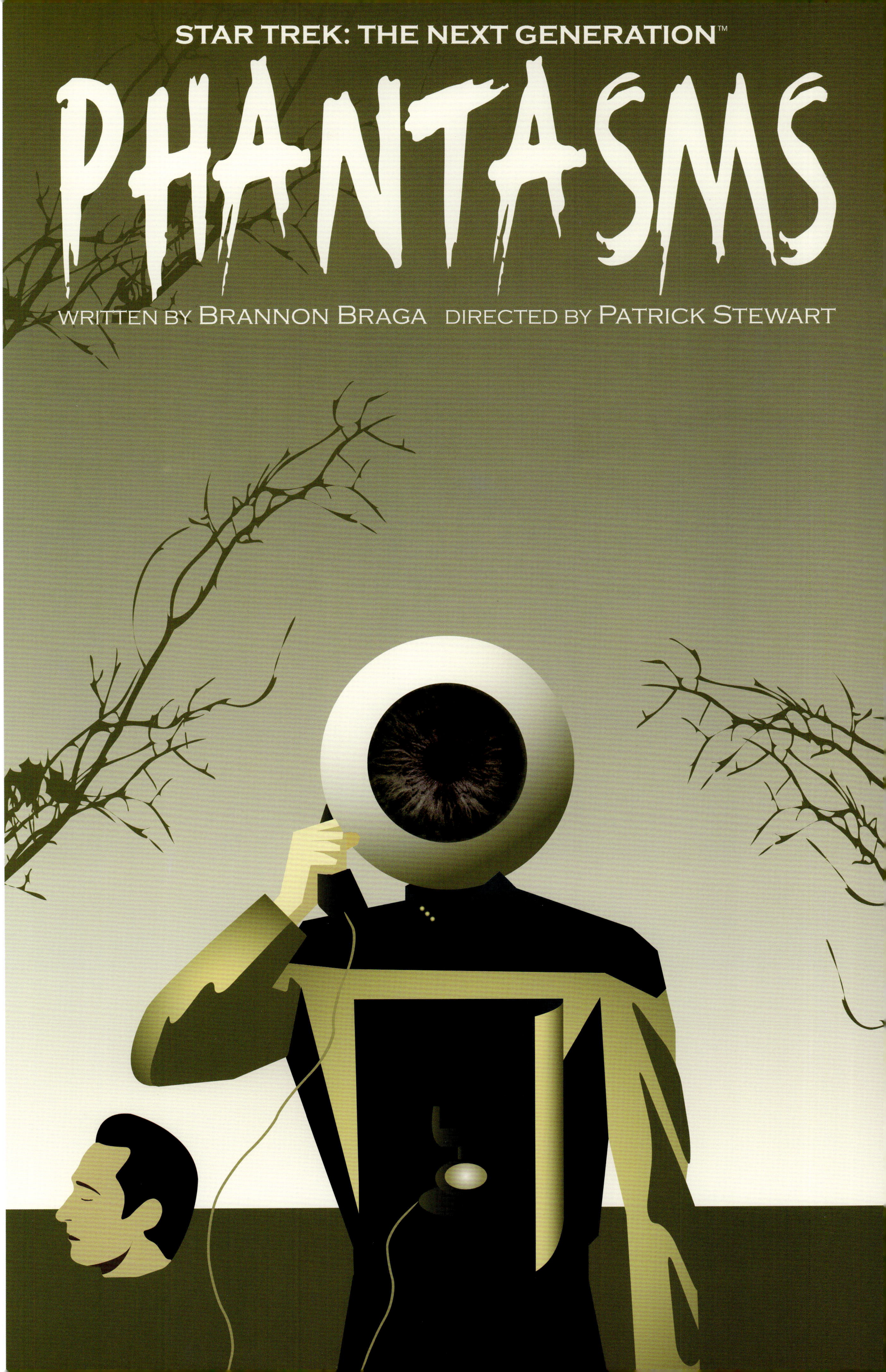
STAR TREK: THE NEXT GENERATION™
PHANTASMS
WRITTEN BY BRANNON BRAGA DIRECTED BY PATRICK STEWART

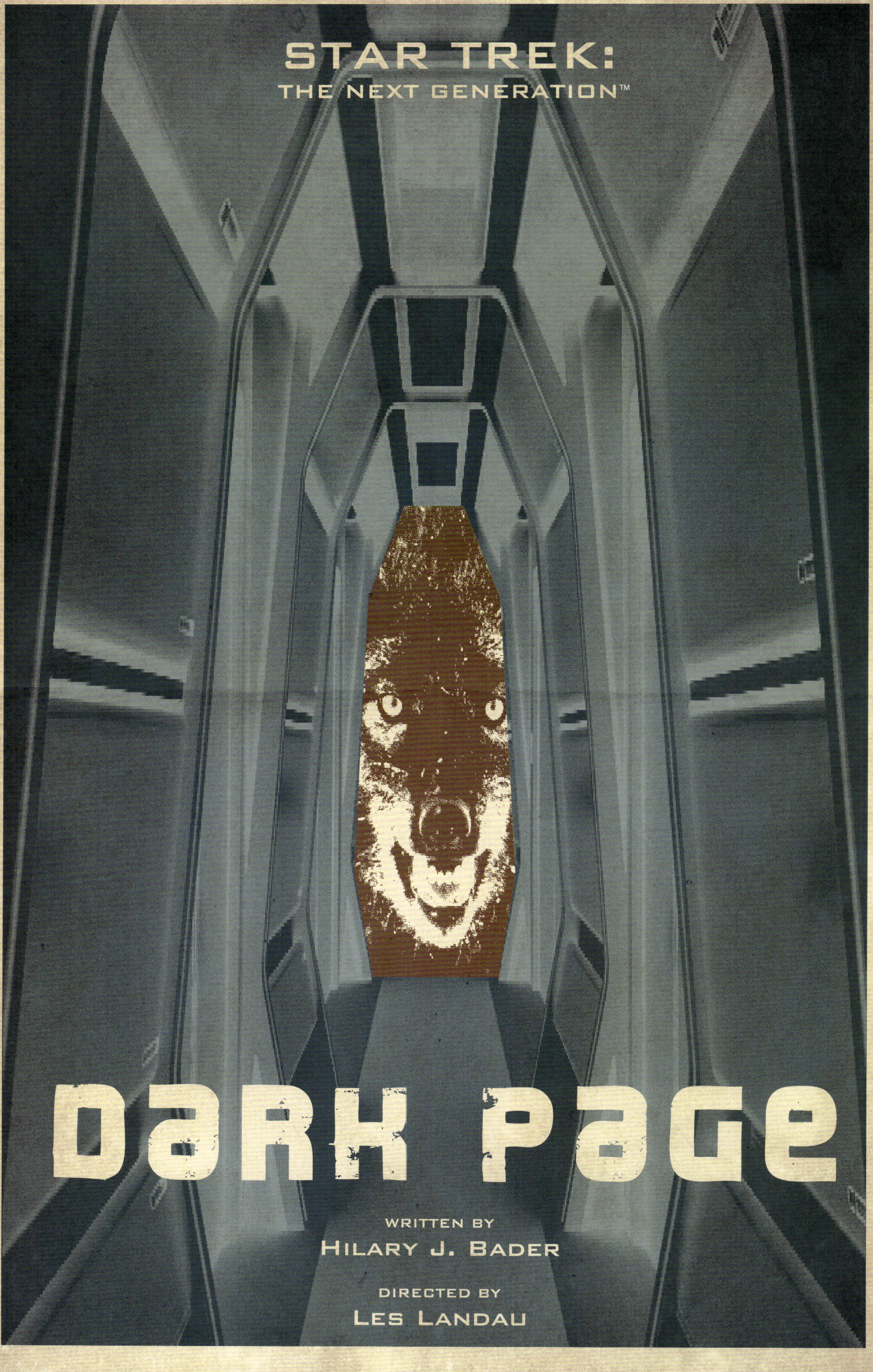
STAR TREK:
THE NEXT GENERATION™
DARK PAGE
WRITTEN BY
HILARY J. BADER
DIRECTED BY
LES LANDAU

STAR TREK:
THE NEXT GENERATION™

ATTACHED

WRITTEN BY
Nicholas Sagan

DIRECTED BY
Jonathan Frakes

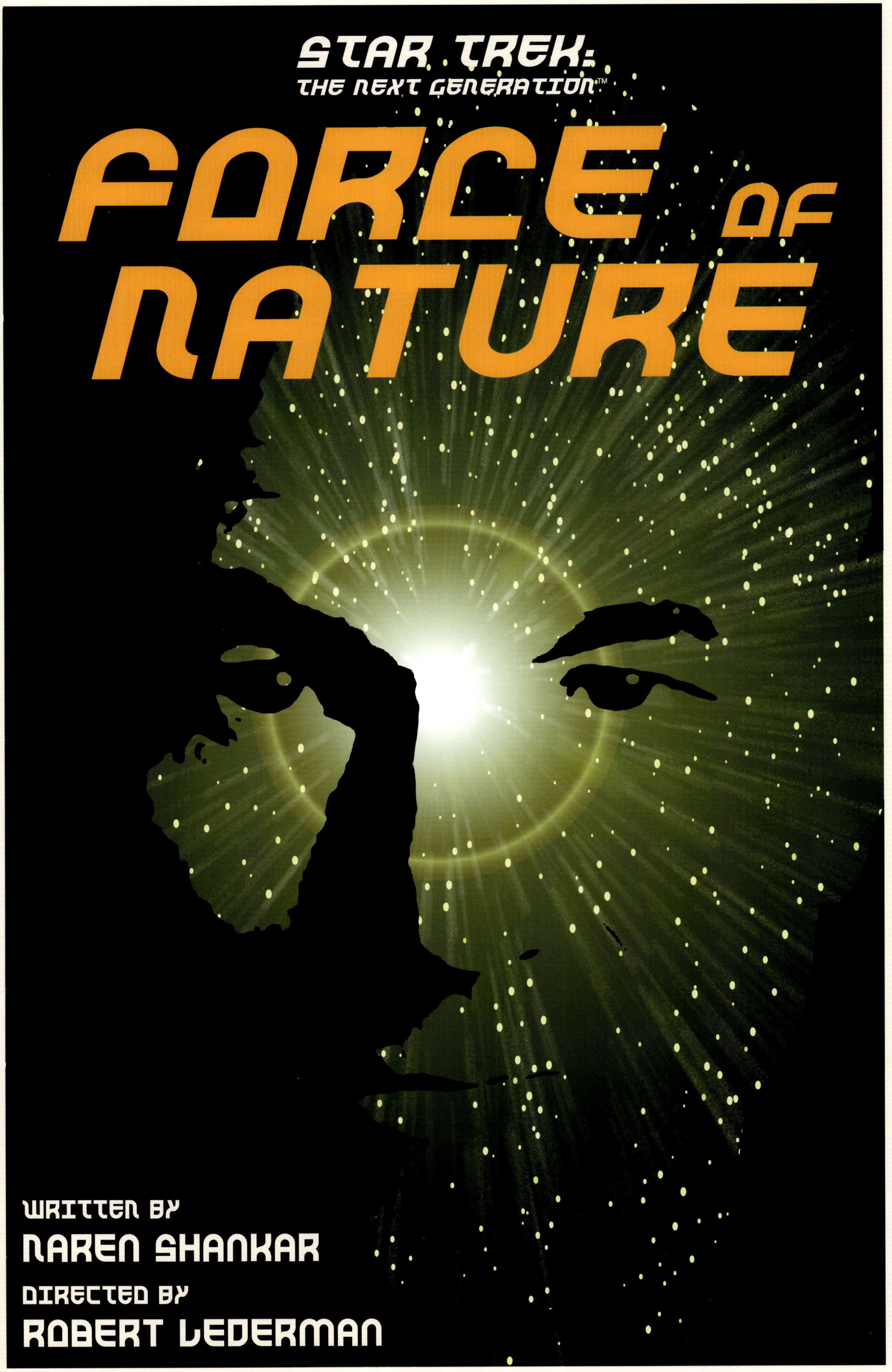
STAR TREK:
THE NEXT GENERATION™
FORCE OF NATURE
WRITTEN BY
NAREN SHANKAR
DIRECTED BY
ROBERT LEDERMAN

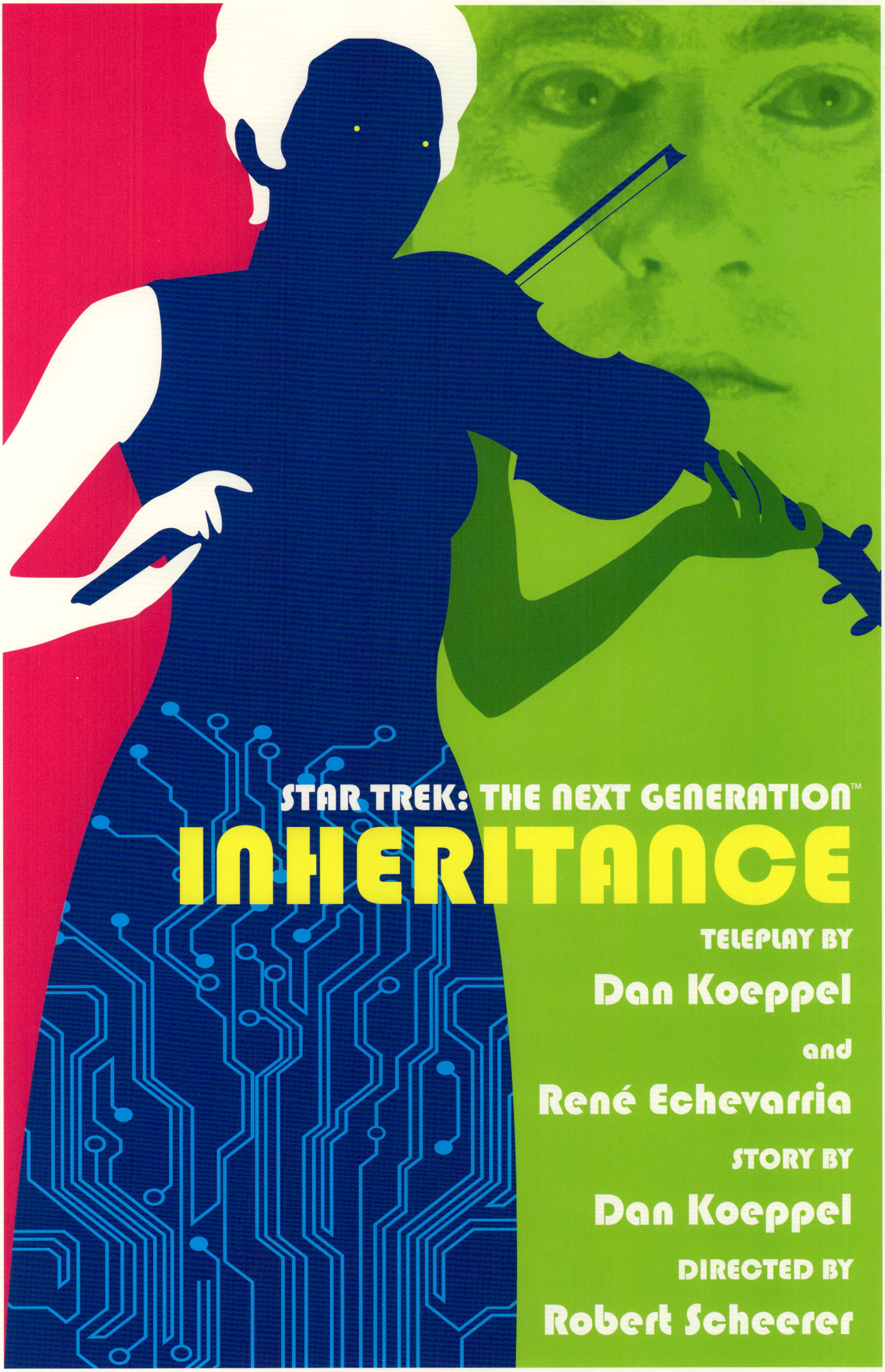
STAR TREK: THE NEXT GENERATION™
INHERITANCE
TELEPLAY BY
Dan Koeppel
and
René Echevarria
STORY BY
Dan Koeppel
DIRECTED BY
Robert Scheerer

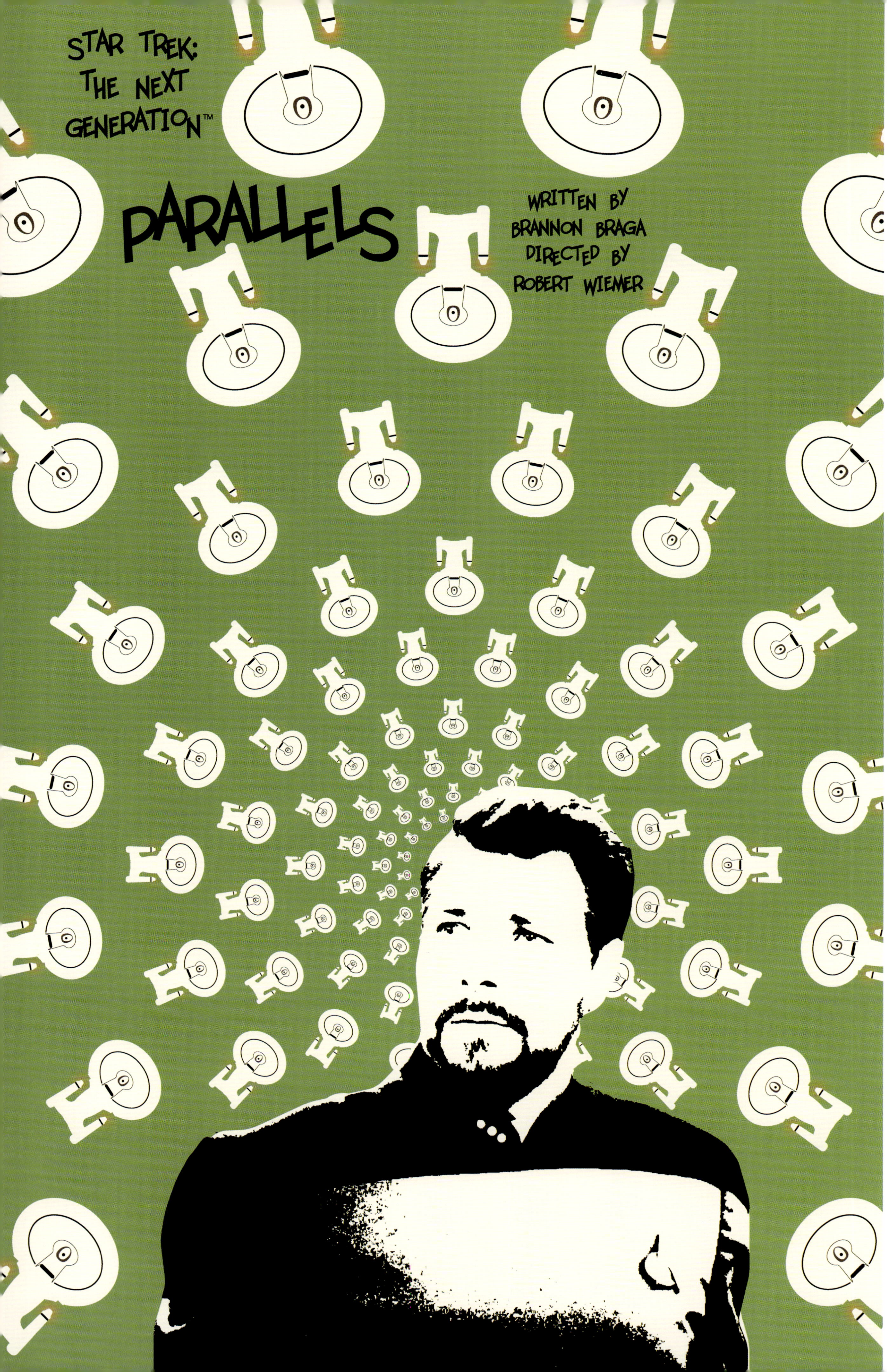
STAR TREK: THE NEXT GENERATION™
PARALLELS
WRITTEN BY BRANNON BRAGA
DIRECTED BY ROBERT WIEMER

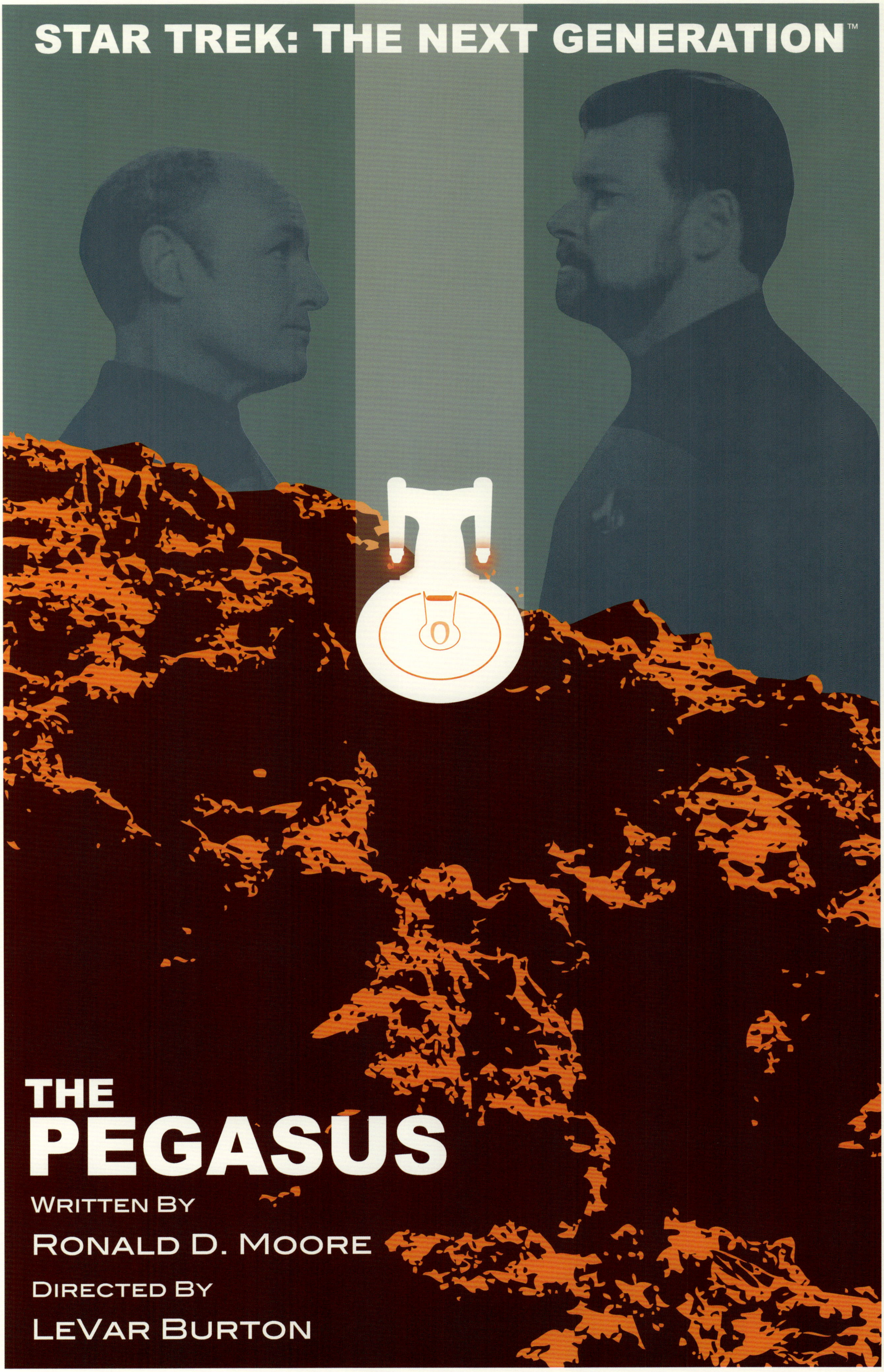
STAR TREK: THE NEXT GENERATION™
THE
PEGASUS
WRITTEN BY
RONALD D. MOORE
DIRECTED BY
LEVAR BURTON

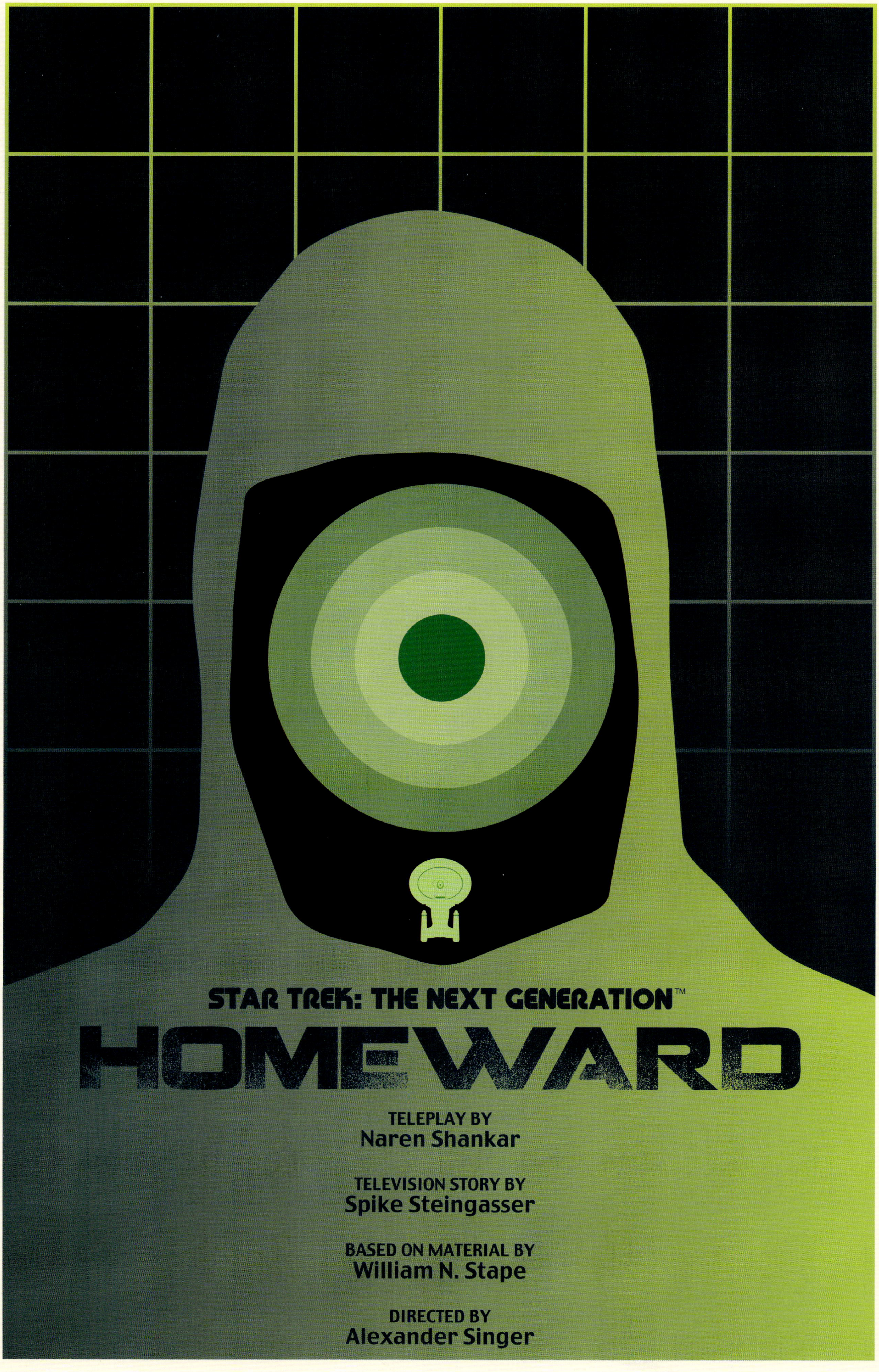
STAR TREK: THE NEXT GENERATION™
HOMEWARD
TELEPLAY BY
Naren Shankar
TELEVISION STORY BY
Spike Steingasser
BASED ON MATERIAL BY
William N. Stape
DIRECTED BY
Alexander Singer

STAR TREK:
THE NEXT GENERATION™

SUB ROSA

TELEPLAY BY
Brannon Braga

TELEVISION STORY BY
Jeri Taylor

BASED UPON MATERIAL BY
Jeanna F. Gallo

DIRECTED BY
Jonathan Frakes

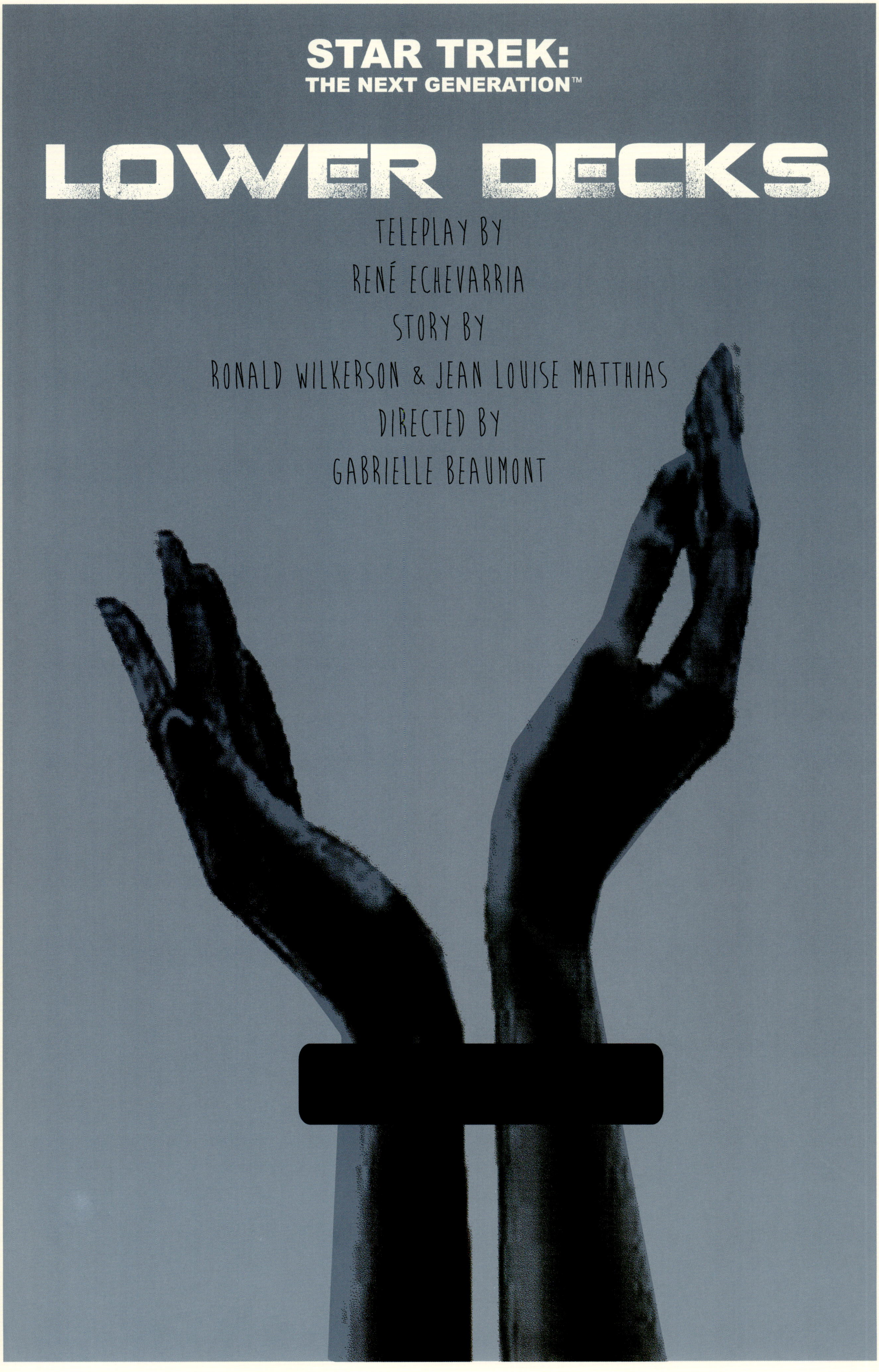
STAR TREK:
THE NEXT GENERATION™
LOWER DECKS
TELEPLAY BY
RENÉ ECHEVARRIA
STORY BY
RONALD WILKERSON & JEAN LOUISE MATTHIAS
DIRECTED BY
GABRIELLE BEAUMONT

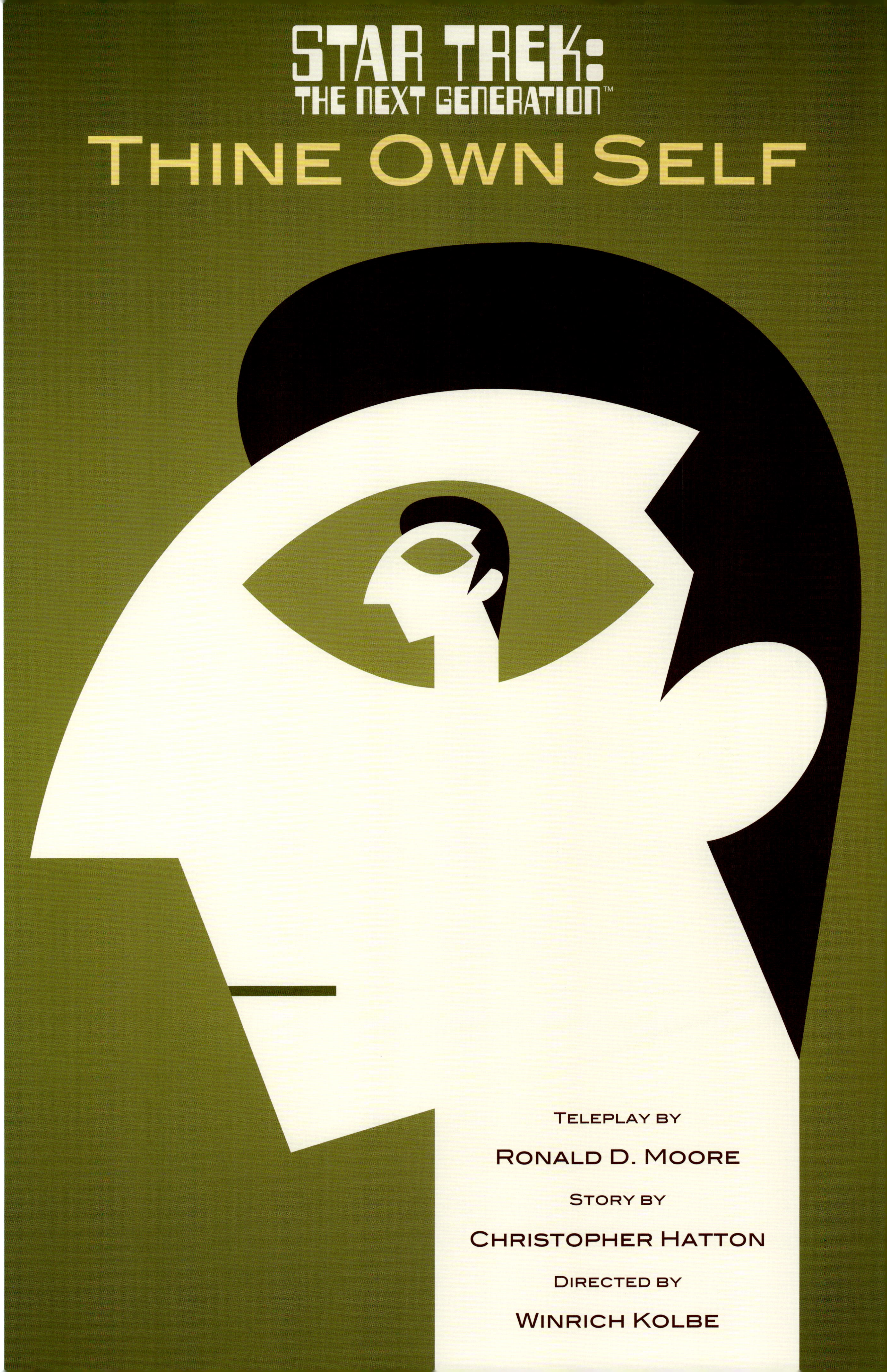
STAR TREK:
THE NEXT GENERATION™
THINE OWN SELF
TELEPLAY BY
RONALD D. MOORE
STORY BY
CHRISTOPHER HATTON
DIRECTED BY
WINRICH KOLBE

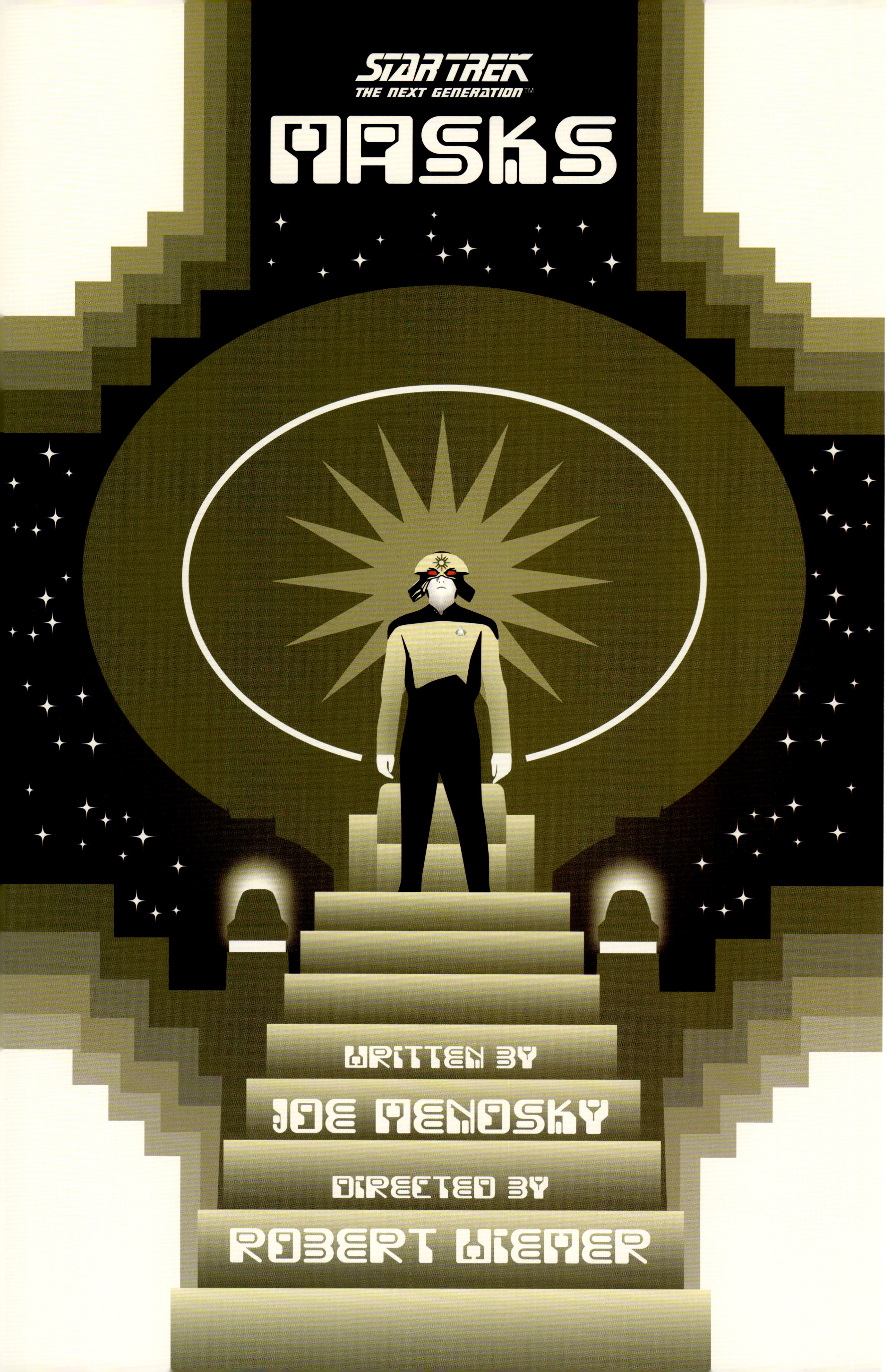
STAR TREK
THE NEXT GENERATION™
MASKS
WRITTEN BY
JOE MENOSKY
DIRECTED BY
ROBERT WIEMER

STAR TREK: THE NEXT GENERATION™

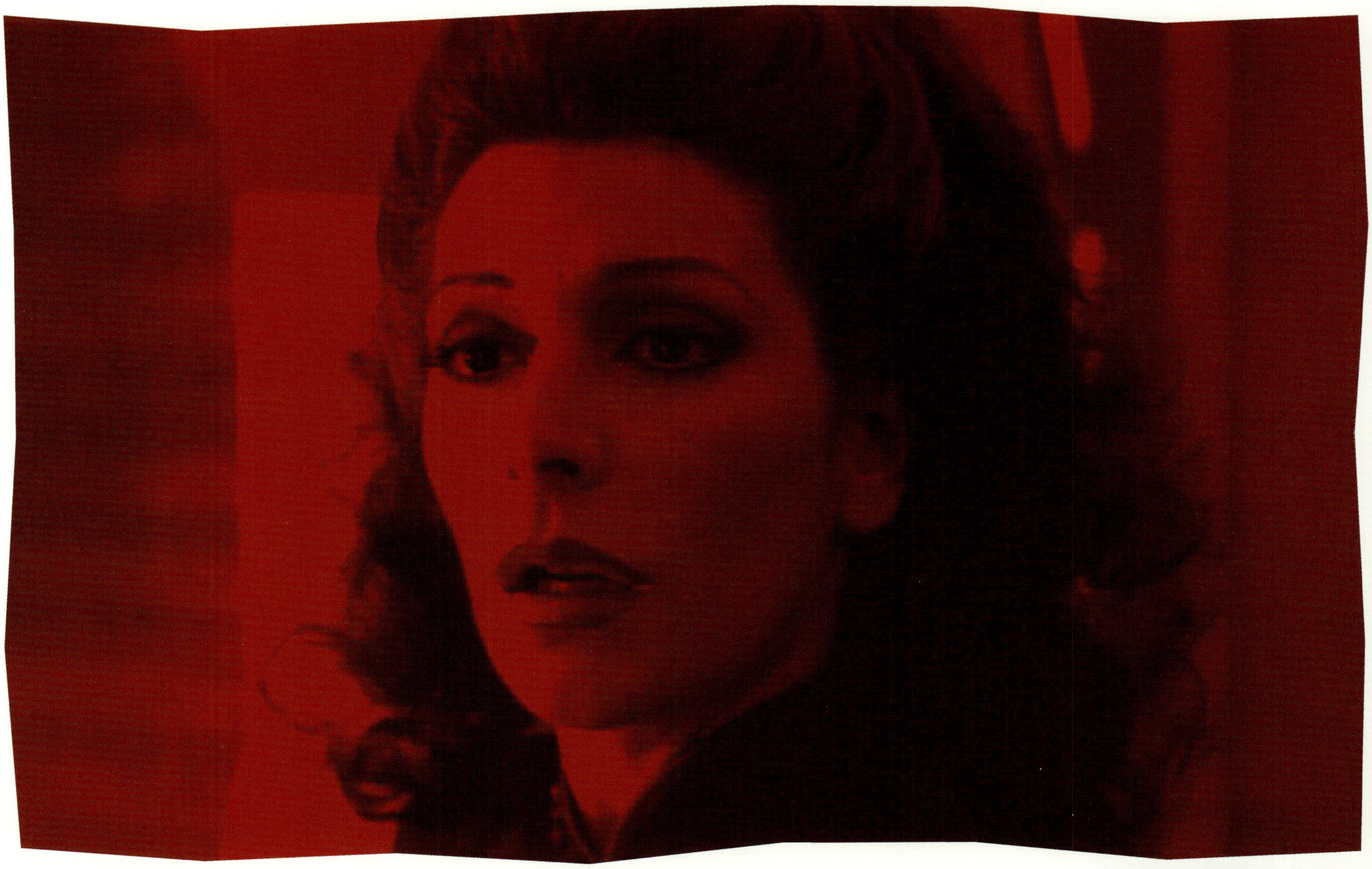

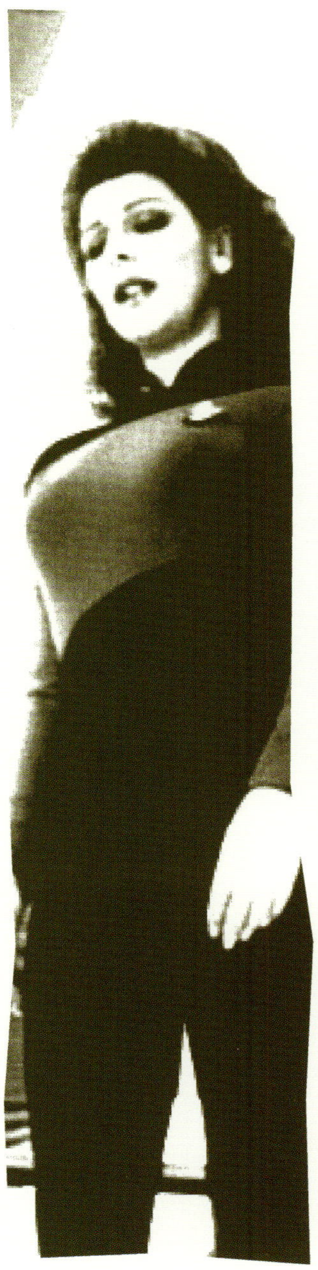

EYE OF THE BEHOLDER

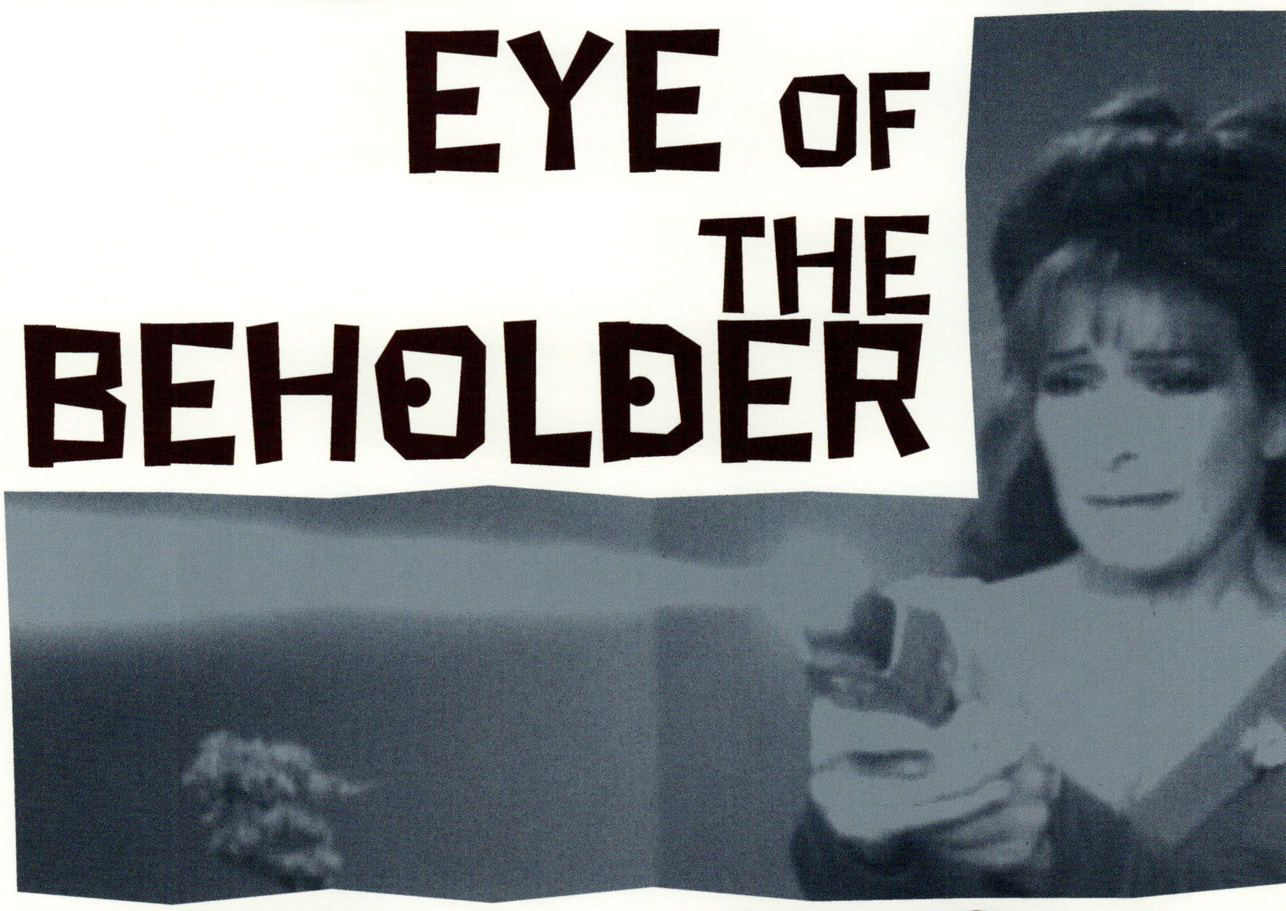

TELEPLAY BY **René Echevarria** STORY BY **Brannon Braga** DIRECTED BY **Cliff Bole**

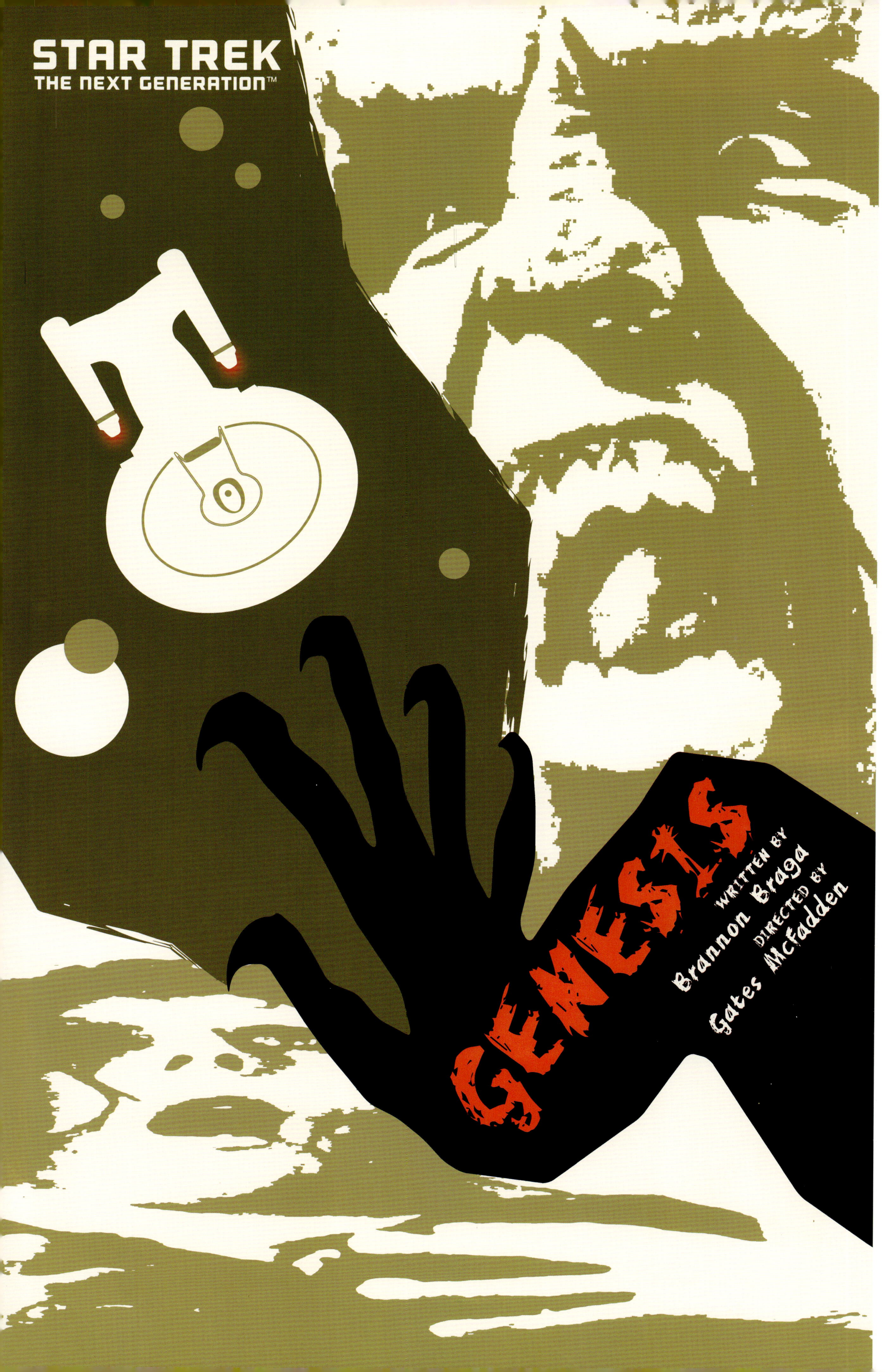
STAR TREK
THE NEXT GENERATION™
GENESIS
WRITTEN BY
Brannon Braga
DIRECTED BY
Gates McFadden

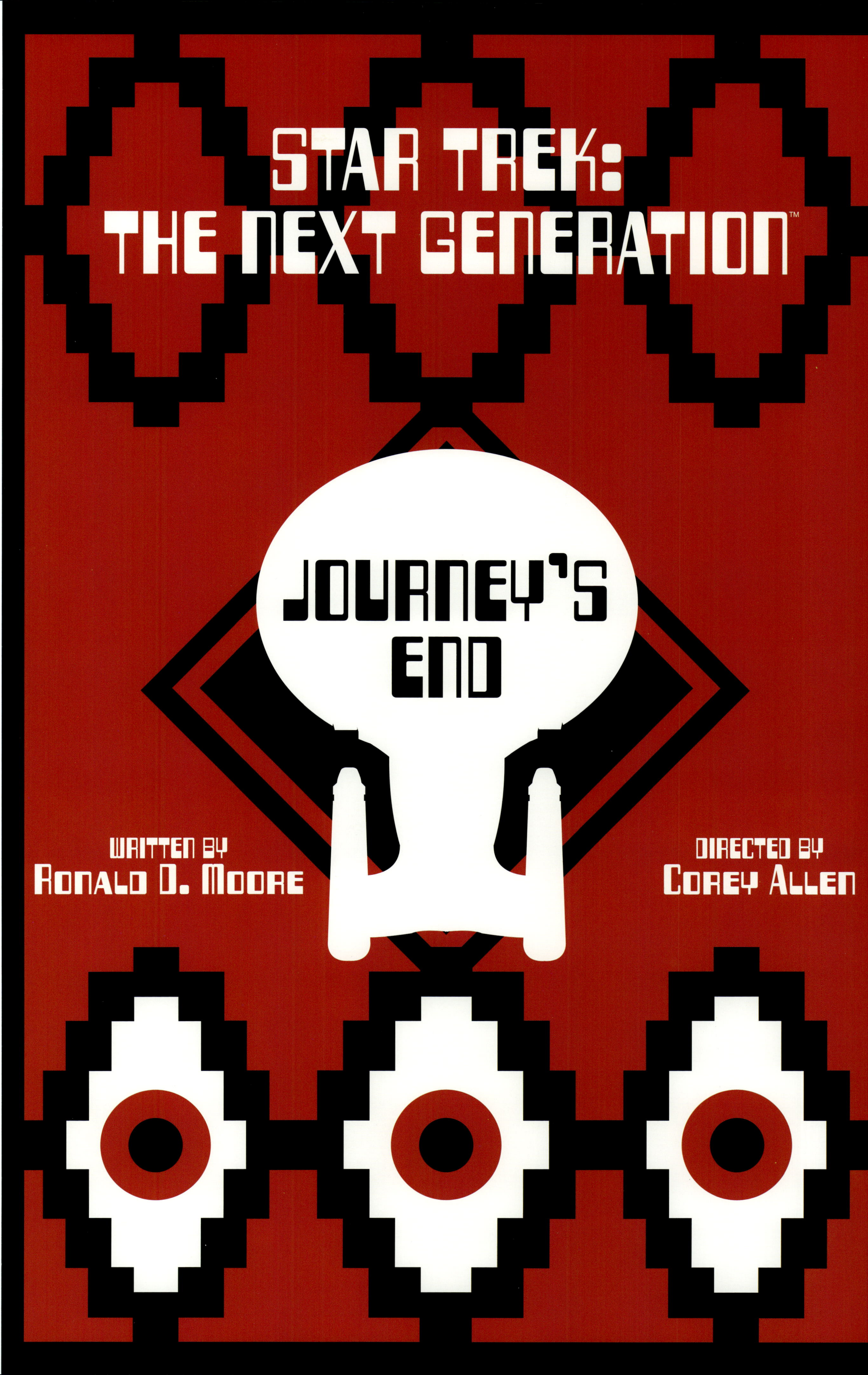
STAR TREK:
THE NEXT GENERATION™
JOURNEY'S END
WRITTEN BY
RONALD D. MOORE
DIRECTED BY
COREY ALLEN

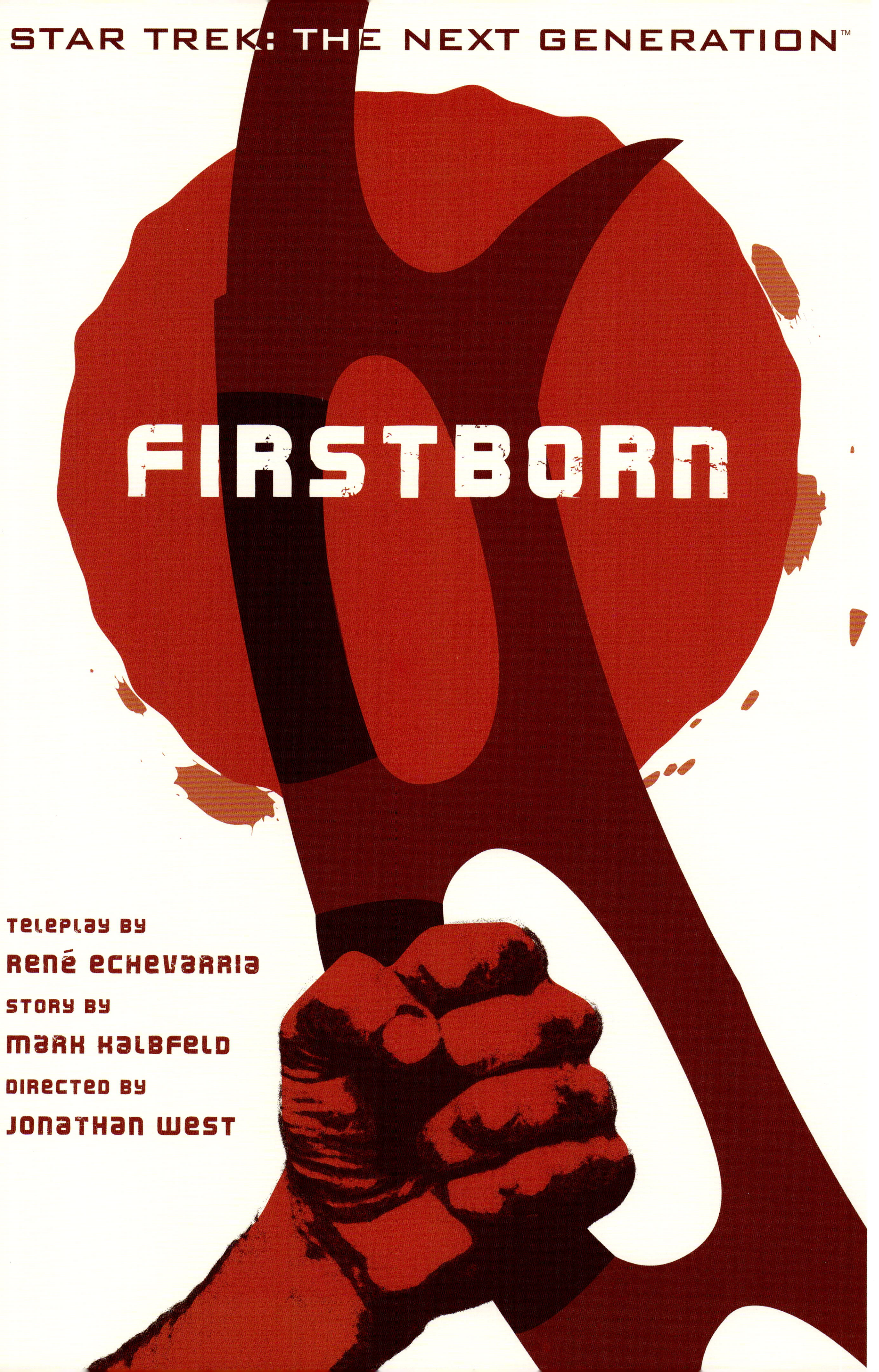
STAR TREK: THE NEXT GENERATION™
FIRSTBORN
TELEPLAY BY
RENÉ ECHEVARRIA
STORY BY
MARK KALBFELD
DIRECTED BY
JONATHAN WEST

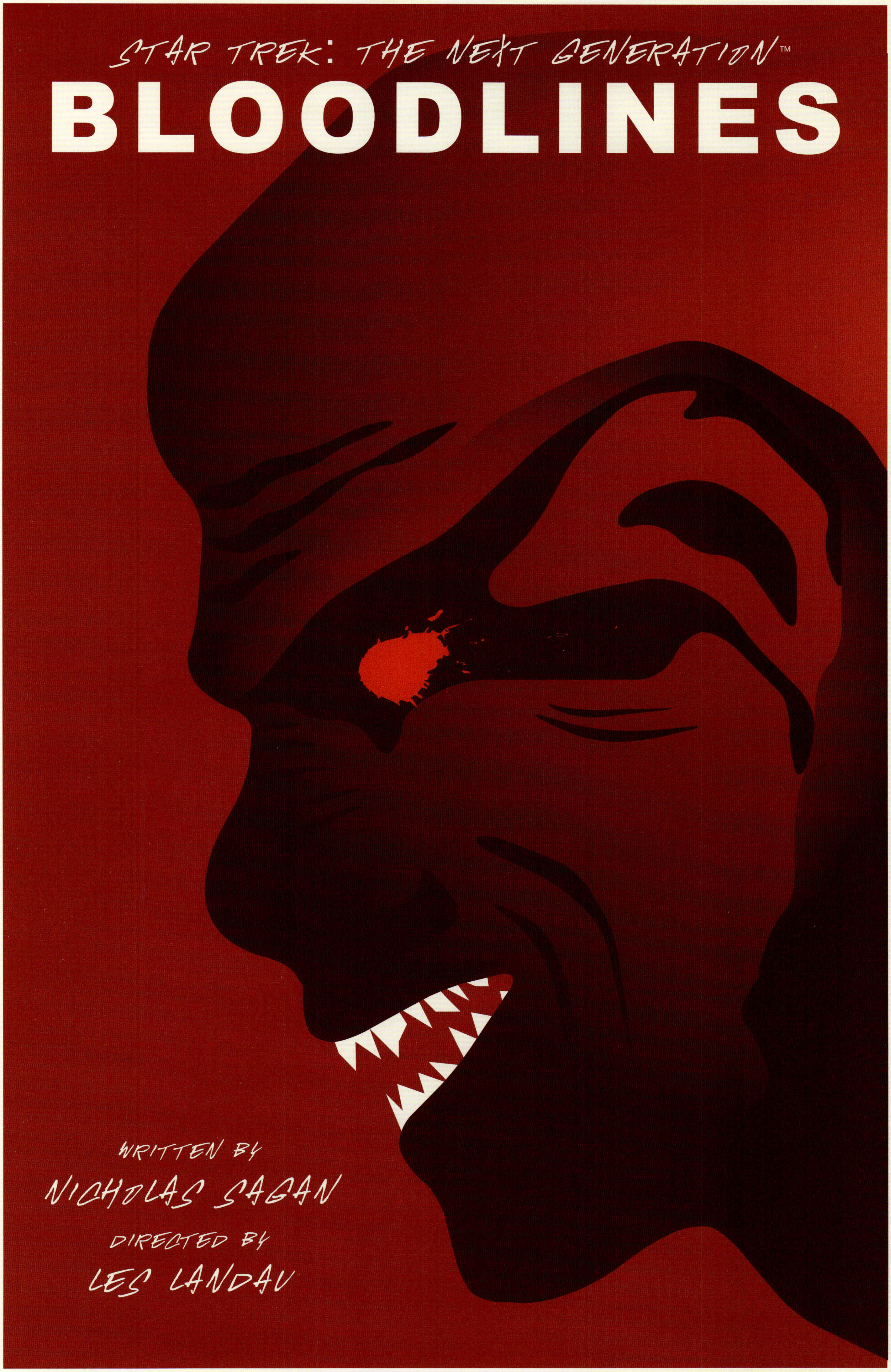
STAR TREK: THE NEXT GENERATION™
BLOODLINES
WRITTEN BY
NICHOLAS SAGAN
DIRECTED BY
LES LANDAU

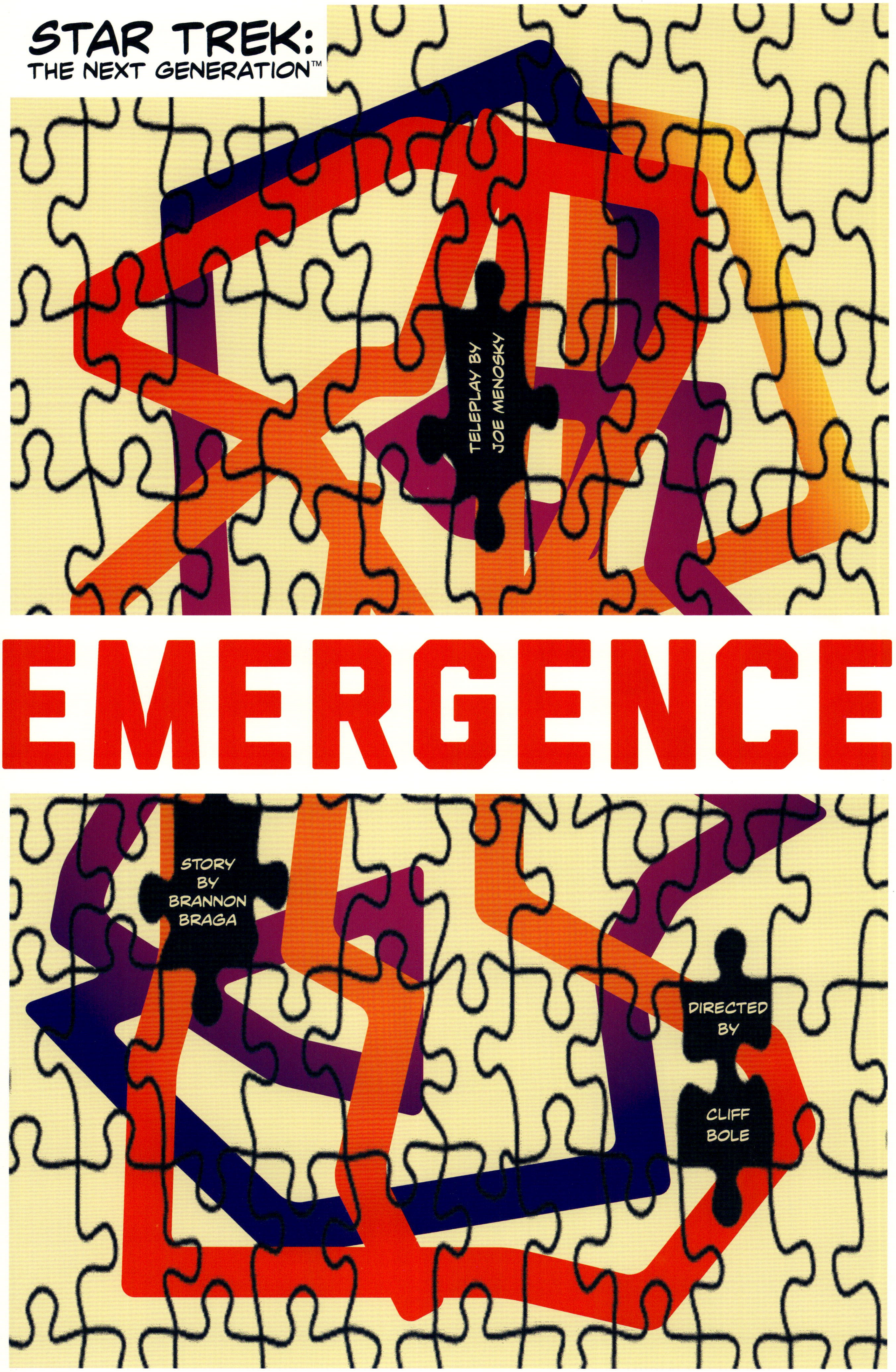
STAR TREK:
THE NEXT GENERATION™
TELEPLAY BY
JOE MENOSKY
EMERGENCE
STORY BY BRANNON BRAGA
DIRECTED BY
CLIFF BOLE

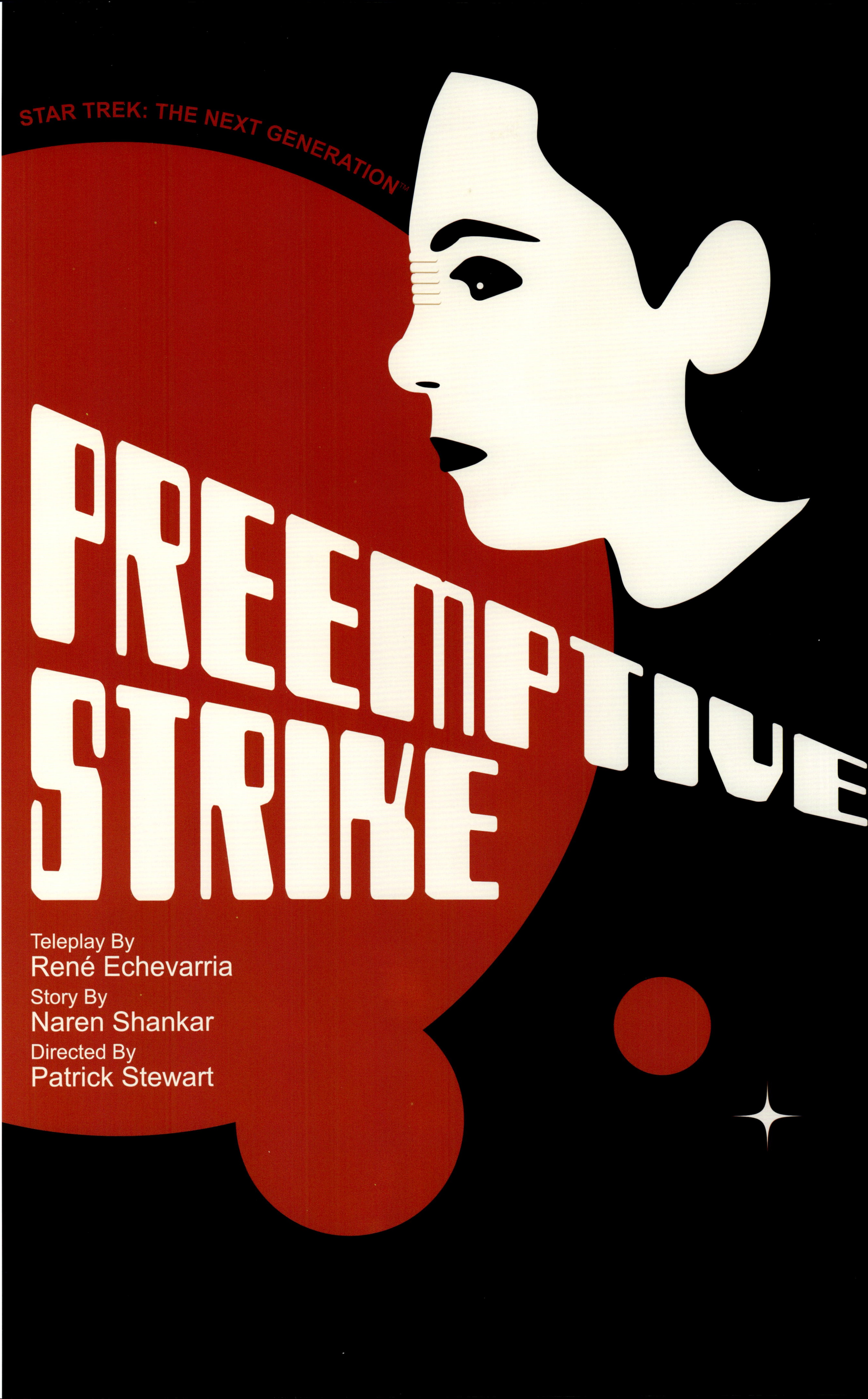
STAR TREK: THE NEXT GENERATION™
PREEMPTIVE STRIKE
Teleplay By
René Echevarria
Story By
Naren Shankar
Directed By
Patrick Stewart

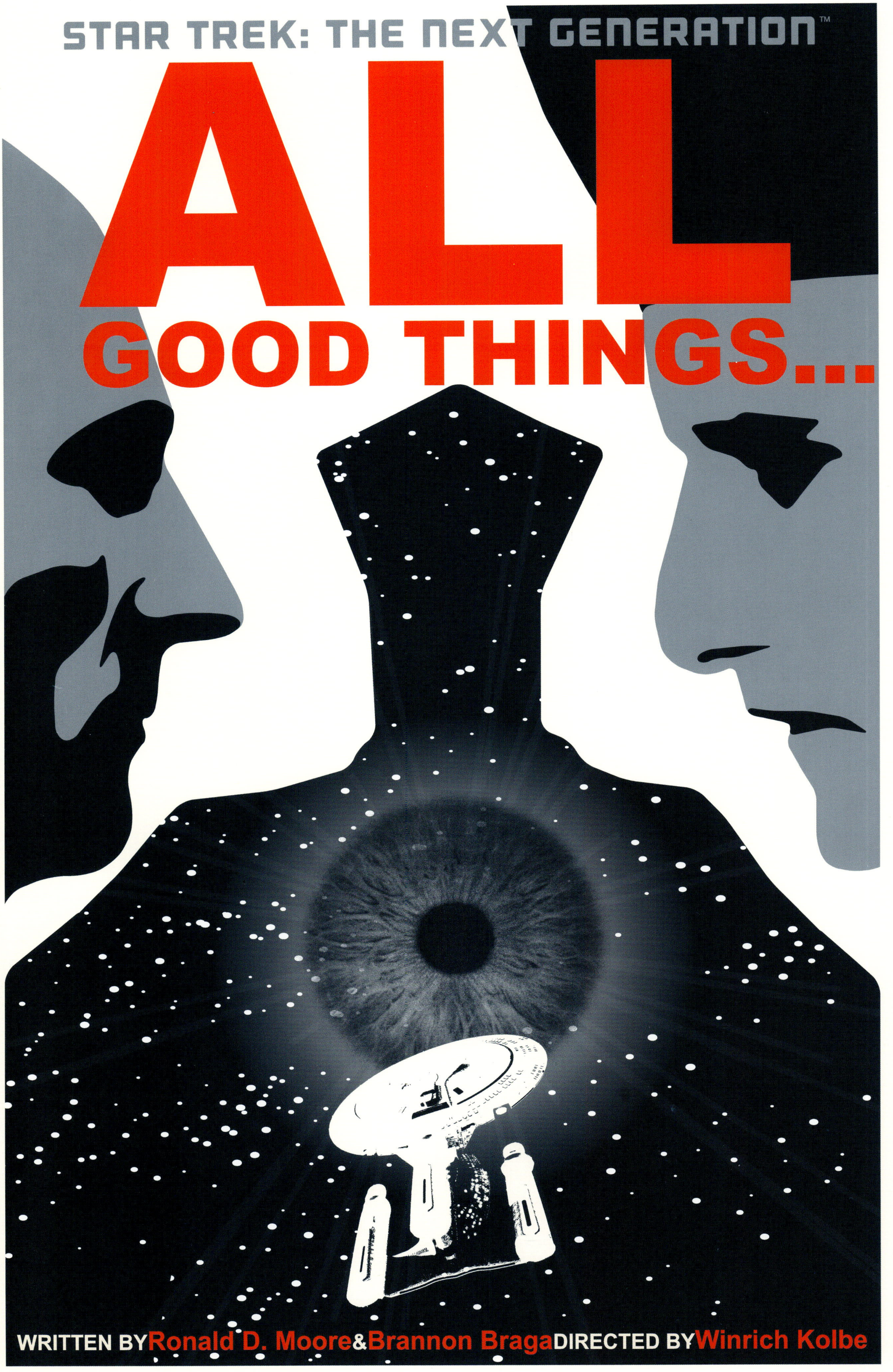
STAR TREK: THE NEXT GENERATION™
ALL
GOOD THINGS...
WRITTEN BY Ronald D. Moore & Brannon Braga DIRECTED BY Winrich Kolbe

Episode Index

Season 1 (1987–89)

No.	Name	Stardate	Director	Written by
1-2	"Encounter at Farpoint"	41153.7	Corey Allen	D. C. Fontana and Gene Roddenberry
3	"The Naked Now"	41209.2	Paul Lynch	Teleplay: J. Michael Bingham. Story: John D. F. Black and J. Michael Bingham
4	"Code of Honor"	41235.25	Russ Mayberry	Katharyn Powers and Michael Baron
5	"The Last Outpost"	41386.4	Richard Colla	Teleplay: Herbert Wright. Story: Richard Krzemien
6	"Where No One Has Gone Before"	41263.1	Rob Bowman	Diane Duane and Michael Reaves
7	"Lonely Among Us"	41249.3	Cliff Bole	Teleplay: D. C. Fontana. Story: Michael Halperin
8	"Justice"	41255.6	James L. Conway	Teleplay: Worley Thorne. Story: Ralph Willis and Worley Thorne
9	"The Battle"	41723.9	Rob Bowman	Teleplay: Herbert Wright. Story: Larry Forrester
10	"Hide and Q"	41590.5	Cliff Bole	Teleplay: C.J. Holland and Gene Roddenberry. Story: C.J. Holland
11	"Haven"	41294.5	Richard Compton	Teleplay: Tracy Tormé. Story: Tracy Tormé and Lan O'Kun
12	"The Big Goodbye"	41997.7	Joseph L. Scanlan	Tracy Tormé
13	"Datalore"	41242.4	Rob Bowman	Teleplay: Robert Lewin and Gene Roddenberry Story: Robert Lewin and Maurice Hurley
14	"Angel One"	41636.9	Michael Rhodes	Patrick Barry
15	"11001001"	41365.9	Paul Lynch	Maurice Hurley and Robert Lewin
16	"Too Short a Season"	41309.5	Rob Bowman	Teleplay: Michael Michaelian and D. C. Fontana Story: Michael Michaelian
17	"When the Bough Breaks"	41509.1	Kim Manners	Hannah Louise Shearer
18	"Home Soil"	41463.9	Corey Allen	Teleplay: Robert Sabaroff. Story: Karl Geurs & Ralph Sanchez and Robert Sabaroff
19	"Coming of Age"	41416.2	Mike Vejar	Sandy Fries
20	"Heart of Glory"	41503.7	Rob Bowman	Teleplay: Maurice Hurley Story: Maurice Hurley and Herbert Wright & D. C. Fontana
21	"The Arsenal of Freedom"	41798.2	Les Landau	Teleplay: Richard Manning and Hans Beimler Story: Maurice Hurley and Robert Lewin
22	"Symbiosis"	Unknown	Win Phelps	Teleplay: Robert Lewin and Richard Manning & Hans Beimler Story: Robert Lewin
23	"Skin of Evil"	41601.3	Joseph L. Scanlan	Teleplay: Joseph Stefano and Hannah Louise Shearer Story: Joseph Stefano
24	"We'll Always Have Paris"	41697.9	Robert Becker	Deborah Dean Davis and Hannah Louise Shearer
25	"Conspiracy"	41775.5	Cliff Bole	Teleplay: Tracy Tormé. Story: Robert Sabaroff
26	"The Neutral Zone"	41986.0	James L. Conway	Teleplay: Maurice Hurley. Story: Deborah McIntyre & Mona Clee

Season 2 (1988–89)

No	Title	Stardate	Directed by	Written by
1	"The Child"	42073.1	Rob Bowman	Jaron Summers & Jon Povill and Maurice Hurley
2	"Where Silence Has Lease"	42193.6	Winrich Kolbe	Jack B. Sowards
3	"Elementary, Dear Data"	42286.3	Rob Bowman	Brian Alan Lane
4	"The Outrageous Okona"	42402.7	Robert Becker	Teleplay by: Burton Armus Story by: Les Menchen & Lance Dickson & David Landsberg
5	"Loud as a Whisper"	42477.2	Larry Shaw	Jacqueline Zambrano
6	"The Schizoid Man"	42437.5	Les Landau	Teleplay by: Tracy Tormé Story by: Richard Manning & Hans Beimler
7	"Unnatural Selection"	42494.8	Paul Lynch	John Mason and Mike Gray
8	"A Matter of Honor"	42506.5	Rob Bowman	Teleplay by: Burton Armus Story by: Wanda M. Haight & Gregory Amos and Burton Armus
9	"The Measure of a Man"	42523.7	Robert Scheerer	Melinda M. Snodgrass
10	"The Dauphin"	42568.8	Rob Bowman	Scott Rubenstein & Leonard Mlodinow
11	"Contagion"	42609.1	Joseph L. Scanlan	Steve Gerber & Beth Woods
12	"The Royale"	42625.4	Cliff Bole	Keith Mills
13	"Time Squared"	42679.2	Joseph L. Scanlan	Teleplay by: Maurice Hurley Story by: Kurt Michael Bensmiller
14	"The Icarus Factor"	42686.4	Robert Iscove	Teleplay by: David Assael and Robert McCullough Story by: David Assael

15	"Pen Pals"	42695.3	Winrich Kolbe	Teleplay by: Melinda M. Snodgrass Story by: Hannah Louise Shearer
16	"Q Who"	42761.3	Rob Bowman	Maurice Hurley
17	"Samaritan Snare"	42779.1	Les Landau	Robert L. McCullough
18	"Up the Long Ladder"	42823.2	Winrich Kolbe	Melinda M. Snodgrass
19	"Manhunt"	42859.2	Rob Bowman	Tracy Tormé
20	"The Emissary"	42901.3	Cliff Bole	Teleplay by: Richard Manning & Hans Beimler Story by: Richard Manning & Hans Beimler and Thomas H. Calder
21	"Peak Performance"	42923.4	Robert Scheerer	David Kemper
22	"Shades of Gray"	42976.1	Rob Bowman	Teleplay by: Maurice Hurley and Richard Manning & Hans Beimler Story by: Maurice Hurley

Season 3 (1989–90)

No.	Title	Stardate	Directed by	Written by
1	"Evolution"	43125.8	Winrich Kolbe	Teleplay by: Michael Piller. Story by: Michael Piller & Michael Wagner
2	"The Ensigns of Command"	43133.3	Cliff Bole	Melinda M. Snodgrass
3	"The Survivors"	43152.4	Les Landau	Michael Wagner
4	"Who Watches the Watchers"	43173.5	Robert Wiemer	Richard Manning & Hans Beimler
5	"The Bonding"	43198.7	Winrich Kolbe	Ronald D. Moore
6	"Booby Trap"	43205.6	Gabrielle Beaumont	Teleplay by: Ron Roman and Michael Piller & Richard Danus Story by: Michael Wagner & Ron Roman
7	"The Enemy"	43349.2	David Carson	David Kemper & Michael Piller
8	"The Price"	43385.6	Robert Scheerer	Hannah Louise Shearer
9	"The Vengeance Factor"	43421.9	Timothy Bond	Sam Rolfe
10	"The Defector"	43462.5	Robert Scheerer	Ronald D. Moore
11	"The Hunted"	43489.2	Cliff Bole	Robin Bernheim
12	"The High Ground"	43510.7	Gabrielle Beaumont	Melinda M. Snodgrass
13	"Déjà Q"	43539.1	Les Landau	Richard Danus
14	"A Matter of Perspective"	43610.4	Cliff Bole	Ed Zuckerman
15	"Yesterday's Enterprise"	43625.2	David Carson	Teleplay by: Ira Steven Behr, Richard Manning, Hans Beimler and Ronald D. Moore From a Story by: Trent Christopher Ganino & Eric A. Stillwell
16	"The Offspring"	43657.0	Jonathan Frakes	René Echevarria
17	"Sins of the Father"	43685.2	Les Landau	Teleplay by: Ronald D. Moore & W. Reed Moran Story by: Drew Deighan
18	"Allegiance"	43714.1	Winrich Kolbe	Richard Manning & Hans Beimler
19	"Captain's Holiday"	43745.2	Chip Chalmers	Ira Steven Behr
20	"Tin Man"	43779.3	Robert Scheerer	Dennis Putman Bailey & David Bischoff
21	"Hollow Pursuits"	43807.4	Cliff Bole	Sally Caves
22	"The Most Toys"	43872.2	Timothy Bond	Shari Goodhartz
23	"Sarek"	43917.4	Les Landau	Teleplay and Story by: Peter S. BeagleFrom an unpublished story by: Marc Cushman & Jake Jacobs
24	"Ménage à Troi"	43930.7	Robert Legato	Fred Bronson & Susan Sackett
25	"Transfigurations"	43957.2	Tom Benko	René Echevarria
26	"The Best of Both Worlds: Part I"	43989.1	Cliff Bole	Michael Piller

Season 4 (1990–91)

No.	Title	Stardate	Directed by	Written by
1	"The Best of Both Worlds: Part II"	44001.4	Cliff Bole	Michael Piller
2	"Family"	44012.3	Les Landau	Ronald D. Moore
3	"Brothers"	44085.7	Rob Bowman	Rick Berman
4	"Suddenly Human"	44143.7	Gabrielle Beaumont	Teleplay: John Whelpley & Jeri Taylor. Story: Ralph Phillips
5	"Remember Me"	44161.2	Cliff Bole	Lee Sheldon
6	"Legacy"	44215.2	Robert Scheerer	Joe Menosky
7	"Reunion"	44246.3	Jonathan Frakes	Teleplay: Thomas Perry & Jo Perry and Ronald D. Moore & Brannon Braga. Story: Drew Deighan and Thomas Perry & Jo Perry
8	"Future Imperfect"	44286.5	Les Landau	J. Larry Carroll & David Bennett Carren
9	"Final Mission"	44307.3	Corey Allen	Teleplay: Kacey Arnold-Ince and Jeri Taylo. Story: Kacey Arnold-Ince
10	"The Loss"	44356.9	Chip Chalmers	Teleplay: Hilary J. Bader and Alan J. Adler & Vanessa Greene Story: Hilary J. Bader
11	"Data's Day"	44390.1	Robert Wiemer	Teleplay: Harold Apter and Ronald D. Moore. Story: Harold Apter

No.	Title	Stardate	Directed by	Written by
12	"The Wounded"	44429.6	Chip Chalmers	Teleplay: Jeri Taylor Story: Stuart Charno & Sara Charno and Cy Chermak
13	"Devil's Due"	44474.5	Tom Benko	Teleplay: Philip LaZebnik Story: Philip LaZebnik and William Douglas Lansford
14	"Clues"	44502.7	Les Landau	Teleplay: Bruce D. Arthurs and Joe Menosky. Story: Bruce D. Arthurs
15	"First Contact"	44575.2	Cliff Bole	Teleplay: Dennis Russell Bailey & David Bischoff and Joe Menosky & Ronald D. Moore and Michael Piller Story: Marc Scott Zicree
16	"Galaxy's Child"	44614.6	Winrich Kolbe	Teleplay: Maurice Hurley. Story: Thomas Kartozian
17	"Night Terrors"	44631.2	Les Landau	Teleplay: Pamela Douglas and Jeri Taylor. Story: Shari Goodhartz
18	"Identity Crisis"	44664.5	Winrich Kolbe	Teleplay: Brannon Braga. Story: Timothy De Haas
19	"The Nth Degree"	44704.2	Robert Legato	Joe Menosky
20	"Qpid"	44741.9	Cliff Bole	Teleplay: Ira Steven Behr. Story: Randee Russell and Ira Steven Behr
21	"The Drumhead"	44769.2	Jonathan Frakes	Jeri Taylor
22	"Half a Life"	44805.3	Les Landau	Teleplay: Peter Allan Fields. Story: Ted Roberts and Peter Allan Fields
23	"The Host"	44821.3	Marvin V. Rush	Michel Horvat
24	"The Mind's Eye"	44885.5	David Livingston	Teleplay: René Echevarria. Story: Ken Schafer and René Echevarria
25	"In Theory"	44932.3	Patrick Stewart	Joe Menosky & Ronald D. Moore
26	"Redemption I"	44995.3	Cliff Bole	Ronald D. Moore

Season 5 (1991–92)

No.	Title	Stardate	Directed by	Written by
1	"Redemption II"	45021.3	David Carson	Ronald D. Moore
2	"Darmok"	45047.2	Winrich Kolbe	Teleplay: Joe Menosky. Story: Philip LaZebnik and Joe Menosky
3	"Ensign Ro"	45076.3	Les Landau	Teleplay: Michael Piller. Story: Rick Berman & Michael Piller
4	"Silicon Avatar"	45122.3	Cliff Bole	Teleplay: Jeri Taylor Story: Lawrence V. Conley
5	"Disaster"	45156.1	Gabrielle Beaumont	Teleplay: Ronald D. Moore. Story: Ron Jarvis & Philip A. Scorza
6	"The Game"	45208.2	Corey Allen	Teleplay: Brannon Braga Story: Susan Sackett & Fred Bronson and Brannon Braga
7	"Unification I"	45233.1	Les Landau	Teleplay: Jeri Taylor Story: Rick Berman and Michael Piller
8	"Unification II"	45245.8	Cliff Bole	Teleplay: Michael Piller. Story: Rick Berman and Michael Piller
9	"A Matter of Time"	45349.1	Paul Lynch	Rick Berman
10	"New Ground"	45376.3	Robert Scheerer	Teleplay: Grant Rosenberg. Story: Sara Charno and Stuart Charno
11	"Hero Worship"	45397.3	Patrick Stewart	Teleplay: Joe Menosky. Story: Hilary J. Bader
12	"Violations"	45429.3	Robert Wiemer	Teleplay: Pamela Gray and Jeri Taylor Story: Shari Goodhartz and T. Michael and Pamela Gray
13	"The Masterpiece Society"	45470.1	Winrich Kolbe	Teleplay: Adam Belanoff and Michael Piller Story: James Kahn and Adam Belanoff
14	"Conundrum"	45494.2	Les Landau	Teleplay: Barry Schkolnick. Story: Paul Schiffer
15	"Power Play"	45571.2	David Livingston	Teleplay: Rene Balcer and Herbert J. Wright & Brannon Braga Story: Paul Ruben and Maurice Hurley
16	"Ethics"	45587.3	Chip Chalmers	Teleplay: Ronald D. Moore. Story: Sara Charno & Stuart Charno
17	"The Outcast"	45614.6	Robert Scheerer	Jeri Taylor
18	"Cause and Effect"	45652.1	Jonathan Frakes	Brannon Braga
19	"The First Duty"	45703.9	Paul Lynch	Ronald D. Moore & Naren Shankar
20	"Cost of Living"	45733.6	Winrich Kolbe	Peter Allan Fields
21	"The Perfect Mate"	45761.3	Cliff Bole	Teleplay: Gary Perconte and Michael Piller Story: René Echevarria and Gary Perconte
22	"Imaginary Friend"	45852.1	Gabrielle Beaumont	Teleplay: Edithe Swensen and Brannon Braga Story: Jean Louise Matthias & Ronald Wilkerson and Richard Fliegel
23	"I, Borg"	45854.2	Robert Lederman	René Echevarria
24	"The Next Phase"	45892.4	David Carson	Ronald D. Moore
25	"The Inner Light"	45944.1	Peter Lauritson	Teleplay: Morgan Gendel and Peter Allan Fields. Story: Morgan Gendel
26	"Time's Arrow, Part I"	45959.1	Les Landau	Teleplay: Joe Menosky and Michael Piller. Story: Joe Menosky

Season 6 (1992–93)

No.	Title	Stardate	Directed by	Written by
1	"Time's Arrow, Part II"	46001.3	Les Landau	Teleplay: Jeri Taylor. Story: Joe Menosky
2	"Realm of Fear"	46041.1	Cliff Bole	Brannon Braga
3	"Man of the People"	46071.6	Winrich Kolbe	Frank Abatemarco

4	"Relics"	46125.3	Alexander Singer	Ronald D. Moore
5	"Schisms"	46154.2	Robert Wiemer	Teleplay: Brannon Braga. Story: Jean Louise Matthias & Ron Wilkerson
6	"True Q"	46192.3	Robert Scheerer	René Echevarria
7	"Rascals"	46235.7	Adam Nimoy	Teleplay: Allison Hock. Story: Ward Botsford & Diana Dru Botsford and Michael Piller
8	"A Fistful of Datas"	46271.5	Patrick Stewart	Teleplay: Robert Hewitt Wolfe and Brannon Braga. Story: Robert Hewitt Wolfe
9	"The Quality of Life"	46307.2	Jonathan Frakes	Teleplay: Naren Shankar. Story: L.J. Scott
10	"Chain of Command, Part I"	46357.4	Robert Scheerer	Teleplay: Ronald D. Moore. Story: Frank Abatemarco
11	"Chain of Command, Part II"	46360.8	Les Landau	Frank Abatemarco
12	"Ship in a Bottle"	46424.1	Alexander Singer	René Echevarria
13	"Aquiel"	46461.3	Cliff Bole	Teleplay: Brannon Braga & Ronald D. Moore. Story: Jeri Taylor
14	"Face of the Enemy"	46519.1	Gabrielle Beaumont	Teleplay: Naren Shankar. Story: René Echevarria
15	"Tapestry"	Unknown	Les Landau	Ronald D. Moore
16	"Birthright, Part I"	46578.4	Winrich Kolbe	Brannon Braga
17	"Birthright, Part II"	46579.2	Dan Curry	René Echevarria
18	"Starship Mine"	46682.4	Cliff Bole	Morgan Gendel
19	"Lessons"	46693.1	Robert Wiemer	Ronald Wilkerson & Jean Louise Matthias
20	"The Chase"	46731.5	Jonathan Frakes	Teleplay: Joe Menosky. Story: Ronald D. Moore and Joe Menosky
21	"Frame of Mind"	46778.1	James L. Conway	Brannon Braga
22	"Suspicions"	46830.1	Cliff Bole	Joe Menosky and Naren Shankar
23	"Rightful Heir"	46852.2	Winrich Kolbe	Teleplay: Ronald D. Moore. Story: James E. Brooks
24	"Second Chances"	46915.2	LeVar Burton	Teleplay: René Echevarria. Story: Michael Medlock
25	"Timescape"	46944.2	Adam Nimoy	Brannon Braga
26	"Descent, Part I"	46982.1	Alexander Singer	Teleplay: Ronald D. Moore. Story: Jeri Taylor

Season 7 (1993–94)

No.	Title	Stardate	Directed by	Written by
1	"Descent, Part II"	47025.4	Alexander Singer	René Echevarria
2	"Liaisons"	Unknown	Cliff Bole	Teleplay by: Jeanne Carrigan Fauci & Lisa Rich. Story by: Roger Eschbacher & Jaq Greenspon
3	"Interface"	47215.5	Robert Wiemer	Joe Menosky
4	"Gambit, Part I"	47135.2	Peter Lauritson	Teleplay by: Naren Shankar. Story by: Christopher Hatton and Naren Shankar
5	"Gambit, Part II"	47160.1	Alexander Singer	Teleplay by: Ronald D. Moore. Story by: Naren Shankar
6	"Phantasms"	47225.7	Patrick Stewart	Brannon Braga
7	"Dark Page"	47254.1	Les Landau	Hilary J. Bader
8	"Attached"	47304.2	Jonathan Frakes	Nicholas Sagan
9	"Force of Nature"	47310.2	Robert Lederman	Naren Shankar
10	"Inheritance"	47410.2	Robert Scheerer	Teleplay by: Dan Koeppel and René Echevarria. Story by: Dan Koeppel
11	"Parallels"	47391.2	Robert Wiemer	Brannon Braga
12	"The Pegasus"	47457.1	LeVar Burton	Ronald D. Moore
13	"Homeward"	47423.9	Alexander Singer	Teleplay by: Naren Shankar Story by: Spike Steingasser. Based on material by William N. Stape
14	"Sub Rosa"	Unknown	Jonathan Frakes	Teleplay by: Brannon Braga Story by: Jeri Taylor. Based on material by Jeanna F. Gallo
15	"Lower Decks"	47566.7	Gabrielle Beaumont	Teleplay by: René Echevarria. Story by: Ronald Wilkerson & Jean Louise Matthias
16	"Thine Own Self"	47611.2	Winrich Kolbe	Teleplay by: Ronald D. Moore. Story by: Christopher Hatton
17	"Masks"	47615.2	Robert Wiemer	Joe Menosky
18	"Eye of the Beholder"	47622.1	Cliff Bole	Teleplay by: René Echevarria. Story by: Brannon Braga
19	"Genesis"	47653.2	Gates McFadden	Brannon Braga
20	"Journey's End"	47751.2	Corey Allen	Teleplay by: Ronald D. Moore. Story by: Shawn Piller and Antonia Napoli
21	"Firstborn"	47779.4	Jonathan West	Teleplay by: René Echevarria. Story by: Mark Kalbfeld
22	"Bloodlines"	47829.1	Les Landau	Nicholas Sagan
23	"Emergence"	47869.2	Cliff Bole	Teleplay by: Joe Menosky. Story by: Brannon Braga
24	"Preemptive Strike"	47941.7	Patrick Stewart	Teleplay by: René Echevarria. Story by: Naren Shankar
25 / 26	"All Good Things..."	47988	Winrich Kolbe	Ronald D. Moore & Brannon Braga